CHINA IN AFRICA

CHINA IN AFRICA
IN ZHENG HE'S FOOTSTEPS

LI XINFENG

TRANSLATED BY SHELLY BRYANT

Published by BestRed, an imprint of HSRC Press
Private Bag X9182, Cape Town, 8000, South Africa
www.bestred.co.za

First published 2017

ISBN (soft cover) 978-1-928246-10-7

© 2017 Human Sciences Research Council

The author acknowledges the support of the Chinese Fund for the Humanities and Social Sciences (本书获中华社会科学基金资助)

The views expressed in this publication are those of the author. They do not necessarily reflect the views or policies of the Human Sciences Research Council (the Council) or indicate that the Council endorses the views of the author. In quoting from this publication, readers are advised to attribute the source of the information to the author and not to the Council.

The publishers have no responsibility for the continued existence or accuracy of URLs for external or third-party Internet websites referred to in this book and do not guarantee that any content on such websites is, or will remain, accurate or appropriate.

Copy-edited by Mark Ronan
Typeset by Damian Gibbs
Cover design by Nic Jooste
Printed by Shumani Mills Communications, Parow, Cape Town
SW64499

Distributed in Africa by Blue Weaver
Tel: +27 (021) 701 4477; Fax Local: (021) 701 7302; Fax International: 0927865242139
www.blueweaver.co.za

Distributed in Europe and the United Kingdom by Eurospan Distribution Services (EDS)
Tel: +44 (0) 17 6760 4972; Fax: +44 (0) 17 6760 1640
www.eurospanbookstore.com

Distributed in North America by River North Editions, from IPG
Call toll-free: (800) 888 4741; Fax: +1 (312) 337 5985
www.ipgbook.com

No part of this publication may be reproduced, stored in a retrieval system, or transmitted by any form or by any means, electronic, mechanical, photocopying, recording or otherwise, without prior permission from the copyright owner.

To copy any part of this publication, you may contact DALRO for information and copyright clearance.

Tel: 086 12 DALRO (or 086 12 3256 from within South Africa); +27 (0)11 712-8000
Fax: +27 (0)11 403-9094
Postal Address: P O Box 31627, Braamfontein, 2017, South Africa
www.dalro.co.za

Any unauthorised copying could lead to civil liability and/or criminal sanctions.

Contents

Tables vi
Acronyms and abbreviations vii
Foreword: From the Human Sciences Research Council viii
Foreword: From the Chinese Academy of Social Sciences xii
Prologue: Four visits to see 'relatives' xv

1	The journey to Pate Island	1
2	Discovering the Chinese Village	20
3	Redefining 'Chinese'	35
4	Further exploring Pate Island	49
5	Search for a sunken ship	68
6	Refugee camps	82
7	Insight into Somalia	95
8	Revisiting Somalia	114
9	Exploring Sofala	126
10	Visiting four island nations	137
11	Round the Cape of Good Hope	152
12	Northward search for the Zheng He Monument	167
13	Travelling in the interior of Africa	182
14	TAZARA Railway: Conveyor of friendship	195
15	Searching for roots at home	212
16	A historical record of China–Africa relations	235
17	The Chinese in Africa	270
18	Significance of China's long history in Africa	296

Postscript: Final reflections 313
Notes 321
Bibliography 344
Index 351

Tables

Table 17.1 Total population of Overseas Chinese, 1950–2008
Table 17.2 Distribution of Chinese diaspora, 1950–2000
Table 17.3 Overseas Chinese population and distribution by continent, 2006–2007
Table 17.4 New Overseas Chinese population and distribution by continent, 2006–2007

Abbreviations and acronyms

ANC	African National Congress
DRC	Democratic Republic of the Congo
EU	European Union
EXCOM	executive management committee
FOCAC	Forum on China–Africa Cooperation
MNC	Mouvement National Congolais (Congolese National Movement)
NGO	non-governmental organisation
RMB	renminbi (Chinese currency)
TAZARA	Tanzania–Zambia Railway Authority
TCM	traditional Chinese medicine
UK	United Kingdom
UN	United Nations
UNESCO	UN Educational, Scientific and Cultural Organization
US	United States

Foreword
from the Human Sciences Research Council

The dominant 'discovery' narrative for global exploration remains almost naturally personified in the achievements of individuals such as Christopher Columbus, Vasco da Gama and Bartholomieu Dias. Columbus is almost indelibly embedded in the pages of our histories as the founding father of the great opening up of what we know today as the Americas. Da Gama and Dias sit, similarly inscribed, in our physical and mental archives as the resolute explorers for the world east and south of Europe. They sit there in the points of departure of our founding tales. They animate the discourses of our beginnings. They give the vocabularies of those discourses their subjective and embodied amplitudes – raced, gendered and cultured. Always coloured, always sexed and always (to coin a term) entempered. White, male and civilised. The Vitruvian ideal. The ontological apex.

Almost naturally, almost indebly.

Enter then the extraordinary figure of Zheng He and the *almost natural* cadence has to change. The register we use to account for the beginnings of the socio-political spaces that we inhabit in the political south, and most significantly, the continent of Africa, has to give way to a much more considered one. Zheng He was by any measure, and I am mindful of the pitfalls of ethno-centric comparison of any kind, one of the expanding human universe's most important *connectors*. I am aware, for example, of the caution urged by commentators such as JR Masson (see http://www.sochistdisc.org/2006_articles/masson_article.htm), which questions interpretations of the evidence of Chinese exploration and which attribute to it cartographic discoveries). But on the basis of what we now know, it is necessary to use the term *connector* here to describe the work Zheng He did to distinguish it from the *discovery* work that came to be associated with the expeditions undertaken by the European empires and kingdoms. Zheng He gave the challenging work of moving out of one's zone of comfort into spaces inhabited by others a sociable purpose. It was about building connections. It was about learning about difference and managing it on the basis of respect. He embarked on his missions not to conquer but to connect with new people. Discovery for him was about learning about *others*, not disrespectful comparison. At the First International Academic Conference on Zheng He held in Malacca, Malaysia in 2010, the head of the Malaccan State, Tun Datuk Seri Utama Mohd Khalil bin Yacoob, a 'self-proclaimed "super-fan" of Zheng He', said at the opening ceremony that 'during its voyages on the Western Ocean, "Zheng He's fleet was able to conquer everyone, but did not conquer anyone, bringing peace wherever it went. In the eyes of the world, Zheng He was a messenger of peace, revered and admired for his style as a general and for his superior strength"' (p. 310-311).

But who was Zheng He? Zheng He was an entrusted envoy of the Chinese Ming dynasty appointed in 1405 to undertake a diplomatic mission to what the Chinese physical archive described as the 'Arabian countries' west of China. Between 1405 and 1433 he undertook seven westward expeditions, four of which reached the African littoral. These expeditions took him into what the Chinese called the Western Ocean and what we would today call the Indian Ocean. He journeyed all along the African coast and reached as far north as the Cape Verde archipelago. There is the possibility too, as yet unconfirmed, that his fleet split into three groups and that one group completed an almost-circumnavigation – that he had reached the American continent. Aside from being intrepid, he was, in relation to the Vitruvian ideal, a Muslim and a Eunuch. On his journeys into the Western Ocean he had alongside of him Arab language translators. When he made contact with the people all along the western coastlines of the Western Ocean it was with an awareness that he needed to understand the languages and the customs of the people he met.

This book is about another Chinese journey. It has its beginnings in the amazing curiosity of Li Xinfeng, a Chinese journalist based in South Africa, about the Chinese presence in Africa. This curiosity leads Li Xinfeng, almost compulsively, to excavate as much as he can about this history and to seek out the most remote and interesting parts of the continent. He undertakes this journey from 2002 into the present with a *brotherly* and *sisterly* sensibility which connects him strongly to the sensitive diplomacy of Zheng He – literally in the footsteps of Zheng He. It takes him to the Kenyan Islands of the Lamu Archipelago, a group of five islands off the Kenyan coast where a ship in Zheng He's fleet, the date is not known, had foundered on the rocks of Pate Island on one of the four expeditions to Africa. The survivors of the wreck made it to the island and there, in the Zheng He style of managing new encounters, integrated into the local population. On the Lomu Archipelago the journalist seeks out the descendants of the ship-wreck and finds extraordinary traces of Chinese culture, most particularly that of Chinese Traditional Medicine. The chapters in the book which describe Li Xinfeng's visits to the Lomu Archipelago are intense. They reach a high point with the description of the missions undertaken by a team of Kenyan, Chinese and South African underwater experts to find the remains of the Chinese wreck. Sadly, this mission, a modest one, did not yield anything. *China in Africa* could almost have ended there but it becomes clear that the Chinese presence in Africa over the last 600 years is a good deal more extensive and influential than had previously been thought. What comes to light through the author's journey all over the continent is the extensive reach of this influence. It is supported by a thriving literature, mainly

Chinese, which has begun to document this experience. It includes, of course, the work of Gavin Menzies *1421: The Year China Discovered the World*, which is critiqued by JR Masson, referenced above. But the point about this literature is that it is not known widely. *China in Africa* is an enormously valuable attempt to change that situation around. It constitutes a valuable contribution to what we know. And even if it will be challenged, as Masson does, it puts forward a set of cues with which a proper discussion can proceed. At its core is the thesis that the China–Africa encounter is founded on very different principles than was the case with the European encounter with Africa. Most powerfully, the author makes no pejorative judgements about the Africa he experiences. His observations lead him to conclusions of sadness and disappointment but they do not begin with a sense of superiority and patronisation. Judgements made are utterly human ones. There is sadness at the degree of poverty and misery that is there to be seen on the continent. There is also disappointment at what could have been achieved. But neither of these sentiments *other* the people that are the subjects of discussion. This is what makes this book such an important contribution to the discussion of the relationship between China and Africa.

A final comment about what I call the Columbine legacy is in order. Hyperbolic as the allegory of Columbus is in the explanatory logics of who we are as a modern world, we must not in our aversion to what it represents be so unwise to want to efface it, erase it and to behave as if Columbus did not help to inaugurate a phase of global development that has unleashed intensely complex effects in almost every aspect of our lives as human beings. These effects were both good and bad. They are deeply part of who we are as a modern people living in a modern world. We are in the inescapable and never-to-turn away from embrace of the technologies that supposedly defined the making of the Columbine legacy – from navigational instruments to guns. We are also in the embrace of the complex of ideas of what human life is all about. And these ideas range from the extremely offensive to the most hospitable. These ideas, which sometimes developed into technologies, provided the frameworks for classifying and placing human beings into hierarchies of worth in many different ways, from looks to physical ability. This complexity is all ours now – all of it. We might reject part of it, but we cannot pretend it away. It is our task to work critically with this history. Working critically with it demands we understand it better. Understanding it better, and critically, we will learn, for example, that the idea of a pristine and self-constructed Europe – its technology and its knowledge base – is false. Europe was the inheritor of global developments – Egypt, Mesopotamia and in more recent times, the Islamic world. It built on them in wondrous and important ways. From the printing press to the rifle.

Li Xenfing's work helps us to take the critique further. It helps us to unravel our entangled human legacy, the legacy of the last 600 years of living together across the globe. To avoid the hubris of superiority of one group of human beings over another, the hubris of 'race', of purity, of gender, of culture and of class, we now have to be deeply aware, too, of how we tell the stories of these last 600 years. We are in the deep age of globalisation. This book makes available another way of telling this story. It is a response to the Columbine tradition. I am honoured that the Human Sciences Research Council (HSRC) Press is publishing it. The HSRC is dedicated to the ideal of unconditional equality and unconditional dignity. This book exemplifies that HSRC spirit.

Crain Soudien
Chief Executive Officer, HSRC

Foreword
from the Chinese Academy of Social Sciences

It gives me great pleasure to know that Dr Li Xinfeng's monograph *Following Zheng He's Footprints through Africa* (English edition titled *China in Africa*) is soon to be published by the Human Sciences Research Council Press in South Africa. As the first joint publication by the China Social Sciences Press and the Human Sciences Research Council Press, it marks the successful launch of the cooperation in publishing between think tanks in China and Africa.

Working as an accredited journalist for the *People's Daily*, *Global Times*, and people.com.cn at the turn of the century, Dr Li Xinfeng lived in South Africa for eight years, travelling across half the African continent to report on and record major changes in South Africa and other parts of the continent. The forthcoming English edition of the monograph, a record of his pursuit of Zheng He's footprints there, has been reprinted several times in China and has garnered great attention, having won multiple national literary awards as well as a warm reception by the general reader. Professor Fan Jingyi, the late renowned editor-in-chief of the *People's Daily*, applauded the publication, saying that 'he [Dr. Li] has presented an epic of Chinese history to the world and added a new chapter to Chinese history'. I would like to add that it has also contributed an epic story to the history of Sino-African relations. The publication of its English edition in South Africa will bring Zheng He's story in Africa back to the continent for the reading public there.

Six hundred years ago, Zheng He, a great Chinese navigator in the Ming Dynasty, led a large fleet to set sail from a harbor city in China and blaze the trail across the Indian Ocean to the coast of East Africa. This remarkable feat opened up the Maritime Silk Road between China and Africa, initiated their official diplomacy, and tapped into a new realm of economic and trade exchanges between China and other countries. Through his travels, Zheng He built a bridge of friendship, based on goodwill and equality, that linked the Yangtze River to the Cape of Good Hope. At the present historical stage, 600 years later, President Xi Jinping has proposed with great vision 'the Road and Belt Initiative', in which 'the 21st Century Maritime Silk Road' recalls Zheng He's earlier voyage. When talking about Zheng He's four visits to Africa, people may ask: What is the heritage of Zheng He's visit to Africa? Are there any inspiring stories during the journey? What is the relevance of these visits to Sino-African relations today? *China in Africa*, ably answers all these questions.

Zheng He, in his visits to Africa decades earlier than the European colonists, brought silk, porcelain and tea to Africa, along with the notion of equality, mutual respect, mutual benefit and win-win progress, forming a striking contrast to the actions of later colonisers to Africa. China, with the world's strongest naval fleet and most sophisticated weapons, had no intention to invade, plunder or colonise Africa. This firm historical evidence manifests that the Chinese, as true friends to the African people, will hold onto the long-lasting friendship between the two peoples on equal footing, and that the so-called theories of the 'China Threat' and 'neo-colonialism' are merely fabrications out of thin air.

Through research, Dr Li Xinfeng argues that the descendants of Zheng He's crew living in Pate Island, Kenya, today are descendants of the first Chinese immigrants to Africa, decades earlier than the western colonisers, and that Zheng He's four visits to Africa marks the first peak in the history of Sino-African relations. Later, direct contact between China and Africa was blocked by the western colonisers until the founding of the new China. As South African President Jacob Zuma stressed in his remarks at the opening session of the 5th Forum on China-Africa Cooperation (FOCAC) on July 19, 2012, 'When FOCAC was launched it marked a consummation of Africa–China friendship dating back to the famous Chinese navigator, Zheng He, who reached the African coast four times during the Ming dynasty.'

Since the launch of FOCAC in November 2000, Sino–African relations have witnessed a rapid, soundand comprehensive development. As a key national think-tank, the Chinese Academy of Social Sciences has conducted research in cooperation with the South African Human Sciences Research Council to provide policy advice and counsel to the governments of the two countries and to facilitate the sound, steady development of the bilateral ties, generating positive early results. The publication of the book marks the beginning of a rewarding cooperation in publishing between the think-tanks of China and South Africa, and of China and Africa, with the former setting an example for the latter.

In 2013, China President Xi Jinping proposed the Road and Belt Initiative based on the wealth of Chinese history and traditional culture, which was warmly welcomed by countries along the route. China rolled out the 'Strategic Planning of Silk Road Economic Belt and the 21st Century Maritime Silk Road' in 2014 and the 'Vision and Construction of Silk Road Economic Belt and the 21st-century Maritime Silk Road'. The Road and Belt Initiative, starting from scratch to connect the dots, has proceeded faster and seen better results than expected. More than 600 years ago, Zheng He's fleet arrived at the East African coast, opening up a Sino-African maritime Silk Road, and fuelling the cultural exchanges between China and Africa. With cross-cultural communication as the long-valued tradition for the Maritime Silk Road, the construction of the 21st-century Maritime Silk Road requires the help of the humanities and social sciences. It is the responsibility of social scientists to make their due contribution to building a sound and green Silk Road, featuring peace and intellectualism. And the publication of the English edition of this book will definitely further the understanding and communication between China and Africa.

At the Johannesburg Summit of FOCAC in December 2015, a milestone in Sino-African relations, China President Xi Jinping, the Chairman of the African Union Commission, and the leaders and heads of delegations from 50 African countries renewed their traditional friendship and sought mutually beneficial cooperation for common prosperity, forging Sino-African relations as a comprehensive strategic partnership. This marked a new era of Sino-African relations, geared towards win-win cooperation for common progress. At the summit, President Xi Jinping announced the 'top ten cooperation plans' and 'cultural cooperation plan' as part of the endeavour, which is a great inspiration and encouragement to us researchers of philosophy and social science. With the heavier burden and greater responsibility, we should step up our efforts to accomplish the great mission of our times. We are convinced that the all-round strategic partnership between China and Africa, including cooperation on humanities, will yield win-win or multi-win results to benefit China, Africa and the world as a whole.

Wang Weiguang
President, CASS

Prologue: Four visits to see 'relatives'

AUTUMN 2012, BEIJING

When the pleasant autumn wind had dyed Xiangshan Hill red and turned the surface of Beijing's Kunming Lake flowery, a special guest visited a media company nestled among the hills and between the waters. Though she came from distant Africa, she had deep roots in this land. She was not Chinese, but spoke fluent Mandarin. She hoped to become a Traditional Chinese Medicine (TCM) physician, but had never dreamt she would have the chance to study TCM in China.

This person was Lali Mwamaka Sharif, originally from Pate Island, in Kenya, and now a postgraduate student in Nanjing University of Traditional Chinese Medicine. Her teacher had given her the name Xia Ruifu, which sounded close to her surname, but she called herself Xiao Xia, after the customary Chinese mode of address.

It was a special gathering, in which every guest had an African background or an interest in Africa. Xiao Xia was African. Professor Qin Dashu, from the Archaeology Department at Beijing University, had twice led research teams on archaeological excavations in Kenya, searching for historical evidence of early connections between China and Africa. Yuan Xibo, president of the October Media Company and general manager of the African branch of the Qingdao Beer Company, had worked in Africa for eight years, at around the same time that I was working as a reporter in Africa for the Chinese newspaper the *People's Daily*. The Shandong Television Station was keenly interested in Xiao Xia's continuing studies and wanted to present the story to the public as a cross-cultural interest piece.

Between 1405 and 1433, explorer, mariner and diplomat Zheng He made seven voyages across what the Chinese called the Western Ocean (today the Indian Ocean). During four of these expeditions he reached the coast of East Africa. On one voyage, one of the ships struck a reef and was wrecked off the Kenyan coast. The sailors escaped in small boats and made it to nearby Pate Island. They exchanged their cargo of Chinese silk, porcelain, tea and other treasures to the local people for daily necessities, and often ended up marrying local women and had children there.

Even today, the descendants of those sailors have maintained their Chinese traditions, including the use of Chinese medicines and herbs, skills that were passed down from their ancestors. These medicines and herbal remedies have long been used to cure illness and ward off diseases, winning unanimous praise from the islanders. The local people named the earliest spot where the sailors settled the China Village and called their descendants Chinese. Sharif was one of the descendants of those unlucky sailors, and was widely known as the 'Chinese student' in her home town.

This was the fifth time I had met Xiao Xia. Though the others were meeting her now for the first time, it still felt to me like a gathering of old friends who had not met in some time. They chatted at leisure; the atmosphere was relaxed. Before we took our seats, our loquacious host, Yan Bing, asked, 'Xiao Xia, did you just call him "Uncle"?', pointing at me.

Caught off guard by this, Xiao Xia smiled shyly. Zhang Yin, the attentive organiser of the event, helped the embarrassed young woman out of the predicament by indicating that we should all take our seats.

Once we were seated, Yan Bing came straight to the point: 'Xiao Xia, your "uncle" has published his reports as a series entitled *Following Zheng He's footprints through Africa* in the *People's Daily* local and overseas editions. It has caused quite a stir, and there have been at least two direct results. One is that you have realised your dream of studying TCM. The other is that an agreement for a joint archaeology study has been made between China and Kenya. We have invited Mr Qin, the head of the China archaeological research team, to this event. Please tell us about your study and work in China. When did you arrive in the country?'

'I came to China in July 2005, when I was invited here to attend the commemorative events marking the 600th anniversary of Zheng He's journeys on the Western Ocean. In September that year, I began my studies at Nanjing University of Traditional Chinese Medicine. I have been in China for seven years. For the first few years, I studied Chinese language, then I spent five years studying TCM as my major. I started postgraduate studies in September this year,' she replied.

'Why did you want to learn TCM? Do Africans know about it? Are there TCM practitioners among the local people on your island?' asked our curious host.

'There is TCM on our island, brought there by Zheng He's fleet. It has been there for 600 years.' Saying this, she looked to me to continue the story.

By the time I had finished telling the story, I found myself thinking about Fakii Maka Mohed, a TCM physician I had met on Pate Island. I asked Xiao Xia whether Fakii had returned home or whether he was still in Malindi.

'He's still in Malindi. When I made my last trip home, I went to see him and his family. He's my aunt's ex-husband. His daughter Zaujat Fakii Maka is three years younger than me. She often visited me at my home,' Xiao Xia said.

On Pate Island, Fakii was a well-known doctor. A descendant of a member of Zheng He's crew, he had a medical family background. He was diligent in his studies, and skilled in traditional Chinese massage and diagnosis. He made his own medicines from local plants to cure his patients, and his treatments were very effective. Xiao Xia's dream of learning TCM had grown under his influence.

Our host asked, 'Xiao Xia, what courses are you taking this semester as a postgraduate?'

'Treatise on febrile diseases, theory of warm ailments, traditional Chinese paediatrics, traditional Chinese internal medicine, Western internal medicine ...' She went on listing course after course.

The inquisitive host asked, 'But are you learning TCM without practical lessons? How will you be able to treat patients when you graduate?'

'During my studies at college, I practised at a large hospital in Nanjing, and this summer I practised at a clinic near the university, treating patients myself,' she explained, assuaging the host's doubts.

Yuan Xibo interjected, 'Can you check our pulses and see if we have any illnesses?'

The host, Yan Bing, rolled up her right sleeve and smiled, inviting Xiao Xia to feel her pulse. A bit shy at first, Xiao Xia was finally persuaded to diagnose Yan Bing. Seeing her actions and facial expressions, we could not help but feel that she really was like a TCM doctor!

But when we asked for her diagnosis, she hesitated. Yan Bing said, 'If it is not convenient to say it in front of everyone, you can tell me later.'

Xiao Xia then asked for a cotton pad to cushion my wrist, to make my diagnosis easier. Someone fetched a sofa cushion, which sank as I rested my arm on it. We all laughed.

'If there's not anything suitable, we'll make do without it,' she said, removing the cushion.

Nervously, she extended her right arm, and placed her ring, middle and index fingers on the acupuncture points known as the *chizhong*, *guanshang* and *cunkou*. Her expression made me feel as though we were in a hospital and I was her patient. Observing her attentiveness, our initial laughter soon muted into silence.

The smell of tea filled the room. Its fragrance mingled with the silence, refreshing us. It is widely known that tea makes people feel refreshed and relaxed, but the scientific reason for this sensory perception was not revealed until quite recently, when two American scientists, Robert Lefkowitz and Brian Kobilka, won the 2012 Nobel Prize in chemistry for their breakthrough in the study of a certain receptor that enables humans to distinguish colours and flavours.

As I recalled these things, I was reminded of Liu Yuxi's poem in praise of autumn, composed perhaps under the influence of the chain reaction initiated by these receptors after a cup of tea: 'From ancient times to the present, autumn brings lonely feelings. But, to me, autumn is lovelier than spring. A crane soars above the clouds in a clear sky, bringing poetic romance to the blue expanse.'[1]

As the tea was placed on the table, steaming and fragrant, my mind drifted back to my previous meetings with Xiao Xia.

The fourth of these was in November 2009. I visited her at the Nanjing University of Traditional Chinese Medicine when I was attending the First Science and Technology Forum. By then she had grown accustomed to college life and was speaking fluent Chinese. When we met she called me 'Uncle' (see Chapter 15).

The third was when she visited Taicang in July 2005. Sharif came to China on an invitation to attend the activities organised by Jiangsu Province to mark the 600th anniversary of Zheng He's voyages on the Western Ocean. I was there gathering information. When we met at the press conference, she was so excited she couldn't say anything and her eyes were moist with tears. Those glittering tears may well have made it impossible to meet then, had we not already become acquainted in Kenya (see Chapter 15).

The first and second meetings occurred in May 2003 at the Lamu Girls' Shool on Lamu Island, Kenya. In early March 2002, as the first Chinese reporter to visit Pate Island, I went to the 'Chinese Village' and met 'Chinese' people in nearby Siyu Village. Sharif's mother was farming in the fields, so I missed the chance to meet her.

Then, in May 2003, I made a second information-gathering trip to Pate Island. When I visited Sharif's home, her mother, Baraica Badi Shee, received me warmly, as if I were a relative from her home town. After she showed me around her house, we chatted about daily life. She told me the legend of her ancestors, and we talked about her family's living conditions. She told me that her family was poor and depended entirely on her husband, a fisherman. Not only were they trying to earn enough to feed the family, but they also needed funds to keep Sharif in school. She sighed, saying that Sharif was her 'only hope' in life.

That evening, as soon as I returned to Lamu Island, where my hotel was, I hurried to Lamu Girls' School, where Sharif was studying. The school was in the suburbs of the sandy town of Lamu. It was dark by the time I stumbled up the sandy path to the school gate. Sealed off from the outside world, the school greeted me with a tightly closed door. Sharif, the 'Chinese student', was located by her friendly schoolmates and they brought her to me. We spoke through the iron bars of the gate. On the morning of 13 May, I went to the school again and visited Sharif and one of her teachers. To help relieve her difficult financial circumstances, I donated money for her school expenses and tuition fees the following semester. I also told her to contact me or the Chinese Embassy in Kenya if she needed further help during her secondary or college education. I assured her that she would receive a favourable reply (see Chapter 3).

In December 2004, having not been able to get a place in college after leaving school, Sharif returned home to Pate Island. Undeterred, she plucked up her courage and wrote a letter to the Chinese Embassy. And that is how this dialogue between China and that distant, secluded African island began.

This story has a long history and far-reaching significance. In 1405 (the third year of the Yongle reign), Zheng He began his voyages across the Western Ocean, possibly one of the greatest pioneering undertakings in human history. Between 1413, when Zheng He set out on his fourth expedition, journeying all the way to the East African coastal city states, and 1433 (the eighth year of the Xuande reign), which marked the end of his seven voyages, he visited Africa four times. In 2013, we celebrated the 600th anniversary of the first of Zheng He's four visits to Africa.

This anniversary seems to have brought me back to Africa, to the occasion of the Chinese fleet arriving on the East African coast, and to the African people's warm welcome for their friends from afar.

1

The journey to Pate Island

A CHINESE CREW'S AFRICAN DESCENDANTS

On the morning of 28 February 2002, my flight took off from Johannesburg International Airport and headed north. Though the scenery was beautiful, I was too excited about reaching the destination to really notice. I was heading to a Kenyan islet where Zheng He's footprints could be found and where descendants of his crew still lived – though their presence was a little-known fact. Despite three years of diligent preparations, I was still unsure whether this adventure would prove fruitful. My main concern was safety, which was by no means assured, considering I would be travelling alone by boat on the vast sea. I had been drawn by reports of descendants of Zheng He and his crew living on this island, and as I headed towards my destination, my mind was filled with these reports.

On 12 and 15 June 1999, two articles had appeared in South Africa's Chinese newspaper, the *Overseas Chinese Daily*.[1] These articles – titled 'Descendants of Zheng He's crew living in Kenya' and 'Shanga Village in Kenya derives its name from Shanghai' – reported that descendants of Zheng He's crew lived on Pate Island, off the coast of Kenya.[2]

These were translated from '1492: Prequel',[3] an article that had appeared in the *New York Times Magazine*. In his research for the articles, the author, Nicholas D Kristof, relied mainly on information gathered from authenticated materials in academic journals, a year-long dialogue with a Kenyan acquaintance in which Zheng He's story was mentioned and American author Louise Levathes's biography of Zheng He, *When China ruled the seas*.[4] When Levathes was invited to revise the technology section of Joseph Needham's series of academic books *Science and civilisation in China*[5] in the 1980s, she took an interest in the study of Zheng He. In her book, Levathes argues that China was able to rule the world during Zheng He's time, but did not do so. She goes on to speculate about how events might have unfolded if Zheng He had lived 80 years later and had met Vasco da Gama on the seas. Had da Gama been aware of the might of the Ming Dynasty and the colossal ships that made up its armada, would he have dared cross the Indian Ocean in his own small craft? Had Zheng He seen the Spanish ships, even armed to the teeth as they were, would he not have easily swept the 'little snails' from Europe aside and prevented them from opening up their eastern trade route?[6]

In the course of her research, Levathes visited many African countries. In Kenya she met a man who claimed to be the descendant of a Chinese sailor who had survived a shipwreck near Pate Island hundreds of years ago. A ship in Zheng He's fleet sank near the island and several members of the crew made it ashore, where they settled down and married local women. Several generations of their descendants have since lived on the island. When the *New York Times* reporter Kristof learnt of this long-forgotten event in 1999, he travelled to Kenya and the wild jungles of Pate Island. There, he discovered a group of people with obviously Asian features, evidenced by their eyes, hair and skin tone. Although reports of this event were sketchy – and barely recognisable when translated into Chinese – they attracted my attention. Might I be forgiven for assuming that my own closer connection to China and its cultural background would be an advantage when investigating the findings?

On 10 August 1999 the *Overseas Chinese Daily* then reported that a Chinese merchant had met a writer in Mogadishu who claimed part-Chinese ancestry. According to the writer's reports, there were people in parts of Somalia who had Chinese surnames, such as Lin or Huang. He made specific mention of a place called Zheng He Village in Kismayo, a city 500 km south of the capital, where most of the villagers were of Chinese descent. Taiwanese journal *Rhythms Monthly* had dispatched reporters to the site in 1998, but the team was diverted to the coastal area because of unrest in Somalia at the time. Unable to reach Pate Island, they had to gather information through more circuitous methods. The journal promised more in-depth articles at a later date.

Professional instinct and personal interest pushed me to journey towards the Zheng He Village, said to be nestled on that Kenyan islet.[7] Unfortunately, political unrest delayed the quest numerous times.

THE CHINA ROAD AND BRIDGE CORPORATION PROVIDES ACCESS

On 28 February I arrived in the Kenyan capital, Nairobi. When I enquired about the situation on Pate Island, I was repeatedly warned not to attempt a journey to the politically unstable island, so I altered my itinerary, travelling instead to Burundi and Rwanda on a fact-finding mission. In the Rwandan capital, Kigali, I approached the China Road and Bridge Corporation and asked them to present my request for assistance to their Kenyan office.

On 6 March I returned to Nairobi and was met by a staff member from the China Road and Bridge Corporation's office. I was aware that my proposed land–sea–air itinerary for the upcoming week would be confronted with endless roadblocks and frustrations, but the journey held great potential to progress my research.

I listened to the droplets patter on the window that rare rainy Kenyan night while I waited for the company's vice general manager, Xue Tiezhu. Xue, who was bringing information that would be helpful for my journey, was leading a project in Tanzania and was extremely busy with his own preparations. When he rushed in at ten o'clock, I went straight to the point, expressing my aims for and my misgivings about the mission to Pate Island. After hearing my spiel, he had several observations, the most significant of which was that he had personally travelled to Lamu Island and found Islamic Arab inhabitants there. Security would not be a problem, but there were bandits who occasionally roved along the coastal areas of Kenya, so it was advisable to fly to Pate Island rather than travel overland.

Having majored in Arabic, Xue took great interest in my story and very much wanted to travel with me as my interpreter, but was unable to take time off from work to do so. Had my itinerary been more flexible, he would have gladly accompanied me on the journey. The China Road and Bridge Corporation had withdrawn its Mombasa Division, and it was difficult to arrange for a local guide but, fortunately, a staff member was travelling to a work site near Mombasa the following day and offered to help get a local driver to take me to Malindi. He could guarantee my safety as far as Malindi, but having never been to Pate Island himself, he couldn't vouch for the situation there. He advised me to exercise great caution as I proceeded.

According to the agreed itinerary, I was to set off on the afternoon of 7 March and stay overnight at the China Road and Bridge site near Mombasa. The dorm was a collection of converted containers in the middle of the sultry jungle, an area frequented by wild animals. These flimsy structures could easily be overturned by the swipe of an elephant's trunk. To secure the area from such an incident, a pile of old tyres was kept on site. At the sound of an approaching elephant, staff would burn a tyre, and its pungent fumes repelled the creature.

I passed a muggy, restless night in the dorm. At eight o'clock the next morning, I set off in the company of 28-year-old Edward Ogel to visit the Mombasa Museum, housed in a former Portuguese castle. Mombasa first appears in historical records in 1154. By the 15th century, it had developed into a prosperous commercial centre for Asian, African and Arab trade. Chinese silk and pottery were often exchanged for local spices, gold and ivory. The well-known Yuan Dynasty traveller, Wang Dayuan, once visited the site.[8]

Zheng He's fleet visited Mombasa,[9] which Portuguese navigator Vasco da Gama likewise passed on his eastward journey to India. In the 16th century, Portuguese invaders burned and plundered the city four times, occupying it in 1589 and moving their headquarters from Malindi to Mombasa. In 1593, the Portuguese conquerors invested a great deal of human, natural and financial resources in the large-scale construction of a military defence fortress in Mombasa. The project was completed three years later. Over a century later, in 1697, Arab forces defeated the Portuguese and seized Mombasa. In 1888, the British captured the city from the Portuguese. Mombasa was returned to its rightful owners only when Kenya gained national independence from the British in 1963.

The first artefact that caught my attention in the museum was a sailing boat. A closer look revealed that it was the vessel in which Vasco da Gama had travelled to Mombasa in 1498. Turning away from the boat, I noticed a jar inscribed with two Chinese characters, *sheng qiao* (盛桥). The information placard described it as a piece of 17th-century Chinese porcelain unearthed in Mombasa. As I ventured deeper into the museum, I discovered a porcelain exhibition hall filled with a large range of porcelain pieces, including a finely wrought glazed plate with a dragon motif. The introduction to the exhibition stated that Chinese celadon ware was more popular in 15th-century Mombasa than was Islamic glassware. I had previously read *Chinese porcelain in Fort Jesus*, which describes pieces of Chinese porcelain discovered at Mombasa Fort inscribed with the characters 中 (*zhong*), 国 (*guo*), 磁 (*ci*) and 器 (*qi*).[10] This was convincing evidence of the abundance of Chinese porcelain unearthed in the area.

When I left the museum to head to Malindi, I came across a Chinese restaurant. I stopped there, not for the food, but to seek insight into the security situation in the coastal area. As I was leaving, a man from Hong Kong warned me that though he had been in Mombasa for many years, he did not dare attempt the trip north to Malindi. He warned me that 'bandits' were rampant and advised I proceed with extreme caution.

MYSTERY OF THE ZHENG HE MONUMENT

My driver, who was an honest, able young man, had moved with his family from his birthplace in Malindi to Mombasa. Here, in Mombasa, he had worked for the China Road and Bridge Corporation for five years. He told me that the 121-km road from Mombasa to Malindi was safe, but that I must not continue along the road north from Malindi. He insisted that I should fly to Lamu Island, rather than travel by land. I thanked him and assured him I had already bought my air ticket.

Gedi, the renowned ancient city state near Malindi, was a site where much Chinese ceramic ware was unearthed in the 20th century, sparking lively discussion among archaeologists. This, coupled with the fact that Wang Dayuan had toured the area, was enough to establish a long-standing association between Gedi and China. In my search for traces of Zheng He in Africa, I arrived at the remains of this ancient city on 8 March.

From the carved decorations found in the Islamic glazed pottery unearthed from the ancient city, James Kirkman, a British scholar and archaeologist specialising in excavations of Gedi, estimates that construction of the town began at the end of the 13th or early in the 14th century. The city reached its height in the mid 15th century; it was deserted by the early years of the 17th century. The word 'Gedi', meaning 'precious', originates from Galla, now known as Oromo.

Covering 45 acres, the main sites of the ancient city of Gedi are the imperial palace, the Great Mosque, the city walls and the tomb. The imperial palace is made up of 10 structures, two of which – the Chinese Coin Room and the Porcelain Room – have connections to Chinese culture. Archaeologists have discovered a complete Chinese celadon bowl dating from the 16th century, its surface decorated with a lotus motif, representing happiness. In the Porcelain Room, I also encountered an abundance of 15th-century Chinese porcelain ware, including celadon, blue and white porcelain, and decorative blue, white and green bowls, dishes and pots. At the Grand Mosque site alone, as many as 305 ancient Chinese porcelain fragments have been unearthed and are now on display at the Gedi Museum. According to archaeological evidence, porcelain ware was used both as art and as tableware. Archaeologists have found overwhelming evidence for close, prosperous commercial contact between Gedi and China in the 15th century.[11]

Wang Dayuan's presence in the area is attested to in *Descriptions of the barbarians of the isles*, as well as by Yuan Dynasty porcelain unearthed in Gedi, but the question remained whether Zheng He and his fleet had journeyed as far as Gedi. There were still three rooms of artefacts to explore: the Iron Lighting Facility Room, the Scissors Room and the Shell Room. Ironware, silk and porcelain were major export commodities from Ming Dynasty China, and shells were often used as currency in East African commercial transactions. The presence of such items together in one site suggests that commercial trade between Gedi and China might have been common. It is well established that Zheng He's fleet visited Malindi and Mombasa. As the coastal city of Gedi is between these two cities, just 16 km from Malindi, Zheng He's fleet must also have been aware of Gedi. Moreover, the celadon, and the blue-and-white porcelain unearthed there, dating from the 15th century and after, seem to provide sufficient evidence that there was continuous commerce between China and Gedi from the time Zheng He visited the town.

My tight schedule forced me to hurry through the museum and begin my trek to Malindi. Just before we arrived, my driver, Ogel, offered an important piece of information. He said that when he lived in Malindi about 10 years earlier, his friends had mentioned a Chinese monument standing near a beach. It was inscribed with block-shaped Chinese characters. He knew nothing of Zheng He, but our conversations along the way had brought this monument to mind. He suspected it might be a monument to Zheng He, though none of the local people could be sure, since they could not read the Chinese characters. In the area, it was simply referred to as the 'Chinese Monument' to differentiate it from the Vasco da Gama Monument. I was overjoyed to think there might be a Zheng He Monument in Malindi.

Arriving at four o'clock in the afternoon, we got directions from Ogel's friend and made our way straight to the monument. Unfortunately, the open stretch of beach where the monument had once stood was now occupied by the White Elephant Hotel and a smattering of residential buildings. The hotel was still under construction, and the work site was closed, since it was a Saturday evening. We knocked and called before someone finally opened the door for us. We were allowed to enter the site and made a thorough search, but we could not find the monument. Ogel frowned and muttered, 'It must be here somewhere. If only I had seen it with my own eyes, I would know exactly where.'

The hotel guard told us that when the water tower was being constructed behind the hotel, a stone tablet was removed and placed beside the tower. It had sat there for a long time before it finally disappeared once and for all. We continued to question the guard, but he had no further information.

We felt disappointed, but unwilling to give up on this lead. We walked along the beach, entered residential complexes, and walked the streets, asking everyone we met about the stone tablet inscribed with Chinese characters. No one had any information. It was getting very late when we eventually left without having accomplished our mission.

The next morning, we renewed our efforts. We spoke to Ogel's friend, talked to elderly members of the community and looked for the local museum. We hoped to get some clue about the monument. One of the elderly people we met took us to a brick tower, roughly ten or twenty feet tall. At a glance, we knew this was not a monument, but just a tombstone of some celebrated figure. After a long search, we finally made contact with the museum director, Aboalla Ali, who acknowledged that Malindi did have contact with China, but insisted that there was no Chinese monument in the area.

Ogel did not accept the denial, and was frankly puzzled by it. 'I wonder if they're afraid of admitting being involved in the destruction of such a precious cultural relic. The Vasco da Gama Monument at the intersection between Malindi and Silver Sand Bay is half a century younger than the Chinese Monument, but it has received a lot of attention, and even government protection, in recent years.'

Zheng He erected monuments at Liujiagang in Taicang, Jiangsu Province, as a way of marking the beginning of his journey. Similar monuments – more than 10 stone steles – have likewise been unearthed in various parts of South East Asia, demonstrating the extent of his navigations. The mystery of the Zheng He Monument in Malindi has yet to be revealed.

VISITING THE HOME OF THE KYLIN

It is a well-known historical fact that the Malindi king presented a giraffe to the Ming emperor, an event symbolic of good Sino–African relations. This fact is a familiar household story in China, Kenya and many parts of the African continent. Frequently, former South African president Thabo Mbeki delightedly related this tale as he spoke of friendly relations between China and Africa.

'Malin' refers to Malindi, home of the kylin (*qilin*) or giraffe, an auspicious animal in ancient Chinese thought. It should be noted that the Somali word for giraffe, *girin*, is pronounced like the Chinese kylin. In 1414 the Bangladeshi king presented a giraffe from Malindi to the Ming Emperor Zhu Di, causing a great stir in the imperial court. In 1415, when Malindi sent an envoy to deliver a giraffe to the Chinese capital, the Chinese emperor went to welcome the envoy. *The history of Ming* records:

> Malin is very far from China. In the 13th year of the reign of the Emperor Yongle, an envoy was sent to present a kylin as a gift to the Chinese emperor. The Minister of Rites, Lu Zhen, called for a ceremony. The emperor said, 'In the past, Confucian ministers presented us with the *Four Books and Five Classics*, and I accepted it as being good for governance. Whether the kylin exists or not, it means no harm. Let it be.' After that, Malin and other countries presented the kylin, heavenly horse, or holy deer as gifts, and the emperor received them at the Fengtian Gate, while all the ministers kowtowed to express their congratulations.[12]

As I travelled to Malindi, regarded by the ancient Chinese people as the home of the kylin, I listened to folk tales about giraffes. The popularity of this particular story demonstrated to me the importance the Kenyan government placed on Sino–African friendship. *Kenya past and present*, a history book in the form of children's stories about Kenya, displays on its cover a picture of a kylin presented as a tribute to China. The cover artwork is an illustration by Shen Du, an imperial academy lecturer during the Ming Dynasty. It depicts the scene of the Bangladeshi envoy presenting the giraffe to the Chinese emperor in the ninth month of the 12th year of Yongle's reign. *Ki-Lin the celestial giraffe* narrates the story of Zheng He's fleet visiting Malindi and the tale of the kylin being presented to China. It is a fascinating read. The book's author posits that Zheng He's purpose in travelling to Malindi was to find the kylin when the Chinese emperor learnt that it was home to the giraffe he had received from the Bangladeshi king in 1415.

When the Malindi king gave the giraffe to the Chinese emperor, the book suggests, it was Zheng He's fleet that transported the animal home. Two years later, Zheng He made his fifth voyage across the Indian Ocean in a ship 107 m long and weighing 3 000 tons. This voyage was made to send the envoy from Malindi home after they had respectfully presented the giraffe to the emperor.[13]

The reason for the Chinese emperor's interest in the kylin is worth considering. The ancient Chinese people respected the kylin as a totem and revered it as a holy animal. It was seen as a symbol of good luck that could bring great benefits. Even the Han Dynasty philosopher Wang Chong, a well-known atheist, referred to the kylin as a 'holy animal' in his book *On balance*. The ancient Chinese people held the fantastical view that the kylin was the offspring of a cow mated with a dragon, with the 'ky' representing the male and the 'lin' the female. The kylin was said to have the body of an elk, the tail of a cow, and a horn on its snout. It was supposed to be colourful with a yellow belly, and standing ten feet tall. Because no one had ever seen such an extraordinary creature, it became a mythical, divine symbol. The Ming Dynasty painter Shen Du said: 'I have heard that a saint is holy and benevolent, and a kylin is born when the living and dead are in balance.' The Ming Dynasty Confucian minister Jin Youzi is even more specific:

> I have heard that the kylin is a great benevolent creature on earth and when the emperor's merits extend to heaven, earth, and his people, the kylin is born. I have also heard that only when heaven is not affected by its way, earth by its treasures, and man by his affections is the kylin born.

Many officials, prominent figures and imperial scholars of the Ming Dynasty spoke highly of the kylin, and at least 16 anthologies in praise of the auspicious creature were compiled, including *Odes to the auspicious kylin*.[14]

According to research conducted by experts in Zheng He studies, Zheng Hesheng and Zheng Yijun, various African and Asian countries presented Ming emperors with a kylin as a tribute on at least five occasions. The first was in the ninth month of the 12th year of Yongle's reign (1414), presented by the Bangladeshi king. The second occurred the following September, brought by Malindi. In the autumn of the 15th year of Yongle (1417), the people of Adan made the third such gift, and the fourth was bestowed in the eighth year of the reign of Xuande (1433) by several countries, including Calicut and Adan. The fifth and final known gift again came from Bangladesh, presented in the 10th month of the third year of Zhengtong's reign (1438).

The director of the Malindi Museum noted that the story of the giraffe was only one aspect of friendly Sino–Kenyan relations. During the Ming Dynasty, the king of Malindi had dispatched several envoys to China, each bringing animals such as zebras and ostriches. 'Over time, things changed. Without particularly intending it, the emphasis shifted to the interior of Africa and its rarely sighted animals, especially giraffes,' said the director. He then added: 'Malindi envoys brought back Chinese imperial specialties and the Zheng He fleet brought porcelain wares, silk and silk products, which were received enthusiastically by the local people. Chinese porcelain quickly became a symbol of wealth that was highly treasured. Collecting Chinese porcelain became a fashion among the wealthy, as evidenced by the abundance of Chinese porcelain bowls and plates laid in tombstones as a symbol of social status.'

The museum's director led us to Mambrui, a village, 11 km north of Malindi. Crossing a weedy graveyard, we came to a fairly well-preserved cylindrical tombstone, roughly the height of a man. It was inlaid with Chinese porcelain – ten pieces in all, six of which had been stolen; the remaining four were broken into fragments. A celadon pot in the form of a lotus petal was nestled on top of the tombstone. 'The local people take any Chinese porcelain as a treasure, especially complete plates. Even broken shards are carried home and kept as treasures,' the director explained. 'This highlights China's presence in Malindi and the status of Chinese porcelain in the area. Unfortunately, the frequent contact between the two countries didn't last, despite the impressive navigational skills of the Chinese people. China gradually faded from Malindi when the area was occupied by the Portuguese.'

Though the Chinese presence waned, the story of the giraffe has lingered for many generations.

THE KYLIN'S VOYAGE TO CHINA

There is a fairy tale about the kylin in *Kenya past and present*, which goes as follows:

> 'Why aren't we important?' the young spotted giraffe, Raja, asked his mother. 'Why should the lion be king of beasts? We are bigger and our coat is beautifully decorated. We truly are a wonder. We're the tallest of all the creatures, too. Why shouldn't we rule the animal kingdom?'
>
> 'We've already had our heyday,' his mother replied. 'It's time you learn about our ancestor, the kylin. Humans view us as beings from the celestial kingdom. The Bangladeshi king even presented us to the Chinese emperor as a gift. As soon as the Chinese emperor saw the kylin, he bowed to it, respecting it as a holy animal. This happened over 500 years ago, but it remains a fascinating tale.'
>
> 'Tell me the story, Mama,' Raja begged. 'How did the kylin get to China?'
>
> 'It happened hundreds of years ago, back when there were many more animals than there are now,' Raja's mother began. 'The giraffes then were just like us, living only in Africa. People in other parts of the world had never heard of them, because humans didn't have so many planes and boats, and so didn't travel as much.'
>
> 'Did boats have big engines back then?' Raja asked.
>
> 'No, they were wind powered and had long sails made out of cloth or palm leaves,' his mother replied. 'It was a sailing vessel that took the kylin from Africa to China. The voyage took half the year, and they constantly faced

terrible waves. The kylin wasn't used to the sort of tough life one faces on a ship, and he fell ill.'

'Poor kylin,' Raja said, sighing. 'Did he want to travel at sea like that?'

'He was proud to be chosen,' his mother answered.

'Why was he chosen?'

'Humans are adventurous animals who always want to discover new continents. They sailed from India to Africa, exchanging spices and salt for timber and ivory, and even for other humans! The Bangladeshi king came to Africa, and when he stopped at the port of Malindi, he saw giraffes roaming around the coastal areas, munching on the leaves from the treetops.' Raja closed his eyes imagining a huge giraffe standing right before him.

My name is Kylin and I'm going to tell you a story about myself. I am very tall, and my parents are very proud of me. We never go hungry, since I can reach the leaves from the very tops of the trees. We often pass twigs down for other family members to feast on.

One day, I was roaming on the plain, and as I approached the woods, I heard someone calling to me. When I looked back to see who was calling, I heard another whistle. A coil of rope fell around my head, and the knot tightened around my neck. I struggled, but the rope tightened even more, and my front legs started to feel limp. I was afraid I might fall if I kicked, so I kept my peace and bowed my head, trying to maintain my dignity while I looked at my captors.

'He's a beautiful animal,' one of them said.

'This is the best one we've found,' another agreed.

'We can present this one to the emperor,' a third said.

Hearing their conversation, my ears perked up. I knew an emperor was an important person, a king. From their exchange, I gathered I was not destined to be eaten. It was the Bangladeshi king who had ordered my capture, and he planned to present me to the Chinese emperor.

There were a dozen or more people on the site, but I knew they could not move me even if they all worked together. I knew that if I kicked any one of them, he would not survive, but I felt that they meant me no harm. So, when they untied me, I cooperated willingly. They then brought me to a harbour, but were at a loss as to how to get me aboard the ship. Though I had been to many rivers and watering holes in the jungle, I had never been so close to the sea. The ocean is very different from a river, and its white splashing waves and roaring surf frightened me.

One of my captors was appointed to serve as my bodyguard. 'I'll take it for a walk along the shore,' he said, snatching the other end of the rope around my neck and leading me down the sloping beach. My huge hoofs were buried in the soft white sand. Human children surrounded me, stepping into my footprints and staring at me in wonder. They had never seen such a huge creature. I let the sea water swirl around my legs, a cool, comforting eddy. I lowered my head to drink the water, but didn't like it at all. Seawater is salty and doesn't quench your thirst.

My guard took me to a shelter, where I spent the night. On a raised portion in the shelter, there was an earthen pot with clean water and a stack of palm leaves. I was not interested in these refreshments, though. I was homesick, missing my family terribly. I was willing to leave them for the sake of this momentous journey, but I also longed for them. I was very lonely. Gathering all my strength, I kicked the door. It collapsed and fell on me, knocking me to the ground. The guard rushed over and commanded his men to remove the debris from my body and help me to my feet. They were very friendly, and checked me all over to be sure I was not wounded. 'How did this happen?' they asked each other. They did not imagine that I had kicked down the door.

I was not wounded, but I was in shock. Though kicking the door could have injured my neck or legs, I had no trouble getting up. A guard beside me said, 'We are going to China, a foreign land. The Chinese people have made the largest ship in the world. The great sailor and his fleet will take you to China. You are very fortunate, Kylin!'

Within a few weeks, I was used to walking on the beach. One day, when the tide was receding, a guard took me to a submerged rock, near Zheng He and his vessel. Zheng He climbed up the rock and ushered me through the waves, at great risk to himself. The sailors were astonished when I strode onto the ship's deck. Zheng He and his crew took me to the ship's hold. Knowing that I liked to eat bushy, thorny vegetation, they had prepared great stores of it. Zheng He bowed to me and called me 'distinguished guest' and 'revered symbol', and things like 'divine beast' or 'holy animal'. He often referred to me as 'the most precious gift to be presented to the emperor'.

The boat tossed up and down on the sea. It was a long, difficult voyage. I missed having solid ground under my hoofs, and I longed to roam and hunt for the food I liked to eat, but the guards were always there, and they were meticulous in caring for me. I had plenty of food and fresh water, and I was never left alone even for a moment.

The long-awaited day finally arrived. We reached the Chinese harbour. I got off the boat and into the seawater, striding several paces to reach the soft white sand. Having grown accustomed to the ship's tossing, I almost lost my balance when I stepped on solid ground.

Zheng He also disembarked. Bowing to me, he said, 'Holy animal, let's go see the emperor.'

I followed the guard and his men, no rope around my neck and no hand laid upon me. When I came to the imperial palace, I found a large crowd of humans in the compound. Tall as I was, I immediately caught sight of the emperor on his throne, surrounded by his officials.

The crowd separated, creating a path between me and the emperor. As I started toward him, everyone bowed to me. The Chinese people had never seen an animal such as me, and so took me for a sacred creature. The imperial housekeeper walked toward me, gaze shifting between me and the emperor. 'I have seen this sacred animal before,' he said respectfully. 'It came to me in a dream and said, "Only when the ruler of the land is benevolent and upright can the kylin appear".'

As the officials were congratulating the emperor, he received the praise modestly, saying, 'It is because of my wise, benevolent father that the kylin has come, and to you officials, who have helped me uphold his ways.'

All eyes turned to me, expecting a speech. I stood beside the emperor, looking at the crowd.

'My name is Kylin,' I began. 'I have come to China from Malindi, a small city on a continent called Africa, very far from here. The journey was long and arduous, but despite the dangers and diseases we faced on the way, I have arrived safely and in good health.'

Then I was marched from the imperial palace to my residence and made a 'symbol of perfection', not only in China, but throughout the world. In the minds of humans, I stood for perfect benevolent governance, perfect royal power, and perfect harmony.

Hearing this, Raja opened his eyes. 'That happened a long time ago,' his mother said. Raja stood beside her, rubbing her shoulder with his two horns. Having never seen other giraffes, Raja thought his mother was huge.

'That was such a nice story that Kylin told me!' said Raja. 'So the Chinese people think we come from the heavenly kingdom. I wish all humans thought so.'

'Humans are beginning to trust us,' his mother said. 'We are protected by many of their laws.'

'I want to be a kylin,' Raja said. 'I want to be big and strong, and I want to be famous.'

'You will be,' his mother said. 'You are a descendant of the kylin. He told you the story himself.'

THE CHINESE *TITANIC*

The scorching March sun can be unbearable on Africa's east coast, and its nights are humid, sultry and mosquito-ridden. I spent an uneasy, restless night at the Eden Garden Rock Hotel. I planned to travel north the following day, crossing Lamu Island on foot before travelling onwards to Pate Island, where social unrest remained a huge concern. I had to decide that night whether I would proceed on the journey despite the danger, but I was still not sure what I should do.

At ten o'clock, I went to the hotel's rear courtyard to sit beside the swimming pool, which overlooked the Indian Ocean. I listened to the turbulent rhythm of the waves. After great hesitation, I decided I would get more information from the hotel before making my decision the next day. At the reception desk, I asked the night manager, Mr Wanderly, about the political situation on Lamu and Pate islands. He informed me about certain special customs observed on Lamu Island, but assured me that Western visitors had been received there all year without incident. He had been there before, and the Romance Hotel Group, of which his hotel was part, had a branch there, the New Lamu Palace Hotel. He assured me that the situation on Lamu Island was fine, but added that he had no idea about Pate Island and had never been there. After hearing my story and learning of my concerns, he told me frankly, 'Please trust me, friend. Lamu Island is certainly safe. You can go there, then decide your next step. Your story is fascinating. I hope your concerns about safety will not cause you to give up at this early stage.'

Wanderly's advice boosted my confidence. So, at noon the following day, I boarded a 35-seater plane for Lamu Island. I was seated opposite a young couple who were making their second trip to Lamu Island for a holiday. They took an interest in my quest and gave me the contact information of the hotel where they were staying. They were friends with the hotel manager and said he could be of help if I ran into any trouble there.

The Lamu Archipelago is a group of five islands – Lamu, Manda, Pate, Ndau and Kiwayu – of varying sizes, just off the coast, running north to south. Pate, the largest, is about 75 km^2 in area. The two northernmost islands are the smallest. Lamu Town, the only 'city' in the island group, is the seat of government. Our plane landed at Manda Airport, which was very basic, with a runway that looked more like a broad highway.

Geographically, the archipelago is just a stone's throw from the African continent, but, developmentally, people say they remain three or four centuries behind. The islands of Manda and Lamu are merely a nautical mile apart, connected by the hotel ferry. The only other means of transport and communication on the islands was by donkey. At the airport, our luggage was transported by hand carts, and we had to identify our baggage. The fence around the airport comprised a few sticks thrown together in front of the waiting room, which had no proper walls. From a distance, I spotted my name on a board, handwritten by the Palace Hotel staff.

Once at the hotel, I went about gathering information about Pate Island. The hotel's assistant manager said that the island was very safe and that the hotel could arrange transport for me. The challenge lay in the fact that the channel between the islands was narrow and the water level low, making passage impossible even by small craft. We needed to wait for a favourable tide if we wanted to be certain that the water level would allow smooth passage, so she advised me to consider the situation before setting a definite departure time. She took out a calendar and consulted it for some time before telling me that I would need to wait several days before conditions would be favourable for me to begin my journey. When I asked her about Zheng He, she said she knew nothing about him, but her manager was returning from his travels in London the following afternoon, and perhaps he would know something.

It was getting late, and no arrangements had yet been made for the next phase of my journey. The couple I had met on the plane came to mind. I learnt from staff at my hotel that where the couple were staying, the Pelbolis Hotel, was at the southernmost tip of the island, a two-hour walk there and back. Because it was getting late, I gave up on the idea of meeting them.

I spent the night in the seaside hotel, listening to the roar of the wind and waves. Early the next morning, when I was having breakfast alone at the hotel and feeling very anxious, a stout man came down the stairs and greeted me warmly. He introduced himself as David Wheeler, an American businessman who had married a local teacher. He was a frequent visitor to Lamu Island. He offered me a cup of Chinese tea brewed from leaves he had bought on a trip to China the previous month. When he asked why I had travelled to such a remote place, I explained to him how I was in search of information about Zheng He's story. He got very excited. He started clapping his hands and said, 'It's the 'Chinese *Titanic*. Your report will reach the Chinese authorities and they will dispatch people to raise the treasure vessel that has been on the seabed for 600 years. You know I am a businessman. If no one else takes an interest in the ship, I would very much like to raise it and discover what treasures it holds.'

The American rolled up his sleeves and leaned in close, snickering as he said, 'Or maybe we could come to a deal ourselves. You don't have to publicise your findings. We could just raise the ship ourselves. Just imagine the splash we would make then!'

We laughed about that idea, then Wheeler told me that he had been to Pate Island in a small boat, and that he knew the captain, another large, effusive fellow. He told me that the captain was suffering from some discomfort in his leg and had asked Wheeler to get him some herbal medicine from China. When Wheeler brought it back for the captain, he said it had been very effective.

I could not wait to find this man and hear more from him about the sunken vessel, to learn more about the 'Chinese Village' on Pate Island and to hear his tales of the wonderful therapeutic value of traditional Chinese medicine. We wolfed down our breakfast and set out for the seaside, where Wheeler said we were likely to find Captain Abass Makoko.

THE CAPTAIN'S NARRATIVE

The frank, fiftyish Captain Abass Makoko noted that I was from China, and not from the Chinese Village. He had been born on Lamu Island and had gone back and forth between the islands, so he was very well informed about local happenings. He explained that the villages on Pate Island all had some connection to China: 'We do not call the place by its name, Shanga, but simply call it "the Chinese Village". Upon meeting a person, the people of the island always immediately ask, "Are you from the Chinese Village?"'

'The massage therapy doctor there is very professional. If anyone has a twisted, sprained, or bruised limb, he gets on a boat and goes straight to this doctor. I often take people there, and I've consulted him myself many times. I saw him just last week.'

Abass, a plump man, had a chronic ache in his leg that caused him to walk with a limp. 'When I injured my leg, I went straight to the doctor, and he gave me a massage. It was immediately effective. He said it would be even more effective with Chinese herbs, so I asked Wheeler to bring them over from China.'

Wheeler cut in and said it was a medication for injured muscles, but could not remember the exact name.

Abass smiled at Wheeler and said, 'That's how we've become friends. It was because of Chinese medicine that we got to know each other.

'Everyone in Lamu knows the Chinese villages, and knows they are all associated with China. The old legend is that an ancient Chinese ship struck a rock and sank near Pate Island.' He went on to say that the rock was still visible, and that ships plying that section of the sea had to proceed with caution.

I told Abass the names of the five villages I knew, to check the accuracy of my information. He took out paper and pen and sketched the locations of these villages along the coast. As he drew, he explained that Pate, Shanga and Siyu were the major villages, forming a triangle. The other two, Faza and Tundwa, were on the north-eastern coast.

After obtaining this information, I explained the purpose of my journey and asked him for more details about the best route, the amount of time I would need and the costs the journey would entail. Considering the navigation routes and dock positions, he suggested that we start early the next morning, navigate around Pate Island in a clockwise direction, visiting Pate, Shanga, Faza, Tundwa and Siyu, then return to Lamu before dark. I was concerned that we would not have enough time, but Abass did not think it prudent to stay on Pate, where conditions were poor and there were lots of mosquitoes. So he recommended staying on Kiwayu Island, where the treetop hotels were cool and would also shelter us from disturbance by mosquitoes and wild animals.

When I asked about safety issues and water levels, Abass was quite confident, adding that he would send his assistant, Omaly, to accompany me on my information-gathering expedition, since it was advisable to travel with a local companion. He assured me the low water level would not be a problem – he was familiar with routes in that area and could paddle me ashore if the tide was low.

Hoping to make the most of our time, we decided to leave at one o'clock that afternoon, visiting Pate and Shanga villages first, then staying on Kiwayu before visiting the other three villages the following day. Having set our itinerary, Abass began making preparations for our meals and for refuelling the boat.

Meeting these two men, who were like brothers, was a turning point in my journey. At my request, Wheeler accompanied me to the dock to wait for Abass. He told the captain to take good care of me, since he now counted me as a friend. He said that the priority was our safe return. He winked at me and said, 'I'll wait at the docks for your triumphant return, and we can negotiate our plan to raise the Chinese *Titanic*.'

Since I was a stranger in an exotic place, I reminded myself to be cautious. I convinced Abass that Wheeler and I were old friends, and made it clear to him that I had left my cash and luggage, except for the bare essentials, at the hotel, and would pay him when we got back.

The battery-powered boat had seats for five or six passengers. We slowly left the dock near Avicennia Marina, named after the vervain plant, and entered the expanse of the Indian Ocean. The captain accelerated, and a gush of salty seawater splashed onto my face. The tiny craft pushed ahead, followed by a line of white wake breaking the surface of the blue sea. The sun shone brightly, creating a beautiful mirage on the horizon. Near Pate Island, a row of seven or eight rocks looking like sea monsters poked above the surface of the water. Abass said it was one of these that Zheng He's ship had struck, causing it to sink. I asked him to bring me closer, but he said that there were too many hidden rocks, and he did not wish to be grounded on them.

As we approached the island, the water level became lower. The captain turned off the engine and pulled the motor out of the water, then he began to move the vessel towards the shore with a long pole. Before long, we came aground and could move no further. The captain motioned for me to get out of the boat and wade to the shore. I took my camera bag, removed my shoes, and hopped into the water. Before I got out of the boat, Abass told me that the tide was going out, so he would not be able to wait at the spot where he left me. He needed to get his boat away from the shore, so he would wait for me at Siyu Village, on the northern part of the island, where the channel was still navigable.

'You should hurry and make your visit, then rent a donkey or bicycle for your visit to Shanga, before travelling on to Siyu by donkey. I'll wait for you there,' he said, then rowed into deeper waters. These arrangements proved to be tortuous.

THE VILLAGE HEADMAN TELLS OF A SHIPWRECK

In recent years Pate Village had become a must-visit site for foreign tourists. Many Western tourists viewed it as a quaint town three or four centuries behind the modern world, so its primitiveness was the main draw for those seeking untouched nature, relaxation and tranquillity. Because Pate Village was seen as more backward than Lamu Town, it tended to attract many Western tourists.

The tourism business was a source of income for the local people, who often stood at the entrance to the village or on their small home-made boats, offering their services to visitors. When I reached the shore, the village head approached me and introduced himself as Athman Mohd, offering to serve as my guide around the Pate relic site for just 300 shillings (a dollar was the equivalent of 78 shillings).

The relic site was adjacent to Pate Village, along the beach. Mohd led me across the banana grove to the remains of the site. The buildings were mostly Arab in style; there were domestic residences and a mosque. The village head was young and knew little about local history, so he invited an older man along to tell me about the earliest village chief, Batawi, whose descendants had ruled from the early 14th to the 17th century. In brief, when Nabahan (a sultan from Oman) came to Pate Village, he introduced Islam to help facilitate his rule. After converting to Islam, the villagers gradually yielded to him, and he replaced the Batawi rulers. Later, Arabs from Zanzibar overthrew Nabahan, then maintained their rule through British occupation, during which the village maintained its traditions mostly without change.

On our short trip back from the relic site, the village head told me that I would see 'the influence of China, with many people having faces similar to yours'. As he was speaking, we were interrupted by a middle-aged man on his way to work with a straw bag on his back. Mohd asked me if I noticed that the man looked Chinese. As we entered a narrow alley, we saw some women sitting on the ground in front of their doors weaving coconut leaves into bags of various sizes or bed mats; some were weaving containers for holding chopsticks. Seeing a stranger, they dropped their work and disappeared indoors. In front of one of the houses, Mohd pointed out the Chinese-style locks on the doors and the Chinese style of architecture.

When we arrived at the home of the village head, I noticed a lantern hanging from the ceiling. He was surprised when I told him that it looked familiar. He explained that there was no electric lighting in the village, so lanterns were necessary. When we were seated, Mohd explained how the Chinese influence was closely connected to the shipwreck: 'Long ago, a ship drifted off course and struck a rock near Pate Island, where it sank. Hundreds of sailors hastily tried to escape in small lifeboats, carrying porcelain, silk and other valuables with them. Four hundred men rowed to Pate Island, landing on the reedy shore near Shanga. They exchanged their porcelain and silk for food and money. Eventually, 40 of them stayed in Shanga, while the rest left along two routes, 100 heading westward toward Pate Village and 260 northward to Siyu Village. At the time, Shanga was a large village, but a water shortage forced many of the villagers to leave. Added to this problem was a malaria epidemic, which caused the population of Pate Village to decline sharply. Now, only three Chinese families remain on the island.'

As he continued, my mind wandered: all the documents I had consulted suggested that it was not an accident that had driven Zheng He's fleet towards the island. Rather, the fleet had approached the island with a view to conducting trade, but had sunk during a storm. According to those reports, Pate Island had been prosperous at the time, and its wealthy inhabitants took great pride in collecting Chinese porcelain and wearing Chinese silk.

After landing on Pate Island, the Chinese sailors married local women, ultimately settling down to raise their children there. According to Mohd, the population of the island grew to 2 350 at the time, dividing into two tribes known as Nabahan and Pokomd. Among them were three Chinese families bearing the name Wafamau, a term meaning 'Chinese people' in the local language. At this point in the village head's narrative, we were interrupted by a boy who had been sent to contact the Chinese families. He reported that the doors of all the Wafamau were locked, and they were all out working in the fields.

I interviewed the village head so that I could find out more about the local Chinese people. The interview went as follows:

Q: Are the Chinese people here wealthy?
A: As is the case all over the world, we have some rich people and some poor. Comparatively speaking, the Wafamau are rich, aided by the porcelain and silk they carried with them when they arrived. Now they have their own land, and they do well because they are hard-working. (*At this point, the village head went and retrieved a piece of porcelain and asked if I wanted it, for a good price. I looked more closely and saw that it was a recent item, made in Britain. I declined.*)
Q: What sort of food do the Chinese people here eat?
A: Our staple food is corn and bananas. The Wafamau are like the local people not only in their farming techniques, but also in their diet. The people of Pate Island do not grow their own vegetables. Even potatoes and onions have to be brought over from Lamu Island, then sold at high prices because they are

brought over from the mainland. Because transportation is so limited here, we do not have vegetables all year round.

It was four o'clock by now, and Omaly and I had to hurry back. To my surprise, when I proposed renting a bicycle or donkey for the journey to Shanga Village, Mohd made a gesture with his hand and said, 'No, the route is too bumpy for a donkey. And how could you ride a bike there?'

When he saw my surprised expression, he explained that people always travel by boat. When I proposed going on foot, he objected, explaining that the sandy path was difficult to follow and it would take two hours. We would not be able to reach Shanga before dark on foot. We hurried to the beach and were fortunate enough to catch a small boat to Shanga.

2
Discovering the Chinese Village

LODGING IN SIYU UNDER THE STARS

A small boat crept along the coast from west to east amid the amazing scenery. The tiny vessel on the azure waves of the vast Indian Ocean in the evening glow was an uncommonly beautiful sight. Though the boatmen strained hard against the cool evening breeze, I was frustrated by our slow progress. Omaly and I picked up the oars and started to row, hoping to quicken the pace, but the headwind made our efforts futile. As we approached Shanga Village, the boatmen deliberately overshot our destination, so that we could tack back smoothly into the small dock in the south-east wind. However, just as we were about to hoist the sail, a strong gust of wind came and nearly capsized us. We all cried out, and I clutched my camera bag against my body, observing the faces of my three companions who were all pale with fright.

It was dusk by now, so we postponed our visit to the village until the next day and immediately went to find the village head. When we told him about the purpose of our visit, his eyes flashed with surprise and delight. 'You're a Chinese reporter? Welcome to our village! It is getting late, so stay here tonight and, tomorrow, I will take you to the relic site. After that, you can come back here and hear a general account of the Chinese Village.'

I told him that we had to meet Abass at Siyu Village, and that we needed to go there urgently, as he was probably getting anxious waiting for us.

The only road across the densely forested island was the sandy trail between Shanga and Siyu. We went on foot. Omaly was not familiar with the island, so we hired a boatman as our guide. The three of us trekked along the bushy trail covered in weeds, the thick layer of sand making it difficult to walk. The other two walked barefoot and were nimble, while I was too anxious to hurry on and became clumsy in my haste. Sand filled my shoes, causing great discomfort. There was no moon, but the dim starlight helped make the route discernible. I feared wild animals might appear from nowhere and wander onto our path. My companions assured me there were no wild animals, though snakes were not uncommon.

After a 90-minute hike, we reached Siyu Village. We met a middle-aged man, who introduced himself as a fisherman. He said that the captain was waiting for us by the shore and offered to take us to him.

Siyu Village was connected to the jetty by a narrow, snaking trail. When we arrived, the captain was nowhere to be seen but, hearing our voices, he shouted to us from the boat, 'We have to put up in the boat for tonight. Come on over.'

He shone his torchlight onto the sea to guide us across the stone steps. Because his boat was quite large, it could not be pulled ashore. The fisherman jumped into the water and pushed a small boat towards me. When I leapt aboard, he rowed me out to the captain, but the sea was rough and it was very dark, preventing the two vessels from being brought together. When the captain reached over to pull me aboard, the two boats collided so hard we nearly capsized. Unable to swim, I was very frightened, but the captain could not see my expression in the dark. He tried very hard to persuade me to stay in the boat, arguing that it was cooler and that I would not be pestered by sandflies, but I insisted on going back to the village for the night.

Siyu is the largest village on Pate Island, with a population of about 3 500. From a distance, the silent village was veiled in darkness, barring the dim light coming from a few households. There were no guesthouses or hotels, since the place was isolated and seldom had visitors. When a visitor happened to need to stay, he could negotiate bed and board with one of the better-off families. Our guide, the fisherman, proposed that we stay in his home, for which he would charge 500 shillings for the pair of us. We agreed to this arrangement and asked where we could find food – fear having now given way to hunger and thirst. It was eleven o'clock at night, my throat was dry and my stomach empty. I thought of the food I had left in the boat.

We finally located a household that ran a restaurant. The check patterns on the dining table and sitting-room walls were similar to those seen in China. The host's daughter brought us cups of tea brewed from rainwater, which is drunk by the locals here. It was of poor quality in colour and aroma, and had sugar added to it. After some time, a plate of local staple food was brought out: bread made from coconut powder and fried dumplings. It was delicious, hunger being sufficient seasoning for any meal. Breakfast the next morning was coconut cakes, prepared in a style similar to the baked pancakes commonly eaten in China.

Our lodging for the night was with a poor family, their house nothing but bare walls, and it was dark in our room. The host briefly overcame his shyness to ask me whether I would mind paying him, explaining that he did not have enough money for kerosene to light the house. I gave him the money, and he went to buy kerosene. When he returned, the lamp could not be found, since it had been so long since the family had last used it. There were four rooms in the house, and one uneven bed with an old cotton cover on it. The host presented us with two almost-new patterned cloths the size of bath towels, referring to them as 'quilts'. I had left my toiletry kit in the boat, but that was fine – it would not have been of much use without running water anyway. I slept in my clothes, smelly, sweaty and sandy. The house had a single tiny window and when it was closed, the room was muggy. Before I dozed off, mosquitoes appeared to add to the misery. But even without the mosquitoes, there was no hope of falling asleep on that thin cotton pad in such heat. Later, we moved into the sitting room and opened the door, but the mosquitoes would not leave us alone. I dozed intermittently through the night.

YOU ARE MY GRANDPA

Islam was the dominant religion on the island and, early in the morning, I was awakened by the call to prayers. The call was amplified over a generator-powered loudspeaker, as there was no electricity in the village.

In the daylight I could see the true face of Siyu Village. Its houses were almost identical, each made from matting of coconut leaves, or from the leaves themselves. The paths were irregular, winding, narrow and uneven. Only a few of the younger people wore 'proper' clothing; the rest – young and old, male and female – wore no trousers, just a large piece of cloth wrapped about the waist, single-coloured for men and multicoloured for women. People carried water to and fro while donkeys ambled along the paths, creating a memorable scene in the village. While we were eating breakfast, a young man named Mansoor Ile offered to be our guide, saying he had participated in the excavation of the relic sites in Siyu and Shanga, during which he had unearthed a large amount of porcelain fragments. He offered me the fragments, and I asked him to serve as my guide.

There were four 'Chinese' families in Siyu – in other words, four families in which one member had Chinese blood. When I followed the zigzagging path to the home of the first of these families, I found it locked with an iron gate. At the second home, the wife was a 'Chinese' woman, but she had gone to work in the fields, leaving her 16-year-old boy at home. When he poked his head through the door, my guide said, 'Look, this boy's eyes are small, his skin is whiter than his eyes, and his hair is very dark. It's a typical Chinese face.'

When I asked if I could enter the house, the boy replied, 'Mother says not to let strangers in when she's not home.'

I asked if I could take a photo, but he said he would need his mother's consent for that too. Evidently, it was a strictly disciplined home. The house itself was the only one that was fenced in, which might have been a reflection of Chinese architectural concepts.

After my anxiety-ridden, tiring journey the previous day and the sleepless night that followed, my head was numb and my limbs ached. I walked round the village several times before finding the third 'Chinese' household, but the man who lived there was not at home. Being somewhat trained in Traditional Chinese Medicine (TCM), apparently he was quite a celebrity in the area. He had opened a clinic in Malindi two years earlier, and had just left to return there two days earlier, after a visit to his home town. His wife was warm, but not very talkative. She knew little about China or TCM. Her six-year-old son played in the yard, but was too shy to speak to strangers. Walking through the fenced yard into the house, I noticed a heated, raised earthen bed, like a Chinese *kang* bed-stove, and some cubby holes dug into the wall, both of which seemed to have possible connections to China.

As I hesitated on the village path, a lean, elderly man carrying a pole with two buckets of water over his shoulder approached. He had been eyeing me for a while now and as he walked closer, he put down his pole and broke into a trot. He grasped my hands and mumbled excitedly, 'You are very much like my father.' He paused, then added, 'You must be my grandpa. You come from China, where my old home was.'

As he spoke, tears formed in his eyes. The touching scene surprised all who were present, and a crowd started to gather along the path. As we held one another's hands tightly, I studied his appearance closely. He really did look Chinese, with lighter skin tones, long hair, small eyes and thin lips. Standing together on the path, physically we were a clear contrast to those gathered around us. At a loss, I said, 'I'm glad to see you.'

The 58-year-old man introduced himself as Salim Bwanaheri and invited me to his home. He told me that his ancestors had come here many years ago on a ship by way of South East Asia, settling here after a shipwreck. His ancestors had told him that China was a very large and faraway place, and that it could be reached only after a long, arduous journey. They had told him that Chinese characters looked blockish, and that Chinese silk and porcelain were famous all over the world. He did not say much other than this.

Though his house was tall, it looked fairly similar to the others in the village. There was little in the house, certainly nothing of value. On the wall was a clock that didn't work, which he said had been handed down from his ancestor. I took it down and looked at it, but found no writing on it. He took a yellow iron lock from a cubby hole in the wall. It was a three-ring lock, with 'Made in China' written on it in Chinese. This was the only thing his family had from China. He said he had nine children, all of whom had left Pate Island. His youngest son, Ali Salim Bwanaheri, then aged 22, was living on Lamu Island. Hearing the name, my companion, Omaly, said that Ali was his colleague; he worked on board a ship. Omaly found Ali the next morning and brought him to me. Ali said he had travelled to Lamu to study but, having no money to support himself, had gone to work as an assistant on a ship. When I mentioned the story of Zheng He's fleet, he said,

'That happened too long ago. No one on Pate Island will be able to give a clear account of that story. We only had sketchy information about it in the first place.' He did express an interest in learning more, though.

We followed Salim from his house to the place where he drew water. Though we had been acquainted for only a short while, we were reluctant to part company. I asked Omaly to give the elderly man a cigarette. Salim said he hoped we might give him some money, both to commemorate our meeting and as a tip for the photos we took. I agreed.

After nearly 600 years of existence in this remote island and intermarriage with the local people, the Chinese descendants on Pate Island had been integrated into African life over the generations. Even so, they clearly retained some Chinese characteristics, both in tradition and in their physical appearance. Besides the physical similarities – eyes, skin and hair – they also shared what some might term 'Chinese priorities' – in other words, valuing studies, family values, and even familiarity with TCM practices handed down by previous generations. Discontented with local conditions, many of the young people had left the remote island to seek a better future. The domestic features, such as fenced walls and heated earthen beds, were unique in this place, and the Chinese habit of carrying water in buckets on a pole held across the shoulders contrasted with the local practice of transporting water on carts. Even their diet bore some traces of Chinese influence: the coconut-flour cakes, and especially the technique of flattening out the dough with a rolling pin, had been passed down by the Chinese – as is readily acknowledged by the local people.

SIYU VILLAGE, BUILT BY THE CHINESE

After meeting some of the 'Chinese' families, I found it disappointing to discover that they did not know much about Zheng He's fleet. I had learnt from reading about the history of Kenya that there were nine major tribes living along the coast, and that their histories did not exist in written form. Their only recorded histories were in the form of documents derived from stories and archaeological discoveries, so I decided to find some elderly people well-versed in the oral histories of the region. I eventually met 58-year-old Kubwa Mohamed, headman of Siyu Village. He was repairing his boat.

The headman here was similar to the president of an association of elders, a person of lofty values and worthy of respect. Referring to the history of Siyu, Mohamed explained that the village had been established by Chinese people: 'If it had not been for the Chinese, there would have been no Siyu.' He pointed out that the village, which was close to the shore, had once been a stretch of wilderness, but it had an abundant water supply, as there was much rain. Local people stored water in cellars. When the leader of Pate Village attacked Shanga from the west and conquered it, all the villagers, including the Chinese, had fled. Having nowhere to go, they eventually settled here. The residential area was established by the Chinese people, and it eventually developed into Siyu Village.

'If so many Chinese people came here at the founding of the village, why are there only four Chinese families here now?' I asked. The headman continued: 'Later, the Portuguese arrived on Pate Island, moving all the way from Shanga to attack Siyu. Later still, the Arabians came north to the village. Finally, the Swahilis arrived too. Siyu has been the largest and most heavily populated village on the island ever since. According to our history, since it was founded by the Chinese people, Siyu increased in numbers without anyone really noticing. Finally, it became the heart of the whole area in 1873, when its population rose to about 10 000, making it the largest of all the villages on the island. In 1895 a smallpox epidemic killed 1 400 people, which prompted many to flee to the mainland to escape the disease. This reduced the population to about 5 000 by 1897. When the population of Pate Island was at its peak, during the century between 1750 and 1850, Pate Village had between 20 000 and 25 000 inhabitants, and Siyu 30 000, exceeding the total population of Zanzibar in 1890.'

'What happened to the Chinese people after that?' I asked. Mohamed replied: 'Those who came to Pate Island were all men. They married local women and fathered children here. Many who moved to Siyu with their families suffered from unrest or natural disasters, so they soon left the island to seek their living elsewhere. Many went south along the coast on the mainland, settling in one place or another. Some say they went to Malindi; some say to Mombasa or some other coastal city.'

According to the Malindi Museum director, the Portuguese had encountered Chinese people living in Malindi. In light of this, I thought it most probable that at least the bulk of the Chinese settlers had moved to Malindi. After the shipwreck, back in China, the Ming Dynasty changed its diplomatic policy, putting a halt to Zheng He's expeditions on the Western Ocean. It was possible that the Chinese people on Pate Island had given up hope for Zheng He's return after such a long wait, and so started searching along the East African coast for other Chinese communities. With so many tales of the king of Malindi presenting a giraffe to the Chinese emperor, it is reasonable to assume that they might have searched for other former members of Zheng He's fleet in Malindi.

The headman was firmly convinced that Siyu had been established by the Chinese and was deeply influenced by Chinese culture and practices. Some evidence he pointed to in support of his theory were the blacksmiths who forged tools, a skill he believed had been passed down from the Chinese. He also referred to the fact that their dead were not buried in Siyu: the coffins were carried to Shanga for burial – Shanga being the site where they had originally landed. The headman was not sure why this custom was practised, but I suggested it might have come from the Chinese notion that the leaves must return to nourish the roots of the tree from which they fell. Because the Chinese people on Pate Island could not return to their homeland, China, Shanga Village, where they first set foot on the island, would be considered their home.

Our interpreter interjected here, adding that the tombs of the Chinese inhabitants were different from those of the local people. The Chinese tombs, built in hemispherical domes, could still be seen at the Siyu Village relic site. They had been inlaid with porcelain, which had since been looted.

I visited the ancient castle north of Siyu Village. It was believed that the castle was built by the Portuguese, though some thought it had been built by the Arabs. I had also planned to visit the Siyu clinic, which was located in a small house, but it was closed.

At the Siyu relic site, I found several hemispherical tombs, of different sizes. Some had had porcelain inlaid along the outside, some on the inner portions, but it had all been stolen long ago, leaving only the impressions behind. Archaeological discoveries have revealed that the Siyu relic site once included 19 stone-built houses, three mosques and a collection of important tombs. As we approached, the sound emanating from a smithy led us to a thatched cottage, where an elderly man was forging a spade. He told me, 'This skill was passed down from my ancestors.'

When I left Siyu, I recalled how the village had been described by historian J de V Allen, of the University of Nairobi. The town was on a narrow part of Pate Island, facing the northern Kenyan coast, where it was possible to dock in the northern bay at high tide, but more difficult from the east. The name Siyu would inevitably bring to mind the Siyu Fort, which is now a museum. There are different opinions about who built the fort and when it was built. In a paper titled 'Siyu in the 18th and 19th centuries', Allen is of the opinion that the early population fell into nine ethnic categories: Masherifu, Washanga, Waarabu, Wahadimu, Mafazi, Wafamau, Wasegeju, Wakatwa and Waswahili. He writes: 'As evidenced by the prefixes, the population falls into two broad categories, Ma and Wa – the former referring to "outsider" and the latter to "native". The part after the prefix indicates their place of origin, such as "Shanga" after the prefix "Wa", or indicates their language, as in "Swahili" in "Waswahili".'[1]

According to this categorisation, the author divides the people into 'Wafamau' (outsiders) and 'natives', evidence of the long history of outsiders in Siyu Village. In the article, Allen emphasises that 'Wafamau refers to China, and the earthen stone dome is typical of Wafamau tombs'.[2] 'Wafamau' was not originally the family name of the Chinese, but a reference to the category of outsiders. However, over time, the two were collapsed into one.

Allen points out that at the end of the 18th century, when Siyu was invaded by enemies, a young Wafamau named Mataka bravely led the villagers in heroic battles. After defeating the enemy attack, he was elected their leader. The author also notes that Siyu was prosperous for a time, attracting so many craftsmen and scholars that it became renowned as a 'city of craftsmen' and a multicultural centre. The author lists discoveries of artistic works found in Siyu Village, pointing out that the 'high-backed square chair' was a special feature of Siyu.[3] He goes on to add that this type of chair is not of Arab style, nor was it brought in from the Gulf region. Since there is nothing else of its kind in the area, he deems its provenance a mystery. In fact, this sort of chair is common in China and is apparently another contribution of the Wafamau.

SHANGA, THE 'CHINESE VILLAGE'

As I prepared to say farewell to Siyu and head south to Shanga Village, I encountered an elderly man who looked quite travel-worn. Without a word, he offered me a bottle of mineral water. Before I could say thank you, he took out a piece of paper and handed it to me, saying that he was the father of the Shanga Village headman and had come here at the request of Captain Abass to bring me water and information. The water really was a timely gift, and the paper was a handwritten note from the captain telling me he was waiting for me at the entrance to the village. This information put me at ease.

Led by my guide, we started our trip back to Shanga along the same path we had taken the previous night. Walking along the bushy, sandy trail under the bright sun in the breezeless air was like being in a sauna or an enormous greenhouse. Perspiration soaked me from head to toe, my sweaty clothing constantly dried by the sun, only to start the cycle over again. We passed a primary school and saw the children playing during their break. Seeing a stranger with a camera in hand, they scattered like frightened lambs and ran back into the classroom, leaving nothing but a sandy cloud in their wake.

We stopped first at the Shanga relic site. The guide indicated a hollow in the tomb pillar, explaining that this was a Chinese tomb. 'The column used to be inlaid with porcelain plates.'

I asked, 'How do you know? The tombs of the wealthy are also inlaid with porcelain plates.' The guide explained that when he helped the archaeologists excavate the relic site, he had learnt that if the unearthed body was facing north, the deceased would have been a Muslim, laid to rest facing Mecca. If the body inside the tomb was not facing north, it was not that of a Muslim. His logic was that the Chinese were not likely to be Muslims, and were not buried facing north.

When we got to Shanga, there were few people to be seen in the sweltering lanes of the village. In front of the village head's house, we were greeted by several smiling children riding a camel. Their vitality perked us up. A vessel containing water lay by the corner of the house, lonely and silent. It was noon, the hour the head's father had agreed to meet us. Hearing us talking outside his house, the headman came out, smiling and welcoming us inside. His warm greeting made us feel like old friends. We shook hands and fell into a relaxed conversation – it was as if we were family members catching up on gossip.

The 31-year-old village head was called Swaleh Mohamed. He started talking about his village, which now actually consisted of four centres near the Shanga relic site. The combined population was 480 people, all living in the administrative division set up shortly after Kenya gained its independence.

'Shanga Village was originally called Mtangani, meaning "desert land", but was changed to Shanga when the Chinese people came. The new name was taken from "Shanghai".'

I wondered whether the new name derived from the Chinese settlers' nostalgia for home, or from its geographic location 'on the sea' – the meaning of Shanghai in Chinese.

The village head laughed and said, 'When Shanga villagers go to Lamu Town, the people there ask, "Are you from Shanghai, China?", or just, "Are you from China?" Over time, Shanga Village has also become known as "the Chinese Village".'

When I asked how the village name came to be changed to Shanga, he said it had been passed down by local legend, according to what he had read in a locally written book about world history. When I asked for the title of the book and where I might buy a copy, he said that, unfortunately, it would be difficult to find. 'It has been a long time since I read it.'

When I asked how the Chinese sailors got to Shanga, he said: 'Before the arrival of the Chinese, the town was inhabited by Arabs. The Chinese sailors landed here after a shipwreck, it being the closest landing point to their wreck. Their sudden arrival brought many problems, including language barriers, causing difficulties in communication, a lack of sufficient drinking water, and culture clashes between the Chinese and the Arabs, particularly in regard to religion. These problems were intensified by war and epidemics, eventually forcing the Chinese to leave. That's why you will not find any Chinese people in Shanga today.' He added, 'The elderly people in the village often tell a story of the king of Malindi presenting a giraffe to the Chinese emperor. I've read the same story in books about Kenyan history. The time that story took place is the same time that the Chinese landed at Shanga.'

The information I had gathered at Pate, Siyu and Shanga seemed to support the conclusion that, after the shipwreck, the sailors landed at Shanga. After this, for various reasons, some left and headed west to Pate Village, while others headed north, founding Siyu Village. The archaeologists who studied the Shanga relic site believe that it can be traced back to the period between the early 15th and 18th centuries, and that the Chinese porcelain unearthed there comes from the period between the Tang and Ming dynasties, including lacquered pottery, olive-green

Tang Dynasty pieces, celadon and coloured, patterned porcelain. Archaeologists also believe that before the Chinese came to Pate Island, Chinese porcelain and silk would already have been traded on this remote island and other areas along the East African coast. Unfortunately, Chinese silks have not yet been among the archaeological findings, probably because such fabrics would be unlikely to be preserved in the coastal climate.

Historical facts suggest that the shipwreck near Pate Island took place during Zheng He's time. If it had occurred before his voyage, the shipwreck survivors would not have known about the story of the giraffe and, given the transportation and communication technologies of that era, it is unlikely these islanders would have obtained such information from the outside world. If the shipwreck had occurred after the period of Zheng He's voyages, the survivors could not have settled in Shanga Village. Research by British archaeologists suggests that the Shanga relic site already existed between the 8th and early 15th centuries – a conclusion based on the discovery of a crude olive-green ceramic pot from around AD 800, and the unearthing of some Song, early Ming Dynasty and early 14th-century Longquan porcelain, all of which came from China. In other words, the ancient Shanga Village was destroyed around AD 1440, not long after Zheng He's last voyage across the Western Ocean.[4]

CHINESE MASSAGE AT SHANGA

The young headman of Shanga emphasised that, even though there were no Chinese people currently living in the Chinese Village, Shanga was much more influenced by Chinese culture than Pate or Siyu had been. The most obvious evidence of this influence was the use of massage and cupping – two forms of TCM for which the village was known in the surrounding islands. 'Currently, there are 14 massage therapists and seven others who know how to use cupping in the village, most of whom are elderly women,' he said. 'I have made an appointment with four of them, each from different families, and they are waiting for you. Let's go visit them.'

Following the village head, we first went to the home of a doctor who specialised in massage. It was just across the road from the village head's home. Hearing our voices when we arrived at her gate, a woman of about 50 came out from behind the curtained doorway to meet us. It was apparent that the furnishings in her house were unique to her village. After the village head had introduced us, the massage therapist smiled shyly, sitting quietly on the edge of a single bed in the living area. I later learnt that she had the impression that anyone from China – the home of massage – was an expert in TCM, making her feel that talking to me about massage was like trying to teach a fish to swim.

After I had prompted her repeatedly, the renowned doctor opened up, telling me that her skill had been passed down from her grandmother, who, in turn, had learnt it from her own grandmother, who had learnt it from a Chinese person. She cited various cases of ailments she had treated: 'When someone has a dislocated joint, they come to me and I set the bones in the right position, including areas like jaws and elbow dislocations. The first step is to make sure of the precise location by feeling it with my hands, then, with an abrupt thrust, to restore the bones to their proper position. As a general rule, if the patient still feels a little discomfort, it can be relieved with gentle rubbing. Before long, they will feel like everything is back to normal.

'If someone comes to me with a stomach ache, I give her or him a cup of ginger tea, prepared from tea leaves and ginger slices. After the patient drinks the tea, I use massage to relieve the pain. The results are evident. When massaging certain parts of the body, especially if the pain is in the waist or back, I use coconut or similar oil as a massage oil, to make it more comfortable for both doctor and patient, and to heighten the efficacy of the massage.

'The frequency of treatment depends on the patient and his condition. Generally, a patient with a headache receives a massage twice a day. And, for headache patients, I wrap the head loosely with a towel or some similar cloth before massaging, in order to help relieve the pain.'

I asked her, 'Besides applying coconut oil in massage, are there other aids that you use, like acupuncture?'

She replied, 'I don't know how to use acupuncture or other methods, but I do sometimes use Kuumika.'

The village head explained that Kuumika was made from an animal horn with the lower end sawn flush and the tip removed. 'When I treat a patient, I light a flame inside the horn, then press it to the skin and seal the top with my index finger. It seems to me that this is cupping, but I am not sure.'

Later, the village head got a doctor from the village who specialised in cupping to demonstrate the method on his own arm. I realised that this 'horn pressing' technique was a variation of Chinese cupping, or what one might call 'African cupping'.

As our visit came to an end, Mwanabule, the massage doctor, asked me if there were similar therapies in China, and if there were corresponding medicines for these sorts of injuries. She said all the medical knowledge on the island had been passed down from one generation to the next and that no doctors had had the opportunity to engage in advanced studies. They were therefore not well informed about modern practices in TCM, and knew little other than the fact that China was far away and that Chinese massage was as famous throughout the world as Chinese martial arts.

I had never imagined that I would be perceived as a skilled practitioner of TCM. Before I could make my way to the home of the next massage therapist, a masseuse had brought one of her patients to consult me. She asked if I could treat the condition of a young boy whom she had brought along. She said she knew that massage would exacerbate the problem. Her own method of treatment was to pound fresh ginger slices and the leaves from a local tree into a paste before applying it around the eyes and around the temple, in the hope of cooling his inflamed eyes. Seeing the boy, I had an idea. I had brought some cooling ointment with me, which I took out. I told the therapist that she could use this in the same way that she had applied her own remedy and perhaps it would be more effective. My suggestion deepened the impression that I was an expert in Chinese medicine. After talking further to the therapist, I learnt that her treatment included eye exercises assisted by head massage as a means for relieving pain and pressure on the eyes.

The other two doctors received me together. One specialised in eye diseases, the other in gynaecological issues. The latter, holding a baby in her arms, talked extensively, mainly about adjusting foetal positions through palpation to facilitate childbirth, relieve pain and reduce foetus mortality rates. On Pate Island, there was a shortage of doctors and it was poorly supplied with medical provisions, so these forms of therapy were necessary, effective and popular. Shanga's version of Chinese cupping and massage were mysterious to outsiders, adding to the mystique that surrounded the village.

Centuries earlier, when the people of Pate invaded Shanga, they plundered, killed and looted, abusing and imprisoning young and old, men and women. At that time, according to a legend, one of the invaders came across a beautiful woman who was grinding herbs. Just as he advanced to capture her, the ground split open and swallowed her, leaving only a strip of her skirt visible. Surprised by this story, Sudan, then ruler of Pate Village, ordered that a tomb be built for her at the site and that the soldier keep vigil beside the tomb. Unfortunately, the precise location of the tomb is unknown. Even so, the legend has been passed down from one generation to the next, adding to the mysterious aura surrounding Shanga Village.[5]

THREE REQUESTS FROM THE CHINESE VILLAGE

By the time I had finished visiting the massage therapists, it was getting late and I was ready to start my journey back to Lamu, when the village head indicated he had something more to tell me. Pointing at a house across from his, he told me that though this was their video room, they had no way of watching television because there was no electricity on the island. Evidently, watching videos was the villagers' main recreational activity, and most of their knowledge of China today came from watching martial-arts films. Bruce Lee, Jackie Chan, and Jet Li were household names there – and all because of this video room. He told me about the local people's impression of China: 'The elderly people say the Chinese are highly skilled in medicine and that they are all doctors who can cure various diseases simply through massage. The young people say that Chinese martial arts are known all over the world, and every Chinese person is a master who could knock even a huge white man down with a simple move. We all believe these things must be true.'

'How do you show videos, as there is no electricity on the island?' I enquired.

Without answering, the village head led me to a small room in his home where there was a generator. He turned on the machine, picked up a television and video player, and led me to the viewing room. Now that I was in the Chinese Village, and because the harvest time was over, he would show me a scene from their bumper-harvest celebration to give me a broader understanding of the people there. I repeatedly thanked him for his kindness as he adjusted the image on the screen, which continued to jerk up and down despite his attempts to adjust it. I said, 'This is fine. I can get the idea from this.'

The image was unsteady and there was no music. It depicted a night scene where a group of barebacked, barefooted middle-aged men were dancing around a fire in a jungle clearing, waving wooden sticks in time with their merry singing, serving as a simple melody. He narrated as we watched, adding some harmony to what we saw: 'The staple crops are millet, sorghum, a little rice and cotton. Vegetables are rare. We mostly eat seafood.'

Watching the video gave me a good feel for life on the island. As the village head showed me the video of the harvest celebration, a crowd of villagers joined us and sat silently on a long bench, their eyes locked on the jerky image on the screen. Some playful children stood in front of me and struck martial-arts poses. The clever, quiet village head laughed.

When we left the video room, his father was waiting for me, and he led me to the shore at the end of the village. Pointing to a cistern a short distance away, the village head told me that drinking water had been a problem in Shanga for centuries. There had been cistern for drinking water for a long time, but with desert encroachment, rainwater purification remained a problem. As he was explaining this, he abruptly changed the subject: 'Because relations between Shanga Village and China are so deeply rooted, I have been following China's development. I know that China is rapidly progressing towards becoming a wealthy and powerful nation.' He paused and watched my expression, then added, 'For years, I have been harbouring three wishes, or, rather, requests.' Hearing this, I stopped to listen. The three of us looked at one another, then the village head continued: 'As a "Chinese Village", we have always thought of China as our old home, or at least half of our old home. We ask that the wealthy old home would build a water well for us so that we can improve our living conditions. Our next great difficulty is a shortage of doctors and medicine. TCM is well known around the world. We hope that China might establish a TCM school here to train some medical professionals, so that we can improve our massage-therapy and medical skills. A clinic would be our greatest desire.'

I genuinely did not feel he was asking for much. His requests were benevolent and targeted at the long-term development of his villagers. Besides, there really was a special connection between this place and China. Looking into the eyes of these two men, I was at a loss. What could I say that would be both sincere and satisfying?

I said, 'I will relay your requests to the relevant Chinese departments in my report. You can rest assured that I will give my readers a true picture of what Shanga Village is like.'

When I said this, the village head seemed embarrassed, making me feel awkward. His next words explained his embarrassment: 'I have two more requests. My father is going to Lamu on business. Can he travel in your boat? And, when we played the video, we had to use diesel. Could you give me some money to replace it?'

Before he had finished, I promised to reimburse him and apologised for not thinking of the cost.

As our boat set out, I thought of the lines of a Chinese poem: 'Sitting in a boat under the setting sun, it seems I am surrounded by tender greenery.'[6] We waved goodbye, one on the sea and one on land. Seeing Shanga and the village head fade into the distance, my heart felt as turbulent as the sea around me. Sitting in the little boat on the Indian Ocean, looking at the stretch of mangroves and the line of rocks off the coast of Pate Island that sank the ancient Chinese ship, I could picture Zheng He's fleet on its long sea journey to Africa, landing at Lamu Island, where all this started.

Lamu Island was situated at an estuary where three ancient rivers met. The plain topography of the island was formed by fossilised coral reefs and, except for a few sand dunes in the south-east, the entire island was only a few metres above sea level. Over a thousand years ago, Lamu Island was suitable for human habitation. The river flushed fertile soil to the island from the mainland, and the equatorial climate brought ample rainfall, ensuring the growth of crops. Formed by reefs, the island had a hard coastal base, favourable for ships to land at high tide and berth at ebbs, creating several good natural harbours, the best being at Shanga Village. The luxuriant mangrove and lapacho wood were useful for building houses. The local mangrove and elephants were both prized, the latter hunted by those from outside the island. The equatorial monsoon and ocean current provided good natural conditions for trade between Asia and Africa, factors that Zheng He's fleet took advantage of.

All of these external factors turned Pate Island into a commercial centre in ancient times, making the Lamu Archipelago into the gateway to Africa, particularly East Africa. Archaeologists posit that three major cities were prosperous in various periods: Shanga from the 12th to the 16th century; Pate from the 16th to the 18th century; and Siyu from the 16th to the 19th century.

It is often said that good and bad are two sides of the same coin. The fertile land of Pate Island nourished a rapidly growing population, but this expanding population excessively plundered its natural resources and degraded the natural environment, causing desertification and soil nutrient depletion. In this way, Pate Island degenerated into isolation and was left behind in a developing world.

Under sunny skies, our boat surged along the Indian Ocean's swell. The rocks that sank Zheng He's ship hoved again into sight. I could not help but sigh. Those rocks had created an indestructible link between China and Pate Island. The descendants of Zheng He's crew – the offspring of guests from afar – still cherished China as their native land. Chinese culture had taken root and developed here, and it was still present now. Who says there is no monument to Zheng He's African sea voyage still standing today? This reef was the best possible Zheng He Monument. Its foundation in the bottomless abyss was solid, still standing firm 600 years after sinking that ship. It was a monument full of vitality, alive in the daily comings and goings of the people of Pate Island, one that spoke from one generation to the next. It is the historical evidence of the deep friendship and interaction between the Chinese and African people. It is in those reefs that the immortal names of Zheng He and his fleet are engraved. If a treasure ship were one day raised from the foot of those rocks, it would gain fame around the world. And here I was, a Chinese journalist standing there in Zheng He's footsteps.

As I returned from this brief flight of fancy, I noticed that our small boat had sailed through a narrow channel. It was 5 pm on 11 March. Before we docked, I caught sight of Wheeler and the hotel's assistant manager waiting for me. As they pulled us to land, Wheeler said he had been worried, fearing something might have happened to me while I was on the island, since I was alone and a foreigner. 'I feel much more comfortable now that you're back,' he said. I was moved that this foreign friend whom I had only just met would greet me so warmly.

When I was about to set sail from Lamu Island the following afternoon, anxiety gave way to excitement. I felt at ease despite the aches and stiffness in my joints, especially as my journey had been completed so smoothly and fruitfully. As I waited at the airport waving goodbye to my new friends, a thought occurred to me: the Zheng He story has just begun. I will return with this beautiful, tragic Chinese story, this moving tale of friendship between China and Africa. As peace returns to Somalia, I will bring this 'Zheng He Village' to my readers, allowing them to have a full picture of the place.

3
Redefining 'Chinese'

A 'DOUBLE DRAGON JAR' RECOVERED FROM THE SEA

Seen from above, Lamu Airport resembled a highway more than an airstrip. As the plane was preparing for landing, I imagined it was extremely hot in the airport surrounded by lush jungle. On 6 May 2003, over a year after my first visit, I was back in Lamu, one of the Kenyan islands that had a special connection with China.

The purpose of my second visit was no different from that of the previous one: I was retracing Zheng He's footsteps. The only difference this time was that tourism here and everywhere else in Kenya had slowed considerably because of fears stirred up in the face of recent terrorist attacks. On 7 August 1998, the US embassies in Kenya and Tanzania were bombed. On 28 November 2002, an Israeli-owned hotel and a plane owned by an Israeli airline, Arkia Airlines, experienced terrorist attacks in Mombasa. Public safety became a concern in Kenya. Tourists were seldom seen now on Lamu's seaside boulevards. Captain Abass, who had been constantly busy before ferrying visitors about, now sat by the road watching boats sail east from the airport. As soon as he spotted me, he rose to his feet and shook both my hands, greeting me warmly and saying, 'My friend, I am so happy to see you again.'

Perhaps he was genuinely lonely. At any rate, he accompanied me to the hotel, chatting non-stop along the way. Eventually, he said with an air of mystery that he had 'something important' to tell me.

The captain said that some fishermen had discovered a pair of 'double dragon jars' near Pate Island the previous December. It was believed that these items had drifted from an ancient Chinese ship that had sunk in the surrounding waters, especially given that it was common knowledge that the dragon was a Chinese symbol. Word of the find had made its way to a British man living in Shela, part of Lamu Old Town, and he had bought the Chinese jars. 'You can get more detailed information from the Malindi Museum. It's an official building, so it is best I don't accompany you there.' Then Abass spread his hands and shrugged his shoulders, saying, 'Hey, that's all I can do.'

With the news, I rushed to the museum. Lamu Old Town was not a large place, and my hotel was less than 10 minutes by car from the ancient Portuguese castle, which housed the museum. The museum's assistant director, Ghazzal H Swaleh, pretended to be a sophisticated fellow, not saying a word about the two jars as he prattled on about the local response to my last visit. He took an old copy of the local newspaper from a drawer and read me a passage from an article about the Chinese reporter tracing Zheng He's footsteps through Lamu: 'The Zheng He fleet sailed to Lamu from afar, searching the Kenyan coast for a tiger, an animal revered by the Chinese emperor ...'

I could not help but laugh. 'It's not a tiger,' I said. 'It's a kylin. The ancient Chinese people mistook the giraffe for the kylin.'

He said it was a mistake on the part of the woman who owned the hotel. She had written the article. Seeing that I had come for professional reasons, he dropped the airs and graces, and got straight to the point: 'I guess you are here about the double dragon jars. Do you want to have a look?' Then he picked up the phone and made a call.

We then headed south in a small wooden boat, arriving at Shela Town in about a quarter of an hour. After we had disembarked, we travelled along the narrow, sandy lanes, zigzagging our way through the village until we reached a large house.

Gillies Turle, a tall white man in a checked shirt, greeted us warmly and ushered us in through the gate. The large yard was covered with white sand. (Lamu Island is generally sandy, and the city is surrounded by sandy beaches, with lanes of sand linking the various sandy yards.) Squatting in a shady corner, Gillies caressed a pink jar and said, 'This is it.'

The character 龙 (*long*, meaning 'dragon') was clearly engraved on the jar. Keen to see if there were any marks indicating date or place of manufacture, I asked if I could inspect it more closely. Gillies said that all the surfaces – inside, outside and the bottom – were covered in marine life after having been deposited on the seabed. The outside particularly was covered with barnacles and chunks of coral, making it impossible for the jar to stand upright. 'I've put a thick layer of sand below it and filled it with sand to make it stand upright,' he explained.

We emptied the jar and took it into the yard for a better look. It was a six-eared earthenware jar weighing 10 kg and standing 70 cm tall. Its mouth was 20 cm in diameter, and the diameter at the bulge was 50 cm. In the sunlight, the characters for 'pair of dragons playing with a pearl' were clear, despite the effects of corrosion by seawater and marine organisms. A closer look revealed that both dragons had three claws, though one had a claw missing. Gillies touched the gap where the claw was missing and said, 'This shows that the claws were attached after firing, and the fact that there are three claws means the vessel belonged to an ordinary family instead of a courtly one, since five claws were used for the imperial family and represent imperial power.'

From his remark, I could tell that he was a professional antiques dealer. Unfortunately, we did not find any marks on the jar, neither inside nor out, so we could not determine its precise age.

Though many pieces of ancient Chinese porcelain ware and other cultural relics had been unearthed before in the area, they were incomplete fragments. Local archaeologists agreed that this double dragon jar, being the first complete Chinese relic recovered from the sea, filled a significant evidentiary gap in proving that an ancient Chinese treasure ship had indeed sunk near Pate Island. It serves as an important aid for researchers seeking evidence of Chinese cultural relics long situated on the bottom of the seabed. As an antiques dealer, Gillies was overjoyed to acquire the first intact cultural relic discovered at this local site. Anxious to know the economic and cultural value of this rare treasure, he warmly invited me in for tea.

Gillies's yard was littered with tools recovered from sunken ships, including iron balls, wooden wheels and steering wheels. Inside, his home was filled with Asian handicrafts, such as Chinese tea sets and Japanese porcelain vessels. He was interested in ancient Chinese culture, particularly as it pertained to porcelain ware and navigation. He handed me two books about China, one entitled *Chinese porcelain* and the other *Empires of the monsoon: A history of the Indian Ocean and its invaders*.[1] Gillies turned to the illustrated section of the latter. One page contained portraits of Zhu Di, an emperor of the early Ming Dynasty, loading the large vessels of the Zheng He fleet for its Western Ocean voyage. Pictures of the renowned kylin also featured there.

'There's no doubt that these three pictures show that China was ruler of the sea during those times,' he said. Picking up the other book and turning to a page with a dragon-patterned jar, he added, 'On the earlier celadon and white porcelain, the most popular pattern was a dragon with three claws. A five-clawed dragon, the symbol of the emperor, was only permitted on imperial porcelain ware.'

He said he hoped I could help him date the double dragon jar. I promised I would ask experts in the field and have them send him information.

We discussed the background of the double dragon jar. Gillies explained he had first visited Kenya long ago, first Nairobi, then, six years ago, Lamu. Hearing of the abundance of Chinese treasures in the area, he had travelled here to see for himself. He explained: 'Before Christmas 2002, while I was doing yoga, a young man from a hotel rushed over to tell me that two Chinese jars had been recovered by fishermen who were trapping lobsters. Because of their weight, the fishermen had first mistaken them for large lobsters. When they realised it was two jars, they were quite disappointed and almost threw them back into the sea. They were looking for a buyer as the hotel's restaurant doesn't need such things, so the manager had asked him to see whether I was interested.'

Gillies continued excitedly: 'By the time I got to the hotel, the other one had been sold, so I could only get this one here.'

When I asked about the price he had paid for the jar, the shrewd Gillies was evasive, saying that it was hard to place a price on a cultural object. He added that the prices offered by an exporter, an antiques dealer, a lobster fisherman and a hotel might differ hugely, since each had his or her own notion of the value of the piece. He remained silent for a moment, then said, 'To a fisherman, a jar is worth no more than – probably much less than – the price of a lobster, so he might sell it at a price lower than he would get for a lobster.'

Based on the local price for lobsters – $5 a kilo – I guessed that Gillies got his double dragon jar for an extremely low price.

We spoke about the other jar; Gillies said he had seen it. 'It is different from this one – far better,' he said.

When I asked who had bought it, he again evaded the question, though he did confirm that it was still on Lamu Island. So where was it? Was it actually in his home? I wondered. Was he worried that the museum would swoop in and buy it? I knew that the museum had once expressed this intention. Was it possible that he would deliberately show me the poorer-quality jar as a sort of diversion, keeping the better piece hidden away behind the poorer?

TRACING THE ETYMOLOGY OF THE NAME 'SHANGA'

The purpose of this trip was to fill in the gaps from my previous hurried tour. I planned to visit the villages on Lamu and Pate Island to search for all the stories I could uncover associated with China. I also intended to visit the Lamu Fort, which housed a library and environmental museum, in search of information connected to Zheng He's voyages on the Western Ocean. The double dragon jar was a serendipitous find, one that added a new task to be addressed during my travels. I now needed to find the fishermen who had discovered the jar, so that I could get an idea of where the Zheng He shipwreck had taken place.

The next day, I went to Shanga and Siyu, accompanied by the museum's director, Swaleh, and a member of his staff, Swori. Swaleh was from Faza Village, and Swori from Shanga, so they were both familiar with local conditions. Swori had a degree in history and had studied local history, so was already familiar with what was known about the Chinese shipwreck.

Our small boat approached the beach near Shanga. According to legend, this was where the shipwrecked Chinese sailors had landed. As the water got shallower, we could not use the motor. Captain Abass took out a pole and punted us towards the shore until we ran aground on a sandbar, from which we could wade to shore.

Under the hot sun, the water was warm. Even so, when my feet touched the sand, it was so unexpectedly hot that I almost jumped. The stretch of beach was pristine, its powdery white sand flanked by luxuriant vegetation that made one aware of the beauty of natural, untamed spaces. In the distance we could make out a row of rocks of various sizes. Swori told me that the stretch of rocks was called Wahassani or, because of their proximity to the village, the Shanga Rocks.

We walked along Shanga Beach, then through a densely wooded area, and reached the Shanga relic site. Swori informed me that there were more than 120 relic sites along Kenya's coast, Shanga's being the oldest in the Lamu Archipelago. This site was first constructed in the 8th century, then abandoned in the middle to late 14th century as a result of frequent wars and water shortages. This period marked the peak of its prosperity as the region's commercial centre. The ancient Chinese ship had visited the place and, unfortunately, wrecked on the nearby rocks. Two reasons were commonly cited to explain why the ship had come. The first was that the ship had come for trade, since the place was a mercantile centre at the time, then it had run aground on the rocks at night as it sought to navigate towards the lights of the town. The second suggestion was that the Chinese emperor, seeing the giraffe presented by the king of Malindi in 1415, had sent the fleet to find more giraffes, but the ship had lost its way and became shipwrecked here. Swori was emphatic that, either way, the ship obviously would have been stocked with treasure. This had been mere speculation hitherto but, now, the two recently discovered double dragon jars seemed to provide evidence for this as historical fact.

The Shanga relic site, situated as it was along the coast facing the sea, was easy to find. After the Chinese treasure ship had run aground, almost all the sailors escaped to Shanga in lifeboats, it was believed, hoping to settle temporarily as refugees there. It was said that they arrived half naked and frightened out of their minds. They were first refused safe haven by the local people because of the language barrier, their peculiar appearance and their different religious beliefs.

So, why were these strangers later accepted? Again, there are two legends. One story tells that a fierce boa constrictor had been threatening the people for some time. One of the brave sailors killed the snake with a single stroke of his sword, winning so much praise from the local people that the Chinese refugees were then allowed to settle there. The second version has it that the Chinese, after being refused, built a small boat and moved to another part of the island, where they built a small village with their own hands. They called this village Dondo, meaning 'disappointment and loss'. Before long, they found that the harsh climate and ferocious animals made Dondo uninhabitable, so they again petitioned the people of Shanga for help. This time, their request was granted, but only on condition that they convert to Islam. This way, the Chinese sailors were gradually integrated into the local community and settled down to marry local women. When the ancient

Shanga Village was abandoned, the people drifted apart, some heading north to Siyu, others to Pate or Faza Village. Some left the island for Lamu or even for the distant towns of Mombasa or Zanzibar, far south down the coast.

Swori explained that the current villagers living in Shanga were not indigenous inhabitants, but immigrants from the border region of Kenya and Somalia who had settled down near the relic site. But, he added, if the area really had been an ideal place to live, it would not have been abandoned in the first place.

We went to the remains of a mosque, which had three standing walls and a stone pillar in the centre, even after 500 years of weathering. Swori believed that the ruins demonstrated the Chinese influence on local architecture. 'The Chinese are skilled at building thick stone walls with good, adhesive mortar. Their buildings are always grandiose, like the mosque at Shanga,' he said.

As we headed towards Shanga Village along a dirt path, we came upon an ancient tomb by the roadside. 'That's a Chinese tomb,' Swori observed. Unlike local tombs, with their erect tombstones, this one was a mound of earth protected by a layer of sandy gravel, with a stone-built monument six or seven metres high standing in front of it. Most of the stone pillars were inlaid with porcelain to show the prestige and wealth of the deceased. Swori went up to the tomb, squatted and ran his hand over it. Sighing, he said, 'Years ago, I saw Chinese characters inscribed here. They've worn away now, perhaps eroded by rain and wind. I carefully made a copy with pencil and paper and kept it in my office, but I cannot find it anywhere now.'

As I stepped back onto the road to the village, a group of teachers and students approached. They greeted me warmly, several boys running to me asking, 'Where are you from?'

I asked the teacher if he knew the origin of the name of the village. He said he had both heard from some of the elderly villagers and read in several books that the name was derived from Shanghai.

During my research, I asked many Shanga villagers where the village name came from, particularly enquiring whether they thought it was derived from Shanghai. I asked not only Shanga villagers but also people from all over Pate and Lamu islands, as well as several staff members at the museum. They all believed that the name originated from Shanghai, and the local people called the place Chinese Village. Though most local researchers are of the same opinion, many foreign experts and scholars, however, believe the name 'Shanga' has no connection to Shanghai.

One of the other theories about the origin of the name is the so-called bee theory. In Swahili, *shanga* means 'bee', and Shanga Village means 'the place with bees'. However, since no bees have ever been found around the village and no historical records have shown any connection to the Swahili term, this theory lacks evidence.

Another theory is the surprise theory, which connects the name 'Shanga' with an ancient enemy invasion. When Shanga was conquered, the invaders killed all the men, leaving only the women and children alive. This surprising turn of events was described as *shangaa*.[2] This explanation seems improbable because of the extra 'a' at the end of the word. Furthermore, if this became the village name after this event, what was it called before?

The shell-necklace theory is based on a legend that states that *shanga* means 'shell necklace' in the local dialect. Shells were often found on Shanga Beach and were used as currency here and in other parts of East Africa. However, if shells were used as currency, they would not have been used to make necklaces, and no discovery of shell necklaces has ever been made in Shanga Village.

Experts and scholars who favour the Shanghai theory point not only to the historical fact of Chinese settlers in the village and the legends surrounding them, but also to the linguistic differences between Chinese and Swahili. In Swahili, Shanga is pronounced 'shanggai' and local pronunciation would render the second 'h' in the Chinese 'shanghai' silent, making the two words pronounced exactly the same. According to this theory, after settling on the island, the Chinese renamed the village Shanghai out of nostalgia, serving as a constant reminder of their native culture and homeland. Why would they have been able to change the name of the village? One reason was that they were comparatively wealthy, having brought with them porcelain and other treasures. Another explanation is that most of the Chinese people were skilled artisans in one profession or another, so they would have had some influence in the place.

My own theory, which I call the nostalgia theory, differs from those referred to above. I posit that the renaming of the village as Shanga has no connection with Shanghai. I base this on three reasons. Firstly, Shanghai was not an important place in China at that time, so it's unlikely that it would have elicited that sort of nostalgia from the settlers. History tells us that at the time of Zheng He's voyages, Shanghai was nowhere near as well known as it is now. It was called Huating during the Tang Dynasty, and was established as a county under the name Shanghai County during the Yuan Dynasty in 1291. In 1368 the Yuan Dynasty was replaced by the Ming dynasty. In 1405 Zheng He began his seven voyages across the Western Ocean. In the 114 years between the establishment of Shanghai County and the beginning of Zheng He's travels, a long period spanning the end of the Yuan and the dawn of the Ming dynasties, Shanghai remained a little-known place. It became a prominent city, both at home and abroad, only recently, in modern times.

During Zheng He's time, Shanghai was insignificant compared to cities such as Nanjing or Taicang. When Zheng He began his voyages, Nanjing was the capital of the Ming Dynasty and the birthplace of his expeditions. At the time, Shanghai would not have rivalled Nanjing, the capital of the first unified empire in China's history, lying south of the Yangtze River. Shanghai also lagged behind Taicang, the port from which Zheng He set sail on his voyages. During the Yuan–Ming period, Liujiagang in Taicang was a major port, known as the 'throat of the seas and the mouth of the rivers and lakes'. It was renowned as 'an eastern metropolis' and the 'best harbour under the sun'. All this demonstrates Shanghai's insignificance at the time.

Another reason I reject Shanghai as a possible etymological root for the village's name is that the 'ga' in 'Shanga' is identical to the pronunciation of the Mandarin word *jia* (meaning 'home') in some of China's southern dialects, while *shang* is similar to *xiang* ('to miss' or 'to think of'). This might suggest that the term 'nostalgia' or 'homesickness' – pronounced 'shang ga' in some southern dialects – would be a more likely root for the village name. It is unlikely that the Chinese terms used would have been based on modern Chinese phonetics. Most of Zheng He's fleet were recruited from South China, so it is more likely that the name was pronounced in a southern dialect, then rendered into Swahili. The Swahili pronunciation of 'Shanga' is quite close to the pronunciation of the Mandarin *xiang jia* ('thinking of home' or 'nostalgia') in southern dialects.

A final point in my proposal supporting the nostalgia theory behind the name is that it suggests a change in the village's name. Like adherents of the Shanghai theory, I believe this name change did occur, and that the new name expressed a longing for home, not only reminding the new settlers of their homeland, but also expressing their desire to return there.

In my opinion, two factors transformed *xiang jia* into Shanghai in popular thought. First, the descendants of the Chinese sailors lost their connection to the Chinese language, so the original meaning of *xiang jia* was lost. The second factor involves the rise of China's Shanghai as a major eastern metropolis in modern times. Over time, the inhabitants of Pate Island, even those of Chinese descent, conflated the name of this rising metropolis with the name of their own village, strengthening their ties to China in their own minds and making the Shanghai theory the most popular explanation for the etymology of the village name.

A 'CHINESE' STUDENT'S NOSTALGIA

Word went round that a Chinese reporter was revisiting the Chinese Village. As I prepared to leave Shanga Village, a crowd of both elderly and young gathered to bid me farewell. 'You're welcome to come back any time,' they said, and wished me a safe trip.

We left Shanga and walked through a beautiful palm grove, then entered a narrow, sandy trail flanked by thorny bushes, heading towards Siyu Village. During my previous visit to Pate Island, I had been to and fro along this path, so it felt familiar. Siyu is the village lying to the north of Pate Island, established when Shanga was abandoned. The two villages stand opposite one another along the coast.

We first visited the Siyu relic site, where we found the remains of some ancient structures and some scattered tomb mounds standing in front of one large tomb mound. Swori told us it must belong to a female, since there was no stone pillar – the masculine symbol – in front of it. 'This tomb is very large,' he said. 'That shows that it belonged to an important person, which is also evidenced by the large number of porcelain plates and bowls inlaid around the tomb. The Chinese porcelain ware was stolen by cultural relic dealers, leaving only traces of it behind.'

Behind the tomb, near a patch of weeds, Swori pointed to the bottom of a porcelain bowl, saying it was the only remaining material evidence. It was a piece of blue-and-white porcelain ware with patterns on the base.

At the entrance to Siyu Village, I encountered a young man dressed in a white robe heading to the mosque for prayers. When he saw me, he smiled shyly and gestured to tell me that I was welcome to visit his home, where I could speak with his mother. He then continued on his way to the mosque. Swori and his colleagues were surprised by the encounter because this was the same boy who had been left at home alone on my previous visit and had not been allowed to open the door. His family was of Chinese descent.

Unlike most homes in the village, his had a tall, thick fence around it. When we stepped into the yard, a smiling middle-aged woman with a baby in her arms came out to greet us. She invited us into her home. A little over 50, she was of medium build, with dark skin and grey hair. If this were not Pate Island, I might well have taken her for a woman from the rural areas in South China, not from Africa. She looked very different from other local people.

Because it was so hot, we sat on a day bed on the verandah while she stood near by holding her grandson. Her name was Baraica Badi Shee, the final word being her grandfather's name, according to Islamic tradition. 'My ancestors were from China,' she said. 'Long ago, their ships sank in the waters nearby. They came first to Shanga Village, then later settled in Siyu.'

She continued to unfold her family's history for us. 'Hundreds of years have passed since then, so I don't know the specifics of our family background. My grandfather and father told me we are Chinese, but that China is too far away for us to go home. We have been here for generations without returning to China.'

She lamented how the Chinese people here had converted to Islam, were not educated in Chinese ways, and certainly not taught how to read or write Chinese. When I asked if there was anything Chinese left in her home, she said there used to be some old porcelain plates and bowls, but they had all been sold 20 years ago or more. The only Chinese item left in her house was an enamel Harvest brand washbasin made in China. It was in good condition, on the whole, with clear patterns on the base and sides. It seemed to have been made during the Cultural Revolution[3] period.

From my conversation with Baraica, I learnt that her husband was a fisherman and the sole breadwinner in the family; he was not an indigenous African, but was of Arab descent. They had three daughters and two sons. The two older daughters were married and she had five grandchildren from them, including the one she was holding in her arms as we spoke. 'My two sons and my youngest daughter are still at school. The son you saw earlier is the oldest. He's 17. The youngest daughter will graduate from Lamu Girls' Secondary School next year. She is the only upper secondary-school student, and also the only hope of the family.'

She said her parents had three children. Her younger brother was in Mombasa, her younger sister in Lamu, leaving her the only sibling remaining on Pate Island. 'I've done all I can in life. I hope my children will receive more education than I did and can prove their worth.' She then fell silent. Swori explained to me that having a child in upper secondary school was a financial burden, and there were three children in this family who were still at school.

Baraica then invited us into her home to have a look. The family had two houses, constructed of coral with a palm-leaf roof. The main house had a few simply furnished bedrooms. Since it was so hot year round, there were no quilts on the rough palm-leaf mats they slept on, just a few scraps of cloth covering the corners. The house in front was even simpler – a kitchen with nothing but a pot and a few cooking utensils, all on the ground.

As I left Baraica's home, the whole family saw me off at the gate, suggesting I visit another 'Chinese' family. I was once more filled with the realisation that Chinese culture is so broad, profound and full of vitality that, even after hundreds of years, the descendants of a boatful of shipwreck survivors had not forgotten their Chinese roots. As long as there was Chinese blood in their veins, they would not forget their origins, even though they had long settled into the local community and married local people.

After I left Pate Island, I followed a sandy trail to the Lamu Girls' Secondary School to visit Baraica's daughter Mwamaka Sharif. I hobbled along the path, sweating profusely in the heat. By the time I arrived, it was getting dark, and the school's management had locked the gates and the duty staff refused to admit visitors. Mwamaka's schoolmates, however, excited by the prospect of chatting with a Chinese visitor, eagerly helped me locate the girl, but I only had time to exchange a few words with her through the closed gate.

Three days later, I returned to the school. Mr Kingori, the teacher on duty, provided me with information about the school and Mwamaka. There were 18 teachers in the school to 350 students, most of whom were from Lamu, with four from Siyu. The teacher said that Mwamaka stood out, partly because of her family history. Many of her classmates called her the 'Chinese Student'. But she was also known for her diligent studies: the school thought she would be admitted to college after leaving school if everything went as expected.

Mwamaka was of medium height, round-faced, strong and healthy. She spoke little, being every inch an island girl. Being of Chinese descent, her hair was longer and blacker than that of her classmates. She knew the 'Chinese story' passed down from the elderly people in her village. As an upper secondary-school student, she had naturally become more informed about China than less well-educated people in her home town. She said she longed to go to China, the land of her ancestors. She was especially interested in traditional Chinese medicine (TCM), as there was a 'Chinese' family in Siyu skilled in TCM, and their ability to cure people had brought them great esteem.

When I asked about her dreams, she said she wanted to concentrate on her studies and try to get into college, preferably medical school. Unfortunately, there was no tertiary college in Lamu, so she would have to go to Nairobi or Mombasa if she managed to get a place. This would put an even greater strain on her family's financial situation, especially on her father, the only income earner.

Mwamaka told me that the tuition fees for her final semester cost 8 000 shillings, the equivalent of $100. To encourage her, I donated 10 000 shillings towards her education, hoping she would fulfil her dreams after leaving school. Though she was surprised by this gesture, she did not refuse the gift. Meagre though it was, she cherished it. To alleviate her misgivings, I told her I had visited her family and hoped the small gift would be of some help to them. I told her that she was a 'Chinese student' and that if she were in China, she would qualify for a grant from Project Hope.[4] I would consider my gift as an overseas extension of Project Hope. The gift was rewarded with a sweet smile.

MEMORIES OF A LOOM

It was said that when the Chinese sailors arrived on Pate Island, they brought with them skills not only in Chinese medicine and architecture, but also in silk reeling and fabric weaving. These traditional skills, it was said, continued to be passed down through the generations until a time several decades before I visited the island. I wondered whether these legends were factual, and whether any material evidence might exist to prove their validity.

After we left Baraica's home, we visited another 'Chinese' home: that of 58-year-old Jamal Yonus Dumila, manager of Siyu Castle. This talkative fellow had Chinese blood, but knew little about China, or even local legends about China. Other than a large wooden bed, I saw no connection to China in his home. He took us to Siyu Castle, built in 1843 by the chieftain Said. Architecturally, it bore a striking resemblance to Chinese buildings. Dumila pointed out that the castle gate was Chinese in style and that the interior was also different from that of Western castles.

The third 'Chinese' family we visited was that of an elderly woman. Compared with those of the other families we had visited, her home was in even poorer condition, comprising, as it did, basically nothing but walls. She seemed reluctant to acknowledge her Chinese ancestry, preferring instead to show us her porcelain ware and a brass lock. She took an old basket from a corner, carefully removing from it several fragments of porcelain, eyeing each as if it were a great treasure. However, I noted that they were not particularly old – it would be difficult to call them ancient Chinese porcelain. The piece that the old woman treasured most was the better half of a porcelain bowl, covered in a peacock pattern and bearing the English words 'Harmonious Family Utensil'. She also took out a brass lock with the brand '999' inscribed, claiming it was from China.

In a 'Chinese' household, I had expected to find some traces of a rare history, but the evidence before my eyes told me that my wish was nothing more than a pipe dream. Most of Pate Island's inhabitants were poor. The distressed Chinese sailors who came here hundreds of years earlier had integrated into the local community, struggling to survive together with the local people, generation after generation. It was unlikely that they had recorded any special history to leave to their descendants, not least because most of Zheng He's sailors were illiterate. It was also unlikely that their descendants had preserved any of their utensils as cultural relics until now. In an attempt to make ends meet, it seems more likely that they would have sold anything of value. The only few porcelain bowls or plates that remained in a fairly complete state had been purchased more than 20 years ago for very low prices.

Legends about China had been passed down by word of mouth, without any written records or material evidence. That being the case, I decided to visit some of the elderly villagers in Siyu to glean what information I could from their oral histories.

I walked back and forth through the lanes of the village until I found an amiable elderly man named Mwenye Omar. The 71-year-old was sitting on his neighbours' verandah, chatting with them. Mwenye had a bit of prestige in the local community, mostly because he had a wealth of knowledge about the history of Shanga and Pate villages. As we spoke about the Chinese legends, he smiled and said, 'What I mean by "Chinese" is not people like you, but the descendants of the Chinese sailors. After so many generations, they do not have the typical Chinese look any more. Of these three villages, only Siyu has "Chinese" residents – a total of 10 families. Of those, five acknowledge that they have Chinese blood. Though the rest are known as "Chinese", they do not admit their Chinese ancestry. This is because Chinese people are a minority in the village, so they assume that admitting their Chinese roots will bring them some trouble. It is quite feasible that their Chinese ancestors came here as strangers, and encountered great hardships for it.'

I told the old man that during my two visits to the island, I had met a total of five 'Chinese' families, of which three had been proud of their ancestry and warmly welcomed me. I explained that I had not met Fakii Maka when I visited the family of the Chinese doctor because, according to his family, he had gone to Malindi and had not yet returned. The elderly man sighed: 'Since he left the village, he has not been home. Several days ago I went to see him to have an illness cured, and his wife said it would be some time before he is back, as he is working at a hospital. He is getting on well. I don't imagine he will come back any time soon. As you know, most people here are poor and can't afford to see a doctor. Fakii often serves us without charging a cent, so he is spoken well of.'

I knew that TCM was the aspect of Chinese culture that had made the greatest impact on the local community. I asked what the next greatest influence from China was. The elderly man told me that Chinese porcelain had also been quite influential and, until 20 years ago, could still be found inlaid in local tombs or in people's homes, but that was not the case any more.

He recalled, 'Further back, some 40 or 50 years ago, I heard the older villagers say that there used to be silk spinning and fabric weaving – weaving cloths from silk threads. No one had such skills before the arrival of the sailors. Those skills were brought by the Chinese.'

'Were these two crafts flourishing on the island at that time?' I asked.

He replied, 'It was said they flourished for a time, but they were all family workshops. Later, only a few families retained those skills. When I was young, I was curious, so I went to some workshops and saw the looms and silk-reeling machines.'

'What did they look like? I'm curious too, hearing you speak of them.' Mwenye painted a verbal picture of the shape and structure of the silk-reeling machine, trying to recall the scene from long ago. He smiled shyly, as if he had forgotten something, and said, 'There might be a few families who still have those wooden machines. You might go and have a look, but they are not "Chinese" families.'

Taking him up on this suggestion, we went to another house. The old man had done well when he said the family might still have one of these machines. From the look of the house, it was obvious that this family was considered well-to-do in the village. When we told the young man who opened the door what we were looking for, he went to ask his father what we were talking about. His father said shyly, 'There's nothing left. None of them are here now. Years ago, I used them for firewood. They did not seem to be of much use for anything else.'

I wished I had been there a few years earlier to see them with my own eyes.

Making my way around the village again, I found another family, that of Abubakar Mohamed Chuoni, who was at home preparing for his three o'clock prayers. Being a Muslim, he prayed five times a day. He asked us to wait outside until he was finished. After his prayers, we sat in the lane outside his house and started talking. The 50-year-old Abubakar was a clever, capable man. When we asked him about the loom and silk-reeling machine, he said regretfully, 'We used to have those two machines, and my father taught me to use them. Now they are nowhere to be found.'

'Do you think it is possible to find them? Surely they must be somewhere?' I was keen to see the machines.

'We've looked all over, but in vain,' he said, smiling. 'I have asked neighbours, but they all swear they never borrowed them.'

Perhaps to placate me, he said that he could still remember the structure of the machines very clearly, and he planned to rebuild them and hand them down as 'family treasures'. 'I will rebuild it in a few days. You should be able to see it the next time you come here to visit,' he said.

When I asked him to draw a sketch of the loom, he gave a vivid description, drawing it on a piece of paper. Where the two-dimensional drawing was lacking in detail, he picked up twigs and other objects to help illustrate the machine's structure. He said: 'A loom is a simple machine for making cloth. It has a body, a shuttle and a baffle. It is hand-operated, using materials such as cotton or silk to make a whole piece of cloth or an ornamental object, such as a piece of coloured fabric or a headband. A silk-reeling machine is simpler, but I can't quite recall its structure, so it would be difficult to rebuild it.'

A couplet from a Chinese poem aptly describes the scene: 'The sounds of machines squeaked until daybreak, tens of thousands of strands could be woven.'[5] In my mind, the kind of loom that Abubakar described appeared to be the same type and structure as those once used by rural women in northern China. Other than the differences in size and complexity, the major difference was that men had replaced women as weavers here. Men who had braved the waves had turned into weavers, spinning their fluid nostalgia for home into long swathes of silk.

The Chinese people had brought silk-reeling and cloth-weaving skills to Pate Island, but with the lapse of time and changes of fortunes, the machines no longer existed. In spite of that, they had left a memorable mark on the history of Siyu Village, a moving story passed from one villager to another about the friendly ties between China and Africa.

4

Further exploring Pate Island

PART OF THE AFRICAN FAMILY

On a sunny day in early May 2003, we travelled by boat across the azure sea through a long, narrow strait to Pate Village. A 'Chinese' man from Pate Island travelled with us, 52-year-old Abdalla Said. He was strong, of medium build and completely Chinese in appearance, with paler skin and straighter hair than what was typical of the islanders. He said his ancestors had gone first to Pate Village, then to Shanga, and finally on to Lamu. After that they scattered to the four winds. Said remained in Lamu, working here and there as a tour guide or day labourer.

From our conversation, I learnt that he was not married, but lived in a rented home with a woman from the Kenyan mainland. Because tourism in Kenya generally, and the Lamu islands specifically, had been slack over the previous couple of years, it had become harder for him to make a living. He offered to serve as my guide, saying that it was better for a Chinese person to have a Chinese guide instead of employing a local.

Even though he was not very fluent in English, he spoke well enough for us to communicate. I accepted his offer.

On my previous visit to Pate, the young village headman had told me that certain family members of the Wafamau – the term the local people use to refer to the people of Chinese descent – were working in the fields. Because I had to leave to meet Captain Abass in Shanga, I could not stay long enough to meet the family. This visit was meant to make up for what I had missed on my previous trip.

Led by Said, I followed the short, snaking lanes through Pate Village to a workshop, where we found the first Wafamau. Barebacked and sweating, he was repairing a machine in the small, hot workshop. When he stepped out to greet me, I noticed that his appearance was remarkably different from that of other local people. Hearing why I had come, he introduced himself. His name was Mohamed Faruk and he was 67. His brother, Ali Mohamed Faruk, was 75, he told me. 'I will take you to his house to chat. He knows more than I do,' he said.

Ali's two-storey home was built in the typical Arab style. It had a staircase too narrow to allow easy passage for a man carrying a camera bag. Seeing my camera, Ali smiled, hurriedly put on a shirt and gestured for me to take a picture of him with his brother.

Relating his family history, Ali said he knew only that they were not local people, but he did not know where they had come from, nor when they had arrived. Neither brother spoke English, and Said was also having great difficulty interpreting. Ali's lovely, lively granddaughter came to help interpret, but she had learnt only a few sentences of English at school. I was equally embarrassed by my own linguistic limitations.

Feeling helpless, I left his home and we went to look for other Famau villagers. I had heard that there were four or five Famau families here, but they were not easy to locate because their homes were all over the village.

When I found the third Famau person that day, an elderly woman, she was in her yard picking stone fragments from a pile of rice. The quantity and type of rice suggested to me that she was from a wealthy family. Most people's staple food here was corn and bananas, since rice was not grown on the island.

I sat in the yard and chatted with the family while they worked. The elderly woman said that the two men I had just met were her eldest and second brothers. She added that all the Famau people in the village were from the same family.

At that moment, a middle-aged man entered the yard and greeted me warmly. He said, 'I heard you had been to my home and were now at my auntie's home, so I hurried over.'

He was Ali's son and head of the larger Pate Village. His name was Bwanarehema Ali Mohamed. He explained, 'Pate Village consists of two smaller villages. The village head you met last time is from the smaller village. The information he gave you on your last visit was inaccurate. Our ancestors were not locals. They came here from Yemen, settling first in Dundo, on the coast of the mainland, later moving here. They are called "Famau" or "Wafamau" by the local people, but our family has no connection with China.'

His remarks led us to explore the meaning of the terms 'Famau' and 'Wafamau'. In Swahili, *Famau* is made up of two words, *fa* (meaning 'death') and *mau* (meaning 'water'). Combined, they mean 'drowned in water' or 'struggling in water'. The *wa* prefix converts the noun into a first-person plural pronoun, including the speaker and others, but excluding the listener. *Wafamau* therefore means 'we are people drowned in water' or 'we are survivors from the sea'.

'Because our ancestors arrived here from Yemen in small boats that were not very seaworthy, they are called "Wafamau" or "Famau",' the village head explained. 'It was evidently a derogatory term aimed at outsiders. In my opinion, "Wafamau" refers to people from Yemen who now live in Pate and Siyu villages.

There is another term, "Wachina", which refers to the Chinese people on Pate Island. They now live in villages such as Siyu and Faza. There are no "Chinese" people in Pate or Shanga villages.'

Kenyan scholars and experts hold different opinions on the meaning of 'Wafamau', however. According to information obtained from the Lamu Library and from the residents of Pate Island, the opinions can be grouped as follows:

- According to its basic meaning, 'Wafamau' is a general reference to people on Pate Island from distant countries, with special reference to their living descendants. From this definition, 'Wafamau' refers to the descendants of foreigners, including Chinese, Portuguese and Arabs from Yemen, whose ancestors arrived on Pate Island for business and eventually settled there.
- Also derived from the basic meaning of the term, 'Wafamu' is limited specifically to Arab people, excluding Chinese, Portuguese or other 'outsiders'.
- Some see the term as referring specifically to those of Chinese descent for reasons not tied specifically to the basic meaning of the word. Firstly, 'Wafamau' is seen as specifically referring to ethnic Chinese people who converted to Islam, then later it came to apply to all Chinese people. A second version is that the term 'Wafamau' first referred to a Chinese chieftain, and later came to be used for all people of Chinese descent. A third explanation is that 'Wafamau' is a corruption of the Swahili word *Wafamaji*, meaning, literally, 'drowners' (singular form *mfamaji*), and the term was so often misread that 'Wafamau' came to stand for all people of Chinese descent and 'Wafamaji' eventually faded from memory.
- In contrast to the previous view, the fourth theory is that 'Wafamau' does not refer especially to people of Chinese descent, since there is another word, 'Wachina', which serves this function, though there are not particular terms for Yemeni or Portuguese people. In Siyu Village, 'Washanga' is a special term for people from the neighbouring village of Shanga. Since the 'Chinese' people who built Siyu were understood to come from Shanga in the south, the term 'Washanga' includes those of Chinese descent. With both 'Washanga' and 'Wachina' already serving to refer to 'Chinese' people, there is no need for the term 'Wafamau' to include them. There is evidence to support this view, including the fact that the local people from the villages of Faza, Siyu and Tundwa call the 'Chinese' people only 'Wachina', as do the Chinese themselves. Very few in those villages call them 'Washanga' and none refer to them as 'Wafamau'.

Captain Abass shared his own opinion about the various uses of the term 'Wafamau', saying that the difference between scholars and the local people lies in the possession of book knowledge, as opposed to practical experience. For instance, a scholar might tell you of the existence of a cup, but a local person does not only describe the cup, but also its contents. Abass's notion that 'a farmer speaks his own language, which is not recorded in the classics'[1] seemed reasonable to me.

From a practical perspective, 'Wafamau', 'Famau' and 'Wachina' all reveal the inescapable fact that, despite their different backgrounds and historical intentions, these people have long been an integral part of the larger family of Pate Island, Kenya, and the entire African continent and community.

ALL HAVE THE WORD 'CHINA' IN THEIR NAMES

The Lamu Archipelago comprises five islands: Lamu, Manda, Pate, Ndau and Kiwayu. Of these, only Manda is uninhabited. I was informed during my travels that most of the descendants of the Chinese sailors were living in Siyu Village on Pate Island, with a few spread among other villages on Pate. There were also some living on Ndau or Kiwayu. Hoping to visit more Chinese people and gather as much relevant information as possible, and because I wanted to meet the person who had discovered the double dragon jars, I decided to visit all the villages on Pate and the two smaller islands, Ndau and Kiwayu.

These three islands fell under two administrative zones. The Faza District included the villages of Shanga, Pate, Siyu, Faza and Tundwa on Pate Island; the Kizingitini District included two villages on Pate, Mbwajumali and Kizingitini, Ndau Village on Ndau Island, and Kiwayu Village on Kiwayu Island. Since we were on a tight schedule, and the villages were all some distance away from Lamu Island, we set off in a small boat before dawn.

Faza Village, the seat of the administrative Faza District, was on the northern coast of Pate Island. When we were about 3 or 4 km from the village, Captain Abass said regretfully that the water level was too low for us to approach, so we would have to wade to shore. I walked towards the coast with my trousers rolled up, carrying my camera and shoes.

When we finally reached the village head's house, he was out working in the fields. Said knew a shop owner in the area, so we went to look for that shop. In such hot weather, there were few people out in the village, so we had some difficulty locating the shop. After walking around the village several times, we found a house with an open door. This was Said's friend's shop. It was originally a house that the owner had converted into a shop, living out of the back rooms and working out of the front. We went in to find that it was a small grocery store. The owner, Omar Bunu Vae, was a tall man. He welcomed me warmly and introduced himself with great delight. 'You are my first Chinese customer – and my first foreign customer.'

He showed me several Chinese commodities in his shop, including tape measures, cooling ointments, shavers, bicycle parts, sewing-machine parts, light bulbs and small radios. They were all made in Shanghai. I was surprised to find such a large selection of China-made products in this small shop on such a secluded island. Generally, he bought his wares in Lamu, seldom venturing as far as Mombasa or Nairobi to make purchases. 'Owning a small business is painstaking work,' he said. 'It's not conducive to making long, expensive journeys.'

The lively shop owner smiled. He liked China-made products because they are good quality and competitively priced, he said. The special connection between Pate Island and China was incidental – though he did add that the name 'Shanga' originates from 'Shanghai'.

I asked if he knew of any other connections between Faza Village and China, aside from his China-made products. He said, 'There are relics of a mosque and some tombs, but their only connection with China is the porcelain fragments inlaid in the walls. There were a few Chinese families, but I seem to remember that they all left the place. At most, there might be one or two still living here. Most came here from Siyu Village when a family member married one of our villagers.'

He led us to visit a relic site outside the village. In a grove we saw an ancient tomb with recent inscriptions indicating that the occupant had been a revered Arab hero in the 12th century who led the people of Faza to drive out an invading force. After his death, the local people built a monument in his memory. All that remained of the mosque at the head of the village was a huge pile of debris and a wall, looking ready to collapse any moment, with traces of looted porcelain still visible.

On our way back to the village, we came across a tomb made of cement in the middle of an open space. A fragment of a bowl was inlaid in the tombstone. Omar explained: 'The local people here are proud to have Chinese porcelain in their homes, just like the tradition seen in Shanga or Siyu. But this porcelain is new. If not, it would have been stolen long ago.' It seemed the 'Chinese' influence had spread across the entire island.

As we crossed the village searching for 'Chinese' families, unique island scenes constantly greeted me. Under a huge tree at one end of the village, several young men sat weaving their sails and listening to the radio. Most of the villagers made a living as fishermen. There were strings of dried fish, the surplus of their catch. Under a shelter in the centre of the village, an elderly woman was rocking a rudimentary machine, with an iron basket of maize beside her. The locals used this machine to grind cobs free of charge. In another lane, my eyes were drawn to a row of colourful buckets of various sizes. A crowd of women waited there to draw water from a communal cistern. Omar said this was a traditional way of life for the villagers – the women working the fields and fetching the water while the men fished. 'Faza lacks a good water supply. Every household has a cistern to collect rainwater, and there are also collective cisterns in the village,' he said. I followed a woman home specifically to take a look at the cistern and farm tools.

After making several enquiries, I learnt that most of the Wachina people in Faza Village had left Pate Island years ago, with the last remaining family departing the previous year. They had left and not returned; nor had they even contacted anyone in the village. Their whereabouts were completely unknown. It was rumoured they had gone to Mombasa or Zanzibar.

Omar kindly accompanied me to the end of the village and said that he would email me immediately if he came across any information about the Wachina. After shaking hands and bidding him goodbye, we continued on to Tundwa, which, along with Mbwajumali, was one of the two inland villages. We followed a prearranged route, while Captain Abass waited for us off the coast at Kizingitini.

Faza and Tundwa were about 5 or 6 km apart, connected by a sandy trail. On our way, we came across several donkeys, the main means of transport between the two centres. Most of the donkeys were laden with water buckets or plastic water tanks, highlighting the importance of water supply lines in the local people's lives. About 1 km from Tundwa, we found the remains of a mosque half hidden among the weeds beside the road. It was a rather large building, its walls in fairly good condition and with clear traces of porcelain that had since been looted.

When we got to the village, we saw a two-storey mosque built in a more contemporary architectural style, with a large loudspeaker on the roof. The new mosque was larger than the remains we had seen, but its walls were of a thinner construction. Both mosques told of the influence China had had on the area.

Baushi, the village head, was a young man. Inside his house, I noticed that the furniture and decorative wall hangings were like those found in China. Seeing my interest in such things, he got straight to the point, saying, 'Pate Island encountered some Chinese sailors hundreds of years ago. The name of Shanga Village comes from Shanghai, China. Even young villagers, like me, know this.'

When I asked if there were Chinese people in Tundwa, he said that there used to be some – he referred to them as 'China' – who came here for marriage or business, but that they had all left.

'They are all gone?' I asked.

'Yes. All of them. As far as I know, they have gone to Nairobi or Mombasa,' he said confidently.

'Did they ever come back to visit?'

'The year before last, one family came back for their grandmother's funeral. None of the other families have ever been back.' It seemed this village head kept abreast of what was going on with his villagers.

'People in other villages call them "Wachina", but you call them "China". Why is that?' I asked.

'They all have the word "China" in their names, so we are used to calling them that. "Wachina" is used to refer to Chinese people in general, whereas "China" is used specifically for those from Tundwa Village. For instance, we call all the members of their family, young or old, China. Two women have gone to Mombasa and are working at the Fort Jesus Museum. Their colleagues are used to calling them "China".'

'How do you know that?' I asked.

'I have been to the museum to visit the two Chinas,' he answered. Then, taking my interview notebook, he carefully wrote the names of four 'Chinas' – two in Mombasa and two in Nairobi. 'I don't know the addresses for the two in Nairobi, but the two in Mombasa work at the museum,' he said. 'That should make it easy to find them. One was employed there after graduating from a technical college, and the other moved there with her family. When you ask about China at the museum, you'll be sure to find them.'

I took my notebook back from him and noticed that 'China' was a part of all the four names he had written down. Their names were different from local names, which were usually made up of one's given name, followed by the name of one's father and grandfather. The 'Chinese' names, on the other hand, consisted only of a given name followed by China. The village head explained that 'China' functions as the surname for the Chinese people. 'The shared name is a symbol of their nostalgia for their ancestral home,' he said.

Although I did not meet a single Chinese person in Tundwa, the information provided by the village head was very useful. The small number of Chinese-descended families, like those who had gone from Siyu to Faza, were a minority group who longed for their old home and ancestors. They reminded themselves of their roots by using the word 'China' as their surname. Though they had left this place, their influence remained.

I gave the village head a small gift and departed.

SEARCHING FOR THE PERSON WHO DISCOVERED THE DRAGON JARS

After saying goodbye to the village head, I set off for my next destinations: the villages of Mbwajumali and Kizingitini. Since Said had never been there, he recommended Mohd, a friend of his from Tundwa, to serve as my guide. By the time we got to Mohd's house, we were sweaty, red-faced and thirsty. Mohd greeted us warmly, then put a knife in his belt and went to the coconut tree in his yard. Like a cat, he climbed to the top of the huge tree. There was the sound of his blade cutting something, then several fruit fell to the ground. I had never tasted such fresh coconut juice.

People were walking along the sandy path between Tundwa and Mbwajumali. Seemingly used to the heat, the local people walked in twos and threes along the trail under the burning sun, chatting casually. As we walked, I heard several voices drawing nearer; it sounded like they were reading something. It turned out to be a group of pupils reading aloud as they followed their teacher. A group of children then ran out of a classroom, books in hand, shouting noisy greetings. It seemed they had never seen a foreigner; they motioned for me to take their picture.

The tall village head, Kassim Shee Bwana Mohamed, gave me the impression of being an honest man. He had a large yard, accessed by a small door in the wall, perhaps because he was the village head. As I stepped through the door, he ducked and came out from one of the rooms. The door to the room was even smaller and lower than the main gate. Before we could introduce ourselves, he waved and invited us into a linen-walled enclosure.

'This is my office,' he said proudly. 'Please come in.'

The office had three walls, two of which, like the roof, were constructed with pieces of linen sewn together, waving in the wind. The other partition was the yard wall, which was covered in ageing posters advertising a presidential election. The office was furnished with a dilapidated office desk and chair, which stood against the courtyard wall. The village head sat there, while we sat on two simple single beds arranged along the linen walls as guest seats.

The village head treated my unexpected visit as an important international event. He invited his wife to join us; she sat on the other bed. We sat in a triangle, facing one another. The village head gestured for me to speak. After hearing about the purpose of my travels, he shook his head and said, 'There are no "Chinese" people in our village. As far as I know, the "Chinese" people travelled from Siyu as far as Tundwa, but they never came here. There are no traces left behind by any "Chinese" people anywhere around our village.'

'Are there any fishermen who catch lobsters here?' I asked. 'Have you heard of any of them recovering Chinese jars from the sea?'

'Chinese jars?' His wife's eyes opened wide, and her husband also looked quite surprised. After hearing my explanation, he said, 'No, I've never heard of that nor seen it. Our village is not near the sea, and it takes special skills to catch lobsters. Most of the lobster catchers live in Kizingitini.'

He answered quite resolutely, so I hurried to finish the meeting. Seeing him eye my camera, I offered to take a photo of him and his wife. The village head smiled and started inspecting his clothing, a brightly coloured striped T-shirt, and his wife's dress. Seeing that they were spotless, he sat down beside his wife and posed for the camera with a serious expression.

Where the village came to an end, Mohd showed me the path to Kizingitini and accepted the tip I offered him before we parted. Along the way to Kizingitini, I kept thinking back to the village head and the hospitality he had shown me in his office.

Kizingitini, with a population of over 5 000, was known throughout the Lamu islands as the home of fishermen, most of whom were lobster catchers. They did not use modern diving methods to catch lobsters, but relied on traditional skills. Born as fishermen who had lived their whole lives by the sea, they were excellent swimmers and familiar with the local waters, and the haunts of lobsters and fish. Before diving in, they would put on flippers and diving masks, take a deep breath, and then plunge with all their might into the depths, a sharp dagger in hand. When they saw a lobster, they speared it and resurfaced. They obviously had extraordinary skills, remaining under water for long periods with just one breath.

Unlike the other places we had visited, Kizingitini was a true fishing village, worthy of its reputation. At one end of the village, on the sandy beach, people were busy building boats of all shapes and sizes. The quay, constructed of earth and stone, was long and broad. The village was built along the shore, and the beach was bustling. We walked along the village lanes, asking a few of the elderly people we met there if any 'Chinese' people lived in the village. We were repeatedly told that there were no Chinese villagers.

Back at the beach we enquired about the lobster catchers. A large crowd of young men gathered around us, saying they were all lobster catchers, but had never recovered a Chinese jar or any other cultural treasure, although they were aware that there was an ancient Chinese shipwreck in the waters around Pate Island. I told them I had heard that the dragon jars had been discovered by fishermen in Kizingitini, who had then taken them to Lamu Island and sold them to a white man. The group said that the village was large and well populated, so it was likely that someone else in the village had discovered the jars, but it would not be easy to locate him. At any rate, it was probable that someone who had found such an item would prefer to keep the news secret, hoping to avoid trouble.

'What sort of trouble?' I asked doubtingly.

An older man spoke up: 'Those who are religious tend to think that anything recovered from the sea, aside from fish, might bring something sinister with it.'

This remark called to mind the discovery of the Qin Dynasty Terracotta Warriors.[2] A younger man added, 'Any cultural relics recovered from the sea should be submitted to the state and handed over to a museum. It is not supposed to be sold as private property.' This was apparently another source of fear among the local people.

Their remarks suggested to me that they knew who had discovered the jars. In fact, it was possible that the person who had found them was one of them, but was unwilling to admit that he had found and sold the jars.

Captain Abass, who had been waiting for us at the harbour, took us to Kiwayu Island. We arrived ashore at dusk, then spent the night at a hotel by the beach. Abass and Said had been too busy all day even to eat, so they set about preparing supper as soon as we arrived. Said and I were so hungry and thirsty that we ate all the sweets I had in my pockets.

While they prepared supper, I explored the hotels along the beach. They were all very simple, being constructed only of wood and palm leaves. They had been vacant for a long time, and huge swarms of mosquitoes greeted us the moment we entered. A beach terrace offered an extensive view of Kiwayu Village, so I hurried there to find out what I could. It was a small, sparsely populated village. After making enquiries among several people in the village, I learnt that there were no Chinese people living there. When I located the village head, he affirmed that this information was accurate.

Said boiled water in a pot, to which Abass added tea leaves, ginger, milk and sugar from his bag. He stirred the mixture well, then divided it among three cups. He then took baked fish, salad and rice from a cooler, and we picnicked on the beach. After discussing the matter, we decided not to stay overnight there, but left for Ndau Island as soon as we had finished eating, then we hurried back to Lamu.

Not far from Kiwayu Island, Ndau Village faced the sea. In this small, scarcely populated village, the mosques were grander than those found on the other islands and served as the primary architectural landmarks. As we set foot on the beach, several local residents came to greet us. When we asked if there were any Chinese people in the village, they answered unequivocally, 'No, there have never been any Chinese here. They are all on Pate Island.'

The sun was setting, sinking grudgingly into the void. With night descending and the wind and waves rising, Abass picked up speed on our journey back to Lamu. We rode the crests of the waves towards the larger island, making it feel as if we were on a surfboard, or perhaps a horse. Heavy rain and wind beat against my face painfully and I was afraid Abass might get lost in the dark. When we finally caught sight of the dim lights of the town, the captain gave a sigh of relief, putting us all at ease.

It had been an eventful day that had involved sea navigations, wading through the ocean, crossing forests, scouring village lanes, searching beaches for Chinese people and braving sun, rain, wind and the dark of night. It was an unforgettable day. My only regret was that I had not found any Chinese people or the fisherman who had recovered the double dragon jars. Even so, if I had not come, I would not have found out about the actual conditions here. It also gave me a degree of pleasure to learn that all the Chinese descendants had left Siyu Village. They had done well to leave that isolated, poverty-stricken island where their ancestors had been shipwrecked, and to set out to seek new opportunities.

Though I was still exhausted when I awoke the next morning, I felt well, thanks to the ginger tea Abass had prepared. If not for that tea, I almost certainly would have fallen ill after a day spent at sea in the cold and rain.

IN SEARCH OF THE TRADITIONAL CHINESE MEDICINE PRACTITIONER

Having completed my task for this trip, my plan was then to fly to Nairobi that day, but I made a last-minute change to my itinerary, flying instead from Lamu to Malindi, then on to Mombasa. I altered the schedule in the hope of finding the two 'Chinas' who worked in the museum, and because I had twice failed to meet the Chinese doctor in Siyu, Fakii, who had still not returned from Malindi, and I wanted to meet him.

It was after two o'clock when the plane landed in Malindi. Hoping for a speedy journey, I called a taxi and began searching for Fakii. I had no specific destination in mind, but hoped I might find some information at a hospital or clinic. My taxi driver informed me that, with a population of about 200 000, Malindi had numerous hospitals and clinics, some licensed and some not, and that looking for someone in this way was like searching for a needle in a haystack. For good measure, he added that he had never encountered such a passenger. Feeling curious, I asked him his name.

He blurted out, 'Michael M Ngeta', but looked puzzled by my question.

I joked, 'I have been in numerous taxis in Africa, but this is the first time I have asked my driver's name.'

At that, he laughed. We discussed my problem, then decided to start with hospitals and clinics in the downtown area, asking for information from the most easily accessible hospitals.

Malindi was hot and bustling with traffic, but we managed to find a parking space in front of a clinic. The tiny facility was just a room with a sign saying Jambo (Swahili for 'how are you?') in black letters, serving both as a greeting and the clinic's name. Inside, the young woman behind the reception counter asked me what illness I was suffering from. When I told her my purpose, she wrote a number on a slip of paper and handed it to me, asking me to join the queue to see the doctor, just as all the other patients were doing. I waited patiently while the four or five people before me took their turns to see the doctor.

The clinic was small but orderly. There was a laboratory, a nurse's room where injections were done, an X-ray room, and an air-conditioned consultation room, where the doctor attended to patients. The doctor looked to be in his 40s. Seeing his patient was a Chinese man, he stood up to greet me, smiling. From my experience in this private clinic, I got the impression that Africa was clean, optimistic, sincere and hospitable.

When the doctor had heard my enquiry about Fakii, he thought for a moment, then said, 'I don't know him or recognise the name, and I don't know of any doctors from Pate Island here in Malindi.'

He seemed interested, though, and asked about the appearance of the doctor from Pate Island, as well as what diseases he cured and the level of his medical skills. Not knowing anything about these things, I was at want for words.

After having had no luck at the Jambo Clinic, I altered my approach and decided to target the big hospitals first. As they were larger, more people would be gathered there and I might stand a better chance of getting the information I needed, I reasoned. The taxi driver agreed, saying that going to the larger hospitals might save some time. We went to the three-storey Victory Hospital, where there was a long queue in the main hall, with people walking about quickly. Because he seemed quite resourceful, I relied on Ngeta to represent me at each department, asking, 'Excuse me, but does Dr Fakii from Pate Island work here?'

If he got a negative answer, he would proceed to the next department; if he found a lead, he would call me to follow up.

Unexpectedly, as soon as Ngeta enquired at the first department, he came running back to find me. As we rushed into the first consultation room, a short bearded doctor stood up to shake hands with me. Smiling, he said, 'You've asked the right person. I know Fakii, but he is a teacher in Malindi, not a doctor.' He introduced himself as Mohamed Kombo, from Faza Village on Pate Island, not far from Fakii's home village, Siyu.

I interrupted, 'I've just arrived from Pate Island. I've been to both your home town and Siyu.'

This seemed to bring us closer. 'I would never have imagined you would have been to that backward, secluded island,' he said doubtfully. 'What took you to my home town?'

When he heard that I was a reporter and had been to Pate Island for research – and had now come to Malindi in further pursuit of the 'Chinese story', he laughed loudly. 'I know that Chinese story, too. It's well known in Lamu, but Fakii knows more than I do. We used to share a rented room. Finding me is as good as finding him.'

Because he was in the middle of seeing patients, it was not convenient for Kombo to leave the hospital at that moment. I thanked him and we shook hands as we parted. The map he had drawn for me took me to a mosque that housed the Arabic language school, where a veiled woman told me Fakii was in the classroom teaching. I had to wait at the gate for about 10 minutes. A tall man in white cap and robe came out and introduced himself as Fakii. He shook my hand, then took a stool from a room and asked me to have a seat. 'Please wait here while I say my prayers,' he said.

Fakii was a man of few words. When he came out again, he asked me to follow him upstairs. He showed me to a corner room on the second floor, saying it was his office. Inside was a desk, a bookcase and two stools.

'You met Kombo at the Victory Hospital. He's from my home town. He used to be a part-time student in my Arabic class. If not for him, you would not have found me. I came over here two years ago to buy some farm tools, metal wire and things for making wire mesh at home. I decided to try my luck finding a job here, preferably working as a full-time doctor at a hospital. I never expected to find a school in need of an Arabic teacher. I started working here and have stayed here since, never once returning home.'

Fakii was using his break to talk to us, and now needed to return to teach his last class, so I arranged to meet him for a meal, hoping we could enjoy a longer chat then.

After checking in at my hotel, I hurried back to the school to meet him. Being a pious Muslim, Fakii did not drink alcohol, and would not dine at a restaurant that served alcoholic drinks. We went to a few restaurants before we found one that suited him – a stall selling roast chicken, which had only soft drinks on its drinks menu. Fakii ordered a dish that included a mix of chicken, potatoes, tomatoes, rice and salad, with a Sprite to drink.

He acquainted me with his family history. His grandparents were of Chinese descent; both had skin and hair more typical of Chinese people. Both were doctors. His father and uncle both also had typical Chinese features. 'You saw my youngest son, Anas, when you were last there. He is six. When I was his age, I was always called "Chinese". I had long, straight hair, pale skin and small eyes.' Fakii laughed, then added, 'I have four children. The eldest is a girl, 16 years old, and the other three are boys. The oldest boy is 14.'

Fakii was born into a family that practised medicine. 'We have been doctors for generations. My grandfather said his medical skills were passed down from his father. My grandfather, father, uncle, two brothers and I are all doctors – Chinese medical practitioners, to be more precise. My medical skill is a gift from my father. When he passed away, I continued learning from my uncle. He is a teacher, and he also taught me Arabic. Later, he took up Arabic, even though all the local people spoke Swahili.'

'I hear that your medical skills are not only the best in your large family, but also the most renowned in the area.'

'Our medical skill focuses on massage therapy and the preparation of herbal medicines. Besides learning from my father and uncle, I had a chance to advance my studies in Mombasa, which furthered my knowledge of acupuncture and the circulatory system.'

Hearing this, I asked Fakii to check my pulse, with a view to testing his judgement of one's condition by measuring the pulse. He said, 'As a rule, I should put a pad under the patient's wrist to check the pulse, but since we don't have one here, you can put your wrist on the desk.'

I was impressed by his professionalism when he checked my pulse. When he had finished doing that, I asked him to massage me. He massaged me from head to waist, using considerable force and varied movements, and using his fingers, palms and elbows.

'Do you know any Traditional Chinese Medicine (TCM) acupuncture points?' I asked.

He replied that he knew the names of some acupuncture points that his father had taught him. 'Later, from my own reading,' he said, 'I learnt that there are numerous acupuncture points in the human body. I know only some of them. For most, I can find the points but don't know their names.' Then he added, 'Massage is based on acupuncture points. Sometimes an ailment in the leg is treated by massaging the waist.'

The topic of his family's medical skills got Fakii talking. He showed me two small boxes. The first, a plastic film case, contained a yellow ointment akin to a cooling oil; the other was a slightly bigger box containing white facial cream. 'This cream is used externally to treat headaches and skin problems like mosquito bites,' he said.

I took a box of cooling oil from my camera bag and gave it to him, telling him it served the same function as the yellow ointment. He took the tiny box, opened it and smelled it. Finding the smell quite strong, he smiled curiously, like a child.

He then opened the second box, which contained a black decoction. 'This is taken once in the morning and once in the evening to treat poor appetite or malaria.' He said he could prepare more than 10 kinds of medicines to treat dozens of ailments, mostly those common to the region. The preparation methods fell into three categories: boiling medicinal herbs in a small pot for 30 to 60 minutes; grinding medicinal herbs into a powder and blending them with honey or water to make pills, usually black in colour; and blending powdered medicinal herbs with wax and vegetable oil to make an ointment.

'Where do you get the herbal ingredients for your medicines?' I asked.

'They are all collected from twigs, leaves, seeds, roots, vines and flowers around the village.' He rattled off a list of plant names.

'How do you know the medicinal effects of these plants?'

'My father and uncle taught me. I used to go with them to collect these things around the village when I was a boy.'

'Do you know the names of all the herbs?' I asked.

'Only in Arabic, not in English,' he said. At my request, he wrote a long list of medicinal herbs in Arabic – 18 in all.

Fakii then gave me a detailed description of the use and preparation of two decoctions, one for arthritis, the other for hypodynamia and fatigue. His description suggested that preparation of the decoctions involved placing the herbs into the pot in a particular sequence over an extended period. Certain herbs had to be immersed in water for a day before decocting and the mixture had to be stirred as it boiled. Some of the decoctions had to be sweetened with sugar to make sure they were not too bitter to drink, while others had to be diluted with water, so as not to be too strong. 'Their therapeutic effects, preparation methods and the way they should be taken have all been passed down from our ancestors, though I have improved on some of the prescriptions and preparation methods,' Fakii said. 'Besides choosing the right remedy for the disease, the dosage must also be increased or decreased according to the patient's current state of health and his or her general condition.'

Fakii emphasised that the concoction for treating fatigue was used not only for addressing a specific ailment, but also to replenish the body's vigour. In addition to these traditional treatments, he had his own unique techniques, including an oral medication he had developed to help speed delivery during childbirth. Once, his brother was bleeding from a wound at the waist, and the consensus was that surgery would be required, but Fakii had developed a decoction that completely cured his brother of the problem. 'I'm now studying the ingredients of some herbs to address eye problems,' he added.

Many of the villagers in Siyu – and not just the Chinese residents – had benefited from Fakii's medical knowledge. When I asked if his practice had any connection to China, he said, 'Only in the sense of the Chinese medical knowledge passed down from my ancestors. About 20 years ago, there was still some Chinese porcelain at home, but we sold it all.'

When I asked about his future plans, he said he was already 42 years old and intended to continue with his teaching, since the teachers and students he worked with were all satisfied with his work. 'I don't want to go back,' he said. 'I want to move my family here. You have been there and appreciate how poor it is. Most people are too poor even to see a doctor. In most cases, I offered my medical services free of charge. Of course, if something happens that prevents me from teaching and earning my living here, I would have to go back. Because I am a Chinese medical physician, the hospitals here do not want me, but I do offer my medical services in my spare time.'

Because his family had a special connection with China, Fakii said he had been following the country's development. 'If I have the opportunity to visit China and study TCM there, that would be more than I could hope for,' he said.

He added that he would continue studying Chinese medicine and pass his knowledge on to the next generation in his family.

HOSTED BY A 'CHINESE' PERSON

The next morning, after visiting Fakii, I headed south from Malindi in a taxi. The two destinations I planned to visit on this trip were the ruins of the ancient city state of Gedi and Mombasa. Although I was revisiting the same places, my purpose this time was quite different. Previously, I had been pressed for time, so I had made only a cursory investigation of the Gedi ruins. This time, I planned to make a more thorough search. On my previous visit to Mombasa, I had visited only the museum, but now I had the intention of seeking out a Chinese person who was working there.

The Gedi relic site, situated in a jungle, is surrounded by huge trees on all sides. The sunlight was broken by the foliage as it fell upon us, making me feel the weight of the long history this place had seen.

I was the first visitor of the day, and the museum was still closed when I arrived. Upon learning that I was a Chinese reporter, the staff opened the door and let me in. There were four areas in the museum: the Gedi Relics Site, the Cultural Relics Exhibition Room, the Historical Pictures Exhibition Room and the Porcelain Fragments Exhibition Hall. First, I stepped into the relic site and took pictures from every angle. From excavations carried out in the 1940s and 1950s, archaeologists had determined that the Gedi relic site reflected the unique architectural styles of the Swahili city states that prospered from the 12th to the 17th century.

Stepping into the Cultural Relics Exhibition Room, I stopped to read the inscription at the door: 'The cultural relics unearthed at the relic site include porcelain ware, glassware, shell beads, gold and silver jewellery, and coins from China and the Islamic world. Most numerous are local pottery utensils, mainly cookery and storage vessels.'

The cultural relics on display here were from the Chinese Porcelain Room and the Chinese Coin Room. A large, near-complete, colourful bowl lent its brilliance to the room. It was the only near-complete Chinese porcelain piece unearthed at the Gedi relic site. The description below explained: 'This large blue-and-white figured porcelain bowl is decorated with blooming lotus flowers and three curving leaves, while its inside has three figures indicating longevity. This Chinese porcelain ware, dating from the Ming Dynasty, was unearthed at the Gedi relic site.'

Two exhibition cases contained ancient Chinese coins, but the descriptions below them contained contradictory information, confusing the chronology of the Yuan and Ming dynasties.

The Historical Pictures Exhibition Room introduced the history of Gedi, recording the rise and fall of this ancient city from its establishment and development to its prime, and eventually to its extinction. The history of the city was highlighted by two events: the visit of Zheng He's fleet and the arrival of Vasco da Gama's fleet. The pictures of Zheng He's fleet included one of Zheng He himself and portraits of the Yongle Emperor Zhu Di. There were pictures of Zheng He's port of origin in China and of the town of Gedi during that time. There were also pictures of Zheng He's 140-m ship, which sailed in 1431, and of Columbus's vessel, just 30 m in length, skilfully arranged to show the contrast between the tiny ships of Columbus contrasted to the huge Chinese ships.

Among the pictures of Zheng He's fleet in China was one that showed a monument marking the site of Zheng He's incense-burning and prayer service held at Lingshan, in Quanzhou, before he set out for his fifth expedition across the Western Ocean in the 15th year of the reign of Yongle (1417) – a service held to make supplication to the spirits. The painting, titled *Quanzhou Lingshan Islam sage prayer service monument* had the following description alongside it:

> The imperial eunuch Zheng He, an imperial envoy and military officer, was sent to Hormuz and other countries on official business. He came here for prayers on the 16th day of the 5th month in the 15th year of the reign of Yongle, asking for blessings from the sacred spirits. This monument was set up by the town governor, Pu Rihe.

Another of the descriptions of one of the paintings of Zheng He's fleet read:

> The first Portuguese fleet that arrived on the East African coast should have concluded that the Indian Ocean was under Muslim rule at the end of the 15th century. In fact, this was the exact conclusion drawn by Zheng He, himself a Muslim, who made seven voyages on the Western Ocean between 1405 and 1433, some 90 years earlier than the travels of Portuguese sailor Vasco da Gama. But the Portuguese failed to reach this conclusion, deciding instead that the local inhabitants were Christians, since there were Christian merchants living among them.

In the Porcelain Fragments Exhibition Hall, almost all the exhibits, of various sizes, were from ancient China. Some had clear patterns, such as the smooth lines of lotus leaves depicted on blue-and-white porcelain. Some had distinctive Chinese characters on the bottom – in some instances, an almost complete character *fu* (福, meaning 'happiness'), an expression of good wishes. Some had animal figures, such as galloping horses, whose hooves flew wildly in the air. These porcelain fragments were just bits of civilisation, a living record of the oft-told story of Sino–African friendship and communication. It could be argued that the history of the city of Gedi could not be narrated so clearly were it not for these fragments of Chinese porcelain.

I wandered among the exhibition rooms, taking photos from several angles to gather as much information as possible. I moved about the empty rooms alone, communing with the Chinese porcelain and images of China. To maximise my time there, I sometimes read the exhibit descriptions aloud, recording it on my recorder in case my hastily scribbled handwriting should prove frustratingly illegible later.

It was noon and the sun blazed overhead when I arrived at the Fort Jesus Museum in Mombasa. Visitors sat under the shade of trees in front of the gate, drinking cold beverages. But I was eager to find the Wachinas, as the Chinese people were called in Swahili. In the museum reception area, I found out that there were two 'Wachina' here, but that one had gone home for lunch, and the other was on holiday. They said these were the only two who worked there.

While waiting for the return of the Wachina who had gone home for lunch, I had a look around the porcelain exhibition room. As I left, a young woman in a black robe was walking towards the museum shop. Though her skin was rather dark, she appeared to be of Chinese descent. She unlocked the shop door and pushed it open, signifying it was open for business. Filled with curiosity, I approached her. She was very friendly, even offering to share her snack with me. Learning that I was from China, she smiled and asked if we had such food in China. She started introducing the titles of her CDs, accompanying them with a dance and calling 'How are you doing?' as a greeting. As we chatted, I learnt that she was from Faza Village on Pate Island and had graduated from the polytechnic's business administration department. She knew about the story of the Chinese people on Pate Island, and her features were more typical of Chinese people – she had thinner lips, smaller eyes and a slimmer build than the locals. Though she was quite friendly, she refused to have her photo taken, as was typical of her religion. I was sure she was the Wachina the shop owner in Faza Village had mentioned to me. When I asked her about that, she only smiled, perhaps feeling too shy to discuss her family background with a stranger.

At about three o'clock, I went to the museum reception room again and was told that the Wachina who had gone home to eat would not be returning that afternoon. When I explained the purpose of my visit, a helpful staff member phoned the Wachina, who said I would be welcome to visit her home.

The streets were now bustling with people and traffic, so traffic jams were frequent. The taxi moved haltingly over a short distance. As soon as a sign that read Elephant Tusk Street was in sight, the museum employee who had accompanied me said that the home of the Wachina was just ahead. We got out of the taxi and made our way through back streets to the woman's house.

Though the streets were narrow, the houses in Mombasa were surprisingly spacious, and the home of the Wachina even had a backyard. Stepping through the small iron gate, I saw a woman of about 35 sitting in the yard. Her skin, of an obviously yellow tone, told me that she was a Wachina. She wore a dress with a small yellow floral pattern and a white floral scarf on her head. She looked at me in wonder, then stood to greet me with a smile. She invited me in and offered me a seat and as she brewed tea for me, she pointed out that it was Chinese tea.

The house was not large, but was divided into two rooms. The inner room was carpeted, the external room tiled. It was well equipped with furniture and electrical appliances, including a sofa, a refrigerator, a television, a telephone and a sewing machine. The sewing machine, a China-made Bee brand, had an unfinished dress on it. Seeing that I was interested in the sewing machine, she smiled and explained that she made most of her own clothes. She praised the quality of the Chinese machine, saying that it was still as good as new after many years of use. The arrangement and cleanliness of her house suggested that her family was relatively wealthy by local standards, and that she was capable and earnest. I noticed children's things around the house but, as I couldn't see any little ones around, I assumed they were either at school or playing outdoors.

When I asked about her home town, she laughed and said it was on Pate Island, though she acknowledged that she had another home town – far away in China. She had been born in Mombasa and, though she had travelled back to Tundwa several times, she had never been to China. 'My mother came here from Pate Island,' she said. 'She was Chinese, with skin even paler than mine. My skin tone was inherited from my mother, and is quite different from that of most local people. Wherever I go, people think I am Chinese and call me "Wachina". That's why my mother named me Wachina when I was born.'

'Where is your mother now?' I asked.

'She passed away several years ago,' she replied.

'Have you heard the story of the Chinese people on Pate Island?' I asked.

'Yes, from my mother. It was told to me quite sketchily, without any concrete details. I've also heard stories here in Mombasa, very much like those my mother told me. Because I am of Chinese descent, I am especially fond of using Chinese products and have a special fondness for China. I work in the museum, and have a passion for the Chinese porcelain there.'

When we started talking about Chinese porcelain, she asked me several questions about China, which I answered. The conversation brought to mind a poem by the ancient Chinese poet Wang Wei: 'Because you are from my hometown, you should know what is there. Leaning on the windowsill, I wonder if the winter plum has blossomed yet.'

When we parted, I suggested she pose for a photo. After some hesitation, she declined with a smile, saying, 'I don't mind, but my husband might be unhappy if he were to hear of it. It is our religious belief that a woman should not have her photo taken or generally be too much in the public eye. He is not in right now. If he were, he might say it was fine, since you are a reporter from China.'

If I had not been in such a hurry, I would have stayed longer at the Chinese home, at least until her husband came back. If I had, I could have taken her photo, and no doubt heard him heap praise on his Chinese wife.

5

Search for a sunken ship

SCANNING THE SEABED FOR A TREASURE SHIP

On 16 November 2003, a small boat swept the area around the Shanga Rocks, near Pate Island, braving the sun's blaze as it ploughed through the waves, a sonar machine mapping the seabed and noting changes in it.

There were six people in the boat: two Chinese passengers, two South African divers and two black boatmen. Each were at their respective posts as they pursued a common goal: the discovery of a sunken ship from Zheng He's fleet. I reflected how it was Zheng He who had brought these people of different races together, and how the great navigator couldn't possibly have imagined that his legacy would produce such an outcome.

In November 2003, I made my third journey to the Lamu Archipelago and the legendary waters in which a treasure ship from Zheng He's fleet had sunk on the reefs. I had made my first visit in March 2002. A year later, in its March/April 2003 issue, the Chinese newspaper the *Global Times* devoted five pages to my exclusive report, *In search of the descendants of crew from Zheng He's fleet*. At the same time, the *People's Daily* published a four-part series, *Following Zheng He's footprints*. These two reports – the first publications of their kind for a broad readership – of the historical fact that a vessel from Zheng He's fleet had sunk near the coast of East Africa, sparked great interest and found a responsive audience both in China and abroad. The domestic media reprinted these two reports.

With the publication of these reports, a number of enterprises and media representatives contacted me. China Central Television expressed an interest in screening the material from the reports as a documentary. The South Africa Jinchao International Group, the Sino–African Cultural Media Co. Ltd, the Hangzhou Loulanting Science Exploration Co. Ltd and other companies expressed an interest in recovering the sunken ship from Zheng He's fleet. They all agreed that my four-year international adventure in search of the descendants of Zheng He's crew and the information I had collected on my visits to Siyu Village, which people of

Chinese descent had built on Pate Island, were of great significance for Zheng He studies. Because so much surrounding Zheng He remained a mystery, without a single complete ship from his fleet having been recovered, the refloating of the ship that sank off Pate Island – and the opportunity this presented for research after it had been verified – was of great value for enriching our understanding of Chinese cultural heritage and for furthering research into history, archaeology, exploration, navigation and shipbuilding, and ancient China's communication with the rest of the world, particularly Africa. It would provide insight into the contributions the Chinese nation had made to ancient civilisation.

Together, these companies formulated part of the East African Pate Island Exploration Project plan. The plan aimed for a common goal: observation, exploration and recovery of the ship. Documentaries or television programmes were to be filmed based on these activities. A full-length documentary was shot, and large-scale photo exhibitions with pictures based on the report *Following Zheng He's footprints* were organised. Unfortunately, the outbreak of the severe acute respiratory syndrome, first reported in Asia, was a setback and plans were temporarily put on hold.

In May 2003, soon after publicity had got under way, I made my second visit to Pate Island. Kenyan archaeologists and the head of the Lamu Museum expressed their earnest hope that the relevant entities in China would make arrangements to identify the precise location of the sunken ship. When I returned to South Africa, Mr Wang Wei, president of both the Jinchao Group Co. Ltd, and the Sino–African Engineering Association in South Africa related the interest of his Chinese company in Africa that was willing to offer assistance in the form of financial, human and material resources, which would enable us to recover the ship from Zheng He's fleet, salvaging a lost piece of ancient Chinese civilisation. Were the project to be a success, the Jinchao Group intended to donate the ship to our motherland, presenting it as a gift on the 600th anniversary of Zheng He's expeditions on the Western Ocean in 2005. The company busied itself consulting the relevant experts in South Africa, purchasing equipment for the search and contacting skilled divers. Everything was carefully prepared, and the company assigned its office director, Mr Yao Hui, to accompany me throughout the mission.

Our African divers helped establish contact between us and their German colleague, Martin Schultz, a resident of Lamu Island. Schultz was a businessman specialising in the diving business, selling and repairing diving equipment, and training divers. In his grand seaside home, we negotiated the costs for renting his wooden boat and buying oxygen tanks, then installed the sonar on the boat. Schultz's vessel was 15 m long, sufficient for the divers to manoeuvre, heavy enough to resist the waves, and stable enough for our equipment to make accurate measurements of conditions on the seabed. The sonar consisted of an observer and a detector, with the latter installed at the stern, submerged in the water.

On a mid-November morning, we set off from Lamu Town, passing through a narrow strait and headed east towards the Shanga Rocks at a speed of 20 km per hour. Green foliage surrounded us on both sides and the sun was red overhead. According to local legend, the Chinese ship was navigating at night towards Shanga Port, the most prosperous sea harbour at the time, by Shanga's lights. Unfortunately, as it approached Pate Bay, it struck a rock and sank somewhere near the Shanga Rocks. The Admiralty chart 668: Lamu-Manda, and Pate bays and approaches, which we had with us, indicated that the eight or nine Shanga Rocks and the Pazarli Ridge, to their south-west, appeared to form an obvious north-east to south-west barrier between Pate Bay and the open sea. The water depth in Pate Bay gradually increased from below 1 m to 2 m, then to 5 m, 10 m, and on towards the ocean and into the Barracouta Channel, where the depth abruptly increased to 40, 80, then 120 m. Guided by the water depths indicated on the nautical chart, we decided to take a north-west to south-east approach, searching along a straight line in the areas around the Shanga Rocks. In our small boat, we were bound to pass the huge sunken ship hundreds of times, sailing back and forth along the flourishing coast that spring day.

As the boat moved, the two divers kept their eyes glued to the changing digits of the sonar. Its screen displayed the longitude and latitude, water depth, conditions on the seabed, and everything that appeared between the seabed and the surface, along with their positions. Now a fish was swimming 6 m below the surface; now the seabed was white sand, now seaweed and kelp, and now it was like a huge basin, or curve or a smooth ridge. Each feature appeared in turn.

Just before noon, the shape of the Chinese character 山 ('hill') appeared in the sonar's graph where the water was just 4 or 5 m deep. The divers immediately recorded our location: latitude 02°11'938" south and longitude 041°02'438" east. The boat idled here, and the divers said that there might be something at this spot that deserved closer inspection.

According to the divers, the ship might have been broken in half by the rocks it struck, like the *Titanic*. After remaining on the bottom of the sea for centuries, it might have been covered with sea organisms, plants and reefs. This was very likely, as the water temperatures here were high, which promoted development of marine life. Their analysis was that the ship could present the shape of the character 山 that I had observed in the chart, rather than the shape of a boat. However, after they dived in to investigate, we learnt that there was nothing special there, just seabed reef and seaweed.

By noon, the sun was scorching overhead and as the wind died down, the temperature in the boat rose. Yao Hui and I lay on a mat, trying our best to keep still to ward off the seasickness that had overcome us. We fell asleep to the sound of splashing seawater and the hum of the wooden motor as the boat rocked. By two o'clock, the afternoon sun was making me dizzy. The motor had stopped humming, but the boat continued to rock on the waves. Then, the divers hurriedly put on their wetsuits, telling me, groggy as I was, that something was going on and they wanted to investigate. Seeing that Yao Hui was still asleep, I told them to be careful, then drifted off to sleep again too. Later, I was awakened by flea bites, my legs and back covered with huge red welts that were unbearably itchy and uncomfortable.

By sunset, there was a gentle sea breeze that refreshed me. The divers advised me to eat something, but I had no appetite, even though I was hungry. We prepared to head back to shore. When we reached the hotel, the divers said that the ship could not be in the shallow waters, and that the tide must have moved the wreckage into deep waters. 'There is one possible alternative, though,' they added. 'The tide might have carried it in the direction of the Siyu Strait, and it may still be in the bay there.'

This idea made sense, so we decided to go straight to Siyu Bay, our rationale being that if we failed to find the ship in Siyu Bay, we could come back to the Shanga Rocks and search for it in the deeper waters around Shanga.

At that time, it was the hottest season along the East African coast. We searched for four whole days on the sea under the burning sun. Yao Hui and I, not accustomed to the sea, got seriously seasick. There were moments of excitement, including the occasions when we encountered local fishermen and asked if they had seen any sign of the sunken ship or if they knew anything about the discovery of the double dragon jars, but we did not glean any information, much less find a sunken ship.

Our divers expressed their regret, saying their equipment was not advanced enough, particularly on a boat travelling 20 km per hour. What could we hope to find on the open sea in four days? They imagined it would be quite different if we had a plan.

'CHINA' ON LAMU ISLAND

I paid a second visit to the Lamu Museum. The introductory material displayed there explained that Lamu was the birthplace of the Swahili language, which bore influences of Arab, Indian and Chinese cultures.

During my visit, I learnt that Chinese porcelain was a major part of the museum's collection. The information panel on a porcelain-ware set said that between the 14th and 18th centuries, Chinese porcelain was very popular in the Lamu Archipelago and that the Chinese people traded their porcelain for ivory, gold and other things. The description of a large porcelain plate read: 'This plate produces a melodious sound pleasing to the ear when it is struck. If it touches poisoned food, the dish will crack.' Next to a porcelain cup, I read the words, 'In the 18th century, the people of Lamu used Chinese porcelain as coffee cups, a custom continued until today.' Other objects, including Chinese chopsticks and coins, provided even more convincing evidence of a connection between China and Lamu.

The influence of the Chinese was also evident in the architecture and food of Lamu Town. The local double-layered cake and *ugali*, a porridge made from maize meal, were cooked in almost the same way as in China. In a Lamu cookbook, I discovered that the ways in which many dishes were prepared in Lamu were similar to Chinese cooking styles.[1]

Matondoni, the home of handicrafts on Lamu Island, seemed to offer a more direct reflection of the Chinese influence on the islands. This village was well known for building small wooden boats, and for straw mat and basket weaving. The small boats bore a great resemblance to those of southern China's fishermen, and their weaving skills seemed to have been learnt from China. The baskets I saw on Pate Island were almost the same shape as those found on Lamu Island. The baskets were carried on the back when working in the fields or used as containers at home. When I had visited Burundi, some time before, I saw technicians from China's Sichuan Province teaching local weavers a technique more sophisticated than that used by the Lamu Island weavers.

On Lamu Island, I reflected on why the Chinese presence was so strongly felt here in the East African coastal region. The profound Chinese influence seen on Lamu Island has its origins indirectly in China's ancient Land Silk Road opened by Zhang Qian's Unprecedented Journey during the Han Dynasty in the 2nd century BC. However, the Chinese influence was more directly the result of the Maritime Silk Road, the sea route connecting China to East Africa and beyond, opened up by Zheng He's seven expeditions across the Western Ocean. To an even greater extent, though, it was the result of hundreds of years of traditions passed down among Pate Island's 'Chinese' residents.

Zheng He's maritime crew settled down by accident on Pate Island, bringing Chinese culture and tradition to the area. Among the settlers were sailors, cooks, doctors, men of letters and artisans, who, while bringing many treasures with them, such as porcelain and silk, brought none greater than their professional skills, which they passed on to their descendants and their African neighbours as they integrated into local society. Nowhere was this more evident than in the three villages of Pate, Shanga and Siyu.

In terms of direct influence, the people of the neighbouring islands of Pate and Lamu freely came and went. Many of the Chinese sailors travelled between the two islands to make their living, while some went south in search of other sailors, and others fled Pate Island for better opportunities. From Pate, Lamu Island served as their sole point of access to the region beyond the islands. While travelling, the Chinese sailors had naturally left their footprints here.

The renaming of Shanga Village and the naming of Siyu expressed the nostalgia of these children of China for their homeland and their families. As discussed earlier, the name 'Shanga' was associated with *xiangjia* (nostalgia) or, according to some, with the name 'Shanghai'; Siyu was named after their participation in Zheng He's Western navigation (西, *xiyou*, meaning 'western travels'). The village name 'Siyu' recalled one of China's famous novels, *Journey to the west*.[2] The name 'Siyu' was associated with the geographical relationship between China and the village – a name that signified that these Chinese children yearned for home. The western voyage encapsulated in the name referred to a westbound ocean exploration to places west of China. The sailors who settled down in Siyu gave it its name, having built the town with their own hands. In terms of geographical position, Pate Island is south-west of China. In terms of local geography, Shanga Village, where the sailors first set foot, was to the west of the site of their shipwreck. In other words, the whole journey was made from China to the site of the shipwreck, then on to Shanga and Siyu – a westbound trajectory from beginning to end. One can infer from the name 'Siyu' this westbound journey.

Early the next morning, I went to the library in Lamu Fort. As I made my way to the second floor, a huge ceramic jar caught my eye, making me feel very much at home. In the library, I thumbed through some books and documents about the Lamu islands, paying particular attention to those about Pate Island. As I hurried back to the hotel to copy the materials, the hotel manager, Benson Alaiconya, urged me to take a quick break. 'We are planning to tour Lamu Old Town at two this afternoon. You should have your lunch soon. You have been to Lamu several times, but you have not had a look at its lanes. It's something we've arranged especially for you.'

I would always warmly remember this kind of sincere hospitality extended to me by the islanders.

FASCINATING FOLK CUSTOM ON 'DONKEY ISLAND'

Lamu Old Town was the administrative centre of the Lamu Islands District. Because the town was built in a desert, it was called Sandy Town, and because donkeys were a major mode of transportation, it was also nicknamed Donkey Town. The ancient town is the oldest and best-preserved Swahili settlement in East Africa, and boasts unique architectural styles and folk customs. In December 2001 the UN Educational, Scientific and Cultural Organization (UNESCO) listed it as a World Heritage Site. Led by my tour guide, Charley, I went to explore the narrow alleyways of Lamu Old Town, where I gained a greater appreciation for this 'donkey town'.

In the past, Lamu Old Town had just been a place in a secluded islet, but now that it was a renowned World Heritage Site, it attracted an increasing number of tourists from various countries. How did this time-honoured town gain its world heritage status? UNESCO determined that it had various unique features that contributed to its selection: the combination of European, Arab and Chinese cultures, reflected in its architecture, from which traditional Swahili skills were later derived; the rise and fall of the seaports in the East African coastal area, and the communication and mutual influence between the Bantu, Arab, Persian, Indian and European cultures during an important period of cultural and economic development in the area, of which Lamu Old Town was a microcosm; and the important role of the town in attracting scholars and teachers, making it an influential educational and religious centre for Islamic and Swahili cultures.

It was indeed a sandy town, and donkeys roamed along its alleyways, some just a metre wide. That is the first impression Lamu Old Town makes on most tourists. Formed from an accumulation of reef and sand, the town was overridden by sand. Even in the alleyways, sand was everywhere. Beyond the town, it was a world of sand – sand dunes, sandy paths, sandy squares, sandy forests, and naturally sandy football fields. Even the Lamu Girls' Secondary School, the top educational institution in the town, had a reputation for being a sandy building. Both inside and out, the school was covered in fine white sand. It was a scene unique to this town. The locals, accustomed to living in a desert, walked barefoot in the sand, free and at their leisure. Boys played football tirelessly in the sand, a rowdy, handsome lot.

To call the paths in Lamu Old Town 'roads' is an exaggeration, though the Lamu Seaside Avenue is open to vehicles. When I was there, the town was home to two vehicles – a van owned by the administrative commissioner and a tractor owned by the county government. These two vehicles were confined to Seaside Avenue or to certain parts of the sandy terrain that they could get through. Otherwise, the ancient town was 'politely closed' to vehicles in its narrow alleyways. There were no streets as such, just narrow alleys through which people edged their way along.

Because of the narrow alleys and sandy paths, donkeys were the only mode of transport. If anything were not to the donkey's liking, it would lift its head and bray loudly, making one feel as if he had returned to his rural area far from modern life. However, if one looked up, satellite TV antennas stuck out from modern architecture, creating a sense of incongruity.

Everyday life in Lamu Old Town was an endless flow of playing children, veiled hurrying women, and young men leisurely riding donkeys as they listened to music. This was the way of life. Islam being the predominant religion, most residents there are Muslims. Though it was sunny and warm year-round, most of the men, especially the elderly ones, wore long white robes, and most of the women wore black cloaks. The women dressed this way were often called *bui-bui*, meaning 'black spider'. Due to the strong Islamic influence, it was a social norm that women were expected not to show their faces in public, especially to strangers. If a woman came across a stranger in an alley, she hurriedly veiled her face with a handkerchief and moved away quickly. If a woman encountered a stranger before she had time to veil her face, she rushed to cover it with her hand and passed by quickly, clearly feeling quite embarrassed. Children, boys and girls alike, would greet every guest they met with 'How are you?' in Swahili.

Unlike women and children, young men took pride in riding donkeys. Riding a strong, lively donkey through an alley, accompanied by the rhythmic clatter of its hoofs, seemed akin to a young urban man showing off his BMW or Mercedes-Benz in the streets, and it was clear they were putting on airs as they rode. In the busiest alley in town, one young man astride a donkey came towards me, listening to a radio dangling around his neck as he held loosely to the reins in a free, graceful pose. Perhaps because of the crowds in the alley, the donkey slowed and became distracted. The young man pinched its belly, but the beast just looked right and left, slow to react. He then reached back and gave a sharp, sudden slap to the donkey's hindquarters and it immediately quickened its pace. The crowd made way for him as he trotted along.

As the only means of transport, donkeys shouldered the burden of carrying daily necessities and even building materials. Most people on Lamu therefore took good care of their donkeys but, restricted by environmental and economic conditions, a sick donkey was usually treated by traditional methods of therapy, which were not very effective and could be deemed cruel – things like bleeding it or burning it with a hot wire. The number of donkeys on Lamu Island had peaked at 3 000 but, due to the El Niño effect and the backward medical skills, the population had diminished to around 2 200 when I was there.

The British veterinarian Elisabeth Svendsen made her first visit to Lamu Island in 1985 and, seeing the sad condition of its donkeys, established a donkey 'hospital' there in July 1987, offering free medical care for donkeys. She treated over 5 000 cases a year, making great improvements to the animals' living conditions. When I visited the hospital, I found five or six donkeys waiting to be treated. Abdalla, the manager, said that these donkeys were very fortunate, as their living conditions had improved with the opening of the free medical-care centre.

Lamu Old Town is noted for its three-storey buildings, sandy, sunny beaches and its lucrative tourism industry. The life of the Lamu people is inextricably bound to the sea. They have been heavily involved in shipping, fishing and the felling of coastal redwood trees. In addition, the island's mangoes and coconuts are known all over Kenya, and coconut in particular promoted the growth of various family-run businesses, including rope making, mat weaving and oil production. When

Lamu Old Town became a World Heritage Site, tourism became a new industry that led to vigorous economic development in the islands.

The major tourist attractions included navigating through the narrow alleyways of the ancient town, visiting its museums and harbours, and sunbathing on the sandy beaches. The architecture in the town is typical of the Swahili style – mainly three-storey buildings that accentuate the narrowness of the alleys, giving the ancient town its unique atmosphere. The reason for the three-storey structure of the buildings lies in local history, which stretches back 1 000 years. The town was built on its current site in the 15th century; the earlier site no longer exists. In the early 16th century, the Portuguese invaded Lamu and occupied it without firing a shot. At the time, Pate was the political and commercial centre of the Lamu Archipelago, and Lamu was a part of Pate. When the Portuguese lost their influence in the area, Lamu tried everything to avoid wars with Pate Island, Mombasa and Malindi, until it eventually recovered a basic level of stability in the late 17th century. Then, wars broke out between Lamu Old Town, and Pate, Faza and Siyu. Many were killed in a series of fierce battles, with Lamu fending off a robust attack from Pate in 1813. That year, Lamu asked for protection from Oman, and the newly built Lamu Castle was guarded by Omani soldiers.

Without Oman's support, Lamu would undoubtedly have faced a gloomy fate. With the expansion of Oman's power, it ruled over the entire East African coastal area, from the Kenyan–Somali border in the north to Kilwa in Tanzania, with the busy port of Zanzibar serving as the commercial and political centre. This was when the ugly slave trade emerged in the region.

In many ways, Lamu benefited from the slave trade. Cheap labour promoted the town's economic development, with merchants earning enormous profits from the export of ivory, shells and redwood, and from importing silk, porcelain and spices. In 1907 the British forced Zanzibar's authorities to sign an agreement banning the slave trade. With the termination of the slave trade, Lamu's economy gradually declined, never to recover until the recent emergence of tourism and the new life it injected into the economy of Lamu.

The houses of the ancient Lamu Old Town were three-storey structures built of reef material and redwood timber. According to custom, the ground floor was for slaves, the second for the homeowner and the third was an attic. This demonstrates the significance of the slave trade in Lamu.

The narrow alleys were built to deal with the year-round sultry climate. Being close to the equator, Lamu has direct sunlight all year. The narrower alleys meant less space for direct sunlight to enter the interior of the house, an architectural style that has continued to the present day. My guide led me to a place where a family was constructing a new house. Its interior and exterior design was in the same style as the old houses.

To understand a city, one must visit its museums and gain some insight into its past. Lamu had a number of museums, each featuring a different theme. Built in 1892 on the beachfront, the Lamu Museum was of a style typical of the 19th century. Once the residence of a large local family, it later became home to the British East Africa Company representative, a British family and head of the colonial authority. When Kenya gained its independence, this house became the office of the commissioner of the Lamu Prefecture. It became a museum in 1971. The major exhibits in this museum are cultural relics unearthed in the area, many of which were Chinese porcelain.

The German Post Office Museum was in the old town's busiest street. At first glance, I doubted what I was seeing but, after more careful investigation, I learnt that Wituland, an area inland from the Kenyan coast, was once German territory. In the late 18th century, Clement Denhardt and GA Fisher, two German nationals, travelled to Lamu and came into contact with the sultan of Wituland. At the time, Wituland was under threat from Lamu and Zanzibar rulers, so the territory was eager to establish new alliances. Hence Wituland came to be under German protection. This post office was established and remained in operation for the purpose of maintaining communication between Wituland and Germany, by way of Lamu. It closed when the Germans withdrew in 1891. In 1996 it was restored to its original condition and reopened to tourists as a museum focused on that particular period of local history.

After a trip around Lamu Old Town, most tourists head to the sandy beaches to enjoy the activities on offer. Many enjoy sailing, some making their way very far out to sea. Less adventurous travellers prefer sunbathing on the pure white sands of Manda Beach, adjacent to Lamu, faces turned to the sky and their skin caked with sunscreen. Many of them lie with a book in hand, as if in a pretence of scholarly zeal.

Lamu is noted for its yacht races, its donkey races and its festive, foot-stomping singing. These activities reveal the unique culture of Lamu. My time there coincided with the peak of the Kenyan tourist season. As a tourist town, Lamu held celebrations with a strong local flavour. The donkey-riding contest between the young men along Seaside Avenue featured prominently and requires strong, fast animals and excellent riding skills. These riding contests in Lamu were as popular, lively and raucous as football matches in other parts of Africa.

In the boat races, the small yachts competed from start to finish on wind power alone. The boatsmen's sailing skills meant everything in these races. What mattered most in a boat race was the height and angle of the sail, and handling the rudder. These contests were usually won by veteran competitors, who seemed more cool-headed and confident than the novices who busied themselves adjusting sail and rudder.

Alongside these two contests, a crowd gathered, forming a ring on the open sandy beach west of Lamu City. Young and old, men and women watched performances of song, dance and martial arts. Seven or eight men holding wooden sticks and with bells tied to their their legs danced to the thumping rhythm of drums. Every now and then, they stopped to mutter something – perhaps a song, perhaps talking to themselves, or perhaps just keeping rhythm with the drums. The drums were of various shapes and sizes, and were played in various ways – some were held in the arms, some were on the ground, some between the legs, and some overhead. They were played either with sticks or with the palms of the hand. The local people told me that such activities used to be accompanied in times past by a long ivory flute, which had a loud, melodious sound. Unfortunately, those flutes were no longer anywhere to be found, and their music was no more to be heard.

Martial-arts contests also formed part of the song-and-dance performances. Lamu's martial arts could be traced back to a school of stick fighting. In most cases, a loud cracking sound accompanied the contestants' encounter. These contests hardly seemed like martial arts to me, being nothing compared to Chinese kung fu. It was more like child's play, the protagonists retreating when threatened and running away when chased, to the merriment of the spectators. It was a very playful atmosphere.

SHIPWRECK IN SOMALIA

Sightseeing and appreciating the customs of the ancient town of Lamu did nothing to alleviate my gloom, however. The fruitless days spent drifting at sea looking for the sunken ship and the disappointment of that search had weighed heavily on me. Though I had anticipated that the search would be tedious and trying, I had still believed that we would find the ship. I suppose I was secretly hoping for a repeat of the 'miracle' of finding the Chinese doctor by chance in crowded Malindi.

This was my third visit to Lamu. On my previous trips, upon hearing that there were some Somali merchants from Kismayo on the island, I had asked Captain Abass to find out what was known about the Zheng He fleet in Somalia. The captain introduced to me two groups of people from the Somali port town of Kismayo who had information about Zheng He's fleet.

The first pair had come to Lamu from Kismayo as refugees from the civil war in Somalia. One of them, 54-year-old Athumani Ali Famau, said that there were a number of islets off the coast near Kismayo, two of which featured 'Chinese towers'. Both towers bore inscriptions, he said, but he could not be sure if they were in Chinese or other languages. He had never been to the islets, but had seen the towers when he had passed near the islands during his travels at sea. One of these towers was on Koyama Island. 'I saw it when I passed by in 1991. I don't know if it has since been damaged in the fighting in that area over the past decade.

But there is another Chinese tower at the border of Kenya and Somalia. I could take you there,' he said.

Athumani spoke Swahili; Abass acted as interpreter. Abass expressed his doubts about the information concerning this Chinese tower on the border, but Athumani insisted he had seen it with his own eyes during his travels. 'It was not accessible because of the civil war in Somalia, but it was in the border area, and was visible from the Kenyan side,' he explained.

I decided to travel to the border area for a look, with Athumani acting as my guide. We set out from Lamu in Abass's boat, and landed at the Kenyan–Somali border. Because we were concerned about safety in the area, we planned to contact the border guards before landing, then head to the Chinese tower. The round trip would take a whole day. We discussed the precautions we would need to take and the expenses involved, then decided to start early the next morning. That night, when I was ready for bed, Abass came and told me that the information Athumani had provided was wrong – there was a tower there, he explained, but it was Portuguese, not Chinese. It had been damaged beyond recognition and was not at all as Athumani had described. I decided to cancel our trip for the next day and spend the time gathering new information from other Somali people instead.

The second group we met consisted of three Somali traders who had frequently travelled between Somalia and Lamu before civil war broke out. When we mentioned the Chinese tower, 48-year-old Mohamadi Lali Shelali interjected, 'There is a Chinese tower made of rocks on Koyama Island. It is seven or eight metres tall and has a pointed top. I have been to the island and have seen it.'

The other two nodded in agreement.

'Is there any inscription on the tower?' I asked.

'Yes, but I did not recognise it. It was illegible.' Mohamadi drew a few strokes in my notebook. They looked like Chinese script.

Mohamadi said there was a chain of uninhabited islets south-west of Kismayo. Occasionally, fishermen would stay there when they passed by. There was another smaller, shorter 'Chinese tower' on another of the islands, he told us. As he spoke of it, his eyes flashed and he said, 'There was an ancient Chinese ship in the waters between Kismayo and Koyama Island.'

'What? A sunken ship?' I was surprised.

When I questioned Mohamadi, he gave a description of the ship. When he was a child, his grandfather had told him about a sunken Chinese ship in the waters nearby. It had been there for a long time. The elderly local people also said that the shipwrecked Chinese vessel had been loaded with treasures, such as porcelain and silk, all of which had been looted. In his teens, Mohamadi had played in the ship with other children. It was a huge vessel, roughly 70 m long and 30 m wide. It had three layers: an exterior made of iron, now covered with rust; an interior of copper, now green; and a layer of redwood in between, now rotted away after years of exposure to the sea. 'It was close to the shore, so its mast was visible at low tide. Sometimes the local fishermen attached their boats to it and used it as a sort of temporary wharf.'

Hearing such a picturesque description of the sunken Chinese ship from someone I had just met, I was awash with a mix of emotions – happiness, surprise and doubt. I thought to myself, even if they had made it all up, there might be something behind it.

As if they had read my mind, the other two confirmed what Mohamadi had told me, adding that they had no motive to lie, especially since they did not even know my intentions. I told myself that they could not possibly have made up such detailed and convincing tales.

When our talk shifted to the topic of Zheng He Village, they said they had heard tell of a Zheng He Village several kilometres south of Kismayo – a place where Chinese sailors had lived and built a 'Chinese tower'. Unfortunately, none of them had been there and they did not have any more information about the place.

A Zheng He Village, a Zheng He Tower and a sunken ancient Chinese ship: any of those things individually would have been worth making a trip for, let alone all three. But Somalia was immersed in fighting between local warlords – battles so intense that even the Somali people had been forced to flee, and foreigners' travels in the region were completely put to a halt. Abass said to me, 'It is a chaotic situation. Even we don't dare venture there. It's said that any foreigner caught there will be captured and held for a ransom of millions of dollars. If it's not paid ...' He ran his finger beneath his chin in a universally understood gesture. 'An American friend of mine came here and stayed for a month. He dared not travel to Somalia. Even if he had dared, no one would have taken the risk to accompany him. Once, when a captain was taking passengers over there, pirates seized the boat. Fortunately, the passengers were released, but the boat still has not been returned.' From his remarks, I gathered he would not make the journey to Somalia himself.

'Do you three often return to Kismayo?' I asked.

Before I had finished my question, Abass cut in, saying, 'They are Somalis and speak Somali. Somali pirates do not capture other Somalis, because they know they are not wealthy.'

It seemed the trip from Lamu to Kismayo was impossible. To verify my information, I asked Mohamadi to sketch the 'Chinese tower' he had seen. Without hesitation, he took my notebook and drew a pointed tower. When I asked if he could take some photos of the tower and confirm the existence of the sunken Chinese ship on his next trip home, he was quick to promise. However, he would not be going there soon, and he had no camera. In fact, even if he did have a camera, he did not know how to take a photo. I gave him an autofocus camera, but he did not know how to use it. Even after I had spent time showing him, he still could not even take off the lens cap. Nevertheless, I explained over and over again how to use it, cautioning him about the main aspects of photography, and emphasising that his safety was of primary importance on his travels. To ensure the success of his trip, I gave him $100, with the hotel manager, Benson, serving as witness. I also promised him an additional $100 when we next met, if he completed the task. Benson and I both signed our names as surety.

A year later, when we met again in Lamu, Mohamadi told me he had nearly been robbed by pirates on his way to Somalia by way of the island. He had not dared to approach the island, much less land there to take photos of the 'Chinese tower'. He returned the camera to me intact. The $100 I had given him was gone – a sunk cost. I counted it as a form of tuition fee for this life lesson.

But, deep down, I was relieved. Obviously it was naive to let him take my place. I would have to travel there myself.

6
Refugee camps

DISCUSSING ZHENG HE IN A BORDER TOWN ON A WET NIGHT

In December 2000, I had travelled to the Ethiopian capital, Addis Ababa, to gather information on the African Economic Forum hosted by the then Organisation of African Unity (now the African Union). I planned to take this opportunity to visit the Somali refugee camps in Ethiopia and probe for clues about Zheng He's presence in Somalia.

On the afternoon of 8 December, a small plane from Addis Ababa landed at the airport in Jijiga, the capital of the Somali Region of Ethiopia, stirring up clouds of dust as it glided onto the runway. Some time after the plane had come to a halt, the flight attendant opened the door. The sight that greeted me as I disembarked was not what I had expected of an airport. There was nothing but the dusty runway, a waiting room housed in an iron shed and a narrow gate. Still, none of this prepared me for the situation I would later witness at the refugee camp, the memory of which remains imprinted in my heart.

A driver from the UN Refugee Affairs Office in Jijiga, Tesham Bosase, drove me from the airport to the hotel. Seeing a foreign guest, the young attendant was embarrassed as he pointed out that there was no tap in my room, just some water in a bucket. As the local people said, 'Water is life.' It reminded me how precious water was in this arid region. The refugee camp I was to visit the next day was in a drought-prone pastoral and agricultural area.

Before he left, Bosase said that his superior would come to the hotel to discuss the following day's itinerary with me. Since I had arrived on a Saturday, my trip caused them some inconvenience. I had made an application to the UN Refugee Affairs Office in Ethiopia, requesting they apply to the Ethiopian Administration for Refugee and Returnee Affairs to grant me permission to visit the camp. I hoped this would assure the success of my trip, and provide me with a sort of a 'safety guarantee' as I travelled and communicated with the refugees. This was why I had been met by the UN Refugee Affairs Office in Jijiga.

At dusk, it began drizzling in Jijiga, which had been dry for a long time. The UN staff member, Vincent Chorde, came with two other personnel in charge of the refugee office to discuss the arrangements for my trip. When they arrived, the light rain grew into a fully fledged downpour falling on the eaves, grass and flowers in the courtyard, as if treating us to a symphony of pattering rain that formed a sort of countermelody to the rhythmic African drumming coming from the radio. Chorde greeted me and joked that I had brought them good luck. He added that my visit was a token of the special bond between Africa and China. Our conversation naturally turned to the time-honoured Sino–African relationship and the four visits Zheng He had made to Africa. I explained the purpose of my visit and related Zheng He's history to them, explaining that I was tracing Zheng He's footsteps.

I told them that Zheng He had been captured by Ming forces and made a eunuch. When he had served as a eunuch for some years, and because he rendered excellent service as an attendant of Zhu Di, who later became the emperor, he was elevated to the position of imperial eunuch, and was given the surname Zheng as an honour. Throughout much of China's history, imperial eunuchs were special advisors to the emperor, and were even afforded the privilege of accompanying him into the Inner Court of the Forbidden City, where no other men were allowed to linger too long. In his capacity as close advisor to the emperor, Zheng He was later addressed as Sanbao Eunuch. In the period between 1405 (the third year of the reign of Yongle) and 1433 (the eighth year of the reign of Xuande), under orders from the imperial court, he headed a large fleet leading expeditions across the Indian Ocean, between Kalimantan and Africa. He made seven voyages in 28 years, visiting 30 countries. He reached the East African coast on four of these voyages.

Wherever he went, Zheng He exchanged porcelain goods, silk thread and silk fabric, gold and silver for local specialities, developing trade between Asian and African nations. Two or three hundred vessels were deployed on each of his voyages across the Western Ocean, employing the services of tens of thousands of officers and crew members. The largest of his ships measured 44.4 *zhang* in length and 18 *zhang* in width (1 *zhang* was equivalent to 3.3 m). This vessel accommodated over a thousand people. Zheng He's voyages were made more than half a century earlier than those made by Western navigators, such as Christopher Columbus and Vasco da Gama, and the scale of his fleets was hundreds of times larger than their European counterparts. Numerous Zheng He relics are scattered across South East Asia. Imperial files about his fleet's voyages on the Western Ocean were destroyed by war. The main source of information researchers rely on for information about Zheng He and his journeys to Africa are the travel notes written by Zheng He's attendants, such as those by Ma Huan, Fei Xin and Gong Zheng. These documents include titles such as *Overseas wonders, Marvellous views from a starry mast* and

Records of western countries. Other prominent sources of information are *The history of Ming* and some unearthed stelae related to the voyages.

According to existing documents, Zheng He travelled to Africa by four routes: from the western coast of the Indian Ocean by way of western Asia; from Sumatra to Mogadiscio (modern-day Mogadishu) by way of the Maldives; from Sumatra to Mogadiscio via Ceylon (Sri Lanka) and Kollam; and from Sumatra to Brava by way of Ceylon. Of these routes, the first was a traditional one; the other three were new passages across the Indian Ocean opened by Zheng He. The records show that Zheng He's fleet did not navigate as a whole, but that small boats were dispatched on trial voyages. Some were dispersed owing to difficult conditions and some disappeared or were shipwrecked. Given that there were very few ocean-going vessels and many communication constraints, it was difficult for sailors to contact domestic authorities when there was a shipwreck, so many wrecks remain a mystery today. This lack of information is compounded by the fact that records of these voyages were destroyed. It is not untenable to guess, however, that the Chinese descendants living in Mogadishu and Kismayo today are linked to these historical voyages, and that a ship might easily have wrecked near Pate Island when it was navigating along the Brava route.

There are many opinions about the purpose of Zheng He's long history of voyages to East Africa, especially to the coastal areas of Kenya. One popular theory, as discussed earlier, is that the aim of these journeys was to locate the giraffe or kylin, thought to be a holy animal by the ancient Chinese people.

The three UN officials listened to my story, leaning forward, their eyes filled with curiosity, despite the sounds of wind and rain outside. It was obvious that this was the first time they had heard such a story. Chorde was from France and his two companions from Africa. All three were absorbed in the story. Even though I was telling my account in English, I felt like a master storyteller. When I finished, I tried to lighten the mood by expanding the plot from the past to the present, bringing it from sea to land as I spoke of the discoveries I had made on my trip to Ethiopia, like the local flatbread dish, *injera*, which was similar to the Chinese pancake, and noting the similarities between Chinese music and what was being played on the radio at that moment.

Chorde said he would help me search for leads when we parted, but he reminded me that the refugee camps were not orderly, and warned that I must be cautious on my trips, since bandits often showed up in those places. We then shook hands, and he wished me a safe journey.

With everything arranged, Chorde made a classy gesture the following morning in the refugee office, sending me off not in Chinese or English, but with the Swahili *chao*, meaning goodbye.

SEEKING INFORMATION IN A REFUGEE CAMP

Jijiga is the Ethiopian town that is closest to the Somali border. There were eight UN refugee camps for Somalis fleeing the civil war near there, running north to south along a 400-km stretch of the east Ethiopian border. Kebri Beyah and Hart Sheik were the closest.

At seven o'clock in the morning, my guide, Solomon Seyoum, accompanied me as I set out for these two camps south-east of the town. It had rained heavily the previous night, each drop treasured by the local people after such a long drought. Greeting me, Seyoum grasped my hand, smiling so broadly that his large eyes scrunched into a narrow line. It was as if he had met an old friend. He repeated the comment made the previous evening: that his Chinese friend had brought good luck to the local people. The soil, now lightly moistened, was all but bare of greenery. Here and there, groups of three or four women with buckets on their backs walked along the roads or through the fields, while children driving donkeys and carrying even more buckets searched for water. Water was of prime importance to the people here.

Desperate living conditions

A long row of tents referred to as 'tukuls'[1] – a type of domed tent similar to a yurt – of various sizes came into view in the distance as we approached Kebri Beyah. The tents were like a huge quilt spread out beneath the blue sky. A closer look revealed that they were made of worn scraps of plastic cloth, sackcloth, rugs, cardboard and woven bags of different sizes, all held together with rope.

We went to the UN refugee office and found the officials in charge of refugee affairs. We followed them through the refugee camp on a winding road barely wide enough for a single car. The dust from our tyres blew in the light breeze and settled on the surrounding tukul tents. The car horns drew people out of their tukuls; watching guests seemed to be the only form of entertainment they had.

Another distant scene attracted my attention. A row of yellow plastic buckets were laid neatly on the ground, surrounded by dozens of women and children waiting to fill their buckets with water. Two elderly women sold tomatoes and potatoes by the road. A worker from the refugee office told me that water was supplied each day from a nearby pond, and that the people could fetch it at a set time, so they queued here each day to collect it. Those living in the refugee camps were extremely poor; only a very few had potatoes or tomatoes to sell by the roadside.

We then made our way to Hart Sheik Camp, 17 km away, led by a refugee affairs officer, Abraham Melles. This was once one of the largest refugee camps in the world, with an area of 15 km^2 and a capacity for 59 000 refugees. Even after repeated repatriations in recent years, at the time I visited it, 11 488 refugees still remained. Seeing a few people chatting in front of a tukul, I asked if we could have a look inside the tent. The host showed me in. From inside, I could see it was made of twigs bound together with ropes in criss-cross patterns. The tukul was windowless, and had only one door. Unless the door flap was raised, it was pitch dark inside. In the dim light, the inside was faintly visible. This tukul was 10 m in diameter. It was partitioned into two rooms by a twig screen, the inner room serving as a bedroom. Our host kept his house clean, with his bedding rolled up during the day. It seemed the family members all slept together on the ground. In the exterior room, there were some plastic buckets, some simple farm tools, a sack of flour, a bottle of oil by the door and a kerosene lamp for use at night, which was kept in a prominent location. With little furniture or tools, the tukul seemed spacious, but this only made the penniless state of its occupants more evident. It is said that a poor home has four walls; the tukul did not even have that, being nothing more than twigs and a plastic sheet. Our host said that conditions were bearable in the dry season, but in the rainy season, life would be hard in the leaky, tattered tent.

Beside this tent was another even smaller one equipped with only a cooking pot and just large enough for one person to sit inside. This was meant to be the family kitchen, but they preferred to do most of their cooking with the pot in the open air.

Poor as this kitchen tukul was, it was the envy of many families. The refugees in Somalia and the Somali people in Ethiopia were citizens of two countries, but of one ethnicity, sharing the same language, habits and customs. The tukuls of the refugees looked almost like those of the local people, all having a small space fenced in with a partition made of twigs, with some corn growing inside. The leaves of the corn stems were yellow and dry from the drought.

Poor innocent children

Being a Sunday, it was a day off in the refugee camps. Even so, loud reading captured my attention. In an open-air classroom with twig partitions, a teacher was teaching 30 to 40 children the Somali language. The students' tender, silvery voices repeated the teacher's lesson in unison. Moving closer, I saw that there was no platform or desk for the teacher, and no desks or stools for the students. The children sat, backs straight, on a plastic sheet spread on the ground, reading aloud after the teacher. They held their textbooks in hand and kept their eyes glued to the blackboard, which was suspended from a partition woven from twigs. They had no school bags beside them. The sunlight falling through the partition cast mottled shadows on the children's bodies and attentive faces. When I started to take photos, they all turned to face the camera.

It was with a heavy step that I left this special classroom. Those poor children should be going to school like children everywhere, school bags slung over their shoulders as they went to their bright, spacious classrooms – but they lived here in a refugee camp with the adults. This camp had been established in 1988. Judging from the children's ages, I guessed most had been born in the camp.

The UN Refugee Affairs Office had established primary schools in every refugee camp in the Somali Region. Children with excellent academic records could go to local secondary schools when they completed their primary education, joining local children as schoolmates. A few outstanding learners stood the chance of entering university. Up to this point, only a few assisted students had been sent to university after studying in the refugee camps. Because of the conditions in the camps, especially the limited campuses, only 5–6 per cent of school-age children could study free of charge from Year 1 to Year 8. At the time of my visit, there were 6 000 students and 103 teachers, all of whom were selected from among the refugees.

Melles pointed to a large classroom under construction, telling me that an unexpected wind had destroyed the school, and the classrooms were now being rebuilt. He went on to say that, because of the lack of classrooms, the school had been able to enrol fewer than 700 students, with over 70 pupils in each class. To maximise the classroom time, the schools divided the students according to level and taught on a rotating basis, teaching English, Somali, Arabic, maths, natural sciences, social sciences, fine arts and physical education.

In an effort to provide more children with education, the camp ran different types of supplementary classes. While visiting the Hart Sheik Refugee Camp, I found a group of girls having a supplementary English lesson in a simple house, an additional lesson tacked on to the Sunday open-air-classroom lesson. The director of the centre told me it was set up for girls to learn English and Somali on festival days and holidays.

As I was leaving the centre, I came across a 14-year-old middle-school boy who spoke English fairly proficiently. He told me that he knew nothing when the civil war had broken out in Somalia in 1991. Once, in the middle of the night, they had fled from their home on foot as a gun battle raged around them, eventually walking all the way to Ethiopia. 'I was small, and my mother was running fast, with me in her arms,' he said. 'My brother ran close behind, carrying our bags. My parents keep saying that we used to lead a decent life. My father was a businessman, and we had a large house in town, along with other property. As soon as we arrived here, we lived in shabby shelters like everyone else, with hardly enough food and water. I like the UN refugee office delegation better than others. They give us food and build schools for us.'

It was back in 400 BC when the Greek playwright Euripides said that 'the greatest tragedy under heaven is the loss of one's homeland'. The people in the refugee camp would no doubt agree.

A miserable life

In front of a tukul under the burning sun, a young woman sat cooking at a stove, flicking a fan to stoke the flames. Sugary dumplings rolled in the oil. As I lifted my camera, she turned away, apparently unwilling to draw attention to the scene. Rather forcefully, Melles, the camp official, persuaded her to resume her position. A bit embarrassed, she sat down and continued fanning the fire. After the pictures were taken, she answered my question about food provisions for the refugees.

According to the memorandum of understanding between the US Refugee Agency and the World Food Programme, refugee provisions are supplied by the World Food Programme on a monthly basis, consisting of 12 kg of wheat, 1.05 kg of oil, 150 g of table salt, and 750 g of sugar per person, regardless of age. To ensure the provision of these foodstuffs to every family, the refugee agency registered refugees every year, and they encouraged them to grow crops on the camp's idle land as a way to alleviate food shortages.

The limited amount of food provided and prepared was evident in the refugees' diet. They had to be very economical if they wanted to avoid running out of food before the end of the month, being very careful with the ingredients. They ground the wheat into flour using the camp's mill, then mixed the flour, sugar and oil to make dumplings – their staple food. All the families here ate 'sugared dumplings' once a day every day, all year round. The Hart Sheik Camp was established in May 1988, and most of the refugees had spent ten years of their lives there.

Perhaps attracted by the sight of a foreigner, a young man from a nearby tukul came over to us and we chatted. He was a 20-year-old student in Year 7. When I asked about his life as a refugee, he did not answer directly, but talked about his homeland and his future. 'Somalia used to be a strong, wealthy, beautiful nation,' he said. 'In 1988, the Somali National Movement started an armed uprising against the Barre regime. When the fighting came to Hargeisa, in the north-western part of the country, we fled to Ethiopia. At the time, I was in primary school, a Year 2 student. We had a big house with five bedrooms, two kitchens, and two washrooms.' He looked at the shabby tukul in front of us, frowning. 'Now, we are poor, and have lived in a refugee camp for 10 years. I do not want to be a refugee. I wish the situation in Somalia would stabilise soon. I always dream of returning to my homeland.'

His heartfelt words moved all those who were listening; tears came to my eyes.

With the help of one of the refugee teachers, Ahomed Jama Aden, I interviewed Kadique Hardioma, a middle-aged woman from the coastal city of Kismayo, hoping to learn more about the war in southern Somalia and the Zheng He Village. She explained what had happened to her. 'One night in January 1991, I was awakened by a cacophony of gunfire, followed by rapid knocking on our door. My husband, serving with the anti-government forces, had come home. He hurriedly told me to take the children and flee to Ethiopia at once, and he would meet us on the way. I was in such a hurry that I left everything behind. Slinging my youngest onto my back and grasping two others by the hand, I escaped with my eight children. When we were on the street, I saw soldiers charging forward, submachine guns in hand. My terrified children started crying. Even though that was 10 years ago and I am now 48 years old, I remember it as if it were yesterday. The whole family, all 10 of us, begged for food on the long, arduous, 10-day journey to this place. When we arrived, we had nothing, and had to live in the open air for a whole year. Later, the refugee office gave us plastic sheets and blankets, and we built a tukul for shelter.'

'How do you like living here?' I asked, not suspecting that my simple question would touch a sore spot in her soul.

She retorted, 'What sort of life is this? Can it even be called life? When we were home, we had food and drink. Every day, we ate vegetables and meat, and our children went to school. During this past decade, our children have gone to school, but we could not afford textbooks; we ate, but could not afford vegetables.' Saying this, she lowered her head, broken-hearted.

I asked if she could do something to earn money. She shook her head and said, 'I am penniless. I have not seen money in 10 years. You want to know where I get this firewood? I walk over 15 kilometres a day, taking three hours to get to the place where I can gather twigs to bring back to use for firewood so we can cook.'

When I asked her about Zheng He Village, near Kismayo, she shook her head again. 'I lived in town,' she said, 'and rarely went out. I know nothing beyond my own town.'

My interview had been made possible with the help of 21-year-old Mohamed Shake, who had come to the camp in 1991, at the age of 12, and had learnt English in the refugee school. He told me that, 10 years earlier, when they were home, his father was a businessman and they lived a decent life, but then everything changed at the refugee camp. As he spoke of his own situation, his English began to noticeably falter. When Hardioma said her family was ready to go home as soon as the situation was stable, he interrupted and added, 'I hope to go home too. I am looking forward to that day.'

At the end of the interview, I asked if I could take a photo of Aden, Hardioma and Shake. When the first picture was taken, they all looked grim-faced. I asked them to smile for the second photo. I did not anticipate that their smiles would be more horrific than any amount of bitter tears. They looked helpless and sad. How could I ask them to smile? What was there to smile about?

PAINSTAKING MANAGEMENT OF THE REFUGEE CAMPS

The main responsibility of the UN Refugee Affairs Office is to provide refugees with international protection and assistance. As well as temporary homes, the agency provides the refugees with food, enables the children to receive education, provides medical service and gives the refugees guidance in alleviating poverty. In Ethiopia the first challenge for the refugee office was providing the refugees with water each day.

We climbed to the top of the wall of a big dam near the camp. The reservoir, half full of water, sparkled under the burning sun, looking clear and precious. Melles told us that this large pool, 150 m by 100 m and 3 m deep, was completed half a year earlier to collect rainwater and deliver water to the refugee camps. It had taken half a year and $96 000 to construct the pool and its support systems, including the sedimentation and feeding pools. The reservoir had done a great deal to address the water shortage for refugees and residents in the immediate area.

Eleven years earlier, when the refugee camps were being built, the UN Refugee Affairs Office had drilled five pumping wells in a valley 75 km from Jijiga, and later built several small water pools as a more stable water source for local residents and refugees, in an effort to guarantee sufficient water to meet basic needs. Even with all these initiatives, however, it was impossible to ensure timely water supplies because of poor road conditions and the shortage of vehicles, not to mention the time-consuming, labour-intensive work involved in long-distance transportation of water. Because of this situation, the agency took advantage of the different seasons, the major rainy season and minor rainy season, organising labour in 1997 to dig huge pools. On my first visit, five such pools had been completed and the problem of long-distance transportation of water was a thing of the past. Now, refugees and residents could fetch and use water where they lived. To ensure an economical use of water and to keep the process of fetching it orderly, the camps had established water-use associations, with a water-management committee in charge of the pools and establishing water regulations.

Besides the water-management associations, the refugee camps also established organisations such as refugee committees, elderly committees, youth associations and women's centres. The latter two were meant to stimulate and enrich the lives of the young men and women, organising them and helping them get through the difficult times and to generate some income. The former two aimed to share the responsibilities for camp management on behalf of the Refugee Affairs Office, settling disputes among neighbours. To avoid conflict erupting among refugees from different ethnic groups, the agency tried to arrange the refugees from different areas into different parts of the camp.

We went to one of the camp's women's centres. It was a Sunday, and the centre was especially busy. The director took us to a sewing room, where women were making clothes on Butterfly brand sewing machines made in China. Melles told me the machines had been purchased with funds from international aid. The sewing machines were seen as a means of providing skills training and an income generator, encouraging women to be self-reliant and ambitious. Near the sewing room there was a typing room. The youth centre focused on study and recreation; it had organised football teams and reading teams. Young men and women could study in the libraries any time they wanted.

I asked what happened when refugees fell ill. I was shown to the in-patient room of the Hart Sheik Refugee Camp clinic, where I saw several patients, both adults and children, being treated. Though the facilities were simple, with nothing more than sickbeds, plastic sheets, and water buckets, the clinic could accommodate over 40 patients, including children suffering from severe malnutrition. The clinic treated patients in accordance with the severity of their cases and gave preferential diets to those in need. Severely malnourished children were fed six times a day with a diet that included milk, rice, vegetables, noodles and protein-rich mixes. We were told that the refugee agency had established a clinic in every camp. An ambulance and medical staff were provided for each camp, which could perform basic tests on patients and provide facilities for sending severely ill patients to Jijiga Hospital or Dire Dawa, the second largest city in Ethiopia, for treatment.

The influx of refugees and their long-term stay there was not a negligible threat to the local ecological environment. This resided in the improper use of large areas of land, felling trees for constructing dwellings and to use as firewood or to sell, and in overgrazing of cattle and sheep.

Ethiopia is on a dry plateau with declining vegetation and a deteriorating ecological environment. In recent years, the refugee agency had learnt of the serious consequences arising from excessive depletion of natural resources in the immediate area and, in 1997, began taking measures to make up for the loss. On the one hand, they set up seed gardens in every refugee camp and planted 500 000 trees in the refugee camps and their surrounding areas. On the other, they actively promoted energy-saving stoves and organised local production of these appliances. The energy-saving stoves reduced wood consumption by a third, reducing the need to fell trees for firewood.

Other non-governmental organisations (NGOs) worked alongside the UN Refugee Affairs Office to help provide support for the refugees. These NGOs included the American Save the Children Fund and Handicap International, headquartered in France. Save the Children built recreational spaces and facilities for children; Handicap International focused on disseminating information about landmines and worked to facilitate the refugees' safe return to their homelands. Juliane Shookey, from France, told me that their organisation, Handicap International, had 27 people working there, two to each camp. They initiated teacher training, then developed their programme to include training in every household, informing the people about landmines and how to mitigate the danger they posed. Since the outbreak of the Somali civil war, landmines had been laid all over the country. To educate the people about landmines and the hazards they presented, the organisation adopted many methods of disseminating information, such as signboards, brochures, posters and banners. Education among the children was conducted through the distribution of free materials about landmine hazard prevention, and through classroom teaching. Their publicity work was welcomed by the refugees, who were all longing for home, and landmines presented their first obstacle to reaching that goal.

On my way back from the refugee camp, my heart was heavy and my expression grave. My driver played a light, lively melody, but it didn't cheer me up. The tragedy I witnessed in the refugee camps played in my mind like a movie on a screen. A sudden jerk of the vehicle reminded me that I had gone without food or drink for the whole day. My mouth was dry, my throat sore and my stomach empty. I seemed to hear an echo in my mind, reminding me to cherish my peaceful life.

AN ENDLESS CYCLE OF REFUGEES

According to the UN's definition, a refugee is a person who is forced to flee from his or her own country out of reasonable fear of serious risk to his or her personal safety or freedom. The reasons for fleeing may involve ethnic conflict, religious issues, political opinions, armed conflicts, external invasion and/or natural disasters. For the sake of survival and freedom, refugees give up everything – property, family, homeland, everything – heading to an uncertain future in a foreign land. As long as war, persecution and discrimination exist on earth, there will be refugees.

The movement of floods of refugees is a great tragedy of the contemporary world. To provide refugees with international protection and assistance, and to obtain a permanent solution to the refugee problem on this basis, the 1950 UN General Assembly decided on 1 January 1951 to establish a UN High Commissioner for Refugees. The major task in the initial period of the refugee agency was to deal with the problem of the refugee crisis following the two world wars. Even so, the best intentions of the UN remained just that, as refugees kept appearing in other parts of the world. The mandate of the refugee agency had to be extended time and again, stretching from the initial three-year term to five-year work terms.

The flood of African refugees occurred in the colonial period. With the surging national liberation movements in Africa in the 1960s and '70s, the number of refugees kept increasing, rising from 900 000 in 1969 to 1 million in 1977, and to 5 million in the 1980s. In the 1990s, as a result of armed conflicts in Liberia, Rwanda, Burundi, Sierra Leone, Guinea Bissau, Sudan and the Democratic Republic of the Congo, the number of African refugees soared to over 7 million, on top of the 20 million people who were rendered destitute and homeless by these conflicts. As of 2000, the number of African refugees was approximately 6 million.

There are three approaches in solving the refugee problem: voluntary return to their respective homelands; assimilation into their country of residence; or settlement in a third country. All over the world, returning home is the preferred solution. Of the three approaches, the refugee agency recommends voluntary return to one's homeland. Once the domestic situation becomes stable, the refugees' safety is ensured once they are back home, and most refugees want to return home. For instance, between 1988 and 1992, when the Somali civil war was at its peak, about half a million Somalis fled to neighbouring Ethiopia. A new round of civil war broke out in 1994, forcing more Somalis to flee to Ethiopia, bringing the number to 600 000, all of whom settled in eight camps along the border. By 1997, when the situation in north-eastern Somalia became relatively stable, many refugees began returning home with the assistance of the refugee agency. By the end of 2000, the number of Somali refugees in Ethiopia was down to about 125 000. As the national situation was then relatively stable, the refugee agency had planned to repatriate all the refugees in Ethiopia within a year or two and close all the refugee camps there.

The UN Refugee Affairs High Commission has been in operation for about 60 years, well beyond the initially envisioned three-year work term. With the increasing number of refugees, the agency is facing growing challenges from all quarters. The Horn of Africa serves as an example. The political situation there is rife with instability and armed conflict. While the Somali political turmoil has been going on for over two decades, the refugee situation remains largely unsolved and large-scale armed conflicts in the border area of Ethiopia and Eritrea have also generated hundreds of thousands of refugees.

In addition, infringements on refugees' human rights have been an ongoing problem, especially the basic rights of vulnerable groups like women and children. Furthermore, anti-foreign sentiment has led governments of certain nations to refuse refugees, and refugees are often the target of discrimination and hostility from local people. Another challenge the flood of refugees poses is the grave threat to the local ecological environment, especially in ecologically weak regions like arid eastern Ethiopia. Finally, there is the enduring financial burden. As the number of refugees has continued to increase, international financial aid has been on the decline, which is a striking problem for the African continent.

In the camps I visited, many of the refugees had spent up to 10 years there. They could not work for a living, and remained helpless and hopeless in their search for employment back home. Would they spend the rest of their lives like this? When would this vicious cycle be broken? Former UN High Commissioner for Refugees Sadako Ogata hit the nail on the head when she said, 'The only solution is to put an end to the vicious cycle of war. Wars generate new refugees and new misery, sowing new seed for further armed conflict.'[2] The aid agencies' efforts seem so pale and weak in the face of the wars that generate more and more refugees, making these agencies appears inadequate and ineffective. In the global setting, it is imperative that we treasure peace and avoid conflict, solving the refugee problem in Africa and across the world.

Solomon, the driver who accompanied me during my tour of the camps, was interested in the legendary tale of Zheng He. He said he had learnt of Confucius and the Great Wall of China at primary school, but this was the first time he had ever heard of Zheng He. As we made our way through the streets of Jijiga, Solomon constantly stopped to ask his friends for information. Two of his friends had come from Somalia many years earlier. They had heard of a Chinese fleet visiting Somalia, and had heard about the Zheng He Village, but had only heard vague word-of-mouth references; they couldn't provide firm details.

Back from the refugee camp, I spent a sleepless night tossing and turning in my bed, even though I was exhausted. I wrote a note: 'A happy, wealthy life is varied and colourful. A sad and needy life is dull and empty.' I noted this as a lesson learnt from my trip to the refugee camps.

It had been an utterly disappointing visit in terms of finding information about Zheng He. When we shook hands in farewell at the airport, Solomon and my friends from the refugee agency all agreed that the story about Zheng He was significant, since it told the history of Africa's early communications with China, long before its connections with Europe. They took great interest in the story of Zheng He and expressed a desire to continue to gather information and let me know if they came across any leads.

7

Insight into Somalia

OFFICIAL SEAL IN A PLASTIC BAG

The white clouds against the blue sky looked as orderly as rows of cotton in a carefully cultivated field, presenting a spectacular view. The plane, flying from Nairobi to the Somali capital, Mogadishu, jerked as it flew through the clouds, but my heart was even more unsettled than the aircraft. I did not have misgivings about a plane accident, but was anxious about my trip to an area that had been isolated from the outside world since civil war had broken out in 1990. Little about events in Somalia was known by the rest of the world at that time.

Driven by my professional mission, my trip in early August 2004 had been planned in such a hurry that I had not been able to contact the authorities in Somalia before setting out. I was urged on by news I had heard at the airport in Kenya of the Somali peace process. I was unfamiliar with Somalia and knew little about it, since I gained most of my information from news reports, which gave me only knowledge gained from a distance. My estimations of the present situation in Mogadishu were based on the fact that three weekly return flights operated between Mogadishu and Nairobi.

There were fewer than 40 passengers on my African Express Airways flight, leaving two-thirds of the seats vacant. Besides me, all the passengers were Africans, mostly tradespeople carrying packages of various sizes. When the plane was about to land, the green foliage of trees and grass below us grew more distinct. We glided onto the runway, with its rough, bumpy surface evident after so many years of little maintenance. Before disembarking, I had expected to be greeted by a wave of heat, but the weather was crisp and slightly humid. To my surprise, I did not see any buildings connected to the airport.

This airport was not particularly small compared with other African airstrips, though the runway was uneven, with exposed sand and stone. There was no perimeter fence and no terminal building – just two small houses a hundred metres or so apart. The larger was half hidden by weeds, with no roof and exposed walls. The other was a windowless thatched hut, with a single opening the size of a door. Upon arrival, the plane's passengers rushed to the two dilapidated minibuses parked by the airstrip. Luggage in hand, I was at a loss where to go. I was entirely out of place here.

While I hesitated, a well-dressed elderly man of medium build approached me, carrying a plastic bag. He asked me who I was waiting for and which company had invited me. When I told him I had come alone and without an inviting company, he shook his head, obviously puzzled. He mumbled a kind warning, 'You're in trouble here with no one to receive you.'

I became acutely aware that nothing good was waiting for me here. I wondered if I should turn back, board the plane I had just come from, and immediately leave this troubled place. The flight was scheduled to travel on to Dubai. I could fly to Dubai, I thought, for the sake of my own safety. I kept looking back at the plane, embarrassed. The old man spoke up again. 'I'm in charge of entry visas,' he explained. 'Come with me and we'll settle your formalities.'

A short distance from the small airport was a thatched building of about 40 or 50 m², its earthen floor a series of lumps and holes. Several white plastic chairs lay scattered about the floor, and a round white plastic table and a few chairs stood in the corner near the entrance. The old man gestured for me to sit to one side in what I came to realise was the waiting room; the table was his office. He sat at the table, casually placing his plastic bag on top. He took out a battered invoice book and another, smaller, worn plastic bag. 'Hand me your passport and $25 for your visa fee.'

He read my passport details and found a blank page. He took an oblong seal from the smaller bag and stamped my passport. The words were blurry, the stamp having too little ink. He looked at the results, made a second stamp, then gave up. He reluctantly handed the passport back to me and picked up the seal, turning to leave as the plane took off behind us.

Anxiously, I asked, 'Is it safe in the city?'

'Sure, if you have someone to protect you,' he replied.

'Is there a Chinese restaurant here?' He shook his head.

'Are there any Chinese people here?' He shook his head again.

'Are you a government official, an immigration officer?'

He looked at me in surprise. He did not shake or nod his head, and did not say a word.

'I'm new here. Please help me find a safe hotel.'

'If no one has come to meet you, you are considered a guest of the airline. Go downtown, and they will help you,' he said firmly.

I relaxed a bit. When I asked him to help me get a taxi to go downtown, he pointed to the two minibuses. 'Those airline buses are free of charge for passengers.'

He added a sincere word of advice: 'Years of civil war have left the capital in a mess. While you are here, don't trust anyone, and don't go out on the streets alone. People can become quite nasty when they see money. Be more cautious.'

Before I boarded the bus, he demanded a tip for his service.

ARMED CONVOYS ESCORT PASSENGERS TO THE CAPITAL

What was happening right in front of me was completely foreign to me. With my camera bag over my shoulder and luggage in hand, I elbowed my way onto one of the minibuses, which were waiting with a load of passengers. To my surprise, there was no gate to the airport, just a wire fence at the entrance, where armed guards kept watch. In a dirty, worn, disorderly square outside the airport, a group of women in gaudy local dress stood in a long queue. Each held a small yellow cup and had a small plastic bucket. They were selling camel's milk. Their brightly coloured clothing, yellow cups and dark skin combined to form an image that reminded me I was in an exotic land. Several times I moved to take my camera out, but each time I refrained, fearing that it might be snatched away. I regretted it, thinking that I would not be facing such dangers if it were not for my rash decision to come here. I resolved to keep a cool head from here on.

About half an hour later, we set off. There were four vehicles in our convoy, the front one a truck loaded with luggage guarded by several gunmen seated on the truck bed. Behind the trucks were the two minibuses packed with passengers, followed by an old van carrying six gunmen, their chests and waists girded with ammunition belts, and holding pistols or submachine guns. They kept watch in all directions. We bumped along the rugged road, sometimes detouring through cornfields or stretches of woods to avoid huge potholes in the road. As we made our way through the parts without a road, the bouncing and rocking of the vehicle made it seem we were travelling at great speed.

The numerous roadblocks set up by various groups suggested that gangsters or bandits were everywhere. When we encountered these roadblocks, the van would rush to the front of our convoy and the gangsters, seeing our fully armed escort, would hastily remove the roadblocks. Once the other three vehicles passed, the van resumed its place at the rear.

There were four airports in Mogadishu. The Aden Adde International Airport, located in the urban area, was a focal point for tensions during the civil war. Its building had been destroyed and its runways damaged by bombs. Out of service when I arrived, it was under the control of a military faction. The other three – Esaleey Airport, 18 km north of the capital, the K50 airstrip south-west of the capital, and Baledogle Airfield, 105 km north-west of the capital – were all under temporary control of separate military factions. The latter two were transfer stations of Daallo Airlines, with its headquarters in Dubai, and African Express

Airways, headquartered in Nairobi. The apparently fake customs entry–exit seals were made by these respective factions.

After a bumpy three-hour ride, I came to the African Express Airways office in the city. As soon as our bus stopped, a group of local people rushed over, surrounding the bus in a tight circle. I nearly panicked. When the door opened, the passengers thronged to exit. I seemed to attract every eye in the vicinity. I stood motionless, clutching my camera to my chest for fear it would be stolen. I reminded myself that it would be worse than useless to resist – it would actually invite trouble, so I felt the best thing to do was cooperate with whatever was demanded.

Once the passengers alighted, the people around the bus scattered. It turned out they had just come to meet friends and relatives. Since they were not allowed at the airport, they had to wait for travellers here at the airline office. A member of the airline staff came and told me to get off the bus, and the armed guards motioned to the people on the ground to make way for me. Under the guard's protection, I walked to the office, luggage in hand, feeling insecure and uneasy.

After five or six minutes, the office manager came out and informed me that there were two relatively good hotels there. He asked me to select one. Thinking only of my safety, I instinctively chose the one near the presidential palace. He and two armed guards escorted me to the Sahafi Hotel[1] in a car.

The hotel manager, Aweys Abdulkadir, informed me that the hotel had 75 rooms and 150 people on staff, most of whom were armed guards. He said it was perfectly safe inside the hotel compound, which was guarded by armed guards on all sides, 24 hours a day. He added, 'Under no circumstances should you go out alone. When you go out, you must be accompanied by armed guards. If you go out after dark, you will require twenty or thirty bodyguards to protect you.'

Looking at the airline's office manager, the hotel manager said to me, 'To my knowledge, there have been several Western reporters in Mogadishu in recent years, but you are the first Asian reporter to come here in the past 14 years, since civil war broke out. Your courage is admirable.'

Saying that, he gave me a thumbs up. But I was still in a panic.

GUNFIRE AT MIDNIGHT

At about four o'clock, I went to my room, hunger and fatigue giving way to fear. I switched on the television and chanced upon a CCTV 4 broadcast. I soaked in the pictures of my distant homeland and imbibed the tune of the Chinese language. It all seemed so dear to me at that moment.

I was too nervous to sleep. I tossed and turned in my bed until midnight, despite the busy day I had endured. At that moment, I heard gunfire in the distance. The silence that had seemed impenetrable before the shots was now replaced by the hum of the electric generator.

The next morning, the hotel manager told me the gunfight that took place the previous night had been about 20 km from the capital. Six or seven men had been killed in the factional battle. He added nonchalantly, 'We're used to it. It happens all the time. If you had been here three years ago, you would have heard machine guns rattling every day.' He gestured with his hands as he said these words, acting out an army forging ahead, machine guns in hand. Then, sitting back down, he sighed and said sadly, 'The numbers of casualties and losses during the war are unknown. It is beyond calculation, so no one has bothered to keep count.'

The 50-year-old hotel manager had been a history teacher at a high school. In the mid-1980s, he gave up teaching and started working for a US oil exploration company in Somalia. 'The government was quite annoyed when I quit teaching, but I had 12 kids to feed and a large family to support. I had no choice.'

He went on to describe the situation before the war: 'Christmas 1990 foretold the coming of a storm. I was a storekeeper at my company's foodstuff storehouse in the capital then. At noon, a sick American staff member rushed to me and begged me to take him to the airport and buy him a plane ticket back to the US, one for that very afternoon. His payday had not yet come, so he was penniless, but he insisted that he had to leave that day. He was so sick that he was afraid something might happen. I bought a ticket for him, persuading the airline to make a seat available for him. My wallet now empty, I could bring home only three kilos of sugar from the storehouse that day. On Christmas night, I heard rapid bursts of gunfire. The next morning, the streets and side streets were in disorder, everything looted and left in a mess. The looted company storehouse had been completely cleared of everything. Empty beer bottles and pieces of bread packaging were scattered on the floor. It was then that I became aware of the worsening situation, the impending disaster. Over the next few days, the situation took a turn for the worse. Foreigners vied to leave the country, and the local people likewise tried to flee abroad. The overthrow of the government followed, then the escape of the president to Nigeria and the armed conflict. The country spiralled out of control.'

In this state of anarchy, the first to suffer were government bodies, public facilities, businesses, shops and civilian residences. Opposed militia factions were killing each other and tribal conflicts were intensifying, growing more violent and more frequent. There were beatings and looting, and vandalism grew more severe; there was fighting everywhere. Innocent people were wounded or killed, and lives were subjected to relentless, senseless killing. Cities quickly became battlefields.

The civil war in Somalia was deeply rooted in irreconcilable ethnic and factional conflicts. The Siad Barre regime had assumed power in 1969, and remained there for years without oversight mechanisms, resulting in grave corruption and nepotism. These conflicts, mingled with ethnic tensions, ignited complaints nationwide. There was great public outcry demanding a newly elected government, but Barre turned a deaf ear. At a critical juncture in the war, Barre mobilised men from his own tribe and ordered them to press to the capital and help him maintain power. Unexpectedly, other tribes responded to this action by mobilising their own troops and moving in on the capital, while the national military officers and soldiers each turned to his own tribe to grasp for a share of the power. This way, the situation in the capital rapidly worsened. The Barre government immediately collapsed, and all the government officials fled overseas.

With the country in a state of chaos, warlords vied for power and territory. Barre staged a comeback with his residual army following him in a surge towards the capital, but he was dealt a head-on blow. Multinational forces led by the US suffered heavy losses and were forced to withdraw. Due to widespread division in opinions among the conflicting factions, repeated attempts at intervention and mediation by the international community turned out to be ineffective. Reconciliation conferences and continued fighting hampered progress towards peace, turning each small victory into a hard-won endeavour.

When the Barre government was finally overthrown in January 1991, the Chinese Embassy in Somalia and all Chinese construction and medical teams were forced to withdraw from the country. Most had not returned at the time of writing.

THE CHINESE EMBASSY TODAY

Mogadishu was once one of the most pristine cities in Africa, with its beautiful ocean views and idyllic climate. Today it is relegated to the lowest ranks of Africa's cities, a dirty mess of a place.

All the roads leading to the capital are in need of repair, and those in the suburbs are impassable. Buildings in the downtown area and the suburbs are all incomplete, with missing roofs, doors and windows, and every visible surface pockmarked by shellfire. The town is virtually in ruins. The sight of those long stretches of shabby dwellings, in all their decay and misery, is quite unbearable. Vehicles in the streets have been stripped of their license plates, their windscreens shattered and paint peeling off, and rust showing through. They are so worn out and dilapidated that one would think they would have been scrapped long ago. The roads and side streets are dirty and disorderly, with rubbish piled up everywhere. Domestic animals are herded along by their owners. Driving along the bumpy streets feels more like hiking; the dust flies along the rugged streets and one's shoes quickly become covered with a layer of dirt.

The chaos caused by the separatist warlord regimes has reduced beautiful Somalia to a war-torn state. At its heart, Mogadishu has been shattered into tiny fragments, the government overthrown, legislature disintegrated, infrastructure destroyed and the national economy devastated. Even international organisations have fallen victim to the catastrophe.

The Chinese Embassy and the Chinese-built National Theatre of Somalia are in the old downtown area, about 1 km apart and on opposite sides of the street. On the afternoon of 5 August, under the protection of six armed guards, I went into the downtown area, searching for information. Once the busiest part of the capital, it was now devastated and considered the most dangerous part of the city. As we entered the area, the leader of my team of guards warned me not to take photos, adding that the vehicle's windows must be tightly shut. Almost all the tall buildings on the streets were without roofs, and many of them destroyed. Some time-honoured buildings had been mutilated beyond recognition by gunfire and bombing. Those that had suffered less damage were heavily protected to keep people at a distance, particularly foreigners.

I was informed that, during the civil war, armed bandits, looters and rioters ran rampant, beating people, and destroying and plundering property and public facilities in search of wealth. When the buildings they were looting had been stripped of everything of value, they began dismantling roofs, doors and windows, finally reducing them to rubble. They took over the buildings as their own, making it impossible for anyone – local or foreign – to enter unless they paid the bandits. Most public buildings fell victim to this fate, including the Chinese Embassy and the National Theatre of Somalia.

As our van approached the National Theatre of Somalia, we saw some men sitting idly with their guns to their chests as they smoked in front of the theatre. The van parked in the street and the guard reminded me again and again not to get out of the van while they were negotiating with these guards for permission for me to take photos of the theatre. The Chinese Embassy was occupied by another faction, so taking photos there would depend on another round of negotiations. After an hour of bargaining, first among themselves, then between those guarding the door and me, the price for taking photos was lowered from $50 to $40. They said this was a special price for Chinese photographers, and that Western reporters were expected to pay 20 to 30 times more – no less than $1 000.

The National Theatre of Somalia was once a landmark in Mogadishu and a symbol of high standards in construction. But now, all one saw was huge holes in the wall left by artillery shells, missing doors, missing windows, the front entrance secured by nothing more than some branches. Pushing the branches aside, I ascended a flight of stairs and entered the main hall. I was surprised to find there were no seats at all. On the evenly spaced cement steps, there remained only rows of steel bars to which the seats had once been attached, a reminder of the catastrophe that had befallen the place. The stage was likewise bare; all that was left was a nationalistic-style painting. Raising my head, I saw there was no roof, but only a rusty steel tripod structure, exposed to the elements. The once magnificent theatre was now an open-air theatre, with its straight walls and shiny, neat floor tiles the only reminder of the quality of construction and the demanding specifications that had gone into the design of the place by its Chinese architects. The only performance taking place was one of staged dramatic irony: the guards sitting on the stairs next to me joked, 'Hey, reporter! We're here watching the performance. Snap a photo for us!'

The Chinese Embassy, which was adjacent to the Italian Embassy, was a fellow victim of the unrest. It was in a better state than the theatre, though, since it was only a three-storey building. On the way from the theatre to the embassy, a branch from a milflores tree peeped over a high wall, waving in the breeze as if welcoming this Chinese reporter from afar. The iron door to the embassy was still intact, rust showing through its light-blue lacquer coat. The glass display case had been smashed and fragments of glass lay among the weeds. Entering through the door, I felt a springiness underfoot from a thick layer of dry twigs strewn with rubbish. It brought to mind the image of a large carpet lying over the compound. The two-storey reception room at the entrance was now nothing but a windowless cement shell. Before I entered, a rancid smell greeted me – the reception room now functioned as a temporary public toilet.

The embassy faced west, with huge trees in the front courtyard mottling the afternoon sunlight that dappled the wall. A sewage channel ran in front of the building, filled with fallen leaves floating on a putrid pool. The gate, still intact, was locked with an iron chain. The interior was filthy, the two round pillars carved with an iron chain pattern now covered in dust. Peeping through the slit in the door on the left, I saw an empty activity hall with footprints visible in the dust. In the back courtyard, rubbish was piled into small hills, upon which children played. A rope stretched between two of them, laden with washing. A middle-aged woman, baby in arms, called to a grazing calf and two children, who were playing. Seeing a stranger approach, the calf raised its head and the children stopped running, bringing to mind a rural scene. On a balcony on the third floor, several people were moving about. I was told it was the family of a military official and that his residence, housed in the former Chinese Embassy, was closed to all outsiders.

Such was the state of the Chinese Embassy in Somalia. Surveying the place left me with an unutterable sense of distaste. On the left of the front courtyard stood an empty, open garage. Cattle horns lay in a disordered stack in one corner of it. On the other side of the compound was an unusual plant, perhaps a sort of cactus, standing 10 m tall. It had been badly damaged. I was told that it was a type of Chinese plant grown by the Chinese Embassy, a species otherwise unknown to the local people. The Chinese Embassy stood to the south of the Italian Embassy, but the wall that partitioned them had been damaged. The children now repeatedly climbed over it in some sort of game.

I could only lament all the war and chaos here, and longed for the end of anarchy and disorder.

THE WORRIES OF ABSOLUTE FREEDOM

When they came across large potholes in the road between the airport and the capital, vehicles had to slow down or take a detour. In the case of the latter, roadblocks would appear. When I asked who set up these roadblocks, the local people told me anyone who felt like it would do so. In the streets of the capital, animals and people ambled where they liked, heedless of one another. Heaps of rubbish were piled everywhere. Vehicles stopped and started according to the drivers' inclinations, as the traffic lights had long been out of service. One day at noon, five or six vehicles were stuck in a traffic jam, a dusty cloud stirring behind them. A middle-aged man was directing traffic with a whistle. When I asked about him, I was told he was doing it to make money to live on. The hotel guard who was with me smiled wryly and said no one paid him attention any more – or tips, for that matter.

In one particular traffic jam, we detoured along a side street, where there were people with guns everywhere I looked. The guard explained that during the civil war, arms and ammunition had found their way into the hands of the local people, and now every household had a gun and everyone was a soldier in the most literal sense.

Talking of the 'freedom'[2] that I heard and saw everywhere brought to mind the way the hotel manager asked me, after some prevaricating, whether I needed a Somali passport. Seeing my confusion, he added earnestly, 'I can go through all the formalities for you, and can get as many copies as you need.'

The next day, at the office of Daallo Airlines, I noticed some passports stacked up, ready to be issued to passengers who needed them. Seeing my curiosity, the manager indicated that this was what he had earlier referred to.

When I asked about the passport, he added, 'Do you want to be president of Somalia?' I could not help but laugh, but he added seriously, 'Give the newspaper office a little money today and tomorrow, and they will report that you are president. I'm not joking.'

In Somalia, there was absolute freedom of the press. A local reporter told me that the country had 64 newspapers, 10 radio stations and three television stations, most of them based in the capital. Aside from one radio station and one television station operated by the transnational government, all the others were privately owned by groups or individuals. Restricted only by certain practical constraints, these so-called newspapers were all circulated daily, printed on six or seven sheets of A3 or A4 paper bound with staples. They sold for 1 000 Somali shillings ($1 was equivalent to 15 000 shillings). I bought four of them, *Nationality Newspaper*, *National Newspaper*, *Times Newspaper* and *Newspaper of Interest*. They were all printed in black and white, written in Somali and with a blurry portrait on the front page, but no other images.

In this 'absolutely free' – and utterly chaotic – Somali society, the local people were extremely hard up. A person needed to make full use of his or her prowess to survive in such a disorganised, undisciplined society. People often verbally abused one another, or even came to blows, over the smallest of trifles. According to incomplete statistics, since the outbreak of civil war, a quarter of the population of 8 million had fled the country, becoming refugees in neighbouring states. Those left behind had to struggle, trembling in fear as they sought to carry on with life, minding their own business. After more than a dozen years of turbulence, and after repeated regulations and reorganisations, the Somali society at the time I was there was seeking a temporary balance, striving for some discipline and trying their best to find some sort of public order. When power-supply facilities were damaged by war, people had managed to find access to electricity elsewhere. Some residential communities organised 'self-preservation' initiatives, pooling their money to purchase their own micro-generators, significantly boosting Japanese and Korean sales of such products.

The cruel war had devastated the national economy and left the whole country in utter chaos. People looted government organisations, public facilities, state-owned property and private property, dividing the spoils up among themselves. Airports and harbours were also looted and 'privatised', and factories, schools and hospitals likewise. In August 2004, there were only three factories in the capital and its immediate surrounds: a Coca-Cola plant that had begun operations half a month earlier, a water facility and a factory producing oxy-fuel for welding, which had resumed production sometime around 2000. As they provided an urgently needed service, airports and harbours resumed skeleton operations under extremely difficult circumstances. These transport facilities were constantly guarded by armed forces.

When the country fell into an extreme shortage of everyday necessities, Dubai stepped in as the freight-transfer hub that linked Somalia to the rest of the world. Amid utter chaos, foreign trade was operated by individual entities that imported commodities from all over the world to Dubai, transferring them to Somalia by air and sea from there. At the airport, I met an importer who had been to Guangzhou to source clothing. With the opening of the Nairobi–Mogadishu air route in recent years, Nairobi had become a purchasing centre for Somali traders who flooded the planes for Mogadishu from Nairobi, carrying small bags of goods or shipping large trunks. On my return flight, I was on a plane next to a tradesman who was flying to Nairobi to purchase cellphones and telephones. Without a government to administer import tariffs, such traders were effectively free to enter and exit the country, exploiting the wartime situation to make huge profits by selling products to their compatriots.

One morning, under the protection of armed guards, I visited two markets in Mogadishu. One was once a thriving market in an area of the old downtown. Less than a fifth of the stalls were now in operation. Grains, vegetables, fruit and meat were sold here. The newer market in the new downtown area, enclosed in tents, contained twenty or thirty stalls selling clothing, mattresses, books and daily necessities. The markets, protected by guns, seemed quiet and there were few customers.

Amid the chaos of war, the country's public-security apparatus was in tatters and criminals fled from the prisons. In recent years, religious courts had been revived and religious prisons were serving political functions, a kind of stand-in for the government.

Freedom is relative; there is no such thing as absolute freedom. If absolute freedom were possible in this world, it would look something like the situation in war-torn Somalia. What sort of freedom is that? Each did his own thing, taking what he pleased. It was utter anarchy. The state apparatus was no longer in existence, public property had been stripped and looted, cities were ruined, the nation was shattered and the people were exhausted. Foreigners stopped in their tracks, fearing to move, and adventurers fell victim to profiteers.

Anyone who visited that Somalia, withered and ruined, would surely gain a new respect for the value of peace and would learn the true meaning of freedom.

CHINESE HOSPITAL REOPENED

Despite the civil war and the resulting chaos, I found the Somalis very friendly towards the Chinese, regarding the two races as brothers and friends. During my visit, I witnessed the Chinese influence all over Somalia. The local people's admiration for China and their friendly sentiment towards the Chinese people were unforgettable, surpassing words.

At the Sahafi Hotel, where I stayed, a glance at the big red lantern hanging from the ceiling in the reception hall made me feel at home. The manager of African Express Airways and the hotel manager took great pride in talking about Mao Zedong and Deng Xiaoping the moment they saw me. The four major projects China had constructed for Somalia in the 1970s and '80s – the National Theatre of Somalia, the Mogadishu Stadium, the Banadir Hospital, and the 2 000-km national highway – were on everybody's lips, praising both their quality and their symbolic status as milestones in Sino–Somali relations. Now, these four projects had undergone the severe test of war and had become household names in Somalia. The highways that China constructed, referred to endearingly as the 'China Roads', were still completely intact. The Banadir Hospital, called 'China Hospital', remained as good as it had been the day it was completed. It had reopened 10 days before my arrival in Somalia.

On the afternoon of 5 August, under the protection of armed guards and in the blazing heat of the afternoon sun, I went to the China Hospital. There had been seven large hospitals in Mogadishu before the war, but they had been damaged in the fighting. The China Hospital, the largest of the seven, was the least damaged, with almost all the doors and windows still intact and the walls still as good as new. Completed in 1975, the China Hospital was a first-rate construction that overshadowed the surrounding architecture, large or small. Newly reopened, it looked as new as the day it was completed.

It was a fluke that had led me to visit the hospital. Hearing that there was a Chinese reporter visiting Mogadishu, several doctors in the capital warmly invited me to visit the hospital, offering to accompany me. Madina Mohamed Elimi, the head of the hospital, was a middle-aged woman who was clearly influential in town. She welcomed me at the entrance. She was an extraordinary person, working relentlessly to keep the hospital clean and tidy, hoping to bring it back into service. The hospital, previously occupied by five warring factions, was formerly out of commission. When Madina saw so many sick, helpless people in front of the hospital, it struck her as being extremely wasteful. She had done social work before, and the sight of the hospital filled her with a burning need to act. Bravely and persistently, she negotiated with the various factions, all of whom were finally moved by her goodwill. Coming to a sort of gentleman's agreement, they were prepared to allow her to reopen the hospital.

Madina led me around every ward in the hospital, most of which were empty. In a bright, spacious operating theatre, three round surgical lights still remained intact, hanging from the ceiling. Pointing at the light, Madina told me that they had been donated from China. 'After the hospital was looted, these were the only lights left,' she said.

Despite the disaster, signs of Chinese influence were still evident all over the China Hospital. Not only was its architecture of Chinese style, but the doors in the corridors were marked with both Chinese characters and phonetics, reading 推 (*tui*, 'push') and 拉 (*la*, 'pull'). A rusty lock on the door of one room on the second floor was quite conspicuous. Looking closer, I found Chinese characters identifying it as an Earth brand lock made in China.

In a consulting room next to the main door, a doctor was asking a patient some questions in an effort to make a diagnosis. Seeing me standing at the door, she greeted me and introduced herself, saying, 'My name is Muhubo Ahmed Guce. I have been working here since before the outbreak of the war. At that time, there were eight Chinese doctors working in this hospital, all of them very skilled, pleasant, and easy-going. Dr Su made the deepest impression on me. Please say hello to them when you return home.'

She added, 'I know they are all outstanding doctors from China, but I don't know which province they were from.[3] We all miss our Chinese colleagues. They were our good friends. We wish the civil war would end soon, and that the Chinese doctors would come back to Somalia to help save lives and cure the wounded.'

In the in-patient department, I noticed that most patients were children, accompanied by their poverty-stricken parents. Somalia was a country with a high incidence of malaria. The sick children were lying on the bed, receiving injections. Madina said, 'Most adults can't afford to see doctors. But our greatest difficulty here at the hospital is the shortage of doctors and medicine.'

Pointing out the hospital beds, she said that, besides a few newly bought beds and mattresses, all the necessities, such as desks, chairs and benches, had been donated by the hospital staff members. They were all pulling together to reopen the hospital. 'Most of our doctors and nurses were working here before,' she said. 'As soon as they learnt about the reopening, they came back here to work. They know we are short of money, so everyone is working as a volunteer.'

The deeds of those doctors and nurses, who rose to meet the needs of the sick and wounded during the time of their country's greatest need, was quite inspiring.

THE INTELLIGENTSIA'S WORK TO SAVE THE NATION

It is a truism that everybody has a share of the responsibility for the rise and fall of his or her motherland. While some lawless, arrogant gangsters were destroying the nation during this strife at the expense of the nation as a whole, Somalia's intellectuals, both at home and abroad, organised themselves for the sake of their nation's future and the happiness of its people, joining the efforts to salvage the motherland and reduce the misery that war had brought to the people.

One afternoon, I was invited to attend a secondary-school graduation ceremony that was being held at the hotel where I was staying. Like other public facilities, schools of all levels had fallen victim to the war, their campuses looted and left empty. This school had reopened among the ruins of war and amid continuous gunfire. When the civil war was easing in 1999, some teachers felt an urgent need for education to continue, even if a government had not been re-established. They did not want to see a whole generation reduced to illiteracy because of the terrible war. If there was no education, who would shoulder the fate of the nation in future? An old Chinese saying says, 'It takes centuries to cultivate a people; education determines the future destiny of a nation.'

The teachers organised themselves and established this secondary school, starting from scratch in the most extreme difficulties. Through their combined efforts, they rebuilt the campus from its ruins. They brought desks and stools from their own homes, and they compiled their own teaching materials. The principal told me that the enthusiasm and painstaking effort of the staff were truly heart-warming. Then, changing the subject, he told me that enrolment was over 500, but that most families were too poor to keep their children at school, so only a hundred or so graduated. Even so, this graduation ceremony was quite a media sensation, with newspapers competing for coverage and numerous celebrities in attendance. People congratulated the students on having completed their schooling and thanked those who opened the school for their contribution to the cultivation of talent.

There were six universities in the capital before civil war broke out. Resuming classes the year after the outbreak of fighting, Mogadishu University was the first to reopen, but soon afterwards, it was looted by mobs, and classes were once again interrupted. In early 1997, when the situation took a turn for the better, the university staff again pooled their money and energy, and resumed teaching. In some shopping centres that had been reopened in the downtown area, I saw announcements of a new intake at stalls rented by the university. By 2004 two universities in the capital had resumed more or less normal operations.

Hearing that a Chinese reporter had come from afar to visit, five doctors from the Al-Hayat Hospital invited me to visit their facility. The hospital was a joint venture opened in 1997 by senior medical professionals overseas and renowned medical staff in Somalia. These enthusiastic intellectuals worked together to achieve the common goal of rescuing the wounded and saving lives during a time of national crisis. This noble endeavour was praiseworthy. Two years later they united several local organisations to establish the Hayat Medical Foundation. By the time I visited, this medical fund included under its auspices the Al-Hayat Hospital, another hospital 100 km from the capital, a nursing school and a pharmaceutical company.

Of the five doctors who hosted my visit, three were students returning from Britain. Of those, two had been to China, where they had studied malaria treatments with their Chinese colleagues in Shanghai. According to Dr Mohamed Ahmed, president of the hospital, the fund, initiated by 30 stakeholders, was a neutral organisation specialising in medicine, and it kept its distance from major political groups or tribes, remaining just connected enough with each group to gain recognition from all sectors of society and to bridge the gap between contending parties. The Al-Hayat Hospital was the largest, best-equipped and most technically advanced hospital in Somalia, but it was sadly lacking in doctors and medicine. Dr Ahmed cited an example, explaining that malaria is a common ailment in Somalia. 'But even saline solution for injections is in short supply,' he said. 'We have to import it.'

Like all public buildings in Somalia, the hospital remained under armed protection to ensure normal operation. For safety's sake, the hospital's two gates, clearly marked 'Entrance' and 'Exit', were closely guarded by men armed with submachine guns. Accompanied by friendly staff members, I visited every ward and every department in the hospital. At the pharmacy on the first floor, doctors said that the hospital needed to expand in size and in terms of its medical services, but that, under current conditions, the scarcity of doctors and supplies was the norm. The hospital was badly in need of medical supplies when I visited. I asked if there was any medicine from China. One of the staff members took a box from a shelf and handed it to me. It was a box of penicillin injections manufactured by a pharmaceutical company in Shijiazhuang.

In a room used for CT[4] scans, the hospital's only CT machine was out of order. Two technicians were working busily trying to repair it. In the in-patient departments, nurses in each ward were busy examining their patients.

When they spoke of the current situation in the hospital and the nation, they sighed with emotion. A beautiful country with the longest coastline in Africa, Somalia had a comfortable climate and offered a wide variety of produce and natural resources. It was unfortunate that the unthinkable outrage of civil war had ravaged the country. 'We all really hope the peace conference will bring about a new government and restore peace to our country,' they said. 'The war and chaos are negative images reflecting how precious peace is, and showing that humans really cannot afford such tragedies.'

When we parted, they expressed their wish that the disorder would soon come to an end, and that they would again be able to cooperate with their Chinese colleagues to help relieve the shortage of doctors and medicine in Somalia. 'China has stuck with us through fair and foul,' they said. 'We will always remember that.'

A CARVED-UP ANCIENT BORDER POST

At dawn, the vast sea woke after the long, dark night, facing the rising sun as it shifted its glare from the roaring sea to the Arabian castles on the coast. This was Mogadiscio State, or modern-day Mogadishu. Around 600 years earlier, Zheng He's fleet had travelled all the way to this site, leaving some historical relics behind.

According to historical records, a border post at the entrance to Mogadiscio State was established in a coastal hospital, a stone building with a courtyard. Merchants continually came and went, passing through this single post. In the courtyard, coins from China's Tang and Song dynasties were discovered, and pottery and porcelain fragments from ancient China were unearthed.

In the city in which I now stood, white was the dominant colour. Sadly, it had been spoilt beyond recognition by years of war. I had intended to visit the National Museum of Somalia and the ancient border post that marked the entrance to the state while I was in Somalia, but the situation on the ground was not at all what I had expected. The museum had been reduced to rubble, its cultural treasures looted and carried off to unknown locations. The ancient post, which later became the seat of the Mogadishu Municipal Government, had been the focal point of tensions between the warlords. It sat right in the middle of the 'green line' – the demarcation of the division of power among forces vying for control of the capital. Defying all invasions, it was respected by all parties in an attempt to strike some sort of balance. Any action beyond the green line was understood to be an act of aggression and would invite armed conflict.

The hotel manager warned me: 'Crossing the "green line" is extremely risky. It is most dangerous to venture there unarmed or without bodyguards. Even if unarmed, any unauthorised action would stir up the guns.' He made a threatening gesture, fashioning his fingers into the shape of a gun and pointing them at me, wide-eyed.

'How about we negotiate with them before making a decision?'

'The Municipal Government courtyard is now carved up between six military factions. It will cost four or five thousand US dollars per faction to persuade them and, even then, there's no guarantee,' he said. 'As soon as they see a foreigner, they would gobble you up. After all, that's how they make their living.'

It seemed that occupying a place and using the advantageous position to 'pluck the goose feathers' from foreigners had become common practice. One of the hotel guards suggested I hire a local person to take photos, in an effort to keep costs to a minimum. I politely refused this kind offer, preferring to take a look myself at the Municipal Government, since it was also the location of the ancient post.

The manager remained silent for a while, then said that for safety's sake, the Municipal Government area was crowded during the day, so he suggested I might go there at daybreak and have a look, but without actually entering the gate. He advised me not to walk along the street in front of the closely guarded Municipal Government building, allowing myself a quick escape route through the streets if needed. 'I will accompany you there tomorrow,' he said, with the resigned air of a man who had done his best in an impossible situation.

At dawn the next day, we left the hotel and went to the manager's home to pick him up. He told me he lived in a rented house, and that his own home was located downtown. He was prevented from returning home because of fighting in the area. As arranged, we went first to the seashore to take photos of the beach at dawn, then drove through the street behind the Municipal Government.

As soon as we arrived at the beach, people swarmed to us, encircling us in a tight ring. When I raised my camera, I heard someone shouting in the distance, 'Why are you shooting photos?'

Looking around, I spotted the man who had said these words. The day before, he had demanded I pay to take photos when I had done a shoot at dusk. As he approached us, we sped off and drove towards the downtown area, just as we had done the previous day, in an effort to avoid conflict.

The area around the Municipal Government was the part of the city most severely affected by the war. Driving through the streets, I did not see a single building that was intact. The National Museum of Somalia, the Cinema of Somalia, a renowned Italian restaurant and several large supermarkets had all been reduced to ruins. 'Keep the windows closed while you take photos. And be quick about it,' the hotel manager continually reminded me. I asked if I could sit beside the driver, but was sharply refused. I proceeded to snap photos from a bent position, and with my head lowered.

Wending our way through the ruins, we reached the street behind the Municipal Government. The manager reminded me, 'The Municipal Government courtyard is ahead on the right, where all the white stone buildings are. Be quick!'

I seized the opportunity to take photos, but was so anxious I nearly gave myself whiplash. In terrible pain, I snapped the shutter again and again, ducking in the back of the van.

Under such conditions, I was not confident about the quality of the photos. Hoping to get better-quality images, I proposed stopping somewhere near the Municipal Government courtyard to shoot additional photos. The manager told me it was too dangerous to take photos in the street, but that there were the remains of a market nearby, where a few peddlers still gathered to sell odds and ends from makeshift stalls, even though most of the buildings had been destroyed. 'We'll go there and have a look. If the situation allows, you may be able to shoot some photos there.'

Unfortunately, as soon as I lifted my camera at the entrance to the market, a man seized my right shoulder, shouting, 'Capture him! Seize his camera and bag.'

My sharp-eyed, deft-of-hand guard grappled with the man for a while, then managed to smooth things over without further incident. We drove away in a rush.

This war had caused me great trouble – all sorts of worry and fear, and a literal pain in the neck. Since we could not enter the Municipal Government courtyard, it had been impossible to verify or ascertain which stone border-post building had seen the arrival of Zheng He, or where the customs formalities had been performed. I imagined the situation at the entrance to Mogadiscio State at that time must have been very different from this milieu of civil war.

I thought back to what Mogadiscio must have been like at the time. In the fourth volume of *Marvellous views from a starry mast*, Fei Xin, one of Zheng He's attendants, gave a detailed description of the geology, folk customs, climate and lifestyle of Mogadiscio. He writes:

Mogadiscio, a state within a 20-day windward sail from Kollam, is situated by the sea, with cities built of stone, home to many four- or five-storey homes equipped with kitchen, toilet, and sitting room. The men wear their hair long and don aprons, while the women wear their hair knotted, tying it back in a yellow ribbon, with strings dangling from their ears, silvery bangles around the neck, and strings of beads at their chests. They appear in public in black robes, faces veiled in black gauze and feet clad in leather shoes.

The landscape is a stretch of hills and plains, reddish-yellow in colour, barren, or yielding only poor crops. Being an arid territory, deep wells and water wheels are utilised, and water carried in sheep skins. The people carry bows or other weapons in hand, and the wealthy often travel or trade. The poor spread nets on the sea, then dry their catch to keep for food.[5]

Back at the hotel, I asked the hotel manager if there were any people with single-syllable surnames in the area around the capital, names like Gao or Lin or Mao. It was rumoured that many of Zheng He's crew had such surnames. The manager, and everyone else who was listening, responded in the negative, saying that there were no grounds for such an assertion, and that there were no Chinese descendants or people with Chinese names in the area around the capital. As for single-syllable surnames, the manager said, 'I have never heard the surnames Gao or Lin. There are a small number of people here with the surname Mao, but it is not the same as your Chairman Mao.'

Saying this, he added, 'Years ago, people here with the surname Mao used to joke when they met a Chinese person, saying they shared a surname with Chairman Mao. They took great pride in that.'

The manager then explained that the spelling of the surname that sounded like 'Mao' was actually written 'Mocow', adding that the 'c' in the name was pronounced 'ah' in Somali. It was not, therefore, a single-syllable surname. The word meant 'sweet'. As we talked, I learnt that the manager had majored in Somali history, and had been a history teacher before the war. I felt that his elaboration on the etymology of the name was valid and authoritative.

But I wanted to explore the question more deeply and we dug into the Arabic names together. Arabic names are made up of three parts, the name of the bearer, the name of the bearer's father and the name of the bearer's paternal grandfather, in that order. This meant that any surname was a combination of the father's and grandfather's names. In other words, one's own name would naturally become a part of one's children's surnames. This means that Arabic surnames are not fixed from one generation to the next, so, even if Zheng He's fleet had been here, the surnames of the descendants were not likely to have followed the Chinese surname of that lineage, particularly not after centuries of integration into local society and the passing of so many generations.

I was told, however, that some descendants of Zheng He's fleet were still living in the area around Kismayo, the port city in the south. Unfortunately, because the situation in Kismayo was dangerous, with guns and cannons often heard in the area and frequent ambushes on the road between there and the capital, the hotel manager told me again and again that he could not dispatch guards to accompany me there, and he seriously discouraged any notion I might entertain of going there alone, saying it was far too risky.

I had to abandon my hopes of travelling to Kismayo during my first visit to Somalia. The situation in Somalia at the time reminded me of the Yuan Dynasty poem 'Plum revolution' by the renowned poet-painter Wang Mian. It says: 'The northern wind pierces the sandy world. Barbarians lie dead beneath the Great Wall; will spring ever again be seen south of the Yangtze?'[6] I thought that a slight adaptation of the original might fit the situation here: 'Not as cold as the northern wind, sandstorms prevail. People die under wicked gunfire; where is spring in this corner of Africa?'

8
Revisiting Somalia

THE PRESIDENT'S AFFECTIONATE GRATITUDE TOWARDS CHINA

Nairobi in August reminded me of Beijing's golden autumn. The weather was perfect. During my stay in the Kenyan capital on my way back from Somalia, I was given the opportunity to interview the then president of Somalia's Transitional Federal Government, Abdiqasim Salad Hassan, who was attending the 14th Somali National Peace Conference. We met at the hotel where I was staying.

On behalf of his people, the Somali government and himself, the president expressed his gratitude to the government and people of China. He said that the history of friendship between Somalia and China was a long one, evidenced by the visit of Zheng He's Chinese fleet to Mogadishu and Kismayo about 600 years ago. Since Somalia gained independence, it had been an active supporter of China and its return to the UN, and since the establishment of diplomatic relations between the two countries in 1960, China had assisted Somalia in the areas of construction, engineering, medical services and agriculture. He said, 'The National Theatre of Somalia, the Capital Gymnasium, the Banadir Hospital, and the long-distance highways are all household names, well regarded for their outstanding quality. We are eternally grateful to the Chinese people and the Chinese government for the great support and assistance they have extended to us. We hope that the *People's Daily* will convey our sincere thanks to the government and people of China.'

President Abdiqasim was born in 1941 and graduated from Lomonosov Moscow State University with a degree in biology. During his political career, which began in 1973, he worked as minister of industry, minister of mass media and national guidance, minister of culture, minister of public projects, minister of education and minister of presidential economic affairs. In September 1990, he was working as vice-premier and minister of domestic affairs under the Barre government. When civil war broke out, he fled overseas. On 26 August 2000, he was elected president of the Transitional Federal Government. He said, 'I was fortunate enough to be invited to visit China in February 1978, where I was received cordially by the Chinese leader, Deng Xiaoping. He impressed me as a great man.'

Discussing the conflict in Somalia, Abdiqasim said that since the outbreak of civil war in 1990, the international community had been concerned about the situation and supportive of peace efforts in Somalia. The UN Security Council had held repeated discussions about the situation in Somalia, passing numerous resolutions to respect Somalia's national sovereignty and territorial integrity while also calling on other nations to stop interfering in Somali affairs. He said, 'As a permanent member of the UN Security Council, China has always been concerned and supported the Somali peace process. It has also been actively involved in discussions about Somali issues in the Security Council, has played an active role as UN Security Council coordinator on Somali issues since 2003, and has resolutely dispatched peacekeeping troops to Somali. We are grateful to China for its support. From 1992, the Chinese government and its people provided us with medical and material assistance. We will never forget that.'

In 2000, instituted by several NGOs, the Somali National Peace Conference was held in Djibouti. A transnational charter was passed, the first parliament and first president elected, and the first transitional government established since the start of the then decade-long civil war. Since its establishment, the new government had put forward a series of administrative policies, such as restoring order in the capital, disarming civilians and promoting tribal reconciliation, all while actively seeking recognition from the international community. But the transitional government, consisting mainly of intellectuals, was boycotted or rejected by factional warlords, rendering it ineffectual. As a result, the country was still under the rule of the warlords.

The president said that the previous 13 sessions of the peace conference, which had been held over the previous two years, explored the possibility of establishing a Somali federal government. He emphasised that this session of the peace conference broadly represented all sides, including all political and military factions and representatives from various tribes and NGOs. The aim of this conference was to elect a new parliament and president, and form a new cabinet.

From his estimation, Somalia was on a solid path towards national peace. He based his view on two things. Firstly, the Somali nation had one tradition, one religion, one culture, one language and one writing system. Culturally, it was a unified whole, which made strengthening national cohesion and promoting solidarity among all the ethnic groups achievable. Secondly, he said that the Somali people were tired of war, chaos and anarchy after a decade of fighting, and were longing for peace.

When our conversation shifted to the challenges the new federal government would face, the president said, 'First of all, all parties must work together in harmony under the new government. Secondly, a unified national army should be established, weapons confiscated and civilians disarmed. Thirdly, reconstruction of the water and power-supply systems, transport infrastructure, and schools and hospitals must begin.' He went on to emphasise that the reconstruction of Somalia was inseparable from support from the international community, adding that China had great international influence. He said that Chinese construction projects were enjoying a favourable reputation in Somalia: 'We are earnestly looking forward to China's overall participation in the national reconstruction process, and in further developing relations between our two countries.'

The president asked me why I had travelled to Somalia during a period of such chaos. I explained to him my motives, saying that I wanted to see the situation first-hand, so that I could provide accurate reports. I told him that I was following Zheng He's footsteps through Africa, searching for traces of his fleet in an effort to contribute to the research covering friendly historical relations between China and Africa. I mentioned the rumours I had heard of the Zheng He Village and the tower in Somalia, and the fleet's sunken ship. Although the president was familiar with the historical event of Zheng He's fleet reaching Somalia, he had only a vague idea that any traces might have remained in Kismayo. Hearing my story, he asked his nephew, Osman, if he would accompany me to Kismayo for the sake of my safety and convenience, as Osman was from Kismayo. He readily agreed.

Without further ado, I discussed my plans with Osman to travel from Nairobi to Kismayo. There were air cargo flights between the two towns that offered round-trip tickets for $1 750. When we were negotiating with the airline representative, he repeatedly emphasised that there were no passenger seats on the planes. 'We do not ensure passenger safety,' he said.

We hesitated. It was a four-hour flight without any safety equipment for passengers. Who would dare to take such a flight? And the situation was made worse by the warlords, who were then causing trouble in an attempt to derail the proceedings at the peace conference.

Osman suggested we met at Mogadishu after the peace conference and travel to Kismayo overland. 'What about our safety, though?' I asked.

'My older brother is in Mogadishu,' he said. 'He will help us. I am from there. We can hire guards to accompany us. Anyway, after the election, the situation will be more stable.' He seemed quite confident.

SEARCH FOR THE SUNKEN SHIP

Because Lamu Island in Kenya and Somalia's port of Kismayo were only a few hundred kilometres apart, travel by sea might have been more convenient. The problem was that piracy was rife in those waters, which would put us at considerable risk. According to local fishermen, there were sporadic outbreaks of fighting, and pirates and bandits were rampant around Kismayo. If we risked the trip, it might well end up with us being kidnapped and with demands for alarming amounts of money – probably millions of US dollars. Failure to pay the ransom could result in death. Only a brave man would shirk such information and attempt such a venture. It would not be possible to do the trip from Lamu to Kismayo, nor to go there from Nairobi. The only option that remained was to travel back to Mogadishu, then head back south overland to Kismayo.

Our African Express Airways flight landed safely, creaking along the damaged runway, with the passengers in a bit of a panic. It was late November 2004 and I was back in Somalia again, three months after my first visit, hoping this time to make it to Kismayo to fulfil my as yet unsatisfied desire to look for signs of Zheng He's visit.

My mood was quite different from the previous time I had travelled to Somalia, though. Previously, I had been alone and had no one to meet me at the airport, but now I was accompanied by a Chinese friend, Yao Hui, and had Somali friends to greet me upon my arrival.

I watched the old man, plastic bag in hand, come to greet us once again as soon as we got off the plane. I told myself he was here to finalise the formalities for our entry visa, stamping it in our passports in exchange for $25. When he was about to speak, my Somali friend Osman prevented him from contacting us and firmly refused to give him money. As the old man grumbled over his loss, a member of the airline staff came over to mediate the dispute, smiling. After some bargaining we handed them $20 for the pair of visas. This was an interesting aspect of Somalia at that time – the fact that one could haggle over the fee for a visa and other similar formalities. The applicant merely handed his passport over while sitting in the car, and the 'visa officer' stood beside the vehicle stamping the passport with a seal. There was no need for an office.

We got into my friend's car. Osman told me he had arranged for two cars, a van and six armed guards to ensure our safety. As we drove, he provided us with a great deal of information about the situation at that time in Somalia. When we asked about lodgings, he suggested two options. One was to stay in his elder brother's home, a spacious, secure house that was currently unoccupied, as his brother was travelling to Mecca at the time. The other was to stay in a hotel, which was not as safe as a house, nor as convenient for communication between Osman and us. His sincerity, my concerns for safety, and my desire not to burden him with travelling back and forth meant that I acquiesced to his wishes.

Osman had left his home country 15 years earlier, before the civil war had broken out. He had been home only for a short stay since. Being away for such a long period had left him with an ambivalent feeling towards his homeland. I quickly formed the impression that he was a man of few words, sincere and ready to keep his promises. When the peace conference came to a close, he travelled from

Nairobi to Cairo for a family reunion, then a week later travelled via Dubai to Mogadishu, where he awaited our arrival from South Africa, planning to accompany us all the way to Kismayo. His sincerity was touching.

On this visit, he was staying at his brother's house. His brother, an intelligent businessman, owned a two-storey mansion in the capital, and employed cooks, serving staff, drivers and a team of six guards, who worked around the clock in shifts. The mansion had a modern interior, displaying the wealth of its owners with the suggestion that it was new wealth. Situated opposite Somalia's only Coca-Cola factory, the house stood out conspicuously.

Islam is the national religion of Somalia. We arrived during Ramadan, when the local people fast during the daylight hours. At Osman's request, the cooks prepared for us a delicious lunch of mutton cooked to tenderness. Being very hungry by this time, we wolfed down the meat and every drop of soup.

The three of us began discussing our trip to Kismayo. Osman said that, of our three travel options – by water, land or air – the sea voyage would be unfeasible and dangerous, as the waters were teeming with pirates. The big vessels we would need to complete such a journey were not available, and smaller boats would need refuelling during the 500-km journey, and would not be suitable for the large waves on the open sea anyway. The land journey would start with a 300-km stretch on relatively good roads, followed by 200 km on very rough roads, taking a total of about nine hours to complete. We would encounter along the route various dangers in the form of thieves, road gangs, privately manned roadblocks, and all sorts of inevitable trouble and conflict throughout the journey, and it was impossible to predict how much time this might add to the trip. At the very least, it would be a dawn-to-dusk endeavour. Saying this, Osman smiled and added, 'It is Ramadan. We fast, but you do not. We will also need to take time to eat along the way.'

I replied, 'Don't worry about food. We have enough biscuits to get us through. Safety is the major concern.'

Osman said we would need three vehicles, one for us and two for a team of 20 guards. It would take three whole days for the round trip, two of them being spent on the road. It was going to be a very hard trip, costing at least $1 200 a day, which would include vehicle rental, petrol, food and lodging. This was not an unreasonable price given all it included, but the problem was our safety was still not guaranteed: even our 20 armed guards would be no match for the 'local snakes'.

The last option left was to fly. There had been regular flights between Mogadishu and Kismayo before the civil war, but they had been suspended when the unrest started. Weekly flights were later resumed, supplemented by irregular flights by small cargo planes. We were not even sure whether regular flights were still in operation. Though Osman did his best to find out, he was unable to obtain any concrete information. He received conflicting messages from several sources, none of which were especially reliable. We decided that our task the next day would be to find definite information about these southbound flights.

'Once you are in Somalia, you will realise how difficult things are,' it was often heard told. Before setting off for any travels, one had to locate guards, and they had to be reliable. With the prevalence of armed conflict, safety was always one's first concern. The second issue to address was the cost. Most of the armed guards on the streets were in this line of work strictly to make a living. The local people loved to say that only money talked, and that there was no such thing as a free guard service.

We managed to take to the streets the following day and visit two airline offices – African Express Airlines, one of the major international airlines in the area, and a Somali airline – but neither operated flights to Kismayo. They suggested we try two other airlines, Jubba Airways and Jahiila, to see what they offered. Jubba, located on the main street, was easily accessible, but it did not operate flights to Kismayo. The smaller company, Jahiila, was believed to operate a few domestic airlines, but its office kept relocating and was nowhere to be found. Osman suggested we return home and try to contact the company by phone and learn of its current location.

Once we had found the address, we went to the office. To reach the airline's office, we had to take a commercial arterial road, which was logjammed with vehicles, animals and people. The sound of horns was deafening, and the road was riddled with muddy puddles. Unable to pass the busy road in our vehicle, we had to give up for the day. We decided we would have to make the journey by road.

ARDUOUS TRIP SOUTH

The next day, Osman asked his younger sister, the daughter of the former president, Deka, to arrange guards for us. Because the guards had served the former president, they were familiar with the local situation and the idea was that they would make things easier for us. We were already fully prepared for the trip, so we scheduled for the guards to pick us up at eight o'clock, but they did not show up until eleven.

Mogadishu was hot and rainy that November. Watery potholes in the roads made the already congested commercial area even more chaotic. The street was rendered even narrower by vehicles parked everywhere at random. Clusters of pedestrians evaded muddy puddles, donkey carts and vehicles vied to cross the street, and donkeys brayed and horns honked, adding to the chaos. It was hard to imagine how people could live in such an environment.

But it seemed there was a certain method to the madness. Our small car worked its way through the tightly packed vehicles, edging on as slowly as a cow. From time to time, a pedestrian took the opportunity to slip past in front of a vehicle, and a donkey cart laden with firewood jumped queue, making the driver shout as it cut the other vehicle off. As another cart forced its way in front of our car, our driver shook his head helplessly. At one intersection, our fears became reality. Blindly, vehicles moved forward from all directions, each fighting to get ahead of the others. None was willing to give way. Conflict finally broke out between the four cars in front. Even though we were sweating profusely in our car, Osman warned us not to leave the vehicle, saying that each driver ahead was ready for a fight. Each party had its own armed guard, and no one was willing to give way.

Our driver, a man from the presidential palace, walked to the front to mediate between the two sides and clear the gridlock, hoping to find a way through for us. After a quarter of an hour, he came back to the car smiling and gestured for the vehicles behind us to back up to make way for the jam to clear. Moving backwards was not easy either, since a long queue of cars had formed, but it was possible to move the line back single file. The driver said the situation ahead was heating up for a fight. He pointed out that it was Ramadan and, though they were all willing to go without food and drink, they could not go without fighting.

Without a way forward, we could only retreat and find a roundabout path. Our detour did at least lead us away from the centre of conflict.

With great effort, we backed our car into an alleyway. Once there, we found it was a blind alley, packed with a long line of vehicles. There was only one way to turn, and it led to an even narrower alley, which was blocked to vehicular traffic by a metal barrier. Our guards jumped from the car and tried desperately to remove the iron bar. Members of families living in the alley tried to stop them, quarrelling in raised voices, one side insisting that it needed to pass while the other resolutely refused to remove the iron bar. Seeing the two sides arguing, some of the Somali people standing nearby sighed and said that if their countrymen were not so stiff-necked and inflexible, the civil war would not have dragged on so long. To save time, Osman called his schoolmate and asked him to go to the airline office to see if he could elicit information.

Finally, our driver suggested a solution. After looking it over, he suggested that by bending the iron bar a little to the left, our car could pass on the right. Our guards pulled with all their strength and succeeded in bending the iron bar outward just enough for the car to pass, leaving barely a centimetre between vehicle and bar. I sighed and said, 'I thought Chinese drivers in big cities were the best drivers in the world. Now I know that the skills of Somali drivers far surpass those of the Chinese.'

This setback cost us hours. While we bumped our way through the narrow street, we came across someone with information about the airline company. He said it had ceased regular flights long ago, but that the company operated a cargo flight to Kismayo, which cost $300 for passengers. For the sake of safety and speed, Osman decided that we should go home while his brother's driver and his schoolmate went to buy the tickets.

The previous night, Osman had been informed that the cargo plane for Kismayo transported a fresh vegetable, known locally as *chaat*. It was said to aid sleep and help calm the nerves, and Somalis often ate it after supper. The flight route went from Mogadishu to Kismayo, then returned via Nairobi. The cost of a ticket from the capital to Nairobi was $1 200. The flights were irregular, roughly once a week, and were not very safe, especially with the social unrest around Kismayo, so it was a risky venture. Osman repeatedly emphasised that although he had informed his friends in Kismayo that we would be arriving and asked them to arrange security for us, such measures could not guarantee our safety because there were so many kidnappings by bandits in the area, according to his friend's reports.

Since Somalia was virtually cut off from the outside world, Yao Hui decided he would remain in Mogadishu while Osman and I travelled to Kismayo, providing us with a hotline. In case of accident or, worse, kidnapping, Yao Hui would then be in a position to organise a rescue from Mogadishu. Without this precaution, news of my plight would remain unknown to the outside world if I were kidnapped, cutting off any chance of rescue. We therefore bought tickets only for Osman and me. If everything went according to plan, we would fly from Kismayo to Nairobi, and Yao Hui would meet us there.

At dusk, the driver came back from the airline office with no tickets, but with a receipt for $400, of which $100 was for Osman's ticket, since he was Somali. The driver did not know what had happened to the rest of the money. I was uncomfortable with the receipt and the missing money. Osman called his classmate, but his phone was switched off.

Deka called and invited us for supper at her home. Since she had had us over for supper on the night of our arrival, we were surprised to receive another invitation so soon. We thought she must have something to tell us. After we were seated in her home, her younger sister asked me, 'Mr Li, aren't you afraid of death?'

Caught off guard by the question, I was uncertain how to answer. I smiled. Seeing my calmness, she grew anxious. 'Kismayo is extremely dangerous! Nobody can guarantee your safety there,' she said.

Before I could reply, Deka cut in and said, 'Mr Li, we have asked you here to advise you not to go to Kismayo. It is too dangerous, and conflicts might break out at any time.'

She went on to say that after she heard that I had bought the air tickets, she had been persuading Osman 'not to take the risk', but he had turned a deaf ear to her because of his promise to me, insisting he 'should not go back on his word'. Deka, aged 26, was not as excitable as her sister. She said calmly, 'Osman is a nice guy, but he is thinking of friendship, not the danger. We had expected the situation here to take a turn for the better, but the fighting in Kismayo is still heated, and armed conflicts might occur at any time. Osman knows this, and his friends have warned him not to give this trip a second thought.'

The two sisters looked at Osman. He sat silently beside me, his head lowered. Then he spoke.

'You know the current situation in Somalia, how utterly chaotic it is, without a government and people everywhere carrying arms. The situation is beyond control. We must be very cautious even here in Mogadishu, but it's even worse in Kismayo, 500 kilometres away. As the capital has been carved into blocks and strips, we have to be extremely careful when we go out. I have been selecting your guards since last night. They must be armed, and must be absolutely reliable. That's why they were late today. One came late, but I did not dare replace him with someone else.'

Deka continued, 'You are our friends, so we are of course concerned about your safety. But if you go to Kismayo, we are as helpless as you are in the face of an incident. They will do anything for money, and kidnapping a foreigner will potentially net them millions of US dollars.'

All eyes in that silent, spacious room were firmly on me, waiting for my decision. There was a fierce struggle in my mind. I had come here for the purpose of travelling to Kismayo. If I did not do it, when would I get another opportunity … ?

Yao Hui then whispered in my ear, 'Xinfeng, let's give up on the trip for now. If we received no call from you, I would not sleep at night. There are too many risks.'

Deka spread her arms helplessly and said, 'You are a reporter, and you have the final say about what you will do. But, as your friends, we cannot guarantee your safety. That's why we give you this advice.'

At that moment, Osman's phone rang. It was his friend. 'The cargo flight to Kismayo tomorrow has been cancelled.'

We stayed in Mogadishu for a week, the last few days of which were spent trying to recover the ticket and missing money. When we left, not a single cent had been returned. Osman sighed over and over, saying, 'Now I see. I cannot trust anyone in Somalia any more.'

I really hoped the dove of peace would soon come to Somalia.

ROADSIDE MAHJONG

I have been to Somalia twice. Both times, my purpose was to travel from Mogadishu to Kismayo in search of traces left by Zheng He's fleet: the Chinese Tower, the Chinese Village, and the ancient Chinese sunken ship, all of which I had learnt of during my visit to Lamu Island in Kenya.

On my second trip, like the first, I had failed to make it to southern Somalia. With great regret, I had to rush to the airport for a flight to my next destination.

When I arrived at the airport, 50 km from downtown Mogadishu, I was informed that the flight would be over two hours late, but was given no explanation. Feeling discouraged as I sat in the uncomfortably hot waiting area, I decided to go out for a walk.

Under a huge tree by the road near the waiting area, four people sat around a table, playing cards and laughing occasionally. Looking closer, I saw that the cards in their hands resembled Chinese mahjong tiles, though somewhat simpler. The cards, made from animal bones, were very thin white squares. I could make out the character 筒 (*tong*, 'tub') inscribed on them, but did not see 条 (*tiao*, 'strip'), 万 (*wan*, 'ten thousand'), or 风 (*feng*, 'wind'). It was a simple game, played much the same way as mahjong.

The players, including men and women, young and old, were surrounded by onlookers who offered sage advice. Upon learning I was from China, one man turned to me and asked, 'Do Chinese people play this too?'

Saying nothing, I smiled and pulled a card from his hand to play on his behalf. Everyone's eyes widened. They probably did not realise that China was the birthplace of mahjong, that it was considered our national game. One of the men present did seem to be aware of the fact, and said it had been taught here by the Chinese. Mahjong is very popular among Chinese people. I had never imagined there were also people enjoying it here in Africa, so far away. It made me reflect on the origins of the game.

Among the various stories about the beginnings of mahjong, I thought that the Zheng He theory might be significant. Legend claims that mahjong originated in the early Ming Dynasty. During Zheng He's voyages west, his crew became homesick on the long, tedious journeys. To kill time and relieve boredom, Zheng He not only allowed his men to play mahjong, but to improve on it. For instance, 条 (*tiao*, 'strip') resembled the ropes in boats; 筒 (*tong*, 'tub') the water buckets; 万 (*wan*, 'ten thousand') the vast crew, and the vast distances they travelled; and 风 (*feng*, 'wind') stood for the winds by which they sailed. He used these as card designs and to regulate the rules of play. Mahjong developed into its present form and rules in the mid Qing Dynasty, when soldiers serving as storehouse keepers began adding sparrows and bamboo chips, expanding the game until the current rules were finally formed.

Legend also has it that mahjong originated in Taicang, Jiangsu, often called the imperial granary. After the eastern Jin Dynasty moved its capital to Jiankang (modern-day Nanjing) in the south, it served as capital of the Song, Qi, Liang and Chen dynasties at various times. It is said that 'the area south of the Yangtze River is prime land, vast and productive, and its people are dedicated to farming. Its annual yield is sufficient to feed the people of several prefectures.'[1] This is evidence that Taicang had become an abundant 'granary' at the time.

Taicang is in the Yangtze Delta. In what is known as China's Spring and Autumn Period, it was part of the Wu Kingdom. After the conquest of the Chu Kingdom by the Yue Kingdom, two granaries were established in Wu territory, the eastern and western granaries, with Taicang serving as the former. In the period between the Three Kingdoms and the Sui and Tang dynasties, the region south of the Yangtze further developed into an area known for its abundance of rice and fish. This area was said to be 'home to plump rice and white corn, with imperial and private granaries that overflowed'.[2]

In the Song and Yuan dynasties, a proverb became popular: 'When Suzhou and Huzhou harvest, the whole country is satisfied.'

The bumper harvests and full granaries would attract many sparrows. The guards shot at the sparrows with home-made weapons, driving both the sparrows and their own boredom away. Seeing that shooting the sparrows was an effective way of controlling them, the officers did not discourage their men from doing so. In fact, they gave the soldiers bamboo chips to keep count of their kills and as a means of compensation. The inscribed bamboo chips served as tickets that could be exchanged for other forms of compensation, and as a means to judge wins and losses in gambling.

A game that began in this way eventually evolved into the mahjong we know today. For instance, the character 中 (*zhong*, 'hit') on the card's face indicated a hit sparrow; 白 (*bai*, 'white' or 'blank') implied a missed sparrow; 发 (*fa*, 'fortune') stood for money; and 碰 (*peng*, 'collision') sounded like the report of a gun. The 条 (*tiao*, 'strip') was known in some places as 索 (*suo*, 'rope'), meaning stringing up a hit sparrow. So 一索 (*yi suo*, 'one rope') meant one sparrow strung up; 二索 (*er suo*, 'two ropes') meant two sparrows on a rope. The latter referred also to a bamboo joint indicating the feet of the sparrows, since the granary officers counted the killed sparrows by the number of feet. Further examples included 万 (*wan*) to stand for money or reward, and 东 (*dong*, 'east'), 南 (*nan*, 'south'), 西 (*xi*, 'west') and 北 (*bei*, 'north'), referring to the direction of the wind, since the home-made guns were not very powerful, and were therefore affected by the direction of the wind. When a match was completed, one is said to 胡 (*hu*, 'win'), which is a homophone for 鹘 (*hu*), an eagle-like bird, implying 'to win'. The *Comprehensive dictionary of Chinese characters* says that 鹘 (*hu*), a predatory bird with quick, light wings, was often trained to capture birds. The new edition of the *Modern Chinese* dictionary offers related definitions for 鹘 and 和 as follows: 鹘 was the original name of the 隼 (falcon), referring to a bird with narrow pointed wings and a short broad beak with denticulations on the upper part. It was a fast bird that preyed on other birds. 和 was a verb pronounced hu, meaning 'win', said upon the completion of regulations in mahjong or cards. In other words, because the falcon (鹘, *hu*) flies fast and captures other birds, winning at mahjong was to *hu*, meaning to have the game or the other players in one's grasp – 'preying' upon them. Mahjong terms such as 吃 (*chi*, 'to eat') and 杠 (*gang*, 'to dispute' or 'bar') were related to sparrow catching. To catch sparrows, people lured them with food and the sparrows ate (吃, *chi*) the bait. The 杠 (*gang*) was related to mahjong through its connection to bamboo. At first, mahjong cards were made of bamboo chips, later improved to bamboo plates inlaid with bone tiles, known as 'bamboo bars'. In a mahjong game, bars were inevitably knocked against each other, causing frequent quarrels. When producing a card, 'two against one' was called 碰 (*peng*, 'colliding') and 'three against one' called 杠 (*gang*, 'dispute').

On his first western voyage, Zheng He set sail from Taicang, and his mahjong could have absorbed some of these elements. The four flowers, 春 (*chun*, 'spring'), 夏 (*xia*, 'summer'), 秋 (*qiu*, 'autumn') and 冬 (*dong*, 'winter'), were added to mahjong in the late Qing Dynasty, gaining popularity during the early years of the Republic of China. During the War of Resistance Against Japanese Aggression (also known as the Second Sino–Japanese War), which lasted from 1937 to 1945, many people in enemy-occupied areas whiled away their time at home, hoping to avoid disturbances by Japanese invaders and Chinese traitors. Avoiding public recreational areas, they would stay at home and play mahjong all day instead. Over time, their skills at the game were perfected.

Zheng He's fleet, along with porcelain, looms and traditional Chinese medicine, must surely also have brought mahjong to Africa, which is how, presumably, the local people learnt to play the game. Fortunately, the African players I saw were playing for fun, not money.

During my earlier stay in Mozambique, I had noticed that white people also played mahjong, following almost exactly the same rules as those observed in China. When I asked where they had learnt the game, they answered, laconically, 'From childhood'. It was evident to me that Zheng He had brought mahjong to the Europeans too, either directly or indirectly.

9
Exploring Sofala

SOLVING THE MYSTERY OF THE DOUBLE DRAGON JAR

I was out of sorts on my way back after my second fruitless trip to Somalia. Feeling cheated as I waited in Nairobi for my connecting flight, my mind went back to my previous trip to Lamu and the double dragon jar that could not be traced. Lamu fishermen had recovered two double dragon jars in the waters immediately off their shores. One had been bought by a British antique dealer living on Lamu Island, Gillies Turle; the other was believed to still be on the island, in the hands of an unknown buyer.

This 'hidden' double dragon jar was on the minds of many people. The Lamu Museum was anxious to find it as evidence that an ancient Chinese treasure ship had sunk in the local waters. Such finds were truly rare, precious objects, but since the collector was unwilling to show himself and the seller had disappeared without a trace, the museum's efforts to find it were in vain. I too very much wanted to have a look at the jar, especially because Turle had suggested it would not be corroded by seawater after hundreds of years on the seabed if the surface was glazed black. The piece that he had managed to buy was not protected by a layer of black glaze. He spoke quite assuredly on the subject, so it was my guess that the jar might be in his own home, but that he was reluctant to acknowledge it in case the authorities came looking. Because he had spoken so openly about the unglazed jar, if the worst were to happen, he could give it up while still holding on to the greater prize. But this was only a guess on my part.

I called Swaleh, the assistant curator at the Lamu Museum, and asked if he had any news about the sunken Chinese ship. To my surprise, he said that the other double dragon jar had been found. I immediately changed my itinerary and bought an air ticket to Lamu.

I stayed at the New Lamu Palace Hotel, as I had before. On one of my previous visits, as I was admiring the dozens of jars on display in the hotel, a member of the hotel staff had told me they had been recovered from the sea. He told me of a jar that had patterns drawn on it, and that its belly was covered in coral reef. The local people imagined there was a dragon under the reef. This jar had been in the hotel until the fellow's boss heard about the dragon jar story and then moved the jar to his own home, where he kept it as a treasured object. The boss, a German, was seldom in Lamu. Each time I had been there before, I had asked to meet him, but he was always away. This time, the delighted attendant told me that his boss happened to be in Lamu.

Jule, a tall, polite man, readily allowed me to have a look at the jar in his home. We decided to drop in at his home after we had looked at the double dragon jar in Shela. His villa was in Lamu, overlooking the sea. Its decor was in the local style, and very beautiful, standing out from the surrounding houses like a crane among chickens. The garden, equipped with a swimming pool with azure water, and sporting a green lawn and blooming flowers, was in sharp contrast to the world outside its walls.

In accordance with the local custom, I removed my shoes and, barefoot, followed Jule to the second floor. A red ceramic jar stood alone in a bamboo basket on a decorative table in the centre of the grand lobby. Pointing to the jar, Jule said, 'This is it. It has a V-shaped bottom, so I keep it in that bamboo basket.'

He took the jar to the balcony, where I could examine it in better light. We leant it against a concrete balustrade. It was 50 cm tall, with a wide mouth, a sharp bottom, two parallel corrugated lines around the neck, and 36 dots placed at regular intervals beneath these lines. The belly of the jar was covered with a protruding piece of coral reef, presumably hiding a dragon beneath it. When I saw the jar, I laughed. Jule asked, 'Why the laugh?'

I explained that the dragon was a long, lithe creature, so if the jar really had a dragon on it, then the small round patch of coral would not have covered the entire length of its form. The coral covered just a part of the surface. The probability of finding a single dragon on the surface of the jar was very low because, as a rule, dragons appeared in pairs. I was aware that my explanation might be disappointing for Jule, as the idea that he had the dragon jar in his possession had now gone up in smoke.

As evidence, I took out my digital camera and showed him photos I had taken of the double dragon jar that I had seen. On the glazed black vessel, two vividly portrayed dragons stood head to tail, ready to soar into the air.

'Ah! So it is,' Jule said, and sighed.

There was a circuitous story behind the discovery of the double dragon jar. Since the jar owned by Gillies Turle, the British antique collector, had appeared on the scene, the Lamu Museum had been enquiring about the other double dragon jar. One day, in Shela, two neighbours who lived in adjoining houses had a dispute over house repairs. One of the women, an Italian, had asked Swaleh to act as a mediator. As they sat in the foyer drinking tea, Swaleh noticed a dragon on a jar in the centre of the foyer. Overjoyed, he went to have a closer look. The vessel turned out to be a real double dragon jar, its profile more distinct than Turle's and the vessel larger in size, with black glazing on the surface.

This being my fourth visit to Lamu for the express purpose of seeing a double dragon jar, I was keen to see the piece. As soon as I arrived, I left my luggage in my room and went straight to the museum, then rushed on to Shela. After navigating the narrow alleyways of the village, we came to the Italian woman's home, a modern Arabic-style house. Swaleh said the woman was overseas, and that two local housekeepers were currently caring for the place. The yard was not large, and we could see the double dragon jar in the foyer. Being an object I treasured greatly, it immediately caught my eye. Its surface was smooth and the black glaze almost complete, making the two dragons visible even from a distance, looking like they were ready to soar up and greet their guests who had come from such a great distance. I hurried to the jar and began to examine it carefully.

It stood 85 cm in height, with a 16-cm inner diameter and a 22-cm outer diameter. At its thickest point, it bulged to 60 cm. The bottom of the vessel was 30 cm across. The neck had had four ears, one of which was now missing. The ears were 6 cm wide, separated from one another by four round dots, each 3 cm in diameter. Along the line where the neck joined the waist, there were eight round dots of equal size arranged at equal intervals. This served as a line dividing the neck from the waist. On the waist were two five-clawed dragons, flying head to tail, separated by two circles of equal size. On the surface of the jar were a total of 14 dots, arranged in groups of two, four and eight.

The surface glaze, still intact, glittered. The inner surfaces were also glazed black, but were not as glossy as the outer surface. Because the bottom of the jar had coral reef attached to it, it could not stand without support. I lifted it carefully. It weighed about 15 kg.

This was the double dragon jar that Turle had told me about. Swaleh told me that Gillies knew the owner of the jar, and that she had the piece in her home. 'He kept it secret to give people the impression that his was the only one, so as to elevate its status and his.'

This pair of double dragon jars, which were made centuries ago, had sunk to the bottom of the sea and were recovered by accident. Now they were again a beacon, rare treasures in which their owners could take great pride. These jars, a symbol of China and treasures of Chinese porcelain, were witnesses of an extraordinary historical event, telling the colourful story of a long friendship.

As soon as I touched the double dragon jar, I was filled with a solemn, noble feeling, and my mind was carried back to Zheng He's fleet travelling across the waves. After all these eventful years, the Chinese tower on an island and the double dragon jars on the seabed were like dutiful historians witnessing six centuries of changes in East Africa's history.

HEAD-ON 'CHINA WIND'

I departed from Mombasa Airport for the Tanzanian capital, Dar es Salaam, in a small passenger plane. Having visited Somalia and Kenya to gather information, I was heading south now, continuing my search for traces of Zheng He's fleet.

There were no exciting legends of Zheng He's fleet having visited Tanzania, but there were records of a visit to Mozambique. As Mozambique is south of Tanzania and Zheng He's fleet was navigating south along the East African coast, it seemed reasonable to assume they had passed Tanzania on their way to Mozambique. Based on this assumption, some foreign scholars are certain Zheng He visited Tanzania's islands of Zanzibar, Pemba and Kilwa, leaving behind historical traces.

Dar es Salaam, or 'Port of Peace', was the terminus of the renowned TAZARA[1] Railway. As soon as I set foot in the place, I felt a strong 'China wind'. At the immigration office, the customs officer looked at my Chinese passport, stamped it and said, 'You are welcome, our Chinese friend!' When I got in the taxi, the driver, Mzezele, said, 'I have grown up listening to reports of the TAZARA Railway. China has built many first-rate highways, railways and buildings here. Chinese doctors are rescuing us from injury and death. China is extending selfless aid to us. I love China and the Chinese people!' It seemed his friendly feelings towards China knew no bounds.

The National Museum of Tanzania was in the centre of the capital. The Chinese relics exhibited there were divided into three sections: Chinese Porcelain, the Influence of the Zheng He Fleet in East Africa and Chinese–Tanzania Friendship.

In the porcelain section, there were flower vases from the Yuan Dynasty, manufactured between 1300 and 1320, blue-and-white porcelain plates from the Ming Dynasty, and porcelain bowls with the four Chinese characters 天下太平 (meaning 'Peace on earth') inscribed at the bottom. As well as the complete porcelain pieces, there were numerous fragments, including a 14th-century vat fragment with a dragon pattern, the bottom of a 16th-century bowl with a human head pattern at the bottom and an 18th-century plate inscribed with the character 寿 (*shou*, 'longevity'). The pieces were so appealing, with their striking Chinese features, that many visitors were reluctant to leave the museum. All the porcelain ware on display had been unearthed in Tanzania, from Pemba Island, Zanzibar and Kilwa Island (listing the sites from north to south). One display board explained:

> As we all know, by the early medieval period, the Chinese were continually travelling along African coastal areas. Chinese porcelain ware unearthed along the East African coast is so abundant that one renowned archaeologist has

said, 'The history of East Africa may very well be said to have been written by Chinese porcelain.'²

British archaeologist Sir Robert Eric Mortimer Wheeler was even more specific, saying, 'Tanganyika's history, buried underground since the 10th century, is written with Chinese history.'³ Wheeler maintained this because archaeological investigations carried out around 1955 had uncovered Chinese porcelain at 46 historical relic sites in Tanzania's coastal areas, enabling dating of the cultural strata of the ruins.

Among the exhibits relating to Zheng He's fleet's visit to the East African coast were two large, conspicuous pictures. One was the renowned *Figure of kylin*, a duplicate of that drawn by renowned Ming Dynasty painter Shen Du. The other, drawn by Tanzanian painter Efdel, was a vivid depiction of Zheng He's treasure ships visiting the East African coastal area in the 15th century. The picture's caption indicated that the Chinese ships had arrived in the East African coastal areas for the first time between 1417 and 1419.

I stood before two pictures in the China–Tanzania Friendship section. One, titled *Ceremony celebrating completion of the friendship textile mill*, depicted a mill built with aid from China. The other was a picture connected to a joint inspection of a TAZARA tunnel worksite by Julius Nyerere, former president of Tanzania, and Kenneth Kaunda, former president of Zambia, accompanied by Chinese officials. The picture depicted two African heads of state extending smiling greetings to Chinese construction workers, suggesting that the Chinese and African peoples are of one family.

The next day, I boarded a nine-seater plane to the Zanzibar Channel, then headed to Zanzibar, known as the Spice Island. There, I visited three museums, the Imperial Palace Museum, the Peace Memorial Museum and the Slavery Museum.

The first was once the palace of Zanzibar's rulers. In an exhibition hall, the former palace bedroom, I encountered a 'love seat', with a tea table on each side. A member of the museum staff said it was a special chair made in China. In the former palace parlour, there were several large flower vases, Ming Dynasty porcelain ware with dragon designs.

Like the National Museum of Tanzania, the Peace Memorial Museum housed several Chinese porcelain pieces, both complete bowls and fragments. There were also many ancient Chinese coins, some of which were inscribed with the four Chinese characters 绍定通宝 (*Shaoding tong bao*, 'Shaoding copper coins'), which were still distinct. The caption said these coins were unearthed in Unguja,⁴ the main island of the Zanzibar Islands, and were said to date from the 6th to the 10th century.

The Slavery Museum was situated in the former Slave Market. It consisted of two parts: the stone rooms where slaves were jailed and the open-air slave-trading area of the former market. The stone room was low and gloomy, with chains dangling from iron columns, demonstrating the miserable lives of the slaves. The open-air trading area had been rebuilt to mirror the misery of slaves who were sold in irons. Simple as it was, the museum served as irrefutable evidence of the terrible misery brought about by the slave trade of colonisers in the West.

Near the first station of the TAZARA Railway, I paid my respects to the martyrs in the Mausoleum of Chinese Experts in Tanzania. The scene reminded me of remarks made by Kaunda, former president of Zambia, in an interview I had conducted with him in August 2000. Kaunda had said that the slave trade, colonial aggression and colonial rule had brought grave disaster and misery to the African people, but that the Chinese, who had arrived before the Western colonialists, carried out trade with Africa on equal terms, bringing to Africa porcelain, silk and Chinese culture, without occupying an inch of African land. Since its founding, the new China, Kaunda said, had been a great supporter of the African people's struggle for national independence and liberation, as well as a selfless provider of aid in the economic construction of African nations, as best evidenced by its assistance in the construction of the TAZARA Railway, and other similar projects. In the interview, Kaunda said that the TAZARA Railway is 'a great monument to China–Africa friendship. We shall never forget the support and assistance our friends, the Chinese people, have given us.'

CHAIRMAN MAO IN AFRICAN HEARTS

On 11 July 2003, I arrived in Maputo, the capital of Mozambique. As I stood in Mao Zedong Avenue, admiring the exotic grace and charm of the city, my eyes caught by the street names in this unfamiliar town, events from my previous stays in other African countries kept replaying in my mind, taking wing on this broad, straight avenue.

The first time I had been here had been four years earlier. Mao Zedong Avenue, 50 m wide and 2.5 km long, was a shady two-way avenue on an east–west axis, with four lanes separated by a green belt and flanked by verdant flowering trees. It joined Lenin Avenue at its western end, forming a T-junction, and Karl Marx Avenue at the other, the three roads forming a double T. Besides these two main roads at either end, 10 smaller streets connected with Mao Zedong Avenue. When Mozambique gained independence in 1975, the streets in the capital were renamed after the world's great proletariat leaders, Marx, Lenin and Mao. Mao Zedong Avenue was named as a token of appreciation for the great contributions the Chinese government and people had made to the national liberation of Mozambique.

I also learnt that there was a Mao Zedong Village in Mozambique. An official from the presidential office told me that in the 1980s, there had been an extraordinary flood in Gaza Province, north of the capital, which destroyed an entire village. When it was reconstructed, the local government decided to give it the name Mao

Zedong as a sign of their gratitude for the support and assistance from the Chinese government and people. The village was home to about 1 000 people. From that time on, Mao Zedong's name was known to all the people of Mozambique because of the village and avenue named after him.

Tanzania is a country familiar to the Chinese people, and its capital is the starting point of the TAZARA Railway. During my visit in May 2003, I felt surrounded by friendliness and affection from the people of Tanzania, a feeling that only intensified when I left the airport. The younger generation not only knew the name Mao Zedong, but also knew that China had constructed a railway, and was also building highways for them and sending doctors to cure their sick.

At the terminal station of the TAZARA Railway in Zambia, the New Kapiri Mposhi Station, I found technicians from Tanzania and Zambia busy renewing the railway's communications system. China's national flag flew everywhere. Upon seeing me, a local friend who had participated in constructing the railway pointed at the five-star red flag and said, 'Whenever I see a five-star red flag, I cannot help but sing "The East is red".[5] It is Chairman Mao who sent workers here to build this railway. We will never forget it.'

Chinese technicians told me that black workers had learnt to sing 'The East is red' in Chinese, so they could express their gratitude to Chairman Mao and China. While the Chinese were renewing the equipment for them, the participants worked with great passion.

Kenneth Kaunda was not unknown to the Chinese. In each of our three interviews in the past, he spoke of Chairman Mao and of the exciting moments during his three meetings with Mao. Kaunda believed that Chairman Mao was a great man. 'He not only saved billions of Chinese people,' said Kaunda, 'but also made great contributions to the liberation of the African people. He loved all mankind, and the TAZARA Railway is evidence of that. I love and respect him. The TAZARA Railway is a great monument to the friendship between China and Africa.'

The friendship Chairman Mao initiated between China and Africa was also evident – along with the railways and highways – in tall buildings and healthcare teams the country helped provide. As wealthy Western countries refused to aid in the construction of the TAZARA Railway, Chairman Mao and the Chinese government made the wise decision to construct the railway. As the Western colonialist states were leaving Africa, Chairman Mao made the strategic decision to advance into Africa. During the Mao Zedong era, Chinese construction and medical teams arrived in this distant new continent, helping to construct halls, hotels and other top-grade structures, as well as providing medical support for the sick. These construction and medical teams popularised the name of Chairman Mao and composed songs in praise of China–Africa friendship across the continent.

When I visited Jijiga, in Ethiopia, a driver told me he knew two Chinese names: Confucius and Mao Zedong.

In Lamu, in Kenya, the islanders, although almost totally cut off from the outside world, knew of Zheng He and the China Road and Bridge Company.

In Rwanda, the national broadcasting station taught its people greetings in Chinese, and the local people said that 'it was Chairman Mao who sent doctors to cure our diseases'.

In Burundi, the national construction minister said to me in an interview that both Burundi and China were developing countries, and that Burundi should learn from and refer to China for experience in national construction.

In the Democratic Republic of the Congo, young people greeted me happily, saying 'China, Chairman Mao!'

In Zimbabwe, when a delegation from the *People's Daily* visited a farm in July 2003, a farmer named Remigious Matangira said excitedly:

> Before the 1980s, every member of Zimbabwe's ruling party had a copy of *Chairman Mao's Quotations* in hand. Chairman Mao's works are not only directions for our revolution, but for our construction. I studied his works when I participated in the revolution with a rifle on my back, and now, when I encounter difficulties, I often thumb through those quotations to find solutions to my problems.[6]

In South Africa, Nelson Mandela studied Chairman Mao's works while in prison. When shaking hands with me during an event, he smiled and said, 'You are from China. You must know Chairman Mao.'

Thabo Mbeki, the former president of South Africa, quoted Mao in a public speech: 'Let a hundred flowers bloom and a hundred schools of thought contend.'

When I was visiting the University of Pretoria during the South African presidential election in 1999, a black student told me, 'The Western democratic system will not bring Africa a bright future, but Chairman Mao's socialist thought applies to the real-world conditions in Africa.'

On his visit to China in 1972, former US president Richard Nixon said sincerely as soon as he saw Chairman Mao, 'The Chairman's works have pushed a nation forward and have changed the whole world.'[7]

Chairmans Mao's work truly has guided an upsurge of national liberation movements. He is loved and admired by many African people.

Chairman Mao created the new China and initiated China–Africa relations. After him, China's second and third generation of leaders, and the leaders now in office, inherited, consolidated and continue to develop China–Africa friendship. A few days before the 110th anniversary of Mao's birth, former premier Wen Jiabao travelled to Addis Ababa, the capital of Ethiopia, to attend the Second China–Africa Forum, opening a new chapter of China–Africa relations.

I wandered along Chairman Mao Avenue, so named because of the friendship between the two lands, searching for something still vague in my mind. My cab slowly moved towards the other end of the street, and the driver asked me where I wanted to go. I said I wanted to go back.

He seemed to have awakened to a thought. He said, 'Each time I drive on this street, it reminds me of China, of Chairman Mao, and of the great support and assistance China has offered to revolution and construction in Mozambique. Through your visit, I have come to a deeper understanding of how sincerely and deeply the Chinese people love Chairman Mao.'

Chairman Mao's name will always be connected with the great name of China. He also lives on in the hearts of African people.

THE MOST DISTANT PLACE FROM CHINA

What was the furthest point to which Zheng He's fleet travelled? What was the ultimate destination of his voyage west? Opinions on these matters vary much among scholars in China and elsewhere. Some say the furthest place he reached was present-day Kenya; some say it is modern-day Mozambique; others say Zheng He navigated the globe, that China discovered the world.

To find a way through this mystery, I continued travelling south along the African coast, from Tanzania to Mozambique, the ultimate destination of Zheng He's voyage – at least according to *The history of Ming*. According to this work, 'Zheng He served three emperors, was assigned seven times to serve as an envoy, and at various times reached Champa, Java, Bilad al-Sham, Maldives, Sinlad, Mogadiscio, and Malindi, a total of thirty countries.'[8] Biography 214 in *The history of Ming* records: 'There are also countries known as Bilad and Sinlad. Zheng He prepared gifts to grant to them. As these countries were the most distant from China, their envoy tributes did not arrive in China.'[9] Today, though the identity of Sinlad remains unknown, popular belief among scholars is that 'Bilad' refers to modern-day Mozambique.

According to records in *The history of Ming*, Bilad, apparently furthest from China geographically, is believed to be Zheng He's ultimate destination. So, for Zheng He, where was the end of the 'Western Ocean'? The fairly popular Indian Ocean and its shore theory is basically the same idea held by the Arabs. Al-Biruni, an Arab scholar from the 11th century, said, 'The westernmost area the navigators on the vast sea ever visited was Sofala, inhabited by the Sengzhis "on the Egyptian side." People could not go further, since the northeastern part of the sea found its entry into the land from many access points.' The *Arabic, Persian, and Turkic oriental document annotation* records: 'The sea extends all the way to Sofala, close to the shore inhabited by the Sengzhis. Due to those grave dangers we had to pass, no ship dared cross this limit. The Western Ocean terminates at this point.'[10]

As is well known, the Arabs were the earliest foreign immigrants to travel south along the East African coast. Many geographical sites are recorded in Arabic, and many geographical concepts have been influenced by the Arab world. Before the 14th century, the Indian Ocean, or the Western Ocean, was defined by the Arab world as starting from 'East China' in the east and ending at 'Sofala inhabited by the Sengzhis'. It was further understood that Bilad, the place 'most distant from China', must be there, and must be the end point of Zheng He's journeys.

The new edition of the *Islamic encyclopedia* is quite authoritative. It states that Mozambique was 'originally named Bilad-al-Sofala'. In this Arabic name, *bilad* is a common noun meaning 'state'; *al* is an article; and *Sofala* is a proper noun. Bilad-al-Sofala represents the full name. The forms of transliteration used for these names in Chinese were commonly employed, making it clear that 'Bilad', in *The history of Ming*, is in fact Sofala.

According to *The history of Ming*, Bilad and Sinlad were adjacent, the latter further south than the former. Though it is difficult to determine an exact geographical position for Sinlad, it can be ascertained from Arabic navigational records that it was 'further south than Bilad'. At the end of the 15th century, an Arab pilot of the Vasco da Gama fleet wrote in his log: 'We sailed toward the mainland and arrived with our fellows at the coast near the renowned Sulanyat, a shoal south of Sofala. All around is sand, no clay, and no coral reef.'[11]

While I was in Maputo, I visited a castle built by Portuguese colonialists, where horrible ghostly artillery, iron shackles and instruments of torture were exhibited as evidence of the huge crimes of Western colonialists. The brutal behaviour of Western colonialists in Africa was in stark contrast to the 'peaceful navigations' of Zheng He and the 'messengers of peace' from China.

In my hotel I thumbed through some leaflets that informed me that Mozambique Island was the seat of the first capital of Mozambique, and was a place of both beautiful scenery and a long, brilliant history: 'It was the Arabians who were first to arrive on the island, followed by the Chinese, the Portuguese, and the Indians. The porcelain ware left on the island by the Chinese is evidence that they traded here hundreds of years ago.'

Documents informed me of a tiny island called Mozambique, sharing the name of the country. It was in the northern coastal area, to the north of the Mozambique Channel, the part of the country closest to Madagascar. Its location made it attractive to many navigators. Because it was the passage of the Agulhas Current, shipwrecks were not uncommon in the waters there. Large quantities of Chinese porcelain and gold bars from the Ming Dynasty had been discovered on the seabed around the island, leading to a lawsuit.

In the latter half of the 16th century, a Chinese ship laden with treasure sank when navigating the waters around Mozambique Island. There were vast stores of treasures of all kinds on the ship. Most had since been plundered by pirates. In May 2001 professional divers searched for treasures on the seabed, hoping to verify the historical facts. As many as 1 500 pieces of celadon ware and 12 kg of gold bars made in the Wanli period of the Ming Dynasty were found, including a porcelain bowl manufactured in 1553 and many other treasures, most dating from 1573 to 1619. After the discovery, a state-owned Mozambican enterprise and a Portuguese company signed a contract to auction these cultural relics in Amsterdam. In May 2004 the first batch was put up for auction, including 125 pieces of porcelain ware and 21 gold bars.

Just as the auction got under way, archaeologists and experts in cultural relics sued the government officials and businesses, citing legal stipulations that 'all archaeological findings are fixed assets of the state and removal from state boundaries is prohibited'. The government officials and the companies involved were taken to court by the archaeological experts and scholars, who deemed that such cultural relics were priceless treasures and, as cultural heritage items, they must be protected and could not be sold for money. They argued that 'selling state treasures for money is a harm done to every national of Mozambique, as it is a loss of part of our cultural heritage'.[12] As of 2005, the lawsuit was still ongoing.

Mozambique has about 2 500 km of coastline. Beira, the seaport of Sofala Province, is roughly in the middle of the coastline. The place names 'Beira' and 'Sofala' captured my attention. I wondered if they had any association with 'Bilad' and whether Beira might even be the 'Bilad' mentioned in *The history of Ming*. Bilad-al-Sofala, in the *Islamic encyclopaedia*, was perhaps the name of this area: the 'Beira-Sofala' area. This question, of course, still awaits academic study and verification.

What was the furthest place Zheng He reached? Academic communities in China and abroad differ in their opinions, but almost all scholars and experts are certain Zheng He reached Mozambique. If so, that his fleet managed to travel so far is worthy of being counted among the greatest human achievements ever. It is a precious spiritual treasure of the Chinese nation, which forever pushes the Chinese people to continue dauntlessly in their efforts for national development.

10

Visiting four island nations

DISCUSSING ZHENG HE AT THE GUANDI TEMPLE

Across the straits from Mozambique, Madagascar has a territory 16 times the area of Taiwan. Some researchers in China believe Zheng He's fleet passed the northern tip of Madagascar on its return from 'Sofala', modern-day Mozambique. Some foreign scholars say he not only sailed past Madagascar, but also made observations concerning the longitude of the island and carried out scientific research there. During my stay in South Africa, I heard some veteran Overseas Chinese scholars say there was a Guandi Temple[1] in Madagascar. All this tempted me to visit the world's fourth largest island.

Situated on seven hills in the central part of Madagascar, its capital, Antananarivo, enjoys a comfortable climate all year round. This island is abundant in natural resources and agricultural produce. Its special geological formation helps preserve varieties of time-honoured fossils of various organisms. The island, renowned for its biodiversity, is home to primates as small as one's thumb (*Daubentonia madagascariensis*) and the elephant bird (*Aepyornis*), the largest bird that ever existed. Madagascar's butterflies include 90 per cent of the species known in the world's butterfly population. Because it is so isolated from the rest of the world, few people realise that Madagascar is a 'treasure island' awaiting development.

In July 2004, I searched all over Antananarivo for local veteran Overseas Chinese scholars who could provide me with information about the history of the Overseas Chinese community there and lead me to clues about Madagascar's interaction with China, including things such as the Guandi Temple and Zheng He's voyages on the Western Ocean. From my conversations with elderly Chinese people there, I learnt that the history of Chinese residents in Madagascar is relatively short. The first generation of Chinese immigrants had moved there from Mauritius at the end of the 19th century. Madagascar was formerly a French colony. When France abolished the slavery system in Madagascar, cheap labour was in great demand for the construction of railways, so large numbers of labourers were employed from Guangdong, China. Since then, many Chinese people emigrated to Madagascar. As a rule, the Chinese labourers arrived at the port of Tamatave,[2] then spread from there to other parts of the country. According to incomplete statistics, tens of thousands of people migrated from Guangdong to Madagascar before it gained independence in 1960.[3] As a rule, the Chinese people who arrived before independence were called 'Old Overseas Chinese',[4] distinguishing them from later waves of Chinese immigrants.

After arriving in Madagascar, the more prosperous Chinese people remained in Tamatave to make their living there. The rest went to mountainous areas to purchase local produce, such as cloves, coffee and vanilla, to trade for French products, such as salt, oil, sugar, candles, matches and soup, which they then sold in the mountain villages at a profit. With their accumulation of capital, some started operating shops in the towns and villages. Most of the Chinese immigrants were men who married local women, had children and became part of local society.

In the 1980s the economy of Madagascar, a poor country by any standards, began declining and life there became very hard. A number of Overseas Chinese left for Western countries, mostly Canada. In the 1990s a new generation of Overseas Chinese arrived in Madagascar, mainly for the purpose of export and trade, but also to open shops or restaurants. They imported hardware, clothing and other daily necessities from China, and exported minerals, timber and other local produce to China.

Both the 'Old Overseas Chinese' and the newcomers believe that the Chinese influence in Madagascar is evident. First, the local language has adopted the Chinese words for 'lychee', 'cabbage', 'vegetable shoots' and 'onions' into its vocabulary. Locals believe the lychee that grows wild in Madagascar first came from China. In addition, there are two Guandi temples in Madagascar. The one in Tamatave is particularly well known, not only to the Overseas Chinese community but to the entire local population. Though it still remains a mystery whether Zheng He's fleet reached Madagascar, some say he arrived at Cap d'Ambre, the northernmost point of Madagascar.

Hoping to clarify facts, I readily accepted an invitation from an early Overseas Chinese, Feng Baoquan, to visit his home. He belonged to the third generation of his family to live in Madagascar, and had taken over his father's electrical-appliance retail business and developed it so that it gained the admiration of the local people. Honest and of good repute among the Overseas Chinese community, he had been awarded a medal. He served as president of the Chinese Federation of Madagascar and chairman of the China Peaceful Reunification Promotion Committee. Because he did not speak Chinese well, he invited Chen Zhaochang, another early Overseas Chinese, to interpret for us.

When we discussed the origins of the lychee in Madagascar, Mr Feng said it was very likely that the Chinese had brought the fruit to the island, and the scattered seeds had then taken root and grown into healthy plants, developing abundantly in the fertile soil and suitable climate of the island. The exact time the lychee appeared on Madagascar has not been confirmed by any scientific evidence to date, however.

Mr Feng told me about the Guandi Temple in Tamatave, and that we could go there for a visit. He had heard talk of Zheng He's fleet passing by Madagascar, but no traces of such an event had been found on any part of the island. He felt the foreign scholars' belief that the fleet had observed the longitude and latitude of the country's north-western coast did not seem sufficiently grounded in evidence. To provide more clarity, he suggested we ask representatives from all over the country, who would be attending the Madagascar China Peaceful Reunification Promotion Conference the following day.

The Overseas Chinese population in Madagascar can be understood in two senses – one broad and one narrow. In the narrow sense, the term refers to people of Chinese descent, a total of about 30 000. In the broader sense, it refers to those who have Chinese blood in their lineage, a figure of between 400 000 and 500 000. These are the descendants of both Chinese men and women. The third and fourth generations have become native Malagasies, and though they know they have Chinese blood, they do not speak Chinese. Their lifestyle is more akin to that of the local people, though their skin tone is closer to that of the Chinese people. Nevertheless, they are still 'descendants of the dragon' and have warm feelings towards China and long for the quick reunification of the 'motherland'.

Closing business for the day, many Chinese people attended the reunification conference, travelling to the capital by car from all over the island, some travelling great distances over mountainous terrain. At a reception hosted by the Chinese Embassy to Madagascar, I spoke with more than 10 representatives from coastal regions. Though they were unable to speak Chinese, their enthusiasm was boundless in the presence of this 'relative from the motherland'. They knew of Zheng He's heroic voyage on the Western Ocean, but had not found any relics in Madagascar that could be linked to his fleet. They said that, as far as they knew, there was no evidence related to the fleet having visited. In light of the information I brought, they promised to look out for possible relics and to contact me if they discovered anything.

While I was at the airport waiting for a flight to Tamatave, I came across an early Overseas Chinese resident named Chen Weitian. He told me he had come to Madagascar in 1939, when he was just 12. Decades later, he could no longer speak nor understand Chinese well. He was, however, still able to write, so we communicated through writing. He had made a special trip to attend the peaceful reunification conference.

The following day, Chen took me to visit the Guandi Temple. Roughly a century old, the temple was a simple structure that had been built in a coastal part of Tamatave but, with growing construction in the town, it now found itself right in the city centre. Where the temple was built was always the first stop for Chinese people who arrived in Tamatave. It was a residential area, an assembly place, an activity centre and the seat of the province's Overseas Chinese Federation all in one. The Guandi Temple consisted of four parts: the Earth Altar, the Guandi Temple, the Buddha Hall and the Overseas Chinese Ancestral Hall. The Earth Altar, standing beside the temple, was built by the Chinese community as a site to pray for favourable winds and rain. The Guandi Temple, the centre of the compound, was home to a Guandi statue for pilgrims to worship. On both sides of the gate were red strips with a couplet on one side that reads, 'Lifted eyes are like the sun and moon above', and on the other, 'Heavy brows are like beautiful rivers and mountains'. A horizontal line of Chinese characters over the doorway reads, 'Eternal loyalty'. I was told that the local Chinese people came here every Spring Festival to draw fortune sticks and receive blessings. Chen told me that the Buddha statue in the hall was brought to the site from Vietnam by a Frenchman in 1960, and was then given to Chen as a gift when the Frenchman left Madagascar. Chen had suggested it be placed in the temple near the ancestral tablets of many deceased Overseas Chinese people, which were housed in the nearby Overseas Chinese Ancestral Hall.

A young Chinese man by the name of Chen Jianjiang accompanied us on our visit to the Guandi Temple. A member of the All-China Youth Federation, he spoke Chinese passably. When we spoke of Zheng He, they all said the Guandi Temple was built much later than the time of Zheng He's travels. They were sure the Chinese people there were not in any way connected to Zheng He's travels, and were not descendants of his crew. Even so, they took great pride in the seaman's remarkable achievements. Chen gave me a gift – it was the information he had collected on Zheng He and his fleet.

It was popularly believed by the Chinese community there that the three so-called elderly grandpas in the public cemetery were the first Chinese people to arrive in Tamatave. During certain Chinese festivals, the local Chinese people worshipped these three as ancestors, who, along with two 'uncles', were together considered the first Chinese settlers in Madagascar. Later, Chen and I paid our respects to them with a visit to their tombs. Unfortunately, the dates of birth and death had become blurred beyond recognition, and the only characters that were legible were 'Tomb of the Eldest Grandfather of the Han Race', alongside the date the monument was erected.

Standing in front of the Guandi Temple, Chen told me that, years earlier, a student of mixed Chinese race, while studying at University of Toamasina, had written a thesis on the history of the Chinese people in Madagascar. In it, he related the traditional lifestyle of the Chinese people living in the mountainous areas, including their propensity for porcelain ware and tea. Chen said he did not know the precise content of the thesis, but that the Chinese consul to Tamatave, Wang Jinqing, had read it. Unfortunately, I did not get the chance to meet Consul Wang as planned. He had to depart to take office at the Chinese Embassy to Comoros when I arrived. I was also not able to locate the student who wrote the thesis at his remote home in the mountains.

I went to the University of Toamasina to try to locate the thesis, but it was closed for the holiday. I decided to carry on to Mauritius and Comoros to continue my own investigations.

THE LEGEND OF PARADISE ISLAND

Mauritius is home to beautiful scenery and unique social customs. It is renowned as a paradise island that attracts large numbers of tourists year round.

This beautiful country was once just a barren, uninhabited island, however. In 1598, it became a Dutch colony, named after a Dutch prince. It was occupied by France in 1715, and renamed French Island. In 1814 it became a British colony, resuming its original name. English was adopted as the official language at this time. In March 1968, Mauritius gained independence. Ethnically, its inhabitants are mainly Indians, Pakistanis, Creoles, Chinese and Caucasian. It is popularly said that the earliest people to arrive on the island were the Dutch.

When I arrived in Mauritius, I heard another story, however. According to this version of events, the first people to reach Mauritius were Zheng He's crew. Support from scholars and experts comes in several layers. Firstly, Zheng He's fleet sailed roughly two centuries before the time the Dutch ruled Mauritius. Secondly, in light of the technical level of and distances travelled by Zheng He's fleet, Mauritius was clearly not out of reach. Thirdly, Mauritius is in the monsoon zone, an ancient seaway. After much study, some foreign scholars believe that Zheng He's fleet, or at least part of it, was the first to sail round the Cape of Good Hope by one of two possible routes, one through the Mozambique Channel and the other navigating south-east around Madagascar, which would pass Mauritius to the east.

I travelled twice to Mauritius, in September 2002 and January 2004. When I first arrived, the Chinese and Overseas Chinese Forum was going on in the capital, Port Louis. The moment I arrived, I was surrounded by welcoming Overseas Chinese people. Zhu Qingqiu, an Old Overseas Chinese man took me to his home, located in the downtown area. The entrance area of his house was decorated with scrolls of Chinese calligraphy on the walls and there was a gold statue of Buddha on a table. He explained, 'We businessmen all hope to be blessed by Buddha.'

With the Mid-Autumn Festival drawing near, Zhu offered me mooncakes of various flavours. Zhu said, 'My shop is in Chinatown. My mooncakes are in season now. All 30 000 Chinese people in Mauritius will eat mooncakes during the festival. The local people like mooncakes as well, so business always booms at this time of year.'

When I asked about the Chinese influence on Mauritius, Zhu did not answer directly. Instead, he took me to the Heavenly Altar. When I saw it, my eyes widened in surprise. Zhu smiled and said, 'This Heavenly Altar is no rival for the one in Beijing, but it is an expression by the local Chinese people of their affection for the "Maternal Home". Usually, we call Mauritius "my husband's home" and China "my maiden home". We pooled our money to construct this Heavenly Altar to provide a site for our overseas compatriots, especially the young people, to remember our roots.'

The Heavenly Altar constructed by the Chinese community in Mauritius was a copy of the ancient architectural style of the Heavenly Altar in Beijing, though not as large and imposing.

In Port Louis's Chinatown, Heyan Street is the central artery, with row upon row of Chinese shops, restaurants and hotels along the cross streets, one of which was called Dr Sun Yat-sen Street. Strictly speaking, 'China Street' would be a more appropriate name than Chinatown, though it was like a town within a town. It perhaps ranks first among all Chinatowns and 'China Streets' in the world, in terms of scale and influence.

Walking through Chinatown, I noticed many striking features of Chinese culture in the names of the shops. The street names can be categorised into three types. The first was names of places or people connected with China, such as Hong Kong and Mong Kok. The second was a group of streets named after traditional Chinese values, such as Virtue, Benevolence, Harmony and Victory. The third group of names focused on the revitalisation of China, such as Xinhua Xuexiao ('Chinese Revitalisation School') and the Lihua ('Favour to the Chinese') Travel Agency.

Were the Chinese people here in any way connected with Zheng He's travels on the Western Ocean? When I asked this question, the local Chinese people told me not only the above-mentioned story of the possible routes the fleet took, but also emphasised that the Chinese people had emigrated to Madagascar via Mauritius. This meant their arrival in Mauritius pre-dated their arrival in Madagascar.

The origin of Chinatown was connected with the misery and humiliation the Western colonial powers inflicted on Mauritius, a history of tears and blood. The history of the Chinese community here began during the period of French rule. In the middle of the 18th century, when Port Louis was under construction, the French began employing cheap labour from Asian countries, bringing in the first batch of Chinese labourers, including Chinese women who worked as domestic servants.

Over the next century, a constant stream of Chinese labourers arrived in Mauritius in an initial wave of Chinese migration to the island, mostly by force of necessity. An upsurge of emigration from China followed in 1836, with Chinese sailors and artisans travelling south to the Indian Ocean to work and settle. It is said that one group of Chinese emigrants arrived in Mauritius at this time not by choice, but because a strong wind blew their ships off course. They ended up settling on the island. The third period of migration was between 1840 and 1843, when British authorities stopped recruiting sugar mill workers from India and started recruiting from China. A total of 2 701 Chinese workers landed in Mauritius. When their contracts were terminated, they scattered and settled in rural areas, later becoming merchants or artisans.

Under the tyrannical rule of white colonialists, the Chinese who arrived in Mauritius wearing pigtails were discriminated against and exploited. As a minority ethnic group from an alien land, they were forbidden to own fixed assets and were permitted only to operate retail businesses. Even then, that was based on the conditions that they had the necessary capital, that their rented houses were in conformity with police regulations and satisfactory to the authorities, and that they lived in harmony with the local residents and provided conveniences to their customers. To ensure their own survival, the Overseas Chinese banded together for mutual protection, which naturally gave birth to 'Chinatowns' – like the one in Port Louis – in which they lived and worked. When they were denied loans from banks, they pooled their resources and gradually expanded their business activities from resale to wholesale operations, moving from sales of small commodities to sales of Chinese products, such as porcelain, antiques, clothing and stationery, continually increasing the range of products they offered. With this steady growth over the years, shops and restaurants opened. In 1847, the first Chinese-owned factories were opened, first a cigarette factory, followed by wineries, shoe factories, biscuit factories, beverage factories and soap mills, all on a large scale. With their diligence and wisdom, the Chinese people put down roots and gained respect in Mauritius.

Wherever they go, Chinese people always keep their origins in mind, living in a Chinese way and spreading the influence of Chinese culture to the surrounding society. A couplet written on the gate of the Nanshun Club House reads: 'Benevolence begets happiness, and happiness nurtures fortune.' The words tell of the heritage honoured among the Chinese people in that alien land, while reflecting their method of integration into local society. In the process of integrating into the larger community of Mauritius, the Chinese people there have brought Chinese culture to the island, as seen in the abundance of Chinese food and tea, which form an integral part of the local diet.

The Chinese, accounting for 2.9 per cent of the nation's population, hold colourful celebrations on traditional Chinese festival days. These activities are not just an attraction for the local people, but are also admired by tourists from all over the world as part of the country's rich tourism resources. The leaders of Mauritius have, on many public occasions, praised the Chinese community for its great contributions to the economic, social and cultural development of the country. Mauritius has become more colourful because of the Chinese people and their unique culture.

LIVING BIOLOGICAL LABORATORY

The Comoro Islands are at the northern end of the Mozambique Channel. Seychelles is situated between Comoros and the Maldives. The name 'Comoros', derived from Arabic, means 'land of the moon' and its capital, Moroni, means 'source of happiness'. It is an indisputable fact that Zheng He visited the Maldives and Seychelles; legend tells us that his fleet passed by Comoros and Seychelles. Some foreign scholars even believe that Zheng He's fleet observed the longitude of the Seychelles in its scientific research, and that the accuracy of the measurements was on par with that of today. I decided to fly to Comoros and the Seychelles to verify these facts.

From west to east, the four main Comoro Islands are Grande Comore, Mohéli, Anjouan and Mayotte, which is administered by France. Since the independence of Comoros in 1975, the island of Mayotte decided to remain under French control as a *département* of France and is home to a French naval base.

The Comoro Islands were formed 2 million years ago by sub-oceanic volcanic eruptions in three stages. The first stage was a Hawaiian-type eruption, forming a lava flow. The second was a Strombolian eruption, forming volcanic gravel, and the third was a cone eruption, forming many crater lakes. The geographical position bestows Comoros with a unique landscape. Grande Comore is an active volcano, which last erupted in 1978, leaving in its wake the world's largest crater, more than 8 km wide, and numerous crater lakes on its 2 361-m main peak, Mount Karthala. These high mountain lakes are known as living biological laboratories. The seabed in the immediate area around the Comoro Islands is unpredictably varied. Anjouan Island is honoured as the bright pearl of Comoro, with beautiful scenery consisting of undulating hills and bubbling brooks. The small Nirumaswa Island, near Mohéli Island, is known as 'Paradise Island' and is recognised by the UN as a sea park. Tourism is a key industry for Comoros; aromatic crops are another resource of the island.

In the 10th century, Omanis travelled south to Comoros and settled there as the first inhabitants, founding a sultanate. In 1750 the Portuguese invaded Comoros. In 1841 France occupied Mayotte, and in 1912, the four islands of Comoros became colonies of France. On 6 July 1975, the country gained its independence, becoming the Federal Islamic Republic of Comoro Islands. China was the first country to recognise this four-island nation, and the people of Comoros remember this warmly and gratefully.

In January 2005, I visited Comoros. When I got off the plane at the Prince Said Ibrahim International Airport, Wang Jinqing, the former Chinese consul to Tamatave, was waiting for me. I asked him if he knew whether the Chinese student in Madagascar had spoken of Zheng He in his thesis. Consul Wang replied that, despite what is said about Zheng He visiting Madagascar, the Chinese people studied in the thesis had no connection with the ancient mariner.

I went on to ask him about the Chinese people in Comoros. Zhao Chunsheng, China's ambassador to Comoros, said, 'The earliest Chinese migrants came here from Madagascar, and only travelled to Mayotte Island. The Chinese people on the other islands are all newcomers, arriving in the past 10 years or so. Whether or not Zheng He passed by these islands is a question still awaiting scientific evidence.'

My visit to Comoros was fruitless in terms of finding out about Zheng He's journeys. Even so, Ambassador Zhao, and my Comoros counterparts, told me that, as I was the first Chinese reporter to visit the Comoro Islands, mine was a long overdue visit. 'This is the 30th anniversary of the establishment of diplomatic relations between China and Comoros. The completion and delivery dates of three China-assisted projects in Comoros are all set for February,' he said.

The three projects were the delivery of the Comorian National Broadcast Television Station, the acceptance inspection of maintenance at the People's Palace and the start of the Comoro International Airport expansion project. I gathered information about these three projects and wrote reports about them.

According to the UN, Comoros is among the world's least developed countries, ranking 139th in the Human Development Index. The Comorian economy is facing grave challenges due to its weak economic base, its heavy dependence on external aid, its political instability in recent years, cessation of aid from the World Bank, a decline in tourism and, most markedly, the sharp decline in the price of spices in the international market, resulting in export revenue losses. The government faces great difficulties in stabilising the political situation, developing the economy and enhancing the livelihood of the people. Hopefully, with the convening of round-table conferences among countries that provide aid to Comoros and the revival of its inbound tourism industry, the Comorian people will overcome these difficulties, entering a new period of national construction and development.

A GREAT CONTRIBUTION TO HUMAN HAPPINESS

Seychelles, an island nation in the western Indian Ocean, consists of 115 islands of various sizes. Its position makes it a communication hub between Asia and Africa.

It is popularly believed that the Portuguese arrived there in the late 16th century and named it the Seven Sisters. It was occupied by France in 1756 and renamed after the Vicomte de Seychelles. In 1794 Britain ousted France as the controlling power. After that, rule changed hands between Britain and France until 1814, when it became a British colony. In June 1976 Seychelles gained national independence as a sovereign state.

Some scholars believe that Zheng He's fleet arrived in Seychelles before the Portuguese. My own investigation into this began with gathering information about the Overseas Chinese community living in the Seychelles. The island nation is home to fewer Overseas Chinese people than in Madagascar or Mauritius. The local people all know that on the country's third largest island there is a cemetery in which the earliest Chinese residents were buried. Cantiral, a renowned local scholar specialising in the history of immigrants in Seychelles, told me that the earliest immigrants there had come from Mauritius. He also said that he had not made any investigation into the truth of the rumours of the presence of Zheng He's fleet there. I wondered how to go about obtaining such evidence for myself.

Seychelles is home to the unique sea coconut, a source of pride for the people of Seychelles, and which holds special appeal to tourists from all over the world. The fruit grow on separate trees, native to the Seychelles, as male and female, and their shape resembles the human genitalia. The sea coconut is a large, beautiful plant, growing as heavy as 22.5 kg. The male fruit resembles a phallus, the female a human female's pelvis. It takes two years for a female tree to germinate and 25 for it to blossom. The tree's average life span is over 300 years. After nine to 13 months, the fruit of the female tree begins to turn yellow and the juice inside is ripe for consumption. Beyond this period, the juice thickens. The fruit and leaves are used to make various products, such as straw hats, handbags, soft furnishings, and coconut juice and wine. The female fruit is also used to craft souvenirs for tourists.

The sea coconut was originally called the 'double coconut'. Around 1519 the French found the peculiar-looking fruit in the sea not far from the Seychelles and, mistaking it for something that grows in the sea, named it the sea coconut. It bore that name for many years until people realised it was the fruit of a Seychellois tree whose fruit is dispersed and washed out into the open sea.

Visiting Seychelles without seeing a sea coconut grove is like going to Beijing and neglecting to tour the Great Wall. On a sunny afternoon in March 2004, I went alone to look at a sea coconut grove on the second largest island in the archipelago. The forest of straight boughs stretched across hills and valleys. The sky-high trees stood close together in a howling wind, as if bent towards one another in unending conversation. Because there were no tourists at this late hour, I walked alone along the trails in the valley, surrounded by the straight trees under shady foliage. As I stepped on the yellow leaves, I was occasionally startled by a tremendous thud of falling branches and leaves. The panic I felt in the depth of the forest made me stop when I reached a path crossing my own.

Sitting at a distance from me were a man and a woman; they appeared to be workers on the plantation. They greeted me warmly. Instead of telling me about sea coconuts, as one might have expected, the woman pointed at a plant as tall as a man and said, 'This little tree with pointed leaves is from China.'

Saying so, she started laughing uncontrollably. She took for granted that any Chinese person would know the medical uses of the little tree from China, but I had never seen it before, and knew neither its name nor its use. The man then filled me in on the story, saying that its leaves can be used to cure impotence. 'People here all know this tree. See how it makes her laugh?'

The man found another kind of tree from China. 'These two trees are common in the coconut grove. We know they have been here for a long time, but we don't know exactly when they came. No one has ever looked into it.'

The Chinese species, which added to the biodiversity of the coconut grove, reminded me that Zheng He had not only brought spices to China from exotic lands, but had also taken Chinese plant species to foreign countries, introducing and exchanging species between two regions, and thereby broadening people's understanding of the world's plants and benefiting humans by diversifying ecosystems. Experts and scholars around the world have come to a consensus that the two species of plants in the coconut grove are very likely to have been brought there by Zheng He's fleet.

Some scholars believe that, before the adventurous voyages of European sailors, Zheng He had introduced the lotus to Oceania, the mulberry and rice to the Pacific islands and South America, sugar cane and ginger from India to the islands of the North Pacific, corn from America to China and South East Asia, and sweet potatoes from Mexico to the Philippines.

Some Chinese scholars have pointed out that Zheng He, during his voyages on the Western Ocean, carried out extensive, long-term studies on the biological resources in the places he visited, emphasising rare species, particularly plants and animals with economic and medicinal values, and introduced into China what it needed at the time by collecting, purchasing or gathering tributes for the Chinese emperor. A typical example was the giraffe presented to the emperor by the king of Malindi. Plants introduced from foreign countries, including the carrot, pumpkin, balsam pear, ebony and cotton tree, were included in the *Compendium of materia medica* compiled 90 years later by Li Shizhen, under the same dynastic rulers as during Zheng He's time, to enrich traditional Chinese medicine. The grain tree, now growing in the Zheng He Memorial in Nanjing, Jiangsu, is an incredible plant transplanted by Zheng He from overseas. According to *The history of Ming*, there were two trees of this species, one growing in the Heavenly Temple and the other in the Temple of Great Gratitude and Longevity. According to Ming Dynasty scholar Zhou Hui's *Jinling trivia* and the Qing Dynasty scholar Chen Wenshu's *Moling collection*, there were two trees of this species, one in each of those two temples. This tree not only 'bears fruit the shape of grain, fish, or crab',[5] but also 'tells the crop yields of the year'.[6] A paraphrased poem about the tree says:

> Back from the West in countless colossal vessels, driven by huge ship paddles. Transplanted from the parrots' home, it sets roots beside Phoenix Palace. Both grow old at their temples; still blooming, they tell of bumper harvests. Histories tell of Sanbao, an imperial eunuch of no ordinary talent.[7]

One of Zheng He's great feats was the promotion of species exchange between China and other countries all over the world. In the long term, this brought great happiness to countless generations.

THE TECHNOLOGY OF ZHENG HE'S NAVIGATIONS

Leading his huge fleet, Zheng He made seven voyages on the Western Ocean, reaching the East African coast after sailing day and night across the vast ocean. He probably navigated around the Cape of Good Hope, travelling the globe and 'discovering the world'. How did the Chinese people at that time navigate, and by what means did they determine their location during that first great voyage of human history? Scholars around the world have reached almost identical conclusions. Some have suggested the theory that Zheng He not only defined the earth's latitudes, but also its longitudes, based on records compiled by Mao Yuanyi in the Ming Dynasty in *Treatise on military preparations*. Gavin Menzies, a contemporary British scholar and author of *1421: The year China discovered the world*,[8] fully agrees with this conclusion and claims to provide new evidence for it.

As far as I have been able to discover, Zheng He's crew established longitudinal observation stations in African countries, such as those I visited in the Comoro Islands, Tanzania, Mozambique, Madagascar and Mauritius. As a rule, they chose sites with wide open spaces and excellent visibility for their observation stations. Their measuring devices were fairly functional, reliable and portable, though not as sophisticated as those used today.

During my stay in Seychelles, I had intended to find the observation stations, but failed. Due to hundreds of years of weathering and human factors, these relics were now beyond recognition. Even so, we know that the voyages were supported by the most advanced navigational technology and skills humans possessed at the time, including knowledge and application of the earth's longitudes and latitudes, allowing Zheng He's fleet to accomplish those seven great voyages.

Throughout these voyages, the science and technology Zheng He possessed included rational use of monsoon and ocean currents; use of 更 (*geng*) and 托 (*tuo*) (explained below) to calculate voyage range and measure water depths; use of the compass; positioning by landscape; navigating by landmarks; creative use of astronomical piloting by referring to the stars; discovery and observation of longitudes; and the Nautical Chart of Zheng He's Navigations.

The huge Zheng He fleet consisted of wooden sailing ships. 'Wind comes from all directions, and head-on wind is not for sailing' is an old saying that demonstrates the use of wind for sailing at that time. To take advantage of the common monsoon, there were as many as 12 sails on each treasure boat. China is in a monsoon zone, with an obvious seasonal variation of wind direction due to shifts in barometric distribution in the coastal waters. Northerly winds prevail in winter, southerly in summer. As early as the Song Dynasty, a poem tells us: 'Sailing in northerly winds and returning in southerly winds, merchants are happy with their commodities as they come and go from afar.' In each of Zheng He's ocean voyages, he set sail in the north-east monsoon and returned home in the south-west monsoon. When navigating to the Persian Gulf and the East African coast, he sailed his boats by the monsoon winds on the Indian Ocean. At the turn of the season, he took time to rest and reorganise his fleet. At the same time, the fleet made timely use of China's coastal currents and the Indian Ocean's monsoon circulation to ensure their safety and speed.

Zheng He adopted 更 (*geng*) to calculate water speed, navigating speed and navigating distance. *Geng*, originally a unit of time, was one-tenth of a day-night cycle. It was later used to measure speed, meaning the distance covered in one *geng*. The *geng* was 60 *li*, or 30 km, the distance covered in 2.4 hours. The *geng* was first calculated by the number of incense sticks burnt in a day. In Zheng He's system, the distance represented by a *geng* was dependent on the strength and velocity of wind and currents. Therefore, 'a decision on navigations is preceded by an estimation of wind speed and degree of positive or negative action of water flow. When a decision is to be made, a strip of wood is dropped at the prow while a sailor walks toward the stern from the prow, determining the number of *geng*.'[9]

Measuring water depth, an important part of water safety, was used to avoid rocks and running aground, and to choose a suitable site to drop anchor. Zheng He used a plummet method to detect water depth, which involved dropping a roped lead plummet to the bottom of the sea and reading the water's depth from the rope. The unit of measure for water depth was the *tuo*, a dialect term referring to the distance of the arms when outspread, or about 1.7 m. This method of determining water depth was adopted by navigators until the 1970s or 1980s.

Sailing was directed by flags in the day and by lanterns at night. These were the methods of communication used by Zheng He's fleet. Oceangoing vessels were veiled with red cloth, and over twenty flags of various colours were suspended on all four sides of the deck. The flag atop the mast was the commanding flag.

At night, pine or resin wax was ignited to provide the signal light. This ancient method of maritime communication is the early form of what is used on modern ships, marking the birth of modern maritime communication systems.

During its voyages, Zheng He's fleet used many orienteering and piloting skills to ensure correct orientation. 'Versatile in geography, the fleet sailed during the day by referring to the sun, by stars during the night, and by the compass when it was overcast.'[10] *Records of countries in the Western Ocean* points out:

> East and west are determined by the rise and fall of sun and moon, and distance is estimated by the height of the stars. The compass is carved of wood, engraved with heavenly stems and earthly branches' indices; compass hands float on water to orient ships day and night, for months at a time. Islands or hills of different shape in front of the vessel, or to left or right, are references for steering toward one's destination. With correct calculations of variables for stopping and starting, all destinations are accessible.[11]

These remarks reveal several facts, including orientation by observing the sun and moon, orientation by compass, recording coastal topography, observing islands, rocks, mountain peaks, ports and towns as landmarks for positioning, using *geng* to calculate navigational distance, and observing the stars (or astronomical piloting) for positioning.

Chinese sailors were able to position their ships in the early period of their ocean navigations by referring to the sun, the moon and the stars. Based on the achievements of his predecessors, Zheng He developed this navigational skill to the technology of oceangoing navigational astronomy, or sailing by reference to the stars. This technology was used to determine the latitudinal position of the fleet by observing the elevation of the stars above sea level. Polaris, or the pole star, was the main star Zheng He referred to in his navigations. The apparatus used to measure the elevation of heavenly bodies was known as the navigation astronomy board, with 指 (*zhi*) and 角 (*jiao*) as measuring units. One *zhi*, corresponding to today's measure of 1.9 degrees, was equivalent to four *jiao*. There are four oceangoing navigational astronomy charts in Zheng He's navigational chart.

In navigational astronomy technology, positioning was achieved by referring to Polaris. When Zheng He's fleet entered the southern hemisphere, crossing the equator, the correct positions of Canopus and the Southern Cross were defined as references, as was Polaris.

Zheng He's navigational chart was the fruit of the science and technology used in his navigations. It was produced a hundred years before the so-called World's First Navigational Chart compiled by the Dutch cartographer Lucas Janszoon Waghenaer. Zheng He's chart was found in the *Treatise on Military Preparations*, a book on the art of war, the last volume of which was titled *Ocean-going*

Navigation. The map is on the last page, titled A Chart of Treasure Ship Navigation from Longjiang Shipyard to Foreign Countries. Well-known British scientist and sinologist Joseph Needham highly praises the Zheng He navigation chart, calling it 'the world's earliest truly scientific navigation chart'.[12]

Menzies believes that the greatness of Zheng He lies not only in the fact that he bequeathed to us this navigational chart, but also in his discovery and mastery of many crucial points that are indispensable to cartography – calculating longitude and latitude, and dimension and orientation – which prepared him to make such an accurate navigational chart, to make global voyages, and to discover such a world of wonder. Menzies points out that before Zheng He's voyages on the Western Ocean, there is convincing evidence of the ability of the Chinese to calculate longitude, since they possessed knowledge of astronomy, astronomical construction and timing methods: 'The fact that the ability to accurately calculate lunar eclipses and simultaneous observations of eclipses at different positions on Earth is testimony that it was the Chinese who first discovered the crucial steps to discovering methods to calculate longitude.'[13]

To prove that Zheng He discovered longitude, on 16–17 July 2000, when an eclipse occurred, Menzies went from Tahiti across the Pacific to Singapore, established an observation team, and adopted Zheng He's observational positions to show the reliability and accuracy in observing lunar eclipses and determining longitude. Menzies and the other observing scholars were astounded by the results of the observation.

Six hundred years later, the observational positions Zheng He had selected have been proved to be applicable to observation of longitude with extremely high precision, convincing the world that his navigations on the Western Ocean were made not only on the basis of a fearless spirit and unyielding heroism, but also on the most advanced navigational science and technology of the time.

11

Round the Cape of Good Hope

AFRICA AND THE MING DYNASTY WORLD MAP

When the Amalgamated Map of the Great Ming Empire was exhibited at the Perspectives on and of Africa exhibition held in South Africa's Parliament in 2002, it attracted great attention, and was the main reason the exhibition was extended several times.

When I looked at the ancient map, the guide explained that it had been made in 1389, the 22nd year of the Hongwu reign in the time of Zhu Yuanzhang, founding emperor of the Ming Dynasty. The 4.57 m by 3.87 m map was a same-size copy of the original. 'This extremely rare, precious map is the earliest and largest map of the world in which Africa is depicted in its correct shape and geographical position. This is indisputable evidence that it was the Chinese who first set foot on the African continent, not the Europeans, who have often been thought to be the earliest arrivers,' explained the guide.

European maps: A distortion of Africa

Around the beginning of the new millennium, the African National Congress (ANC) held Congress Millennium Project activities to challenge or renew people's ideas and perceptions of both the history and current situation of Africa, and answer questions of concern to the African people, including the perceptions of Africans both within the continent and overseas. The goal was to promote racial reconciliation, national reconstruction and the democratisation process in South Africa. The Perspectives on and of Africa exhibition was a key activity in the programme.

The ANC collected over 130 maps, all from Europe, donated 87 years earlier by Sidney Mendelssohn, a former mining magnate. The guide told me: 'These maps were drawn in the 16th century, beginning 450 years ago. Most were small in size, such as the five maps from books exhibited here. These maps, marking the beginning of map drawing by Europeans, reveal their bias and ignorance of Africa, and their attempts to justify the idea that they "discovered" Africa.'

When we came to a map of North Africa, the guide said: 'This map was drawn in 1486, about a hundred years after the Amalgamated Map of the Great Ming Empire.' Though names of towns and rivers were indicated on the map, its southern part was marked 'an unknown land' and southern Africa was not on the map at all. 'This clearly proves the ignorance of the Europeans concerning southern Africa,' said the guide.

Another map, drawn in 1535, entitled Map of Part of New Africa, included Africa from the equator to the Cape of Good Hope. In this map, the fairly clearly drawn coastline reflects the Europeans' intense interest in the coastal areas. The interior of the continent bears a description of three kings who ruled there, along with a picture of an elephant and two snakes. 'The snake is used in the Bible to indicate an unknown area inhabited by monsters,' said the guide. A further indication of the mapmaker's meaning is even more starkly expressed in the words of a note on the side: 'Area of barbarians'.

A third map was the complete Map of Africa, drawn between 1544 and 1545, after Portuguese navigators Bartolomeu Dias and Vasco da Gama had sailed round the Cape of Good Hope, when it was believed that Europeans had 'discovered' Africa. Even so, the figure of Africa in the map is of abnormal shape. There are great disparities between the map and reality, including a description of 'single-eyed people' inhabiting the interior of the continent. This demonstrates the obvious bias and ignorance of the cartographers.

A treasured map from Japan

At the World Economic Conference in Tokyo in 1988, Dr Frene Ginwala (who later became Speaker of the National Assembly of South Africa) was meant to fulfil a specific task: to enquire among high-ranking officials from China and Japan about an ancient Chinese world map, which was supposedly kept in a Buddhist temple in Japan. Her agenda was to present facts to rectify the erroneous belief that it was Dias who had 'discovered' Africa.

The reason Ginwala was so drawn to this ancient Chinese map was that it really was an extraordinary piece, the earliest known world map to have accurately depicted Africa.

Events had been unfolding for some time. In 1969, a Professor Zheng, from Washington University, had delivered a lecture in Canada in which he spoke of an ancient Chinese map of the world that distinctly depicted the African continent. It had been made in 1402, three years before the first of Zheng He's fleet's voyages on the Western Ocean. Ginwala was a historian with a keen interest in collecting and researching maps, particularly ancient African and world maps. Hoping to find this particular map, she sent a special assistant to the US in 1988 to ask Professor Zheng where the map was. He said he believed it was kept in a temple in Japan.

Ginwala tried everything she could think of to find the map, hoping to provide the South African people with historical evidence of the friendly communications between China and South Africa. Painstaking effort is always rewarded. In this case, after repeated visits and investigations, the map was finally found in the library of a Japanese university. In 1999 the university gave Ginwala a high-resolution copy of the map, fulfilling her dream after many years of searching for it.

There is an intriguing story behind how the map found its way to Japan. Drawn by Chinese cartographer Li Kai, the map was taken to Korea by a Korean envoy. Over time, a Japanese warlord who invaded Korea plundered it and took it to Japan. After an eventful journey, it was moved to safekeeping in a temple, where it was stored in the private library of the abbot. Later, he donated it to the university.

The Amalgamated Map of the Great Ming Empire actually came in two versions. I am still awaiting research and verification concerning the first, supposed to have been made in 1389. The second was smaller than the first, and more accurate in its descriptions of Africa. Ginwala insisted on finding the earlier Chinese map of the world.

World map from the Chinese government

In November 1999, then chairman of the National People's Congress of China, Li Peng, gave Ginwala a special gift during his visit to South Africa, a copy of the *Ancient Chinese Atlas* (Ming Dynasty volume), which showed a copy of the 1389 version of the Amalgamated Map of the Great Ming Empire on the first page. Given her knowledge and appreciation of ancient maps, Ginwala was overjoyed to receive the treasure after her long search. Praising the cartographic skills of the Chinese people from 600 years earlier, she asked for permission from China to display the map at the South African exhibition, to provide the public with a first-hand representation of Africa before the arrival of European colonialists. The Chinese government promptly agreed to her request.

In 2002, the then Chinese ambassador to South Africa, Liu Guijin, told me in an interview that the original version of the Amalgamated Map of the Great Ming Empire, which was produced in silk and kept in the First Historical Archives of China, is the largest and most complete ancient map of the world in China. It is a national historical and cultural treasure, but due to its huge size and the effect of ageing, it was not fit for exhibiting, though it was still in its complete form. The map exhibition had been scheduled in South Africa during a summit conference on sustainable development, and Ginwala asked Premier Zhu Rongji for China's assistance to enable the map to be exhibited.

In response, China decided to produce for the South African exhibition a copy of the Ming map. In an effort coordinated by China's Ministry of Foreign Affairs, the State Archives Administration, the Dunhuang Research Academy and Zhejiang

University, experts carefully made a digital replica of the map, a faithful copy of the original in appearance, size and colour.

On 1 November 2002, the map was placed in the hall of Parliament. Senior ANC researcher and special assistant to the Speaker of the National Assembly Heindri Bailey carefully opened the map with gloved hands. As soon as the African continent came into sight, Ginwala could not hold back her excitement at seeing such a distinct, exquisite piece of work, exclaiming, 'Africa is now before your eyes. I do not claim to be an expert, but the image on the map is an exact copy of the actual Africa.' Nelson Mandela was likewise delighted when he visited the exhibition in Cape Town and had a look at the Amalgamated Map of the Great Ming Empire.

Accurate depiction of Africa

The map covers a large territory, with the area under the control of the Ming Dynasty at its centre, Japan to the east, Europe to the west, Java to the south and Mongolia to the north. There are no distinct boundary lines between territories on the map; territorial divisions are indicated by colour. The map indicates positions of administrative areas, mountain ranges, towns, villages and other place names. There are over a thousand names in all.

The map features Manchu script for the names, without a single Chinese character, besides the title of the map at the top: Amalgamated Map of the Great Ming Empire. This title was deliberately added to the map by the Manchu rulers to indicate their conquest of the country when the Qing Dynasty replaced the Ming.

On the African part of the map, mountains, rivers, lakes and capes are a very close reflection of African topography in terms of their position and relation to one another. Pointing to the lower left-hand side of the map, the guide told me: 'This is the African continent, with its distinct contours. It bears great likeness to the actual land, with the direction of the river's course close to that of the Nile, the direction of the mountain range basically identical to that of the Drakensberg mountains, and the tip of the continent consistent with the well-known Cape of Good Hope. The trees in the interior tell of thriving vegetation on the African continent. Look, this large lake in the south might have been drawn based on the Arabian legend that says "south of the Sahara Desert there is a lake much larger than the Caspian Sea".'

After a pause, he posed the question, 'Is such an accurate, detailed depiction possible for someone who has never been to Africa? European maps of Africa were drawn much later than this, but are much less accurate.'

The Amalgamated Map of the Great Ming Empire, with its faithful depiction of the African continent, its lucid lines, its natural variations of colours and shades, its picturesque marks, its great durability, its completeness and its clarity, reflects the superb skills of ancient Chinese graphic artists.

Rewriting African history

On 12 November 2002, when the 600-year-old map drawn by Chinese cartographers first appeared before the public, the ANC held a grand opening ceremony. At the event, Ginwala said: 'The Amalgamated Map of the Great Ming Empire, drawn by Chinese artists, was made a hundred years before the arrival of Western explorers. The history of the discovery of Africa by Europeans has been rewritten.'

Ginwala emphasised that the discovery of Africa was made a century before the arrival of Europeans, and that what the Chinese brought to Africa was not war and slavery but Asian civilisation. The Ming map is convincing evidence of friendly communication between Africa and China, and exhibiting the map in South Africa another example of that friendship. Ginwala expressed her hope that the South African people would know the historical facts and learn more about China and the East, further strengthening cooperation and exchange between Africa and China.

As a historian, Ginwala knew that Zheng He's voyages to Africa were made more than 80 years before Europeans navigated round the Cape. The Chinese were not only the first to 'discover' Africa, but possibly rounded the southernmost tip of the continent long before Western explorers. There were two other Chinese exhibits on display: a picture of Zheng He's fleet and a picture depicting the king of Bangladesh presenting the auspicious kylin to the Chinese emperor. The guide said that the longest boat in Zheng He's fleet would have measured 140 m, whereas the longest in Dias's fleet was only 23.5 m, one-sixth of the length of Zheng He's treasure boat.

Ginwala was also of the opinion that there was another world map drawn in ancient China around the year 1320 by the geographer Zhu Siben during the Yuan Dynasty, even older than the one on display in South Africa. In *Science and Civilisation in China*, Joseph Needham mentions that Zhu Siben indicated the African continent in his map.[1] Two other contemporary geographers, Li Zemin and Shi Qingrui, correctly depicted Africa as an inverted triangle on their Large Coverage Map and Complete Territorial Map, each with dozens of place names, and made much earlier than those of the European geographers. South African historians are now studying this period carefully.

After visiting this exhibition about China, in a foreign land, I felt excited. I had had my doubts as my guide led me into the ANC Research Centre, but the researchers there offered convincing evidence. As shown by the Amalgamated Map of the Great Ming Empire, Zheng He's navigational chart, large quantities of ancient Chinese porcelain and the historical fact of the king of Malindi presenting a giraffe to the Chinese emperor, it is indisputable that the Chinese were the earliest foreign explorers to reach Africa. The great scale and advanced equipment of Zheng He's fleet also strongly suggests the possibility that the Chinese navigated to the Cape of Good Hope before European sailors. Even so, some Europeans are not willing to admit that fact, since to do so would be to acknowledge that they were lagging behind China at that time, economically, technologically and in national strength. On the contrary, they want to justify their invasion and colonisation of Africa with a theoretical basis. Nevertheless, as historical facts are unchangeable, many insightful Westerners have expressed their respect for these historical facts, and most of the world's people will surely come to doubt the fallacy that Africa was first discovered by the Europeans.

A ZULU KING JOKES ABOUT HIS QUEENS

My car crept along the highway towards the interior as sugar-cane plantations, cornfields and orange orchards appeared in turn through the window. The green fields were dotted by groups of thatched igloo-shaped structures. Row upon row of short, tidy papaya trees impressed us with their bountiful fruit and thriving vigour. With raindrops pelting the car windows, and cattle roaming casually in the middle of the highway as vehicles patiently waited for them to make their way, I found myself in a typical rural scene, tranquil and lovely. This was the nurturing land of the Zulu people, the largest black ethnic group in South Africa.

The vehicle was wending its way up and down hills. As we reached the bottom of a basin from the top of a hill, in the distance there appeared a typical traditional African architectural complex, the Zulu palace in eNyokeni.

The Zulu king had five queens living in five palaces dozens of kilometres apart. The queens did not interfere with one another and would only gather on special occasions. This traditional palace seemed graceful and representative of Zulu culture. Perhaps this was the reason the Zulu king chose to receive us there.

The walls of the palace compound were built with logs of the same diameter, spaced evenly and in fine order, the lower ends in the ground and the middle part reinforced by brackets to make them sturdy and durable. At the sight of the king's foreign guests, the guard at the gate gestured for us to drive directly into the yard. The yard had a large circular cattle pen in the centre, with two concentric circles around it, one tidy and one messy, adding brilliance and harmony through contrast. Since cattle were the sign of wealth and social status for the Zulus, the king's cattle pen was larger and rounder than those of the common people. Beside the cattle pen were stacks of reeds, which young girls would wave to the king as they danced, a symbol of the 'triumphant return'. The ritual invoked the true story of invaders who, growing lascivious at the sight of the young girls, were beaten to death with reed stalks by the girls, who then reported their victory to the king, celebrating with a dance to the king, reed stalks in hand.

Though it seemed we were enclosed once inside the yard, a more careful examination revealed many narrow passages leading to numerous igloo-like structures. The central passage led to a thatched house where a BMW sedan was parked. I was struck by the juxtaposition of modernity and tradition. The king and his youngest queen stood at the door to the reception room, warmly greeting Yu Zeming, Chinese consul to Durban, as their 'brother'. They happily took a picture with Yu and his wife, Hou Bing.

The reception room consisted of three sections, a lobby, a dining hall and a bar. Being in a good mood, the kindly king created a relaxed atmosphere. I brought the king a replica of a Terracotta Warrior cast specially for him. He looked at it carefully, stroked it admiringly, and placed it in the centre of twelve British statues, saying that those were a gift from the British royal family. I joked that the Terracotta Warrior had become 'king of British kings'.

The king gestured for us to take our seats in the lobby. The unique layout of the lobby greatly interested us. The king's throne was a red sofa with a leopard skin beside it, a symbol of prestige, power and strength. The red sofa was opposite a special seat for the queen, and there was a long sofa beside both of these for guests. The centre of the floor was covered with a colourful carpet, the end of which had Zulu handicrafts such as woodcarvings and braided tassels – it was all very dazzling.

On the walls were thirty or forty photos that told of the glory of the royal family. The king took pride in introducing these photos of his family to his guests, a sort of 'opening remarks'. The king's introduction informed us of the history of the Zulu Kingdom. The wise, brave King Shaka kaSenzangakhona, or Shaka Zulu, four generations earlier, founded the Zulu Kingdom through heroic struggles, the king told us. The grandfather of the current king had fought the British invaders with various tactics. Fearing the weapons and ammunition hidden in the palace, the British demolished the site and dug deep into the ground in search of them. The king's grandfather moved the stones of the palace dozens of kilometres away, reconstructed it and later participated in the founding of the ANC.

While the Zulu king was introducing his family history, I said to myself that the British had left no stone unturned, plundering everything precious. I had intended to see if there was any ancient Chinese porcelain in the palace, but it seemed that was a lost cause.

After the lecture on his family history, the king invited us to have dinner with him. The dining room was furnished with two dining tables arranged in a line, each large enough to seat more than 10 guests. The king gestured for us to help ourselves to the food. We replied, 'Ladies first.' Just then, a female servant on her knees arranged the knives and forks for the king, then the queen came over to serve his food. The dinner had eight courses, including roast beef, chicken, steamed pumpkin, a South African spinach purée, salad and steamed rice – basically Western food with African flavours. Our conversation began with the diet of the king, who was mostly a vegetarian, eating only a little chicken or beef. He did not usually eat breakfast, only lunch and supper. He drank mostly mineral water. 'I have a special liking for Chinese tea,' he said, 'especially ginseng tea, which is an effective refresher, though not very tasty.'

When we asked about physical exercise, the king smiled and said that he often took a walk around the palace in the morning or at night, or exercised on a treadmill or exercise bike. He went hunting on holiday and, on occasion, was a 'lead dancer'. He said, 'Zulu dance not only boosts morale, but also builds up the dancer's muscles.' With his moderate diet and proper amounts of physical exercise, the 55-year-old Zulu king looked much younger and stronger than his age.

My visit to the royal palace had been arranged months earlier at the wedding ceremony of Princess Nandi Zulu, during which the king said he would visit China and then I would be invited to his royal palace after his trip to China. As it was now shortly after his trip to China, our topic naturally shifted to his travels. In April 2004, the Zulu King, King Goodwill Zwelithini kaBhekuzulu, visited Beijing, Shanghai, Guangzhou and several other cities, and was deeply impressed by China's Reform and Opening Up, especially by the vigorous development of agriculture and the measures taken to solve the basic problems of food and clothing. During his visit, which had been at the invitation of Fujian Province, he reached some agreements of intent. He told me, 'My trip left a wonderful, deep impression on me. The Chinese government has solved the problem of food for a country with a population of 1.3 billion. This great achievement has real significance to us as a reference. China's mushroom-planting skills, modern chicken farms, and reasonable development and utilisation of land and traffic infrastructure are all of interest to us and merit study and emulation.'

He paused, then added, 'A king should be concerned and anxious about his subjects. Enhancing people's livelihoods is always my priority, and I have been enlightened by China as to how to solve such problems.'

The Zulu king does not hold real power, but is a figurehead and representative of the 8 million Zulu people in South Africa, with authority or status in name only. The democratic regime in South Africa has reserved a position for the Zulu king, and the Constitution has ensured him the benefits of a vice-premier. This provision, made by the new government at the beginning of South Africa's democracy, was understood and supported by the people as a symbol of respect for kingship in a modern democratic country, for the sake of social stability, national cohesion and the good of the nation. Although he does not have an official post, he was as busy as the next man. During our conversation, he frequently answered calls. He was unhurried and calm. He even took the time to sign his name in the royal commemorative albums given to us as gifts.

The king gestured for us to have dessert, and our conversation shifted from domestic affairs to the international situation and the Iraq crisis. It was 19 March

2003, just before the outbreak of war. When we asked his opinion, he replied, 'If I or any other head of state demanded the Bushes, father and son, to leave the country within a fixed time, would that work? Is there any justice or morality in this world? Does international society observe any objective standards?'

'What can we do to stop them?' I asked.

He smiled. 'We can all go to Korea.'

After the meal, as the king walked out of the house, a female servant fell into a prostrate position and the two beside her went down on their knees. The male servant beside them took off his shoes and sat down where he was. Once the king had walked past them, they returned to their original positions. It was a royal custom for subjects to fall to their knees or onto their front or buttocks at the sight of their king. After a while, he came out of the front room with his youngest son in his arms, smiling. When I asked the age of the prince, he smiled and replied, 'He was born on 5 July last year, the day the African Union was founded. His name is Langlanu, meaning "union".' We each held the prince in turn, but when I took him from the king, the baby screamed, making everyone in the room laugh.

When the laughter had died down, in the relaxed atmosphere, I asked the king, 'May I be blunt with you?'

He nodded, smiling. I said that, as he had visited the Forbidden City in Beijing, he knew that the Chinese emperors had their wives and concubines living together, but that he had five queens in separate places. I asked why.

He replied, 'It is to keep me closer to the people. Going to and fro between the palaces keeps me in their sight. Otherwise, they would have little opportunity to see their king.'

'Are you worried there will be rivalry between the queens?'

'I am not trying to avoid problems among the queens. If there are any tensions, they inevitably surface at gatherings.'

I probed further into his private affairs. 'The king of Swaziland has eight queens. Do you plan to have more than the five you already have?'

He smiled and said, 'No, at least not for now. But I am still young.'

In this delightful relaxing atmosphere, three hours had passed without us realising it. We rose to say goodbye, but the king, still in high spirits, insisted we should stay longer. But we were in a hurry to start our journey and needed to leave. The king took out a great number of souvenirs, gave them to us, and took group photos with us by the gate, explaining that some of the souvenirs had not been packed properly because the queens were too busy to see to it. The king and queen saw us to the gate, shook hands with each of us, and happily waved goodbye as we drove away.

Leaving the royal palace, we felt a little sorry we had only seen the king's fourth and fifth wives, missing out on the other three. But we felt he was an easy-going man, amiably sitting on his 'throne' and smiling. We enjoyed the delightful day at his palace.

SOUTH AFRICA'S ZHENG HE VILLAGE

In February 2005 the Chinese ambassador, Liu Guijin, told me there was a Zheng He Village in South Africa. Overjoyed, I asked for more information. Ambassador Liu explained that a politician had told him at an ANC ceremony that there was a Zheng He Village 80 km from Port Elizabeth, and that the residents there had light skin and long hair, that they looked more like ethnic Chinese than locals and lived a lifestyle more common to Chinese people, which had been passed down from their ancestors.

Because the village was in an undeveloped rural area, the road leading to it was unsuitable for ordinary vehicles. The politician offered to take Ambassador Liu to the village in his own off-road vehicle, but I had to postpone my visit there when I could not get in touch with the politician, as I would not have been able to find the village without his help.

I had previously been to Port Elizabeth and visited a farm in the Eastern Cape, home to a species of Boer goat, but had not heard tell of a Zheng He Village there. News of it filled me with joy and curiosity. From the information provided by Ambassador Liu, I estimated the position of the village in relation to Port Elizabeth and East London. It was probably a small fishing village, I reckoned, because there was a rather large population of early Overseas Chinese in Port Elizabeth and East London. I contacted Professor Baojin Zhao, dean of the Geology Department at the University of Fort Hare, near East London. When I told him the nature of my enquiry, he said enthusiastically, 'There are two local students in the department who look very much like Chinese people. Now that you mention the Zheng He Village, I think there might be some connection.'

The university was closed for vacation, but after several phone calls, he managed to contact one of the two students. Unfortunately, the student knew little about his family history. With Professor Zhao's help, I located a professor of history at the university who provided me with information about Overseas Chinese in Port Elizabeth.

In my search for information about the exact location of the Zheng He Village, I called on several of the veteran members of the Overseas Chinese community. The Chinese population in South Africa can be divided into two categories – early and new. The early Overseas Chinese were the descendants of those who had come to South Africa over 100 years ago, now the third, fourth and fifth generations. According to historical records, the first Chinese people to arrive in Africa came in 1658, when the Dutch East India Company needed labourers to construct their base in Cape Town. They transported thousands of prisoners, some of them

Chinese, to South Africa from Indonesia. These 'criminals in exile', generally people unable to pay debts, became the first batch of Chinese settlers in South Africa.[2]

In the early part of the 19th century, the British replaced the Dutch as rulers of the Cape Colony. At that time, the Chinese population in South Africa was less than 100. The British authorities, badly in need of cheap labour for construction projects, transported 50 Chinese artisans from Guangdong to South Africa in 1815. Arriving in two batches, the first, including 23 workers, were smuggled in by an Englishman named Captain TT Harington. In response, the Cape governor, Lord Charles Henry Somerset, decided to bring in a similar number of Chinese workers.[3] Profiting from the low cost, diligence, capability and obedience of the Chinese workers, the British authorities recruited an additional 250 Chinese labourers between 1849 and 1882, distributing them between their two colonies, the Cape and Natal, to work as contracted labourers. Most of these returned home when their contracts expired.[4]

With the discovery of diamonds and, later, gold in South Africa, groups of miners swarmed to the country between 1867 and 1886. Many Chinese people, lured by their dream of gold, left China and travelled to South Africa to seek their fortune. According to incomplete statistics, between 1888 and 1898, about 1 800 Chinese people travelled to South Africa by way of Mauritius. These gold miners, the first Chinese immigrants who came to South Africa of their own accord, formed the early Overseas Chinese population in South Africa. They were categorised into two groups, the Hakka and the Cantonese, each of which retained their own lifestyle and dialect. Now, most of the former live in the mining towns of Johannesburg and Pretoria, and the latter have settled in Port Elizabeth, East London, Cape Town and other coastal cities.[5]

Under apartheid in South Africa, the Chinese and other Asian people, like black people, were exploited and oppressed by the racist white regime. Chinese people were forbidden from owning assets and from independently operating in certain trades. Chinese-operated restaurants or shops had to be registered in the name of a white person, who would then profit from the enterprise without putting any effort into it. The language barrier, along with their shortage of capital, added to their misery in this alien land. Under these arduous conditions, the Chinese realised their potential for survival and development through hard work.

With the new democratic dispensation in South Africa, and especially since the establishment of diplomatic relations between China and South Africa in 1998, bilateral relations between China and South Africa have continued to develop and deepen. The Chinese population in South Africa has rapidly increased, and their social status is also on the rise. The new Overseas Chinese, who arrived in South Africa over the past 20 years or so, are different from the early Chinese community in terms of education, age and experience in life. Different as they are, the two groups are united and have coordinated their efforts in generating success and making positive contributions to the economic development and social progress of the nation. Their diligence, wisdom and hard work have won the respect of the local people.

As news of the Zheng He Village got around, both early and new Overseas Chinese were excited. Many of the elderly people were as surprised and enthusiastic about the news as I was, making numerous calls to contact members of the community who might have some information.

The information suggested that, though we had not managed to determine its location, the village did exist, because it was supported by archaeological discoveries made by various academic departments. In the border area between South Africa and Mozambique, Song Dynasty earthenware had been found. Among Bushman rock paintings, figures have been found wearing pointed, Chinese-style hats. A few years earlier, Chinese porcelain ware and other daily items pre-dating the Song Dynasty were discovered by archaeologists at the foot of Table Mountain. All of these are evidence of a Chinese presence in early times. In a research paper titled 'Early Chinese mariners, Natal and the future', South African scholar David Willers writes: 'The first batch of newcomers to the renowned Table Mountain were a Chinese emperor's sailors. They, under the leadership of Zheng He, the imperial eunuch of the Yongle Emperor, came to Africa before 1431 and navigated around the Cape of Good Hope.'[6]

WHO FIRST FOUND A ROUTE AROUND THE CAPE OF GOOD HOPE?

Many people hold two erroneous ideas about the world-renowned Cape of Good Hope. One is that it is at the southernmost tip of the African continent, the other that it was 'discovered' by Europeans. In 1988 some Europeans and white Africans held ceremonies in celebration of the 500th anniversary of the 'discovery' of the Cape of Good Hope by Bartolomeu Dias. Commenting on this, Nelson Mandela said ironically, 'Long before the arrival of Europeans at the Cape of Good Hope, we Africans had been here.'

Of course Africans had long been there, but which foreigner was the first to navigate it? In light of continuous discoveries of ancient cultural relics, and studies and scientific findings by experts and scholars, the idea that Europeans 'discovered' the Cape has been shattered. At Cape Agulhas, about 150 km east of the Cape of Good Hope, at the southernmost point of the African continent, I visited a sunken-ship museum that contained recovered items from the Cape of Good Hope and its immediate waters. Exhibited there were broken ship hulls, rusty anchors, everyday necessities for ship life, life buoys and almost everything one could imagine. I noticed that most of the recovered porcelain was made in China, some of it inscribed with recognisable Chinese characters.

In *Shipwrecks and salvage in South Africa*, the author lists the locations and dates of about a thousand shipwrecks. As the Preface points out,

> This book of course does not include all the shipwrecks along the South African coast. The first shipwreck occurred in 1505 when a Portuguese ship, fully loaded with spices from India, sank in Mossel Bay on her way home [...] Apparently, this is not the first ship that sank in South Africa. Long before this shipwreck, Chinese porcelain ware had been discovered in South Africa. Chinese fleets were very likely to have navigated around the Cape of Good Hope earlier than 1420.[7]

To explain why no sunken Chinese ships had been discovered in South African waters if Chinese fleets had been the first to navigate around the Cape of Good Hope, the author offers the following explanation: 'The ancient Chinese sail boat building industry represents the world's supreme level in shipbuilding, a level not attained in Europe until the 19th century.'[8]

Historical records indicate Zheng He's fleet was large and had sturdy ships. Gong Zhen, an attendant of Zheng He, wrote in his *Records of Western Ocean countries*: 'The treasure ships are grandiose and unparalleled in size, with sails, anchors and rudders that take two or three hundred sailors to operate.'[9] *The history of Ming records*: 'The ships, 44 zhang long, 18 zhang wide, and 62 in number, set sail from Liujiahe, Suzhou.'[10] Converting the measuring units of the Ming Dynasty, Zheng He's ships were 138 m long and 56 m wide, with a loading capacity of 2 500 tonnes and a displacement of 3 100 tonnes for the largest ship.

To fulfil the mission of navigating the Western Ocean, Zheng He built a huge oceangoing fleet that was unprecedented. The fleet consisted of a treasure boat, a water boat, an official boat, a horse boat, a food boat and a battleship, all of sound structure and coordination. In each of his ocean voyages, 62 ships formed the main body of the fleet, a record number of vessels.[11] There were more than 208 ships deployed on the first voyage – the most on any of the seven missions.

By contrast, Italian navigator Christopher Columbus had only three ships in his fleet, and the flagship, *Santa Maria*, was less than 100 tonnes in displacement when he sailed to America in 1492. Portuguese navigator Vasco da Gama had only four ships in his fleet when he sailed in 1497, which were all less than 25 m in length and had a loading capacity of about 120 tonnes. These were the best-equipped boats in Europe at the time. When Da Gama returned to Lisbon, less than half his men had survived, and when Ferdinand Magellan returned to Spain after his voyages, few of his men remained on the ships. Zheng He, on the other hand, brought back not only most of his sailors, but also many foreign envoys, safely to China. This suggests there was great disparity between China and Europe's shipbuilding skills, navigational science and technology, and nautical knowledge.

Some scholars, after in-depth study and field investigations, agree that the first navigation around the Cape was made by Zheng He's fleet, and not by European sailors. They believe the Europeans navigated the Cape of Good Hope only after obtaining Zheng He's navigational charts. Gavin Menzies was convinced of this fact when he wrote his book about the events of the voyage.[12]

When Zheng He's ships arrived at Calicut, India, in 1421, Niccolò de' Conti, a young Venetian merchant, was there.[13] He had studied Arabic in Egypt, married a Muslim woman, converted, and travelled to many countries as a Muslim merchant. He made the acquaintance of the Chinese sailors, boarded a Chinese ship at Calicut and travelled safely to Sofala (part of modern-day Mozambique), then travelled south and west, round the Cape of Good Hope, and arrived on the West African coast.

De' Conti took with him the nautical knowledge he had gained and several copies of the Chinese nautical charts. He gave one of these charts to Fra Mauro, who was working for the Portuguese royal family. Mauro, in turn, gave the chart to a Portuguese prince, Henry the Navigator, who was fascinated with navigation. Mauro had printed De' Conti's travel notes and, in 1459, drew a world map based on the Chinese nautical chart. In this world map, he accurately represented the triangular shape of the Cape of Good Hope, which he called 'Cap de Diab'. He drew there a picture of Chinese sailing boats and made a note, describing Chinese sailors involved in organising and restocking activities at the Cape of Good Hope, or 'Cap de Diab', and making special mention of the sailors' discovery of large birds (ostriches) and their eggs. Hundreds of years have now passed since that time, but the ostriches are still there, extending their necks to greet visitors.

Because of Niccolò de' Conti, the original nautical charts drawn by Chinese cartographers were copied, redrawn, reprinted and circulated in Venice and other European cities. It was called a nautical map in some places and a world map in others, depending on the translator's choice.

In 1428 Dom Pedro, Prince Henry's older brother, brought home a world map to Portugal from Venice. While in Venice, Pedro had bought a world map, which depicted all parts of the world. On the map, the Strait of Magellan was named 'the Dragon's Tail', and the Cape of Good Hope was called 'the Cape of Boa Esperance', an alternate name for the Cape of Good Hope, along with 'the forefront of Africa'.[14]

From this, it is evident that, in 1428, 60 years before the Europeans made their first navigation around the Cape of Good Hope, the Strait of Magellan, the Dragon's Tail, and other well-known marine communication hubs had already been drawn on world maps.

To validate his theory, Menzies travelled around the world along the route he believed Zheng He's fleet had taken and estimated that the date of the Chinese fleet's navigation was August 1421, travelling at a speed of 6.25 nautical miles per hour after it left Sofala. Menzies believes that Zheng He's fleet not only reached the Cape of Good Hope, but also the American continent, marking humanity's first circumnavigation of the globe. He and other Western experts have offered substantial evidence for these views.

When famous navigators such as Columbus, Dias, Da Gama, Magellan and other European explorers made their voyages, it seems they carried with them copies of Zheng He's navigational charts. Because the Cape of Good Hope and the American continent were marked on these charts, these navigators located the places by following the charts – they did not make the first navigations around the Cape of Good Hope, it seems, or discover a new continent, or 'discover the world'. Their names were left in history because they followed the footsteps of a forerunner, and their fame is based on their forerunner's attainments.

Menzies and some other scholars around the world are crying out for this part of history to be corrected:

> Those men should have attributed their success to the Chinese people, the earliest explorers, the epoch-making navigators who made the first ocean voyages in the 19th through 21st years of Yongle's reign, AD 1421–1423 [...] The Portuguese led a European upsurge of exploration and colonisation. Of so many countries, Portugal was the greatest beneficiary of the endeavour and pursuit of the Chinese for new lands and new waters.[15]

It is widely acknowledged that the Chinese initiated these oceangoing navigations, but they did not continue after Zheng He. After his time, Europeans took advantage of the nautical knowledge the Chinese had accumulated, including Zheng He's nautical chart, and started another seafaring era. On the negative side, this brought Asia and Latin America under savage conquest and initiated the African slave trade and endless disasters, leaving a painful scar on human history. On the positive side, it continued great geographical discovery, helped trigger and promote development in industry and trade, and provided a broad and profound impetus for the progress of human history.

It should be pointed out that the impact and significance of Zheng He's seven voyages go far beyond navigation. Chinese expertise in navigation, and mastery of navigational science and technology, enriched the knowledge store of humankind, promoting the development of human civilisation. Is it too much to acknowledge Zheng He's expeditions as the 'fifth great invention'[16] that ancient China contributed to the world?

12

Northward search for the Zheng He Monument

GRUNTING HOGS BESIDE CAPE CROSS

Our car travelled along the sandy coast, which looked like a plateau of a dark golden-yellow colour, the vast desert on our right and the stormy sea on our left, with the sea's white-crested waves crashing onto the shore. The blue sea was veiled from sight by a heavy fog. Far ahead was an endless stretch of desert. Misty rain from the cold Benguela current fell on the windscreen and was swished away by the wipers, revealing the reach of our headlights.

The Namib Desert stretches from north-western South Africa in the south to south-western Angola in the north, running the length of Namibia's coastline. The desert landscape along the Namibian coast is quite unique. The Benguela current emanating from the Antarctic seas and the invasion by Western colonialists have added detail to the desert, including Cape Cross, Seal Island, Angling Bay, the tourist city of Swakopmund, and the large port of Walvis Bay.

Cape Cross is 115 km north of Swakopmund. Being in a desert, the tarred road we drove along was covered with fine sand. There were no road signs or residential buildings interrupting the endless desert. Because we had not counted the miles since leaving Swakopmund, our guide was filled with misgivings. He had once overshot Seal Island by 100 km, he told me. A house came into sight, so we stopped to ask the way. Three dogs barked, summoning our host, a tall white man, from the house. Before we had even opened our mouths, he held up his hand and, with fingers spread, said, 'Three kilometres ahead.' It seemed his household had become a living road map for confused travellers.

When we got out of the car at Cape Cross, a strong, foul smell greeted us, the offensive fishy smell of the seals. Amid the roaring Atlantic waves stood a cross made of granite blocks, aged, alone and mottled. In 1486, Portuguese adventurer Diogo Cão had first landed here. In memory of his discovery and the expansion of Portuguese territory, he built the cross with in that desolate, barren cape and named it after the Portuguese king, John I. The place has been called Cape Cross ever since.

Over the next 500 years, Western colonialists, under all guises, landed at this 'bridgehead' and from there staged all their ugly schemes for the cruel plunder of Africa. In 1878 British colonialists seized Walvis Bay. In 1892 German colonialists took Swakopmund. In 1915, the white racist regime of South Africa invaded and occupied Walvis Bay, when it was mandated by the allies to annex South West Africa (now Namibia), given German hostilities around the time of World War I. It was ironic that thousands of seals were on the beach in this now world-renowned tourism area, barking loudly day and night as if angrily condemning the colonial invasion and its rule for hundreds of years.

Over 100 000 seals live on the plankton at Seal Island. Across the beach and over the low partition wall, seals of different sizes were huddled together on the shore, in the seawater, and between reefs, grunting like hogs or bleating like sheep, calling, courting, teasing, abusing and attacking one another, or seeking milk from their mothers. Lazy, fleshy and clumsy, most lay idle on the beach between the reefs, paying no heed to anyone else. A few wiggled their bodies forward, looking quite amusing and clumsy. Watching the seals, I could not help but think that whoever had translated the name into *haibao* (sea leopard) in Chinese must have never seen a seal; *haizhu* (sea pig) would be more appropriate.

According to the guide, an average male seal weighs 187 kg, with the heaviest weighing 360 kg, while an average female weighs 75 kg. Seals follow the rule of the jungle, with one male generally mating with between five and 25 females, on a beach or in the water. A seal's gestation period is nine months. A female seal gives birth to one cub at a time, weighing 4.5 to 7 kg at birth and covered with short black fur. Seals are fat creatures, and have a high daily food intake, consuming 8 per cent of their body weight. A male seal eats an average of 15 kg of fish every day, and a female eats 6 kg of plankton.

The reason I thought the seal would be more fittingly called 'sea pig' was not because of its fat or its diet, but because of its friendliness toward humans. Even when a human is up close, they will not attack. They live in harmony with people, and are quite willing to be photographed close to humans, just going about their own business as if nobody were there. When people clap their hands or shout, the seals will respond in kind.

The Namibian seal is unique among the world's seal population. They are classified as haired or eared seals, one of three haired species along the southern African coast. Seals in other parts of the world are without both hair and auricles. These seals have two layers of hair, one long and thin, and the other short and thick. Seals are warm-blooded animals with a body temperature of 37 °C. When they prey on food in the sea, the outer layer of hair protects them from the cold Benguela current, and their body temperature remains constant in currents that originate from the cold southern seas, whose temperature is 10 to 15 °C. Their inner thick fur and their thick flesh and surface layer of fat insulate them against the cold currents when they spend long periods in the water. Their four limbs are wing-like to increase buoyancy when swimming, and strong enough to support their body weight when waddling on land.

The cold Benguela current, the nemesis of the seals, provides them with abundant food in the form of a large variety of plankton. This is the main reason the seals prefer this particular coastal region, and why they have developed layers of fur – which, incidentally, makes their skins valuable to humans. There is a row of buildings built as sealskin shops for tourists. Sealskin, like ostrich skin in South Africa, is made into leather caps, shoes, belts, handbags, briefcases, leather jackets and fur coats. Whole sealskins for interior decoration and ornaments are also available. Sealskins are not expensive, at just RMB 300, which was about $40 at the time, and they were pure, shiny, soft, durable, warm and pliable.

Rare things are precious, while abundant things are cheap. Large numbers of seals at this site provide a large volume of sealskins. Because the seals there are not endangered, the Namibian government allows an annual catch of 3 000 young seals, to maintain the ecological balance in the tourist area. This has led to low prices for sealskins. It seemed ridiculous to me that one could even buy fly swatters made of seal skins.

FLOWING OIL AND GLITTERING DIAMONDS

Nature has endowed Angola with abundant natural resources. It is home to mineral reserves such as petroleum and natural gas, and diamonds, in which it ranks first in Africa. It also has sizeable reserves of iron, copper, gold, marble, granite and quartz – over 30 mineral types in total. It has fertile land, criss-crossed by rivers, and a climate suitable for growing many tropical and subtropical crops, including coffee, sugar cane, cotton, sisal hemp and peanuts. Angola has become the fourth leading coffee producer in the world. With 50 million hectares of dense forests, it also produces ebony, African sandalwood, narra and other valuable timber. Hydropower and marine resources are abundant, with many rivers to provide ideal irrigation conditions for agricultural development and generation of hydroelectric power. With a coastline of 1 650 km, Angola is one of the African countries with the most abundant marine products, averaging 0.6 million tonnes a year. This used to be a main pillar of the national economy.

An official from the Angolan Ministry of Telecommunications and Information Technology told me that his country had great potential for economic development, with oil and quartz as the country's pillar industries. Oil prospecting in

Angola began in 1906, but oil wells did not come into operation until 1955. With the discovery of huge oil reserves in the Cabinda Gulf in 1966, oil's contribution to the national economy grew rapidly, replacing coffee as the number one export from 1973 onwards. In 1975, when Angola gained national independence, it had been the third largest oil producer in Africa, next only to Nigeria and Gabon. Now it is the second largest oil-producing country in Africa, with a daily output of 1 million barrels at the time of writing. In recent years, new offshore oilfields have been discovered with a total reserve of 17.7 billion barrels. Alongside oil, natural gas reserves are as large as 50 billion m³.

In 1912 diamonds were discovered in Angola, and excavations began five years later. Before World War II, diamonds had been the country's major export item. After the war, diamonds gave way to coffee. Today, after oil, diamonds are the largest export. Angola's diamonds are first-rate in brilliance, colour and purity. Diamond ore is concentrated in the northern and north-eastern parts of the country.

Unfortunately, the endless flow of oil and the glitter of diamonds lured Western colonialists, eventually becoming their property, an object for them to exploit and a source of lucrative profits for their wallets. Since 1482, when the Portuguese explorer Dias's fleet arrived at the estuary of the Congo, they targeted this oil-rich, glittering, fertile land. The Portuguese, Spanish, British and Dutch colonialists came one after another and began their evil slave trade, with Angola serving as an unfailing source of black slaves.

In 1576 the colonialists began building Luanda, from where they proceeded along the Cuanza River into the interior, extending their evil hands to the highlands. Over 3 million black people were sold in the slave trade at different times to Portugal, Brazil and Central American countries. For Angola, the abolition of the slave trade in 1836 and its formal termination did not bring about any substantial changes because, under the guise of contract labour, large numbers of Angolans were still under cruel oppression and exploitation.

By the 19th century, as a result of their crazed plundering of the land, the colonialists had obtained an accurate map of the Angolan territory. At the 1884/85 Berlin Conference to determine how to divide Africa among the colonialists, Angola was designated as a colony of Portugal. In 1922, Portugal occupied the entire territory of Angola, and the abundant mineral resources went to the Portuguese.

In the 1950s there was an upsurge in resistance to Portuguese colonial rule in Angola, and three national liberation organisations were formed: the People's Movement for the Liberation of Angola (MPLA); the National Front for the Liberation of Angola (FNLA); and the National Union for the Total Independence of Angola (UNITA). In the 1960s huge armed struggles for national independence unfolded. In January 1975, the three national liberation organisations achieved mutual recognition in Mombasa, Kenya, and on 15 January, they signed the Alvor

Agreement with the Portuguese government, marking Angolan independence. On 31 January, a transnational government was formed. However, in August 1975, the three nationalist organisations fighting for control of Luanda entered into armed conflict and disintegrated the cooperation. On 11 November that year, the MPLA announced the founding of the Angolan People's Republic, which the other two parties refused to recognise. The other two organisations planned to found an Angolan Democratic Republic in the name of the coalition government, but because they could not reach an agreement, UNITA unilaterally announced the founding of the Angolan Black People's Democratic Republic in Huambo. The next year, the armed wing of the MPLA defeated the FNLA forces and drove UNITA forces out of the city.

An official from the Angolan Ministry of Petroleum told me in an interview that his country had been mired in civil war because the government and anti-government forces each controlled one of the country's two main economic resources – petroleum and diamonds – which served to finance the war. Despite the UN's punitive measures on arms and diamond embargoes against UNITA, some countries acted out of their own interests to maintain contact with UNITA, ensuring it a continued financial flow for long-term armed struggle against the government.

Fortunately, Angola is now seeing the glimmer of peace. As President José Eduardo dos Santos said on 11 November 2000, the 25th National Day:

> With social and economic wounds resulting from the forty-year war, Angola is crying for peace and progress. We are pressing toward this goal and our government is going all out to create an atmosphere of peace so the nation can march toward reconciliation, economic stability, and development. We have put forward a solution in light of the great challenges the nation is facing.

On 22 February 2002, the government troops defeated UNITA leader Jonas Savimbi, ending the 27-year-long civil war.

In June 2006, Chinese Premier Wen Jiabao visited Angola with a government delegation. At the time of the premier's visit, Luanda presented a new look of peace and prosperity for national reconstruction, entirely different from the situation a decade earlier. Li Zhaoxing, who was with the premier as minister of foreign affairs during the visit, wrote the following poem:

An aria for Angola

After thirty years of confusion
A new century born of chaos

Civil war bred costly reconciliation
Foreign aggression opened the national consciousness

A lowland aims high
For solidarity and development,
The supreme bliss of the nation

On 21 June 2006, I flew out of Luanda (which means 'lowland'). Angola, a country abundant in natural resources, is known as the treasure bowl of southern Africa, but nearly three decades of civil war, in contrast to this natural backdrop, stagnated the economy and made the people's lives hard. A decade later, I found it in an encouraging stage of peaceful development.

SLAVERY MUSEUM ON THE COAST

About 30 km south of Luanda, a building stands alone on the Atlantic shore, its foundation washed by roaring waves from the sea. An ancient melody of sea winds fills it. On a misty morning, I walked up the stairs and entered this weather-beaten building, the National Museum of Slavery.

The two-storey structure, less than 100 m^2 in area, is a record of the history of the brutal, inhuman slave trade, of the struggling cries of millions of black slaves, their indignation and helpless tears of humiliation. The museum director told us that the colonialists brought slaves here from all over, detained them in ships, and sold them across the Atlantic in America. They began their miserable life in this place of utter darkness. This museum marked the site where they stepped into an abyss, never to return to their homes.

There were not many objects in the museum, so the ground floor was closed. We climbed a steep, narrow staircase to the second floor. A number of pictures greeted us. One depicted a slave in irons, head thrown back in defiance of a white colonialist as he cried, 'I am a human being, not a beast.' The iron-faced colonialist, pointing his gun at the slave, forced him to move forward. Below the picture was a set of guns that had been used to capture slaves and suppress slave resistance.

Between their landing in Angola in 1482 and the completion of the construction of Luanda in 1576, the Portuguese began to penetrate into the interior of Angola, where they started their evil business of slave trading. On the heels of the Portuguese came the Spanish, Dutch and British. In the initial period of the slave trade between the 1400s and 1580, colonialists and slave traders organised so-called hunting teams to capture slaves by violent means. As casualties were common, due to resistance from the black tribes, the colonisers resorted to all sorts of sinister, ruthless schemes. They created conflicts and stirred up fights between the tribes, hoping the surviving captives would be sold as slaves. Other methods included finding agents among the upper classes of the black communities, providing them with weapons to bring their subordinates under control, thus facilitating their slave trade and the profits ensuing from it.

Beside the guns on the floor were sets of ball and chains, which, like the cangue (wooden collar) at the centre of the floor, were used to prevent the slaves from escaping while at sea. If a slave tried to jump into the sea, the iron ball would pull him to the bottom, and his hands would remain helplessly motionless. When the slave trade was rampant, the black African people were in a tragic condition. A black person, once captured, was delivered to a slave trader, who drove slaves into a closely guarded, crowded stronghold, clapped in a wooden collar and shackles, and chained with other slaves to prevent escape as they waited for the ships that would carry them away. There were almost 100 slave-trading posts, large and small, along the 6 000-km stretch of coastline between Cape Verde and Angola. They still stand today as historical relics.

A shabby room in the basement of the museum was the gate to hell, where slaves were led to board the ships, the small ferry door opening onto the water. The stone threshold was worn shiny by the feet of countless slaves, their last footprints on their homeland. Looking over the endless waves of the blue sea, our faces were caressed by the breeze as we sighed. The museum director said in a heavy tone, as if to himself: 'They began their long voyage here, some were tortured to death, and more died in an alien land, ending their helpless, miserable lives. The evil slave traders overloaded their ships with slaves, packing them like sardines in a can. They died of disease and neglect.'

This was why slave-trading ships were called a floating, living hell. Thus, millions of black slaves stepped into endless, inescapable suffering. As living commodities, they were sold to American and Caribbean plantations, and gold and silver mines, living a dog's life until they died. The slave trade took a triangular route. The first leg of the cycle was slave-trading ships bound for Africa, loaded with cheap industrial products which were traded for black slaves. In the middle leg, the ships transported the slaves across the Atlantic to sell them at a high price, and the return voyage saw ships laden with raw commodities, liquor and other goods from the American colonies sailing back to Europe.

This museum is a weighty textbook of human history. When people thumb through its pages with a heavy heart, it unfolds before their eyes facts and data that fill them with mixed emotions. In their book *Angola*, Douglas L Wheeler and René Pélissier note: 'Over several centuries, the total number of black people shipped out from Angola as slaves reached two or three million, according to conservative estimates, but four million is perhaps more accurate.'[1] In pursuit of wealth, the Western colonialists earned their fortunes through the slave trade, causing Marx to say that 'Africa became a commercial centre where black people were hunted'. The slave trade was one of the main sources for the accumulation of capital in Europe.[2]

Chairman Mao said, 'The supreme evil of colonialism and imperialism thrived along with slavery and the trading of black people, and will only end with the thorough emancipation of black people.'[3]

The cruel facts of history show that the skyscrapers of the Western powers are soaked in the blood of black slaves. The slave trade not only helped amass large amounts of early capital but also supplied plenty of cheap labour for the development of capitalist industry. At the same time, this great calamity in human history interrupted the social progress of Africa, destroyed its original social foundation, plundered its labour force, sabotaged solidarity among its people, deepened class polarisation of African society, and led to the resultant stagnation of social development. The colonial rule that followed the slave trade was like adding snow to frost for the African people.

In 2001 the blood debt owed by Western powers to the African people became the theme of the third UN assembly against racism. Faced with just and reasonable demands for an apology to be given to the African people for the slave trade and compensation for colonial rule, the former colonialists shied away, offering evasive, vague answers and trying to cover up the facts, fearing that an 'apology' would require 'compensation' from their own pockets. They are too foolish or stubborn to see that what the African people value is their dignity, which was trampled on, and not the money in someone else's pocket.

MONUMENT TO A NATIONAL HERO

In late February 2001, during my visit to Kinshasa, capital of the Democratic Republic of the Congo (DRC), I kept noticing the tall monument to Patrice Lumumba, the country's first prime minister after its independence and a great national hero. The monument is a reminder of the contributions Lumumba made to national independence and liberation, and of his persistent patriotic spirit in winning national sovereignty and unification.

The DRC was formerly part of the Kingdom of Kongo. The Berlin Conference defined it as the 'private domain' of the Belgian king, calling it the Congo Free State. Lumumba was born to a poor farming family in Sankuru County in 1925. He studied at a Christian school for a short time, then transferred to a vocational nursing school, where he read extensively and was heavily influenced by European bourgeois democratic ideas.

In 1943, at the age of 18, Lumumba left home to earn his living. He first worked at a mining company in the capital of Maniema Province. The following year, he went to Kisangani, to work as an assistant taxman in a post office. As a reward for excellent service, he was sent to Léopoldville (present-day Kinshasa) to study, where he graduated as an outstanding student. In August 1948 he returned to the post office in the capital, where he played an active part in the political movement for independence. He published articles in journals and newspapers to expose and denounce the reactionary Belgian colonial authorities, and was eventually imprisoned in 1956. His book *Congo, My Country*, written in prison, systematically unveils the crimes the Belgian colonialists had committed against the people of the DRC.[4]

After a year behind bars, he popularised his ideas about national independence as he worked as a beer seller, and he founded the Mouvement National Congolais (Congolese National Movement – MNC) in October 1958, guided by the principle of national defence and ethnic solidarity. In December of the same year, he attended the first session of the All-African Peoples' Conference, where he delivered a speech that strongly denounced colonialism and called for a rapid move towards national independence. 'National independence is not a gift given to the Congo by the people of Belgium, but a recovery of the last rights of the people,'[5] he said. He expressed his will for the immediate realisation of national independence. Lumumba's speech was warmly applauded, but the celebration was cruelly oppressed by colonial authorities, and ended in a bloody massacre. The people of Congo's demand for justice shook the foundation of colonial rule, and the Belgian king agreed to work toward independence for Congo, saying it would be done 'without delay, but without haste'.

In October 1959 Lumumba presided over the MNC, which called for a discussion between Congo and Belgium about national independence. He also got the support of several allies to help popularise and lobby for the movement. A rally that he took part in was cruelly suppressed and Lumumba was arrested, this time on the pretext that he was stirring up a revolt.

All countries want independence and liberation, and the people want revolution. This great historical impetus can never be stopped. Amid an irresistible cry for justice, the Belgian government was forced to release Lumumba in January the following year, attended a round-table discussion, and agreed to the national independence of Congo on 30 June 1960, ending 75 years of Congo's colonisation.

In the election leading up to independence, the MNC came out the winner. Lumumba was voted prime minister, and the Alliance des Bakongo Party chairman, Joseph Kasa-Vubu, became president of the country now renamed the Republic of the Congo, also referred to as Congo-Léopoldville.

Just a month after independence, a nationwide anti-Belgium struggle broke out, with rioting among black soldiers in the Congo security forces who could not stomach the insults of their white officers. The Belgian government, on grounds of safeguarding its nationals, resorted to force, resulting in a bloody conflict and national secession. Lumumba called for UN intervention. The UN, under US manipulation, did all it could to protect the Belgian army, ending in more rampant separatist activities. To maintain national sovereignty and unity, Lumumba announced that the country would be placed under military rule for the next half year.

It was then that an acute, irreconcilable conflict broke out between the prime minister and the president. On 5 September 1960, the president announced dissolution of the cabinet and, on the same day, Lumumba announced his non-recognition of Kasa-Vubu's presidency and declared the president's cabinet dissolution invalid. The armed forces of the two parties prepared for war, and gunfire was exchanged in the capital. UN Secretary General Dag Hammarskjöld said at the UN Security Council meeting: 'The Lumumba government is illegal and nonexistent, and Kasa-Vubu is entitled to dissolve the cabinet.'[6] With this, Kasa-Vubu issued an order to have Lumumba arrested. On 14 September, the army chief of staff, Colonel Joseph Mobutu, launched a military coup and temporarily took over the government. On 2 October, Lumumba published a speech, stating that the evil hand behind his removal from office had been the US, which was intent on obtaining uranium from Congo. Lumumba was placed under house arrest at the prime minister's residence.

On the night of 27 November 1960, Lumumba escaped the prime minister's residence in pouring rain and went to Orientale to propagate his nationalist policies. He was heartily welcomed by his supporters. Four days later, news of his arrival had got round. He was arrested again on false charges and, while incarcerated, subjected to all sorts of cruel torture. On 12 December, the pro-Lumumba vice-premier, Antoine Gizenga, acting in his office, proclaimed that Lumumba's government would be moved to Stanleyville.[7] From that time, the two governments in Congo have been there in opposition, neither acknowledging the other. Seeing Lumumba grow in power, the Léopoldville authorities stepped up their persecution.

On 17 January 1961, a mysterious plane flew to Elizabethville with three special passengers on board. The trio were tied together, each of them beaten black and blue, and each blindfolded. Upon landing, they were pushed into a waiting car. The three men were Lumumba and two of his comrades in arms, Joseph Okito and Maurice Mpolo. Soon after, the scheming authorities announced that they had escaped from prison. A few days later, it was announced that they had been found killed by villagers near the airport.

Lumumba and his comrades were killed in cold blood. In February 1963, though an investigation group consisting of Myanmar, Mexico, Ethiopia and Togo was established by the UN, it was not allowed to enter Congo to investigate the crime scene, due to interference from the Congolese authorities. As a result, the death of Lumumba and his comrades is a mystery waiting to be solved. Some say that they were shot execution-style, others that they were thrown into sulphuric acid, others that they were buried alive. Since facts have not yet come to light, none of these theories can be verified.

People have a clear memory of Lumumba's farewell letter to his wife:

My dear wife,

I wonder if this letter will ever reach your hand, or if I will still be in this world when it does. Ever since I committed myself to the cause of independence, I have never doubted the final victory of our sacred cause, to which my comrades and I have contributed all we have. Our sole ambition for our country is that she be a nation with significance, dignity, and independence.

But this is not the will of Belgian colonialists and their Western allies. Such people, directly or indirectly, openly or covertly, are supported by high-ranking officials of the United Nations. We placed our full trust in this international organisation when we requested assistance from it, but it has cheated some of our compatriots, bribed them, and perpetrated all manner of evils.

I have put aside life, death, freedom, and prison. I have my compatriots and my motherland in my mind. We are trampled underfoot, but we are not alone. People in Africa, Asia, and the world are with us, supporting us in our struggle until our final victory.

No cruel torture or flogging or insult will make me yield. I would rather die with my head held high than live in humiliation or give up my sacred principles. History will tell the truth in the end. It will not be narrated by Brussels or the United Nations or the United States, but will be told by the people, the winners of history.

Long live Congo! Long live Africa!
Patrice Lumumba
Thysville Prison[8]

This farewell letter, full of patriotism, internationalism, heroism, awe-inspiring righteousness and great faith in victory is so thought-provoking, inspiring and worthy of respect that Chinese military commander Marshal Chen Yi composed a poem in response:

Reading Lumumba's farewell letter[9]

4 March 1961

A modern-day hero, Lumumba
Admired by the people of the world
His blood shed
To irrigate Africa's floral plain

> The People's Congo, such small demands
> Only resisting aggressors and traitors
> Great Africa awaits the dawn
> Under the brilliant banner of Lumumba
>
> Defense of territory is a rule
> With no willing concession of land
> Every drop of fantasy, poison
> Proved in the bleeding letter of Lumumba
>
> Inspecting the Congo murder
> The killer's time-killing scheme
> Cheating the world's people, and the killer too
> Bringing down a west wind, and a setting sun

The murder of Lumumba filled the people of the world with righteous indignation and initiated an upsurge of protests against such brutal acts. On 15 February 1961, the Chinese government issued a public condemnation denouncing the murder: 'This atrocity of the old and new colonialists is a petty, cruel attack on the cause of national independence for Congo and all the African people, and is a severe challenge to the peace-loving people of Asia and the world.'[10]

On 18 February, grand rallies of more than 500 000 people were held in Beijing to denounce the murder of Lumumba. Flags flew at half mast out of respect.

Forty years later, after a two-year inquiry, a Belgian Parliament investigation committee came to the conclusion in November 2001 that, despite the lack of evidence of Belgian government participation in Lumumba's murder, some Belgians did participate in hostile acts directed at him. The Belgian Parliament had allotted a secret fund of 270 million Belgian francs to support the factional opponents of the Congo government.

On 5 February 2002 the Belgian government made a formal apology for the murder of Lumumba. Belgian Minister of Foreign Affairs Louis Michel, in a speech made to Parliament, said that the Belgian government offered its profound apology to the people of Congo and to Lumumba's relatives for the pain caused by his murder. He said that some Belgian government officials had been 'unsympathetic' to Lumumba, that they were 'indifferent to his fate' and that the Belgian government 'could not shirk' its responsibility for the death of Lumumba. The Belgian government made a decision to establish a Lumumba fund of €3.75 million to support the DRC in preventing conflicts, strengthening the rule of law and training youth, as a form of compensation for the blood debt caused by the murder.

Lumumba and his comrades gave up their lives for independence and the unity of their motherland, composing a triumphant song of patriotism. Their spirit is an eternal encouragement to the people of the DRC and everywhere, challenging all people to overcome difficulties and obstacles in their advance towards national independence and sovereignty, and towards the final victory of their lofty cause.

ZHENG HE MONUMENT ON THE BANKS OF THE CONGO

Some scholars believe that, after navigating around the Cape of Good Hope, Zheng He's fleet headed north along the West African coast aided by the Atlantic Benguela current and the south-eastern trade wind, that they stayed for a time at the estuary of the Congo River, then put in at the Cape Verde Islands by way of the Gulf of Guinea, whence the fleet then navigated in a south-western direction, driven by the north-eastern trade wind, sailing south along the South American coast to the southern end of the South American continent by way of the Strait of Magellan, and then returned across the South Atlantic to the Cape of Good Hope.[11]

In the DRC, the heart of Africa, the 4 640-km Congo runs through the whole country and flows into the Atlantic Ocean. Before merging into the Atlantic, the Congo, with the might of all its tributaries, forms the famed Yellala Falls. Next to a pool of clear water below the falls, there stands a stone monument. According to studies by experts, the stone monument was built by Zheng He's fleet in September 1421.

Because the falls are close to the river estuary, large ships could travel upstream as far as the falls, anchor in the beautiful environment, replenish their fresh-water supply, rest and make preparations. For hundreds of years, navigators have made short stops there. I travelled to Kinshasa so that I could see the monument with my own eyes. At the time, the DRC was in a state of war, however, with fighting between government and anti-government forces. Turbulence prevailed throughout the country. The Congo was only partly open to navigation because of the conflict. The section between the capital and the estuary was blocked. Feeling disappointed, I was unable to visit the spot I admired so greatly.

According to documents, besides the monument at the Yellala Falls, there was another similar stone monument in Cape Verde, often called the Janela Monument or the Pedra do Letreiro (Portuguese for 'inscribed stone monument') by the local people.[12] The monument was of red sandstone texture, about three metres tall, and inscribed from top to bottom. Like the Janela Monument, the Matadi Stone Monument on the Congo was also covered with inscription. The inscription was in two parts, the upper in medieval Portuguese, apparently added in memory of a sailor who had died on the voyage. The lower inscription was illegible due to ageing and weathering, and damage from recent years.

British scholar Gavin Menzies had sent photos of the lower part of the inscription to Chinese and Indian experts for identification. The Chinese experts replied to the effect that there were not any Chinese characters inscribed on the monument. The photos were also sent to Indian experts, the rationale being that large-denomination banknotes in India contain 13 official languages, and Zheng He was known to use many languages when setting up his monuments, including several Indian languages. The Indian Bank experts confirmed that the inscription was written in Malayalam, a language used in Kerala, with Calicut as the capital, a place where Zheng He stayed over during all of his ocean voyages. This language, though used only rarely now, was commonly used in India from the 9th to the 15th century.

Zheng He's fleet respected local customs and employed interpreters who spoke many languages. In 1421 during the sixth voyage on the Western Ocean, the fleet sailed towards the East African coast by way of Calicut. It is reasonable to assume that perhaps the fleet had interpreters of the language commonly used in India. This would be further evidence that Fra Mauro and Niccolò De' Conti were right. They pointed out that before the arrival of the Portuguese, an oceangoing ship from India or China had arrived at 'Garbin', meaning where the Yellala Falls was, and at Cape Verde on another occasion.

Based on the above theories, Menzies writes: 'It is easy to explain: The inscriptions in the Matadi Falls and Janela Monuments were made by the interpreters in the Chinese fleet, just as the interpreters made inscriptions in foreign languages [in] other places.'[13]

For Western colonialists, it was common practice to take other people's property for their own, after some reshaping, and the same had happened to the Yellala Falls and Janela monuments. In America, too, Western colonialists remade buildings of the Native Americans into their own churches. It should be pointed out that the Western colonialists, to satisfy their desire for Eastern spices, gold and wealth, committed monstrous crimes – burning, killing, raping and plundering, committing all sorts of evils on their navigation to the east.[14]

According to historical records, Vasco da Gama, upon his arrival at Calicut, ordered his attendants to insult any opponents they encountered and cut off their hands, ears and noses, and then had the severed organs stacked in his boat. When an envoy came for peace talks, the 'brave' da Gama had the envoy's lips and ears cut off and replaced them with dog's ears.[15] This was just one example of the cruelty of the Western colonialists. As Menzies says,

> The Portuguese, using Chinese maps, found a route to the East. They usurped the spice trade that had taken the Chinese and Indian people hundreds of years to establish. All objectors were eliminated [...] the enlightened Chinese people were educated to cherish people who come from afar, but what replaced the Chinese were the cruel, savage Christians, the colonialists.[16]

Zheng He's fleet was committed to peace, equal exchange, fair trade, and the popularisation of civilisation, which still remain on the lips and in the hearts of the local people. Such great achievements and contributions as those made by Zheng He in his seven voyages on the Western Ocean will forever live in the memories of the people of the world.

Zheng He's seven voyages on the Western Ocean also make it clear that China has never been, and will never be, a threat or a menace to anybody. It has not plundered the wealth of others, nor invaded or occupied an inch of others' territory. Even to this day, some ill-willed people are biased against China, fabricating the idea of a 'China threat' in an attempt to curb China's development. In the face of hard facts, such imaginary fears and fallacies will have no place.

13

Travelling in the interior of Africa

CHINESE PORCELAIN IN A STONE-AGE CITY

With safety my paramount concern, I had been unable to visit to Kenya's Pate Island or Somalia in January 2000, so I decided to make a roundabout return journey. During my visit to Zimbabwe in January 2000, I visited the National Art Gallery in the capital, Harare, and saw ancient Chinese porcelain fragments that had been unearthed from the ruined city of Great Zimbabwe dating from the 11th to the 16th century. This drew me to Great Zimbabwe.

About 270 km south of Harare are the remnants of an ancient stone city. It is the renowned site of the origin of the Kingdom of Zimbabwe and the cradle of its national culture. The reporter in me was attracted by its reputation, but I also wished to fulfil my own special mission of following Zheng He's footsteps.

It was sunny when I set off from Harare in the early morning of 17 January 2000, but the sky soon grew cloudy. By the time I reached the stone city, drizzle had given way to heavy raindrops. As I arrived, the stone tower, faintly visible from some distance moments earlier, retreated from sight, hidden by the rain.

Situated in a hilly area, Great Zimbabwe is spacious, tranquil and beautiful. It consists of three parts – the Hill Complex, Valley Ruins and the Great Enclosure – each unique, yet all harmoniously integrated. With heavy rain pelting my umbrella, I started up the steep, rugged ancient stone steps to a narrow passage just wide enough for one person to pass, formed of two separate, massive stones. This was 'the only road since ancient times' and 'a pass that one man could guard against ten thousand', as the Chinese sayings go. This military post was easily defended, but difficult to attack. Close to the top of the hill, a tall wall constructed of granite blocks met our eyes, with a stone gate through which just one man could pass. Legend says that this enclosure was where the first king lived. A small building still stands in the middle of the enclosure. On the western wall stood four solid cylindrical beacon towers. According to the local people, there had been seven, but three were now missing. Below the northern wall was a small stone gate that led to the 100-m-high watchtower, which overlooked the whole expanse of the site, offering a view that confirmed the creativity and originality of the architects.

Looking at the beacon tower from the watchtower, where I stood in the endless rain, I could not help but reflect on the grandeur and magnificence of the Great Wall of China. Seeing the seamless stone wall here, built without mortar, still straight and sturdy after so many centuries of corrosion by wind and rain, I could only admire the superb architectural skill of the Zimbabwean people who had built it. Taking in the ruins of this architectural complex of 10 000 *mu*,[1] its past grandeur now lost, I uttered a sigh of regret, just as I would at the Yumen Pass or Yang Pass sites on the Great Wall of China.

Viewed from the watchtower, a complex made up of buildings of different sizes was visible at the foot of the eastern wall. This was part of the Hill Complex, where the king, queen, concubines and attendants had lived. A peculiar cave in this ancient regal palace functioned like a loudspeaker. A person shouting into it could be heard by people in the distance. One can imagine that the king's instructions, state laws and decrees were amplified to the people from this spot, serving as evidence of the Zimbabwean people's skill in applying basic acoustic principles.

To the south-east lies the Valley Ruins, made up of 42 smaller constructions, of which two are worth mentioning. In one was discovered the Zimbabwe Bird, a 40-cm-tall sculpture of a bird atop a stone pillar. The bird, with the head of a dove and the body of an eagle, signifies totem worship, like the dragon in China. It has become the national symbol of Zimbabwe, depicted on the national flag, the national seal and the currency – until it was replaced by the US dollar. Carved out of a special African stone, the chimeric bird holds its neck high and its wings close to the body, standing proud on top of a 1-m pillar. The Zimbabwe Bird, the most precious cultural relic excavated from the Great Zimbabwe site, is believed to have once ornamented the Great Enclosure. Eight birds were excavated from the site, seven complete, and half of another. They had survived many dangers, troubles and looters over the years before finally returning to their rightful position.

In the same place, several other cultural relics were found, including Arabian glassware and Chinese celadon and pottery. These Chinese fragments were from the 14th and 15th centuries, two of which were the bottoms of large celadon vases, imprinted in celadon glaze along the centre of the bottom rim with six Chinese characters: 大明成化年制 (Made in the Year of Chenghua of the Great Ming). This provided evidence of direct or indirect communication between China and Zimbabwe in ancient times, with Chinese commodities travelling as far as southern Africa. The question of whether these porcelain pieces had any connection with Zheng He's fleet awaits further study and verification.

Ancient terraced fields and irrigation facilities, such as ditches and wells, were also discovered by the side of the relic site. In the foundations were ancient mud moulds for casting coins.

At the south-eastern end is the oval-shaped Great Enclosure, with a wall around it built of granite blocks. The wall is 10 m tall, 5 m thick, and has a circumference of 225 m. According to historical records, there had been settlement centres of fairly large size around the site in the 5th and 6th centuries, which reached their peak in the 12th century, when the construction of Great Zimbabwe was under way. The Hill Complex was the earliest of the structures, and the Great Enclosure was constructed later, around the 14th century, and is the most magnificent of all the structures. At that time, there were about 15 000 residents living in Great Zimbabwe, including the king and his family of about 100 wives and 1 000 children. The Great Enclosure is said to have been built for the royal family.

There are entrances and exits on the north-eastern, southern and northern sides of the Great Enclosure. A 90-m-long semicircular interior wall forms a narrow passage between the interior and exterior walls, leading to the exit through the enclosure gate. At the beginning of the interior wall, a conical stone tower 20 m in height and 5 m in diameter stands erect and magnificent. This solid tower is the symbol of Great Zimbabwe. Its architectural features are identical to those of the rest of the complex, built with dry-stone blocks without any kind of mortar. Since there are no written records about the tower, its use remains unknown. Today, there are five theories, however. The first, based on the tower's barn-like shape, sees it as a symbol of a bumper harvest and wealth. The second, judging from the function of the Great Enclosure as the royal residence, views it as a symbol of kingly authority. The third theory, noting the fact that an altar was discovered near the tower, views it as a religious symbol. The fourth, taking into account its shape, assumes it is a symbol of masculine culture. The fifth says it must be a watchtower, given its height. All of these theories are based on supposition and not well grounded in evidence. Archaeologists today, unable to provide convincing evidence of the architect's true intent or the stone's real meaning, can do nothing but leave it as an eternal mystery, since Western excavators a century earlier had dug a metre and a half into the ground beneath the Great Enclosure. After this disastrous move, the Great Enclosure was no longer what it had once been, and some historical evidence has been irretrievably lost when the sites were destroyed by the excavators.

Not only is the actual use and reason for the structure a mystery, but who built it also remains unknown. Because there are no written records about or inscriptions at the relic site, the question of who created this great cultural artefact is open to dispute. Some believe it was built by a Western power, but they can neither provide evidence of this nor explain the need and use for such an architectural complex, making the idea seem like nothing but a flight of fancy. Emergent theory that the structure was built by Africans, rather than Europeans or Arabians, has become increasingly popular.

A Chinese poet has observed that 'rise and decline, like birth and death, are natural occurrences, according to the laws of nature'.[2] Similarly, towards the end of the 15th century, the Great Zimbabwe complex began to decline, and eventually the magnificent structures fell into ruin. Nevertheless, it is the largest ancient southern African architectural site, the brainchild of the diligent, wise African people, a symbol of brilliant African culture, and a piece of historical evidence of the brutal plundering of Africa by colonial powers.[3] In 1986 Great Zimbabwe was recognised by UNESCO as a World Heritage Site, and it has since become a renowned tourist destination.

CHINA AS A VALUABLE GUIDE

The Burundian minister of economic planning, development and reconstruction, Professor Andre Nkundikije, said to me during an interview on 2 March 2002:

> Let me take the opportunity to express two sentiments. First, we are thankful to the Chinese people for their consistent, warm support and assistance. Second, the reconstruction and development of Burundi should take China's successful construction as a guide. We welcome more Chinese enterprises to participate in the reconstruction of Burundi, and our door is always open to the great nation of China.

Burundi is one of the world's least developed countries. In 1999 it had a per capita gross national product of $187, ranked 204 in the World Bank's 206 listed countries and regions. Because of continued political crisis since 1993 and the 30-month-long economic sanctions imposed by its neighbours following the 1996 political coup, compounded by occasional disturbances from the Hutu anti-government forces from foreign bases, the economic situation is in continual decline, and the people live in misery.[4]

According to official statistics, the gross domestic product of Burundi in 2000 dropped by 20 per cent against the figure in 1992, and 60 per cent of its people are living below the poverty line. In that same time span, the average lifespan dropped from 53.8 years to 34 years, and primary-school enrolment fell from 67.3 to 52 per cent. The country was locked in a serious international payment imbalance, with high debts and a shortage of foreign exchange. Its total foreign debts exceeded $1 billion by 2000. At the same time, millions of people became refugees in other countries. The minister indicated that the goal of reconstruction was to level the national economy and people's livelihoods by the end of 1992.

Nkundikije said that, since Burundi was progressing towards peace, its national reconstruction and development should include both material and spiritual growth, involving political, economic, cultural, social and other forms of development:

> In the economic field, we should first find solutions to the problem of everyday water and power supply. Highway construction should be resumed to provide a solution to the transportation of agricultural produce. We should carry out agricultural deep processing to provide a solution for the storage of agricultural products. We should invigorate the development of fishing resources to speed the growth of the fishery industry. We should not only provide our people with enough food, but should also earn foreign exchange through exports. We hope to share China's successful experiences in the development of the agriculture and fishing industries.

He added, 'Burundi is a country that has agriculture and animal husbandry as its pillar industries. We hope to duplicate China's experience in industrialisation and make a successful start to industry in Burundi.' He cited the Burundi Bujumbura United Textile Mill as an example to illustrate the need for and the success of economic cooperation between the two countries. The mill was the largest joint enterprise integrating spinning, weaving, printing, dyeing and clothing manufacturing. It had thrice won gold medals at the Madrid International Exposition. Since its establishment in 1979, the company had played an important role in satisfying the people's demand for clothing, earning foreign exchange through exports and promoting the development of the national economy.

As founder and part-time professor of the Burundi University of Economic Administration, the minister was eager to see stronger cultural and educational exchanges between China and Burundi, and continued assistance from China in training economic and technical professionals to help Burundi raise its employment rate. He pointed out that the Kamenge Handicrafts Training Centre in the capital, Bujumbura, had been established in 1985 with assistance from the Chinese government. By the end of 2001, it had organised four training sessions, with a total of 136 learners receiving training in bamboo furniture weaving, bamboo utensil weaving, vine weaving and carpentry. Each time, the Chinese government provided specialists and financial aid, and the Burundian government provided supporting funds. Most of the graduates from such training classes took up jobs in their respective fields, becoming the wage earners in their families and earning the admiration of their community. 'We are thankful to China for providing us with such a training opportunity,' the minister said. 'We look forward to strengthened cooperation and exchanges in the field of education and promoting the development of our educational and cultural causes.'

A short while later, when I returned to Lamu and Pate islands, I saw everyday utensils being made by the local people from coconut leaves. The weaving method, and the size and shape of the utensils, were exactly the same as those I had seen in Burundi. They all had distinctly Chinese characteristics. The minister said:

> While we are thankful for the sincere and friendly assistance China has sent thus far, we also look forward to more Chinese enterprises and businesspeople coming to Burundi for investment. The door of our country is always open to China in all fields. For instance, in the financial field, there is enormous potential for cooperation.

At the end of the interview, he said: 'We admire the great achievements made by China, and we are eager to take China's successful experiences as a guide. We warmly welcome Chinese participation in the national reconstruction and development of Burundi.'

At the invitation of Endayichi Jeye, president of the Burundian News Agency, I visited the agency's simply furnished news office. The president explained that, in May 1999, the Burundian News Agency and the Chinese Xinhua News Agency had signed an agreement for news exchange and cooperation:

> This will provide the Burundian people with information about great changes that take place far away in China, and with opportunities to learn from the Chinese people's successful experiences. It will add courage and confidence to our people in their struggle to overcome poverty and to reconstruct our nation. At the same time, it will provide the Chinese people with information about what is going on in Burundi. We are determined to march toward peace and national reconstruction.

In an effort to achieve lasting peace and begin national reconstruction, in 2000, Nelson Mandela, serving as the Burundian peace-negotiation mediator, had proposed that a conference be held in Paris for assisting nations. Concerned nations and international organisations expressed their willingness to provide Burundi with $440 million for its post-war reconstruction and to help free Burundi from its debts by ensuring that funds would be used in the economic development of the nation. The visionary Mandela also persuaded the World Bank to provide financial aid to 30 young Burundians for their studies in economics, in the hope of cultivating talented people to lead the nation's transition from an agricultural to an industrial economy. He also persuaded six of the world's most prestigious universities to grant scholarships to a number of young Burundians to assist in their studies of economics. As Mandela said, this would 'lay a sound foundation for the economic development of Burundi'.

In his interview with me, Nkundikije called for immediate implementation of the pledges that were made at the Paris conference, so that funds sent in aid would be in place in due time.

A MEMORABLE HISTORICAL TRAGEDY

To commemorate the terrible genocide that occurred in 1994 and to prevent such tragedies from recurring, seven museums were set up in Rwanda. On 20 February 2001, I visited two of them, the Epimaque Museum, 60 km south-east of the capital, Kigali, and the Ntarama Genocide Memorial Centre, 40 km from the capital.

On the evening of 6 April 1994, Rwanda's president, Juvénal Habyarimana, and the Burundian president, Cyprien Ntaryamira, were on the same plane bound for Kigali after having attended a summit in Tanzania on regional peace. The plane exploded upon landing at the airport, killing both presidents and their attendants in the accident. After this event, the situation in Kigali deteriorated rapidly. The next morning, the presidential bodyguards, mainly consisting of Hutus, kidnapped and killed the premier, Agathe Uwilingiyimana, and three other ministers, then founded a provisional government. On 8 April the Tutsi anti-government forces' Patriotic Front rejected the provisional government, which had excluded them, and marched to the capital. This brought civil war to Rwanda. While the two forces engaged in bloody conflict on the political front, the two ethnic groups engaged in ruthless, brutal killings in their respective domains, which turned into widespread genocide. In just 100 days, over 500 000 people were killed in cold blood, over 2 million had fled to other countries as refugees, and another 2 million were left homeless, causing shock waves across the international community. The two museums I visited were the sites of terrible massacres during that horrific period.

The Epimaque Museum used to be a church in the town of Nyamata, with a school on one side and a hospital on the other. As I arrived, my guide pointed to a missing section of the iron gate, saying the gap had been made by bullets. During the genocide, about 3 000 Tutsis, fleeing from the pursuing, murderous Hutus, had flooded into the church and locked themselves in. The Hutus broke the metal chain, swarmed in and killed all 3 000 of them.

Entering the church, I felt horrified by the ghostly atmosphere. The pulpit was covered with a bloodstained white cloth, and the walls around it were dotted with blood. All the walls were pitted with bullets and, with its countless bullet holes, the metal roof looked like a starry sky. The guide told me the church had been crowded with people, young and old, who had hidden themselves there in the hope that God would shelter them but, unfortunately, none of the 3 000 had survived the atrocity. Standing at the site of that massacre, I visualised the crazed, bloody scene, a terrible sight that no one would ever want to recall. It was no wonder mental disorders caused by the massacres had been on the rise in recent years. To commemorate the innocent souls lost, the museum had built a basement mausoleum, where the human skulls and bones were neatly arranged in glass boxes.

Following the guide, I came to the back of the church, where three huge basement rooms were filled with the bones of the victims of massacres in the surrounding area. When the plastic cloth at the entrance was lifted, the smell of a newly opened ancient tomb filled my nostrils. Several minutes later, I entered the basement, which was partitioned into square cells that contained the bones of the victims. According to the guide, as many as 20 000 people from the area were killed in cold blood. Some had been driven to the hills, where they were tortured to death by the murderers with guns, cleavers, spears or sticks. The population in this area dropped from 125 000 in 1994 to 60 000 in 1997.

I walked through a banana grove to the Ntarama Church, which housed the museum. The two red-bricked churches in the town were simply furnished. During the massacre, the people came here to pray for protection. The signage at the site suggested that they were killed while in the act of praying. Bloodstained clothes lay scattered among rows of low concrete benches, corpses lying in a pile at the entrance with flies gathering round them. The people inside had closed all the doors and windows, but the militias, hatred burning in their eyes, broke in and turned all the windows into gaping holes. Outside the church stood a simple reed structure, in which skeletons were arranged in an orderly way on a large table. Some of the skulls still had spearheads in them.

When I left a note in the visitors' book, I noticed that I was the 12 070th person to have visited the museum.

This terrible tribal massacre shook Rwanda like a magnitude-eight earthquake, and left an equally devastating mark on the country that is still evident today in the composition of the Rwandan population, among other things. In 2001 children under the age of 14 accounted for 40 per cent of the population, and 40 per cent of the nation's women were widowed. These figures were just the tip of the iceberg. At the time of my visit, as many as 130 000 criminals involved in the massacre were being reformed through labour and were awaiting trial. Pursuing and arresting Hutu militiamen who had fled to neighbouring countries became a major undertaking that embroiled the Rwandan government in the civil war in the Democratic Republic of the Congo.

The genocide was an indirect consequence of long-time colonial rule. The Hutu and Tutsi tribes were the two major ethnic groups in Rwanda, with Hutus making up 85 per cent and the Tutsis making up 14 per cent of the population. In the 16th century, the Tutsis established a feudal kingdom. In 1840 Rwanda became a colony of Germany and, after World War I, rule was handed over to Belgium. The colonialists made use of the conflict among the local people to rule over both groups by stirring up conflicts among the two ethnic groups, sowing seeds of dissension.

Between the 1950s and 1970s, there were repeated tribal massacres that generated huge numbers of refugees, which, in turn, deepened ethnic conflict.

In the Cold War period, when the two superpowers, the US and the Soviet Union, were contending for hegemony throughout the world, including Africa, tribal, racial and ethnic conflicts were temporarily overlooked. After the Cold War, tribal conflicts suddenly re-emerged. In October 1990, a three-year-long civil war between the Hutu and Tutsi tribes broke out in Rwanda. Though a peace agreement was reached in 1993 between the two groups, it was never implemented because of profound conflicts and prejudice.

In 1994, when the president was killed in the aviation incident, another nationwide civil war broke out. It was evident that the terrible massacre was a striking expression of intensified racial conflict in Rwanda. It cost 500 000 innocent human lives to warn the world that ethnic, tribal and racial problems in a nation, a region and the world must be addressed wisely and solved. Otherwise, disturbances, wars and disaster are inevitable, as evidenced by the continuing instability and unrest in certain parts of the world.

GUARDING AN ANCIENT MAUSOLEUM

When I was in Uganda in February 2001, I visited the ancient royal palace with a view to seeing if there was any ancient Chinese porcelain there and to further my research on the history of communications between China and Africa. I was particularly hoping to uncover more information about Zheng He's voyages.

As early as AD 1 000, a kingdom was founded in the Buganda area in southern Uganda. By the middle of the 19th century, the Buganda Kingdom had become the most powerful and prosperous state in East Africa. Later, as a result of the continual wars caused by British and German invasions, the kingdom rapidly declined and Uganda became a British protectorate.

The Buganda royal palace is on top of a hill in the centre of the capital, Kampala, its grounds covering an area of three acres. In 1884 the Bugandan royal family moved there. The present structure, however, built by King Mwanga II, dates from 1924. When Uganda gained independence in 1962, the Ugandan Federation was founded, with four kingdoms re-established, including Buganda. The following year, the constitution was revised and King Mutesa II became president. In 1966 Mutesa was expelled from Uganda. The next year, the feudal kingdom system was abolished. In 1971, Idi Amin Dada staged a political coup, took over the presidency, and turned the royal palace into a military camp from where he ran the country as dictator. In 1986, Yoweri Museveni took power and restored the kingdom system in a move aimed at relieving ethnic tension and building tribal solidarity. Nevertheless, the king was now only a figurehead, a symbol of culture and tradition. The king's expenses depended on financial allocations and donations. In 1997 the palace was formally returned to the current king, Mutebi II.

The royal palace consisted of 62 rooms, each unique in architectural style. Above the gate were two sculpted lions standing erect, a symbol of Buganda kingship and prestige. Unfortunately, the palace was undergoing repair work, and I did not get to see anything special when I visited. The palace affords the best view of Kampala. The guard, pointing into the distance opposite the palace, indicated the Buganda Parliament building, accessible by a straight road that had roundabouts at each intersection for vehicles to go round as a show of respect for the king, as the king's car cut straight through. The Parliament, the royal palace and the Kasubi Tombs provided a special historical and cultural overview of Uganda.

A visit to Uganda is made in vain if one does not see the Kasubi Tombs. The tombs, on Kasubi Hill in the suburbs, is different from other Ugandan royal tombs. This tomb was the ancient palace of Mutesa I and three of his successors, all of whom are buried at the site. It also differs from other royal tombs in the country in that the king entombed there is guarded day and night by 'royal concubines'. On the afternoon of 25 February, keen to see this ancient site as well as the beautiful scenery, I followed Yu Xueyong, an official from the Chinese Embassy, to visit the Kasubi Tombs, where four kings were buried.

The gatehouse to the royal tomb is designed in a typical local architectural style – primitive and simple. There, the royal guards watch the tomb day and night. The gatehouse leads to a small courtyard, in which trumpet and drum players and other musicians live. In one of the rooms on the left was a large royal drum. Further inside was the spacious royal courtyard, surrounded by palace courts inhabited by the king's queens and concubines. Opposite the court was an enormous conical thatched structure; this is the royal tomb and former royal palace. The palace gate and the court gate stood opposite each other at some distance, separated by a straight passage. The traditional architecture was believed to enable the soul of the king to move in and out, since Ugandans believed the soul could only travel in a straight line.

Traditionally, the gate of a royal palace must face east. The palace of Mutesa I was an exception, however, because when he took the throne, the Buganda Kingdom was at war with the Bunyolo Kingdom in western Uganda. The royal palace was therefore built facing west in preparation for invasion from that direction. The location was meant to meet three conditions: providing the royal family with adequate living space; having a broad road in front of the palace gate connected with roads leading to other parts of the country; and being close to Lake Victoria, so the king could flee to the islands there in case of foreign invasion or domestic unrest.

At the palace gate, we took off our shoes, as local custom required, and entered on bare feet as a show of respect to the king. Our guide, Musokay, pointing at the concrete floor in front of the gate, told us that the palace was built in 1882, but that Europeans had used cement in its restoration and repairs in 1938. Once inside, one has the sensation of being inside half of an inverted orange peel, with concentric circles of woven coconut leaves serving as a roof. Pillars were connected to points in the roof – a form of traditional African architecture. Each of the pillars was wrapped with cloth made from tree bark to symbolise the king's clan. Such thatched buildings, made from carefully chosen, specially treated coconut-tree leaves, provide shelter from rain and sunlight. The environment is cool and cosy all year, with a grassy fragrance that keeps out insects and breezes. Local custom calls for architects to stay away from women, and women are never allowed to approach a construction site, out of a superstition that the structure will leak. Besides these observations for architects, it was also common practice for a king to cut a branch of weeds when the architect had completed the roof, like a modern-day ribbon-cutting ceremony.

The royal palace was partitioned into two sections by a reed wall. The rear section, the mausoleum of the four kings, was off limits for tourists. The front section was further partitioned into two sections by parallel wooden rods along the floor. The front section was meant for royal guests from other parts of the world, the rear section for all other guests. On the reed wall opposite the door hung portraits of Mutesa I, Mwanga II, Daudi Cwa II and Mutesa II. In front of the portrait was each king's collection of favourite weapons, including spears of various lengths, shields of various shapes and sizes, and lances.

The royal palace housed many other royal items. To the left of the front gate was a stuffed leopard, one of Mutesa I's pets, which was said to be a clever beast that had followed him everywhere like a hound, forgetting it was a man-eater. Next to the leopard were different types of drums, and in front of those were two Western-style chairs. The two chairs, along with two desk lamps on the table beside them, were believed to be made in Austria and brought over in 1887 as a gift presented to the king from the British queen. A glass showcase contained an African game called Omweso, made up of a thick wooden board with 32 round pits in four rows of eight for two players. Each pit held 32 round, black seeds from a local tree. This game had been a favourite of Mutesa I. At the end of my visit, I asked the guide to explain the rules. He and another player explained them to me in the shade of a tree in the yard in front of the palace.

While we were sitting on a straw mat on the floor of the royal palace, the old guide told us many thrilling tales of the Buganda Kingdom. Once the most powerful and prosperous state in East Africa, it was reduced to the humiliating status of a protectorate after the British invasion. The Ugandan people struggled heroically against the foreign power and finally won independence in 1962. The royal palace, too, underwent dramatic changes during this period.

There had been 35 kings from Mutesa I to Mutesa II, the last four buried together in the Kasubi Tombs. As the guide spoke to us, the women in the royal palace, the 'royal concubines', whose job was to guard the four kings, sat listening. The guide said that local custom called for a royal concubine to guard the soul of a deceased king day and night. Since a king's queens and concubines were numerous, six were generally chosen to serve as guardians of the king's soul. They were on duty in the royal palace for two months each year, on a rotation basis for each king. There were 24 'royal concubines' guarding the royal souls constantly, day and night, having meals brought to them while all the affairs of the royal palace were looked after by the queen's younger sister.

On the right of the royal palace were three concubines, two of them whispering to each other now and then; the other was asleep on the floor. When I asked if I could speak to them, the guide communicated my request to them. The one who had been asleep awoke, not knowing what had happened. Her bemused look made us all laugh.

I asked them, 'Do you want to be here all day?' They shook their heads silently. It wasn't clear whether they had really understood my question, whether they just did not want to answer it, or whether they did not want to be here as 'concubines'.

When I asked about their income, they remained silent. The guide explained to me that each was allotted a piece of land and that they earned their living by tilling the land; they were not given any special benefits.

I asked if I could take a photo of them. The guide said I should consult them and, before taking the photo, should make a donation to the royal palace. I noticed that there was a bowl on the floor with some small change in it. Although I made a donation, the women refused to be photographed. There was no point taking a photo of the tomb without them in it. Curious, I asked the guide several questions:

'Who succeeds a "royal concubine" when she passes away?'

'A young woman is selected from the concubine clan, usually her younger sister.'

'What are the qualifications for a concubine? What if one of them gets married?'

'Once she is selected as a "royal concubine", she will never marry. If already married, she must divorce.'

'With customs changing, is it possible a time will come when no concubine is chosen?'

'No, they are all from large clans. There is never a lack of young women.'

'Are they willing to become "royal concubines"?'

'There used to be more than there are now, but their clans count it an honour. Although some later gave up the privilege.'

'Why do you keep on selecting concubines like this?'

'To us, the king is immortal. Since he lives forever, he needs "royal concubines" to keep him company.'

As I walked out of the royal palace, I could not keep my mind at peace. Human history has entered the 21st century, yet such an anachronistic custom as women living as 'widows', guarding the souls of the dead, still carries on. How can people strike a balance between restoring a symbol of royal prestige, respecting traditional customs, and at the same time respecting the rights and interests of women? Where is the solution to this tangled knot? How do we find a happy medium between history and modern reality, respect for the king and respect for the women who work as his 'concubines'?

14

TAZARA Railway: Conveyor of friendship

A MONUMENT TO CHINA–AFRICA FRIENDSHIP

It was pleasantly warm in Zambia in July, and the villa in the capital, Lusaka, was blooming with flowers. The former president, Kenneth David Kaunda, just back from a 2001 summit conference of the Organisation of African Unity, granted me a special interview in his home.

This was the second time I had interviewed this old friend of the Chinese people, having previously met Kaunda in Windhoek in August 2000. I would interview him a third time two years later, in July 2003, in Maputo. In our three talks, in different places and on different themes, Kaunda always mentioned the TAZARA Railway, praising it as 'a great monument to the friendship between China and Africa' and 'an example of South–South cooperation'.

The reconstruction of the railway was the shared wish of the two countries. The original tracks had been built by colonialists to transport the local natural resources. The two old railway tracks, the Central Line and the Tanganyika Line, led to the agricultural areas in the north and west, while the country's eastern and southern areas had no railways. Zambia is a landlocked nation, and before gaining independence, its only railway line linked the Copperbelt area to Livingstone by way of Lusaka, offering access to the sea at three points: the northern line to Mombasa, via Tanzania; the western line to Lobito, Angola, by way of the Democratic Republic of the Congo (DRC); and the eastern line leading to Beira, Mozambique, via Zimbabwe. The northern line was a combined railway-highway system, consuming money, time and energy. The western line was blocked by the civil war in Angola. The eastern line offered the shortest access to the sea, at 1 547 km, and was economical and convenient, but blockades by racist regimes in South Africa and Rhodesia, and the Portuguese colonial regime, had prevented the nation's key export commodity, copper, from making its way to the sea for export. Under this great pressure, Zambia decided to join efforts with its neighbour, the newly independent nation of Tanzania, to find a solution.

Kaunda pointed out that, after independence in 1965, Tanzania and Zambia had similar ambitions: firstly, to fight imperialism and colonialism by supporting the national liberation movement in South Africa; then, to break through the blockade imposed by the reactionary colonialist regime and develop the local economy. Kaunda told me in an interview in July 2001:

> These aims called for the construction of a railway to open up a passage between Tanzania and Zambia in order to provide reliable access to the sea for copper ore and other goods from the two countries, to promote their economic exchange and development, and to support the national liberation movements in our neighbouring countries.[1]

The two countries sought aid for the construction of the railway from the Soviet Union and various Western countries, but their requests were rejected because such a railway was difficult to construct and offered poor economic returns.

In 1965 Julius Nyerere, president of Tanzania, visited China. After his visit, he said he planned to seek economic assistance from China but, since China was relatively poor and the construction of the TAZARA Railway involved a huge investment, he did not list its construction in his plan for an aid package. Unexpectedly, the Chinese government not only accepted all his requests, but also asked that if there were any other needs, he should speak frankly.

Nyerere said, 'I was a bit embarrassed, but also very encouraged, so I plucked up my courage and mentioned the construction of the TAZARA Railway.'[2]

He was overjoyed when the request was accepted by China. In an interview with Nyerere, Chairman Mao said that states that had won independence earlier were obliged to help those who won their freedom later. In August that same year, China dispatched a team of experts for feasibility investigations, and they delivered their investigation report the following June. Kaunda recalled:

> President Nyerere told me this. I put forward the same request when I visited China in June 1967.[3] In an interview with me, Chairman Mao expressed his appreciation and support for the idea of constructing the TAZARA Railway. Premier Zhou indicated that, with the determination of the leaders in Tanzania and Zambia, China was willing to assist in the construction of this railway. On my way home by way of Dar es Salaam, I consulted President Nyerere, and we decided to deliver a joint request to China for the construction of the railway.

In August 1967, a joint economic delegation was dispatched to China from Tanzania and Zambia. In Beijing the governments of China, Tanzania and Zambia signed the agreement in September on the construction of the TAZARA Railway. Nyerere pointed out then that China's aid in constructing the railway was 'a great contribution to the African people' and that 'in history, foreigners built railways in Africa to plunder its wealth. Today, by contrast, China is constructing a railway to assist us to develop our economy.'

Thirty-four years later, when recalling those past events, Kaunda could still not conceal his enthusiasm. Speaking of his interview with Chairman Mao, he said, 'Mao is a great man of this generation, and a great strategist. He supports the national liberation movement in Third World countries and helps us in economic construction. He loves the whole human race, as evidenced by the TAZARA Railway.' Kaunda indicated that the railway was an extraordinary project:

> When we were in difficulty, we received selfless support from the Chinese people. The Tanzanian and Zambian peoples will forever bear it in mind. The TAZARA Railway is not only the best symbol of friendship between the Chinese people and the peoples of Tanzania and Zambia, but also a great monument to the friendship between China and Africa.

'STEEL ZEBRA' RUNNING OVER MOUNTAINS AND RIVERS

Dar es Salaam in May had a feel of seasonal change in the 'port of peace', with cool breezes dispelling the lingering heat. I was visiting the Kurasini Railway Station in Dar es Salaam, the terminus of the TAZARA Railway.

What first greeted my eyes were the station building and large square. As I watched the black people coming and going on the square under a blue sky dotted with white clouds in this alien land, the seemingly familiar building and square freed me from the feeling that I was a stranger in a strange land. The woman from the TAZARA Railway Public Relations Unit, who accompanied me, told me that the auxiliary facilities along the railway were all made in China. 'Look at the style of the station building, the gates and everything here,' she said.

In the spacious waiting room, people carried luggage and other bulky items. It was a Friday, and there was an express train due to leave the station. Passengers busily prepared for their journeys. The station director, Harrison Fungo, showed me round the building. President Kaunda had laid the foundation stone on 26 October 1970. The interior layout and facilities were of Chinese style. On the main wall was a bird's-eye-view map of the entire railway network, which Fungo explained to me in detail.

The TAZARA Railway runs in a south-westerly direction, beginning in Dar es Salaam, capital of Tanzania, in the north-east and terminating in the south-west at New Kapiri Mposhi, in Central Province, Zambia, where it joins with track built earlier. There is a total of 1 861 km of track, 976 in Tanzania and 885 in Zambia.

Prospecting of the railway began in May 1968. Six hundred and eighty prospectors and designers were engaged in the long-distance prospecting, measuring, aligning, crossing mountains and rivers, and breaking through bush. On 16 and 18 October 1970, Nyerere and Kaunda, together with a Chinese delegation, presided over the foundation-laying ceremonies at both ends of the railway. In the period between October 1970 and June 1975, the Chinese government provided an interest-free loan of 988 million yuan (about $500 million at the time), donated 1 million tonnes of building materials and construction machinery, and 56 000 manpower hours from technicians and managers, with 16 000 Chinese labourers working on the construction during the height of the building period. The workers arrived by sea, overcoming great difficulties; fought acute shortages of medicine, doctors and food; and braved hot climates and disease. Sixty-five lives were lost in the project, all technicians and engineers. The railway was completed ahead of schedule. The 'steel zebra', as it was known, was finally galloping across the vast wilderness, ignoring predictions from the West that only buffaloes, lions and leopards could run across the African wilderness. A Western visitor to the TAZARA Railway marvelled, 'Only those who built the Great Wall of China could build such a high-quality railway here.'[4]

Pointing to the map of the railway, the station director explained to me that the TAZARA Railway is a trunk line across East Africa and central southern Africa, a single-tracked line with 318 bridges, 2 269 culverts, 22 tunnels and 93 stations, of which 16 were closed in 1994. He said:

> This railway runs through four districts in Tanzania and two provinces in Zambia, crossing the East African Great Rift Valley, which is known as the 'Scar on the Earth'. It passes over high mountains, steep cliffs, rivers, lakes, forests, steppes, and marshlands, all extremely complex topography and greatly varied in altitude. For instance, in the 502 kilometres from here to the first station, Mlimba, the altitude rises to 332 metres, but in the space of just a further 165 kilometres from there to Makambako, it rises to 1 671 metres. In the next 173 kilometres, at Uyole, the highest point of the railway, it is 1 786 metres. Twenty kilometres beyond that is Mbeya, the largest station in the border area.
>
> Starting from Mbeya, it gradually levels off along a low range of hills, then gradually rises to the Makambako Ridge, the watershed of the Ulanga River and the Great Ruaha River, where the railway makes an abrupt rise. In high mountains and lofty ranges, it snakes and winds, rising and falling, with deep valleys running almost perpendicular to the direction of the railway. It then climbs to its peak, then descends to its last station, New Kapiri Mposhi, at an altitude of 1 275 metres. The challenges in constructing the railway and its bridges are beyond imagining.

On the platform, we saw several Dong Fang Hong brand trains, built and donated by China. The station director told me that the two trains on the right, worn and damaged, were now out of commission. I walked to a passenger train that was still in service. It was divided into soft-berth cars, hard-berth cars and seating cars. Some of the seating showed signs of wear and tear. Fungo pointed to the railway tracks, each section of which bore distinct Chinese characters that read, 'Made in the People's Republic of China'.

Stepping out of the station building, we went to the memorial monument marking the 25th anniversary of the operation of the railway. This special monument in front of the square, set up on 19 July 2001, stood erect, with a locomotive chassis bearing Chinese characters that read, 'Made in 1973 by Sifang Locomotive Works, People's Republic of China'.

A TRIBUTE TO THE CHINESE DECEASED

Under the scorching sun, the cemetery for Chinese experts who had assisted Tanzania was quiet, surrounded by the fragrant grass that grew luxuriantly in the tranquil grounds. On 23 June 2006 the Chinese premier, Wen Jiabao, and his Tanzanian counterpart, Edward Ngoyai Lowassa, stood side by side before the memorial, paying silent tribute. The memorial monument was inscribed with the words 'Cemetery for Chinese experts who assisted Tanzania. They died as martyrs.' Before the monument was a wreath placed by Premier Wen, with a ribbon containing the words 'Long Live the TAZARA Railway Martyrs. Written by Wen Jiabao, Premier of the State Council of the People's Republic of China.'

These heroes had answered the party's call to aid in the construction of the TAZARA Railway, crossing the ocean to reach a foreign land, where they laid down their lives for the friendship between China and Africa. The Chinese premier travelled to the site to express the love of the Chinese people. I wondered if the martyrs were aware of this honour.

The cemetery is 24 km south-west of Dar es Salaam; the track runs beside it. There were 69 Chinese experts, technicians and workers buried there, 47 of whom had died during the construction. One of the martyrs had died on the ocean voyage from China to Tanzania. There were another 17 buried in Zambia, the youngest just 24.

After paying their respects, the two premiers walked slowly into the cemetery. The square plot of land, allotted by the Tanzanian government in 1972, covers an area of 14 000 m². Jointly built by the Ministry of Foreign Affairs of the People's Republic of China, the Ministry of Railways, and the Chinese Ministry of Foreign Trade and Economic Cooperation, it was managed by the Chinese. On the fenced green lawn, standing in orderly fashion, were cement tombs and monuments with red letters against white backgrounds. The monuments were inscribed with the martyrs' names, birthplaces, official posts, and dates of birth and death.

Premier Wen reverently placed a bouquet of fresh flowers in front of a martyr named Mao Zhongman. This was not an ordinary bouquet of flowers, but bore the weight of the love of the Chinese heroes who had sacrificed their lives to build China–Africa friendship. Mr Du Jian, leader of the team of experts working on the TAZARA Railway, told the Chinese premier that Mao Zhongman was the first hero who died from an accident on the project, killed by a bulldozer on 4 January 1971 at a worksite 40 km from the cemetery. Premier Wen said to Prime Minister Lowassa, 'Mao Zhongman was born in Liaoning in 1930. If not for the accident, he would have been 76 now.'

After that, Premier Wen placed a bouquet in front of the tomb of Peng Mingliang. Du Jian said that about a third of the heroes had died on railway construction worksites, two-fifths in transportation accidents and about a third from malaria. Peng was the first to die from malaria. Hearing this, Premier Wen's heart grew heavy. This reminded me of a story I had heard of a Chinese worker who had fallen seriously ill. Hearing that he lacked medication, Premier Zhou Enlai dispatched a special plane and a Chinese doctor to Tanzania to save the man's life.

Premier Wen walked slowly through the cemetery, stopping from time to time to look at the tombs. He murmured to himself, 'He's from Hunan; this one from Liaoning; from Shanxi ...'

Mountains and rivers are no barrier for the love the people at home feel for these martyrs. Concerned that they might feel lonely, staff from the Chinese Embassy in Tanzania and all Chinese-government-sponsored workers in Tanzania travel to the cemetery to sweep the tombs and express their sorrow, and all delegations that travel from China to Tanzania go to lay wreaths at the tombs as a show of respect. This time, Premier Wen was paying a special visit to the martyrs. He said with affection in his voice:

> Today we have come to place fresh flowers at the martyrs' tombs to show our endless mourning. As time passes, you spend countless days and nights here, but the people at home and the peoples of Tanzania and Zambia have not forgotten you. They are thankful for your selfless contribution to China–Africa friendship. Your contribution and merits will live forever in our hearts.

Premier Wen's speech moved all those present; many people's eyes filled with tears. Du Fu writes: 'Human life is as affectionate as a tear-soaked soul; is there ever an end to river waters and river flowers?'[5]

The people of Tanzania and Zambia have not forgotten the martyrs. They praise the heroic deeds of the deceased. The Tanzanian guests at the event said that Chinese lives had been sacrificed for their railway. 'We are forever thankful to them,' they said. 'They will live forever in our hearts.' Lowassa said the names of the Chinese martyrs would always be in the hearts of three nations – Tanzania, Zambia and China – spanning borders just as the railway did.

Premier Wen wrote the following words on a blank page in the guestbook: 'Long live the heroic martyrs. Long live the friendship between China and Tanzania.'

Half an hour passed in a flash. When he was leaving the cemetery, Premier Wen could not help himself from looking back over the grounds. People always feel sad at such a parting. The motherland will likewise always look back longingly at those martyrs who gave up their lives for the construction of the TAZARA Railway.

I hope the martyrs may rest in peace in their second home. They loved China, and were devoted to Africa. The TAZARA Railway, the great historical monument to friendship between China and Africa, was constructed with their sweat and blood. It will always stand as proudly on the African continent, and in the hearts of the Chinese and African peoples, as the great Kilimanjaro.

INSUFFICIENT FREIGHT VOLUME AND OUTDATED EQUIPMENT

On 16 May 2003, I went to the head office of the TAZARA Railway, located next to the station. As the director, Charles C Phiri, was away on business, the deputy director, Margaret Banyikwa, received me for an interview. She frankly acknowledged that the railway currently faced numerous challenges, including aged equipment, ageing personnel, ineffective communications, shortage of funds, insufficient traffic volumes, weak support and poor management. In China, we called this the problem of 'two ages, five weaknesses'.

In January 2004, I visited Zambia as a member of the *People's Daily* delegation. At the last station, New Kapiri Mposhi, Sun Wenhua, head of the Zambia branch of the TAZARA Railway Chinese Experts Group, and JM Namoodc, general manager of the TAZARA Railway sub-office in the New Kapiri Mposhi area, both admitted that the railway did indeed face the problems enumerated by the head office.

Passengers using the railway came from not only the two host countries, but also from other parts of the region, such as the DRC, Malawi, Uganda and Burundi. The annual passenger volume had reached a peak of 2.219 million, then levelled off at 1.5 million in recent years. Passenger transportation is generally a business that runs at a loss, and the TAZARA Railway was no exception, having operated at a loss since its inception. In terms of freight transport, the volume was concentrated at the two ends and in the middle sections, in the areas around Mbeya and Makambako. The terminal station in Tanzania ran freight transfer for imports and exports; the centre sections for cement, lumber, agricultural and sideline products;

and the terminal station in Zambia for copper exports. Each section accounted for about a third of the total transportation volume.

The initial planned annual transport volume of the railway was 2 million tonnes in both directions, and the forward transportation volume 5 million tonnes. Since the railway entered formal operation, however, the annual transportation volume remained at 1 million tonnes for seven years, and the peak was 1.27 million tonnes. The period from 1993 through 1994 saw the beginning of a decrease to about 0.6 million tonnes, starting a trend of decline. By 2003, the company had a foreign debt of $70 million, along with overdue export charges, and was unable to pay for power and water supply. As a result, the parlous condition of the railway was often reported in the media, and the head of the general office was sued. Finding it difficult to make ends meet and impossible to make progress, the railway was now in a vicious cycle and seemed beyond hope.

The origin of the crisis of the TAZARA Railway is multi-pronged, including the direct factors of continued decline in transportation volumes and reduction of income. Slow economic growth, acute market competition, and political instability in neighbouring countries were all factors contributing to the declining transport volumes. Significantly, with mines in poor repair and equipment seriously outdated, Zambia's copper output was on the decline, leading to a decrease in the volume of copper transported from 0.4 million tonnes to 0.1 million. With the birth of the new South Africa, the economic boycotts came to an end and the Zambian import and export channels faced more options. Besides the TAZARA Railway, the more efficient, better-furnished southern route was reopened. Slow economic growth and the continuing civil war in the DRC had also discouraged the transportation volume and mobility of the people.

But the main cause of the decline in transportation volume was a shortage of capacity. All the facilities on the TAZARA Railway were in poor repair. The track and some bridges were in need of overhauling, with some sections completely out of service. Over 800 km of the track bed had been damaged, and one 300-km stretch completely lacked ballast. Wooden bridge ties – about 20 per cent in some sections – were decayed and ineffective for reinforcing the steel rods, requiring concrete blocks to be used. The electric system of the communication network had never been overhauled, leaving the wire frames rusty and the electrical porcelain insulators damaged. About 90 per cent of the pull wires had decayed or been stolen, so that inter-station blocking had to be dealt with through the schedule line. Wallboard anticipating signal machines at 40 stations were in ill repair due to theft or neglect.

Inadequate locomotive power caused another bottleneck in the transportation volume of the TAZARA Railway. With a 'rob Peter to pay Paul' approach, the trains were out of commission for lengthy periods, paralysing the entire railway.

According to our guide, most of the locomotives on the railway were provided by China, half of which had now been declared useless. The rest, including those supplied by the US and Germany, were nearly paralysed. By 2003, only 15 of the locomotives were usable, though the minimum number required was 20. The passenger and freight carriages were likewise in poor condition. The passenger cars, with their damaged doors and windows, looked shabby. Poor maintenance and delayed overhauls over the years had caused things to get to a point where immediate repair was impossible, with the demand for urgent repairs, like the replacement of hubs and bearings, rising rapidly.

Wanting to enable self-sufficiency in maintaining the spare parts, China provided assistance in establishing a locomotive factory in Dar es Salaam and a train-car factory in Mpika, Zambia, along with facilities for foundry, smelting, heat treatment, metallographic analysis, electric plating, moulding and metal processing, all in the hope of ensuring the sound condition of the locomotives and coaches. About 95 per cent of the equipment had been made in China in the 1970s, at a low level of automation. After 20 years of use, they were well beyond their service span of 14 years, with no overhaul having ever been performed. With production facilities in poor repair, defective, or damaged, all the facilities were out of service, spare parts were in seriously short supply, and routine inspections, maintenance and service were impossible.

Poor management was another major problem that had led to the shrinkage in transportation volume. Goods were overstocked at the departure station, waiting in vain for transportation. The transportation capacity of the railway could have seen a huge rise if its working proficiency had been enhanced and service improved. Without that, it was bound to lose even more of its market share.

POOR MANAGEMENT AND AGEING WORKFORCE

At New Kapiri Mposhi Station in January 2004, we heard an announcement that was as ridiculous as it was true – because of poor communication and inefficient management, the train would stay put where it was, in order to avoid accidents. Often the dispatcher, uncertain where the train was, would drive a car alongside the track to find out where the train was.

But the joke of driving a car to find a train was just the tip of the iceberg of the management problems experienced by TAZARA. The railway was under the joint management of the Tanzanian and Zambian governments, as specified by the TAZARA Railway rules and regulations. This railway was under a three-tier management system comprising the council of ministers, the board of directors and the railway executive management committee (Railway Bureau). The council of ministers performed the function of macro-regulation and control; the board of directors was the operational decision-maker; and the head of the Railway Bureau was the chief executive in charge of the administrative affairs and the supervision of the board of directors. Institutions directly under the TAZARA Railway Bureau included the two branch offices in Tanzania and Zambia, the engineering workshops, the TAZARA Training Centre in Mpika and the Lusaka office. The financial system was structured for unified income, unified expenses and unified distribution, with the Railway Bureau responsible for all losses and profits, and the subordinate institutions detached from obligations, rights and profits.

Taking locomotive power as an example, the separate management of staff and vehicles was an important factor affecting the quality of trains. The train crews of the TAZARA Railway were not part of the locomotive depot, but part of the management department of the branch office's business-operations institution. The train drivers did not perform locomotive maintenance and were not concerned about the quality of the locomotive. Their indifference often led to minor problems turning into major ones. In a multilayered management structure like this, it was often said that the sub-office is powerless, the rail station penniless and the Railway Bureau inaccessible. Any plan for maintenance, spare parts or funds had to go through three tiers to receive approval before it could be allocated funds. This obviously restrained the enthusiasm and initiative at the lower levels. On the other hand, even with work plans and arrangements, inspection and assessment were completely lacking, leaving everyone to 'eat from the same big pot', which, in turn, resulted in loose discipline and frequent accidents. In the period between 1999 and 2000, there were 246 accidents, of which 115, or 46.7 per cent, were related to collision or derailment cases.

The poor management of the railway was deeply rooted in the administration system. The highly centralised management system did not meet the requirements of a market economy, and the co-management by two countries did not function well in the face of market changes. The co-management scheme called for equal benefits, which naturally resulted in unreasonable allocation of resources, difficulty in raising capital and in material regulation and adjustment, and competition for higher wages and benefits, which all led to greater challenges to management and operations. Both Tanzania and Zambia were interested in management, but not in investment. Further complicating matters, regulations for tax exemptions were cancelled in 1995. At the time of writing, the TAZARA Railway needed to pay property tax, an urban management tax, a fuel oil tax, sales tax and value-added tax. In particular, the fuel oil tax was a challenge, involving payment of a tax for highway construction, an unnecessary additional financial burden imposed on the railway.

Ageing staff was another huge problem confronting the railway. The fixed number of staff was 5 652, in contrast to the 4 600 employees proposed by China or the figure of 3 000 suggested by foreign consultants. The actual number ballooned to 6 700 at its peak, then dropped to 4 995 by the end of June 2000, and 3 900 by the end of June 2003. The TAZARA Railway practised a graduating wage system, whereby wages were not connected to performance, and wage packages increased at an annual rate, accompanied by fat benefit packages.

By 2003 the TAZARA Railway, already confronted by the serious problem of an ageing workforce, was operating at an annual loss of 200 employees to retirement. The experienced, skilled, responsible staff members who had been trained by the Chinese were all due to vacate their positions within the next two or three years. Namoode, the general manager, told me in Chinese that during the period of the railway's construction, 100 staff members had been sent from Zambia and Tanzania to study at the Northern Jiaotong University for three years. Then, between 1987 and 1989, another 10 staff members were sent from each country to China for further studies. Namoode had been fortunate enough to go to study in China both times. He said, 'I have been working for the TAZARA Railway since 1975 and have great affection for China, for the Chinese people and for the railway. Seeing the current condition of the railway, I am very concerned, and eager to see an improvement.'

Workers such as Namoode and those who were trained on site by Chinese experts had been the core managers and the professional backbone of the railway. Before leaving their posts, they all hoped to see the TAZARA Railway returned to its former vitality.

The railway also suffered from a serious lack of talented personnel. When the Chinese-trained staff, the main force, left their posts, the technical strength of the railway would undoubtedly be weakened. In recent years, a small number of young staff members had been recruited and placed on duty without training. This resulted in a severe lack of technical expertise in many areas. Unfortunately, due to the entity's deteriorating financial situation, the problem of the ageing workforce and lack of talented personnel did not concern the Railway Bureau.

THE PRIVATISED TAZARA RAILWAY

Poor management of the railway resulted in a worsening financial position for the company, a heavy debt burden, and a cash-flow crisis, which was reflected in failure to pay wages on time, shortage of funds needed to maintain equipment, and inability to pay statutory expenses.

In an interview, the China International Trade Representative to Tanzania cited three examples that reflected the TAZARA situation. The first was that inadequate capital investment led to a declining rate of available rolling stock and transport capacity. Shipments in the first quarter of 2003 totalled 117 000 tonnes, 73 000 tonnes less than that of the previous quarter and 32 000 tonnes less than the same quarter of the previous year. The average monthly shipments had dropped to 38 887 tonnes, a record low in the history of the railway's operation.

The second example he cited was that two sets of sleeper replacement machines specified in a technical-cooperation loan, transferred from France, had arrived in Dar es Salaam on 20 August 2000 but, due to financial shortages, had not been picked up until nine months later. For the same reason, 21 containers of spare parts had stayed in port for a whole year.

The third example concerned the inability to pay phone bills. Dozens of telephones in the Railway Bureau had been out of service for over a year in 2001, requiring staff members to use cellphones to maintain business operations. Faxing had to be done at a nearby airport.

The problems confronting TAZARA had been there for many years, many having surfaced years earlier. In 1985 the railway drafted a 10-year development plan with a view to commercialising the entity. In the plan, it presented 24 projects and asked for donations from Western countries. Ten countries and organisations made donations to 17 of the projects, which helped maintain normal railway operations. In 1995, the commercialisation of the railway began, aiming to turn it into an energetic, economically independent corporate entity. In accordance with these changes, the TAZARA Railway rules and regulations were revised to expand the rights of the board of directors and the managing director, with units such as sub-offices and factories serving as centres of cost and profit, in a move towards decentralised management and independent accounting, and in an effort to motivate lower levels of the staff. However, restricted by the co-management system and fund shortages, certain reform measures, such as rationalising a fixed number of staff members and reforming the financial system, were not implemented and the commercialisation of the railway came to a halt.

Faced with acute market competition and great difficulties, the TAZARA Railway Bureau tried all it could do to increase its revenue and minimise its expenses, making every effort to keep the whole line operating normally. Even so, the root problems defied solution. Before the beginning of the new millennium, privatisation of the TAZARA Railway was placed on the agenda.

Privatisation of state-owned enterprises is an established national policy in Tanzania and Zambia. Tanzania began privatisation in 1993, selecting 395 out of 425 state-owned companies for privatisation. By late 2002, 300 enterprises had completed the transition into the private sector. The transformation of the TAZARA Railway was moving towards licensed operation. Most of the Zambian state-owned enterprises, including copper mines, had completed the shift to privatisation. After three years of preparation, Zambia Railways began licensed operation in 2003, awarding a 20-year joint contract to South Africa and Israel, under the ownership of the Zambian government. During this period, the operator was meant to submit a total of $253 million and 5 per cent of its turnover to the Zambian government.

In December 1999 the governments of China, Tanzania and Zambia agreed that a Chinese enterprise be entrusted to conduct a feasibility investigation into joint operation of the railway by Tanzania and Zambia. The Shanghai Railway Bureau was entrusted with the task. The initial intent of the investigation had been to attempt to initiate China–Tanzania and China–Zambia joint ventures, following the models of joint-venture textile mills by the respective partnerships. After a 45-day investigation, completed on 29 September 2000, the Shanghai Railway Bureau determined that the joint operation and cooperation of the TAZARA Railway needed a huge capital investment, whereas Chinese railway enterprises, being non-profit public-transport entities, were incapable of making international investments. In other words, the conditions for the joint operation of the TAZARA Railway were so different from that of the textile mills that cooperation was impossible.

In light of the licensed operation of Zambia Railways, which allowed private departments to participate in the operations, the two countries decided to go ahead with privatisation of the railway.

In August 2002, the Tanzanian and Zambian governments held a forum in Lusaka on privatisation of the railway and developed a privatisation implementation plan. By the beginning of 2004, the plan remained only a plan.

On 19 December 2003, aided by the World Bank, the two countries made a feasibility assessment for licensed operation of the railway. The Chinese government expressed its hope that the two countries would finally formulate a plan suitable to the actual conditions of the railway. It said that China would provide every assistance within its capability, and would actively push for collaborations to consolidate the fruits of the cooperation between the three nations. This way, it said, the TAZARA Railway would be assured of renewed healthy operation as a symbol of the friendship between China and Africa.

THE EAST IS RED

The early morning of 14 July 2001 was dim and chilly. We set off from Mulungushi Textiles, a Chinese–Zambian joint venture, where we had spent the previous night. We headed to New Kapiri Mposhi, the Zambian terminal on the TAZARA Railway, for a visit.

The station was quiet in the early morning. An attractive red flag with five stars was flying on the high-rise iron tower. In front of a sculpture called *Spade*, which stood in the station square, several local people were chatting. Seeing me taking photos of the flag, an elderly man some distance away greeted me. Delighted, he said, 'When I see Chinese friends, I always greet them. On this special day, I'm especially excited to see you and your flag. Whenever I see your flag, I sing "The East is red".'

We then sang, 'The East is red, the sun rises ...' The group proudly sang the song in Chinese, their pride showing in their speech and expressions.

The old man told me that he had participated in the construction of the TAZARA Railway, and had then worked for the railway. Pointing at the sculpture, he said, 'Our Chinese friends constructed this railway for us with such simple tools. We still remember this. You Chinese have been extremely kind to us. You are our best friends, our brothers. You helped us build the railway, and are still helping us install its communication systems.'

The communication system consists of three sections: a full-length program-controlled exchange renewal and rebuilding, a microwave communication system between Dar es Salaam and Tunis in the Tanzanian territory, and a microwave communication system established between New Kapiri Mposhi and Serenje in the Zambian territory. Near the station, in a building constructed of containers, I visited the China Civil Engineering Construction Corporation and the technician group for the railway microwave communication project, where I learnt that the project had formally begun in February 2001 and was to be completed at the end of the same year. During my second visit, in January 2004, I learnt that the first two of the three projects had been completed and had been turned over to the administration of the TAZARA Railway on 9 July 2003. At the time of my visit, the last section was facing geological problems due to incorrect topographical data and drawings provided by another party, and was therefore being rebuilt.

The project to reconstruct the communication system was part of the eighth and ninth phases of technical cooperation between China, Tanzania and Zambia. Since the completion and handover of the railway in 1976, the governments of the three countries had been in technical cooperation and were now in their 11th phase.

The group of Chinese experts told me that the Chinese government had planned to cooperate for two phases over four years, then hand over the railway. China meant to withdraw its experts at that time and leave the railway under independent operation and management by the Tanzanian and Zambian governments. Unfortunately, though, soon after the railway was put into operation, many management problems cropped up. Hoping to improve the management situation, the three governments decided to extend each cooperation phase by two or three years, beginning from the fourth phase in August 1983, with Chinese experts staying on to participate in the management of the railway, but not in key posts. This management mode had continued until the end of the seventh phase, at the end of 1995. In the 12 years of management participation, China dispatched experts to the railway's nine departments and factories, and the number of dispatched experts fell from 250 to 122. Aside from providing management consultation, these experts attended meetings of the administration, the sub-administration divisions, factories and regions, and the head of the team attended meetings of the board of directors.

The participation of Chinese experts in management helped improve operations and management, and played a positive role in raising the railway's periodical transport volumes and increasing profits.

Ultimately, though, the Chinese experts' participation in management was not the final solution for addressing the challenges in the operation and management of the railway. The mode of one railway managed by two countries exposed numerous conflicts between the governments of the two countries and their employees, which had a negative impact on the normal management and operation of the railway. To make matters worse, the two governments were concerned only about management, and not investment, which left the railway facilities in a serious state of disrepair. For many years, the only financial aid the TAZARA Railway could get was the loan from the Chinese government. The railway adopted Western management systems, making it inconvenient for Chinese experts to be too deeply involved in such sensitive matters as human resources, financial matters and employer–employee relations.

Such being the case, the governments of the three countries decided that, from the beginning of the eighth phase of technical collaboration, the mode of cooperation would be changed in such a way that, henceforth, the Chinese experts would coordinate projects with Chinese loans, provide technical support to the two Chinese-made locomotive works and attend the TAZARA Railway Bureau meetings by invitation. The number of Chinese experts on the team was 15, distributed among the administration's head office, two sub-administration offices and two locomotive works. In this period, the equipment and materials provided by China played a role in the railway's operations. The $6 million set aside for purchasing fuel and spare parts, and for the repair of six locomotives especially, helped solve the railway's immediate needs.

In the 28 years since the handover of the railway, the Chinese government had dispatched a total of 2 815 experts and provided over 900 million yuan[6] in interest-free loans for equipment replacement and purchasing spare parts and other necessities. The Chinese experts won enthusiastic praise from the TAZARA Railway Bureau and from the people of both countries for their professional commitment, superb skills, sincere cooperation and great friendliness, and for their guidance, assistance and example. During my visit, our friends in the two countries said the fate of the TAZARA Railway would have been unimaginable if not for the help of China and its experts. A metaphor used by the people of Tanzania and Zambia might tell the story better. They viewed the railway as a child and the two countries as its parents, saying China was its uncle. 'The child,' they said, 'was raised by its uncle.'

AN ETERNAL PATH OF FRIENDSHIP

During my three visits to the TAZARA Railway, I got a strong sense of the deep gratitude and friendly sentiments of the Tanzanian and Zambian people towards the Chinese people. In conversing with railway managers, greeting fellow passengers on the train, making small talk with taxi drivers, chatting to townspeople, and the like, this was obvious wherever I went.

One day in July 2001, at the Lusaka railway office, the director, AM Mawere, greeted me warmly in Chinese. Like Namoode, the general manager of the New Kapiri Mposhi zone, Mawere had been to China twice to study and held great affection for the Chinese people. Speaking of the first time he went to study at the Northern Jiaotong University, he recited eight Chinese words meaning 'self-reliance' and 'hard work'. Then, after a moment of thought, he said, 'The significance and influence of the TAZARA Railway goes well beyond the railway itself. China not only built the railway, but has provided us with much experience and knowledge concerning the operation and management of the railway. When I was in China, I felt that China was also a very poor country, but you have done your best to help us. This sincere friendship is more valuable than money. The leaders of the older generation of our three countries have created this friendship, and it has been passed on for several generations. We must treasure and develop it.'

He joked, 'Twelve years later, I went to China a second time, and I found it had changed greatly. Its economy is developing at 200 kilometres per minute. When I saw that I was very excited.'

On the whole, when he spoke of the railway, he shared the view of the administration and sub-administration, saying, 'It is natural for such a huge project like this railway to encounter some problems. In the past, we needed hand-holding from Chinese experts, who led our every step. Now, when the railway is facing such serious problems, we still need help from our Chinese friends. Your help is of great importance to us.'

At that time, the railway had two trains travelling in opposite directions every Tuesday and Friday. They required 32 hours to reach the terminal station. During my visit in January 2004, I saw passengers entering the New Kapiri Mposhi Station to board a train. When I spoke to them, they all complained about the delayed arrival of trains. Some sighed and said, 'If only our Chinese friends would run the railway. Trains in your country must be better operated.'

When I spoke with people in Dar es Salaam, they all expressed gratitude for the Chinese aid in constructing the TAZARA Railway, saying they hoped the Chinese people would continue to give them assistance to help ensure the healthy operation of the railway, so that it would leave a beautiful, lasting memory in the minds of the people of the three countries, serving as a symbol of their friendship. A Tanzanian taxi driver said to me, 'When I was a little boy, I came to know that the

Chinese people are our friends. I am 29 years old now. I know that China helped us build the TAZARA Railway, highways and houses. I often go to the railway station to pick up passengers. When they speak of China, they give a thumbs up, and when they speak of the railway, they say they hope you will stay to help maintain its smooth operation.'

When I asked why, he said, 'The Chinese are friendly, experienced and familiar with the railway. Surely they can keep it running smoothly.'

The TAZARA Railway is a symbol of the great friendship between China, Tanzania and Zambia, a monument to the goodwill felt by the three countries towards one another, and an ode to China–Africa friendship and the path of friendship.

At the time the railway was being built, the two host nations had recently gained independence from long-term colonial rule, and both had very underdeveloped economies. In an effort to help develop their economies, the people of both countries, with the aid of the Chinese, overcame hardships and, gritting their teeth, built this railway to prove their own worth.

The TAZARA Railway defeated the attempts of the South African apartheid regime at the time to block Tanzania and curb the economic development of Zambia. The railway, the 'path to freedom',[7] offered support to the national liberation movement in South Africa, and a symbol of freedom in support of national independence and liberation in the southern African region.

By the end of 2001, the TAZARA Railway had transported, since its inception, 23.5 million tonnes of freight and notched up 37.5 million passenger hours. It has been a main transport artery linking eastern, central and southern Africa, adding, for some time at least, momentum to the economic and social development of Tanzania and Zambia, and the region, even despite the drawbacks in its operations and management examined above.

After three decades of weathering tough times, the TAZARA Railway is still there, with sound water-draining systems on either side, well-preserved vegetation alongside it, station buildings in traditional local architectural styles, strong drainage ditches, a level bedding face, and tidy, unified joints. In 1998, because of the El Niño weather patterns, an extraordinary flood destroyed the railways of many central African countries, but the TAZARA Railway stood solid, providing convincing evidence of its good quality. Forged by the railways, the friendship between the Chinese, Tanzanian and Zambian people stands as firm, majestic and eternal as Kilimanjaro. The tradition of friendship between the Chinese and African people is extending into the future through the TAZARA Railway.

15

Searching for roots at home

On 20 April 2005, I ended my eight-year stint as a reporter in South Africa and returned to my homeland. My first stop was Kunming, birthplace of Zheng He. During my short stay in Kunming, I visited Zheng He Park, his birthplace, and paid my respects at the tomb of the first Xianyang prince, Sayyid Ajjal Shams al-Din Omar, a sixth-generation ancestor of Zheng He.

A SCULPTURE TALL AND HEROIC

On 23 April, I visited Zheng He Park in the town of Kunyang, Jinning County. Kunyang is on Yue Shan hill, and the park is situated on top of the hill, which commands a broad view. Entering the park up a staircase, there is a stone sculpture of Zheng He, tall and heroic, standing on a high platform. With a sword in his left hand and a navigational sea chart in the other, he stares out into the distance, looking courageous.

This 8.5-m sculpture reminded me of how Zheng He was described in Yuan Zhongche's *Insights of Ancient and Modern Times*: 'Strong and handsome, nine feet tall, sturdy and clean-cut with a small nose, he stood out from others, looking elegant. He had large ears and shell white teeth. He walked with a tiger's vigour and spoke in a resounding voice.'[1]

The sculpture also called to mind the picture painted by these famed lines of poetry: 'Braving ocean winds and waves, crossing blue seas in boats with sails that reach the sky.'[2]

A colossal 'treasure boat', anchored on a large level plot, stands in the park – as if, riding strong winds and waves over thousands of miles, it had sailed to Zheng He's birthplace. The Sanbao Lou ('Three Treasures Building'), built in the shape of Zheng He's boat, is a grand three-storey building with flying eaves and milky-white marble fences. Hanging from the top storey was the inscription 'Ocean Giant' by Liang Qichao.

If one looked into the distance from a balcony on the boat, Zheng He's birthplace, the village of Hedai, was faintly visible through a green grove. Standing near the Sanbao Lou is the Zheng He Stele Forest – 64 stelae, upright stone slabs, some of which bear inscriptions about Zheng He written by leaders Liang Qichao, Sun Yat-sen, Zhou Enlai, Zhu De, Deng Xiaoping and Jiang Zemin. The words 'Zheng He, a great navigator of the Ming Dynasty, visited East African countries such as Somalia and Kenya, making great contributions to China–Africa friendship' were taken from a speech made in 1964 by Zhou Enlai when he visited Kenya, Somalia and other East African countries. Deng Xiaoping, one of the great men of the 20th century, said:

> No country will develop with its doors closed to the outside world. We have suffered from trying to do so. Our ancestors likewise suffered from the same ailment. Zheng He's navigations on the Western Ocean represent a period of openness during the reign of the Ming Dynasty Yongle emperor. After [Yongle's] death, the Ming Dynasty began its decline. The period between the middle of the Ming Dynasty and the Opium War was a time of over 300 years of seclusion. Beginning from the reign of Kangxi, the seclusion lasted another 200 years. This long-term seclusion has made China poor, backward, and ignorant. Historical experience and lessons have proven that it does not do to keep our door shut. In an enclosed environment, we will not be able to catch up with economically developed countries – not ever.

Opposite the stelae is the cemetery of Mir Tekin, Zheng He's father. In front of this is the Mir Tekin Monument, a sandstone stela 1.66 m tall and 0.94 m wide, also known as the Late Mr Ma Tomb Inscription, set on a sandstone foundation. Set up in May 1405, it bears an inscription by Li Zhigang, welfare advisor, minister of rights, and Zuochunfang grand secretary. The inscription is laid out in 14 vertical lines with a total of 284 characters. It is a record of Mir Tekin's life experience, disposition, children, family, date of birth and date of death. The inscription also notes: 'Zheng He has been intelligent since childhood and has now been bestowed with the name Zheng and made imperial eunuch serving the emperor. He is diligent, bright, modest and prudent, fearless of hardship. He is praised by all long-term officials.'

On the back is a carved inscription that reads: 'The eunuch Zheng He, second son of the Ma family, as requested, paid respects to the family tomb on 22 November in the 9th year of the reign of Yongle (1411), until the auspicious day in the leap-year month of December. This is a record of the occasion.' These words were left by Zheng He when he swept the ancestral tomb in Yunnan before his fourth voyage across the ocean.

There is also a pavilion in the Zheng He Park, where there is a stela with the inscription 'Home town of Zheng He, Sanbao Eunuch of the Ming'.

MYSTERY OF ZHENG HE'S FAMILY BACKGROUND SOLVED

Because the *History of Ming* offers only a very brief description of Zheng He's life, the 1912 discovery of Mr Ma's tomb inscription solved the 500-year mystery of Zheng He's family background. Originally named Ma He, Zheng He was born in the fourth year of the Hongwu reign in the Ming Dynasty (1371) to a Muslim hereditary official in Hedai, on the banks of Dian Lake. His grandfather Charameddin and his father, Mir Tekin, had made pilgrimages to Mecca, so they were respected as Hajji. Zheng He's mother, surnamed Wen, was a kind, virtuous woman, full of 'feminine charm'. Zheng He had five siblings: his elder brother, Ma Wenming, and four sisters.

The Mir Tekin Monument had traced Zheng He's family history to his grandfather's generation, but the 1983 discovery of the preface to the Zheng family genealogy traced it back 11 generations. The family history points out that Zheng He's 11th ancestor, Su fei-erh, king of the Bukhara Kingdom, in what is now central Asia, who pledged his allegiance to the Song Dynasty in the third year of the Shenzong's Xining period, was authorised as leader of his own kingdom. By the time he died, he had received the titles Marquis of Ningyi, Duke of Qing and King of Chaofeng. Sayyid Ajjal Shams al-Din Omar, the sixth-generation ancestor of Zheng He, was ordered to defend Xianyang as expedition generalissimo, prime minister of the Kingdom of Shangzhu and regulating administer. In the period between 1274 and 1279, he was appointed first governor of Yunnan Province. He regulated administrative matters, stabilised the border, built water-conservation projects, developed education, and brought literacy and culture to the public. All these great projects were welcomed by the people and, at his death, the emperor granted him the title King of Xianyang, and he was buried in the eastern suburbs of Kunming. The water-conservation projects he had built, such as the Songhuaba Reservoir, continued to serve the people for hundreds of years.

Tracing Zheng He's lineage back, his father was Mir Tekin, his grandfather Charameddin, his great-grandfather Bayan, the fifth generation Nasr-uddin, and the sixth generation Sayyid Ajjal Shams al-Din Omar. Zheng He's heir was his older brother Ma Wenming's son. As recorded in the Zheng He family genealogy, 'By the sixth year of the Xuande reign (1431), Zheng He was bestowed the title Sanbao Eunuch and he had his elder brother Ma Wenming's son as heir to mark this imperial granting.'[3]

Some of his descendants, who were bestowed the surname Zheng, resided in Kunming during the Ming and Qing dynasties, then moved to Dongying, Yuxi Province. About 200 of them moved to Chiang Mai, Thailand. About 100 of his descendants currently live in Nanjing, Beijing, Shanghai and other places. There are three main branches of his family, located in Yuxi, Nanjing and Thailand. They have carried on through 21 generations.

On 24 April, I went to Kunming to pay respects at the mausoleum of the King of Xianyang. It is located on a small hill in Majia'an, a village in Zhongba County, Guandu District, by the Songhuaba Reservoir. The mausoleum was small, clean and graceful. An elderly mausoleum guard, Gao Rong, told me he had been standing guard at the tomb of the sage Sayyid Ajjal Shams al-Din Omar for more than 20 years, tending to trees and flowers and keeping the mausoleum safe and clean during the day. He stayed in a small room near the entrance so he could keep guard every minute, except for short meal breaks. His security efforts had thwarted the attempts of grave robbers and scared away thieves three times. In 1992 Gao Rong was praised for his contribution to protecting the cultural relics of Kunming.

The Zheng He Monument in Xi'an

Xi'an was Zheng He's ancestral home, and the place where he was selected as a talented worker. In May 2005, I paid two visits to the mosque in the Daxuexi Alley near the Drum Tower in Xi'an, where I carefully studied the inscription on the rebuilding of the mosque, which is called the Zheng He Monument by the locals.

The Daxuexi Alley Mosque, also known as the Qingjing Mosque, Qingjiao Mosque and Grand West Mosque, stands west of the Great Mosque of Xi'an, at some distance. According to an inscription at the site, the mosque was first built in AD 705 during the Zhongzong reign of the Tang Dynasty, facing east. The rectangular structure, one of the earliest and largest mosques in Xi'an, consists of a screen wall, a stone house, a gate, a three-room hall, the Shengxin Pavilion, the North-South Hall, the Stelae Pavilion, the Imam House, a bathroom and the main service hall, each of which has its own architectural style. The total floor area is 3 000 m² built on a plot of 7 000 m².

Hung on the gate of the main hall was a board with Empress Dowager Cixi's inscription Evolution of Nature. When I entered the mosque and enquired about the Xianyang Prince Monument, an elderly man pointed at the wooden Imam House and said, 'There is no Xianyang Prince Monument here. That is the Zheng He Monument.'

I went to take a closer look. The board was inscribed with six Chinese characters in relief, which read, 'Monument to the reconstruction of the Qingjing Mosque'. In the introduction at the gate of the mosque, it was named Monument to the Zheng He Mosque Reconstruction. Apparently, it was a monument both to Zheng He and to the reconstruction of the mosque.

The Zheng He Monument was built over 400 years ago, during the reign of the Ming Dynasty Emperor Jiajing. It was 2.23 m tall, 0.83 m wide and 0.2 m thick. Its frame was decorated with a twined pattern, inscribed with 15 lines in regular script, a total of 479 characters, a few of which were incomplete. The inscription in irregular, neat Chinese characters was composed by Liu Xu and inscribed by the young scholar Liu Ruqi, in the style of Yan Zhenqing.[4] The inscription gives an account of the origin, structure, size and renovation history of the mosque. It also relates how, as he prepared for his fourth voyage on the Western Ocean, in April of the 11th year of the Yongle reign (1413), Zheng He had the imam of the mosque serve first as his envoy and later as his chief interpreter in his diplomatic mission. The rebuilding of the mosque was ordered by Zheng He as a reward for the imam's outstanding performance in this service. The inscription reads:

> In April of the 11th year of the Yongle reign, the imperial eunuch Zheng He was ordered by the emperor to travel to Arabic countries in the west by way of Shaanxi. He was searching for an interpreter to serve as his envoy, and the imam of the mosque was approved by the imperial court for this post. Finally, Zheng He was praised for his might and virtue, gaining respect in Western lands. On his way home, the sea suddenly grew rough and dangerous, so the imam prayed for help from the religious sage Ma. The sea presently became calm, tranquil, and safe, and he vowed to have the Qingjing Mosque reconstructed.

According to historical records, in the time between the Yuan Dynasty and the end of the Ming Dynasty, the Qingjing Mosque had undergone six reconstructions and expansions, of which two were related to the Zheng He clan. The fourth reconstruction was carried out during the Dade reign of the Yuan Dynasty by Sayyid Ajjal Shams al-Din Omar, the prince of Xianyang. The sixth reconstruction was performed with the approval of the imperial court, by Zheng He, the Sanbao eunuch, in the 11th year of the reign of Emperor Yongle, in AD 1413. The Shengxin Pavilion, one of the major structures of the mosque, was constructed in the Song Dynasty. It is a four-sided tower, with three storeys and triple eaves. The pavilion was reconstructed when the mosque was rebuilt by Zheng He and is still intact after numerous reconstructions.

Zheng Zihai, a descendant of Zheng He, believes that the purpose of Zheng He's visit to Xi'an, aside from looking for talented people, was to pay respect to his sixth-generation ancestor, the prince of Xianyang.

In recent years, rubbings taken from the Sayyid Ajjal Shams al-Din Omar tombstone (also called the inscription of the tomb of Mr Sayyid, Prince of Xianyang and Administrator of Yunnan Province) have been discovered from ancient books. This inscription was carved on the 15th day of the 10th month in the 17th year of the Jiajing reign of the Ming Dynasty (1538). It was believed that the monument had been erected in Xianyang, but at the time of writing, no evidence had been found to prove this. The monument bears a rare and important inscription about the family history of the prince of Xianyang, which indicates that he was 'buried in Shaanxi', contrary to the common belief that he was buried in Kunming. This disparity in the records is awaiting further research.

Origin of the surname Zheng

It was the 600th anniversary of Zheng He's first voyage on the Western Ocean in 2005. Various commemorative activities were held all over China centred on the theme 'Love for the motherland, friendship with neighbours, scientific navigations'. On 11 July, the first day of Zheng He's voyage, grand commemorative meetings were held in Beijing. In China, 11 July was named Navigation Day. From 6 July to 7 October, the National Museum of China held an exhibition called Towering Sails Brighten Oceans Commemorative Exhibition, marking the 600th anniversary of Zheng He's navigation of the Western Ocean, which attracted people from all circles to pay respects to this ambassador of peace.

The exhibition consisted of five sections: Preface – Origin in Beijing and Yunnan; Zheng He's Life – A Brilliant World; Historical Background of the Voyages – Crossing Oceans by Reference to the Stars; Story of the Voyages – Fame Abroad; and The Impact of Zheng He's Travels. In the first section was Premier Wen Jiabao's inscription, made on 30 June 2005, in memory of the 600th anniversary. It read: 'Pioneer in ocean navigation and ambassador of peace'. This section also reflected Beijing's close association with Zheng He's travels.

Beijing, seat of the Ming Dynasty, was not only the place where the Yan Kingdom became a vassal, but also where Zheng He grew up and performed meritorious deeds. In 1381 the Ming Dynasty imperial court started a war to unify Yunnan, sending an army of 300 000 soldiers to march from Nanjing and attack Yunnan. In 1382 Ma He's father died in a battle at the age of 39, and 11-year-old Ma He was captured in battle and castrated. After returning to the capital with the army when he was 14, Ma He marched northwards with the army, and at the age of 19 was selected to serve in the residence of the prince of Yan for 14 years. He was highly praised and greatly trusted by Zhu Di, prince of Yan, for the honesty, sincerity, talent, perseverance and bravery he exemplified in his eventful life.

After the death of Zhu Yuanzhang, his grandson, Zhu Yunwen, was made emperor under the title Jianwen, known in the historical records as Emperor Hui of the Ming Dynasty. To consolidate his imperial throne, Emperor Hui decided to weaken the vassal states by dispatching troops to attack Beijing. Zhu Di, prince of Yan, took the initiative to start the Battle of Jingnan, under the pretext of 'removing evil ministers from the court', thereby starting a rebellion in August of the first year of the Jianwen reign (1399). At the age of 29, Ma He served in Zhu Di's army in the four-year-long Battle of Jingnan, fighting in Hebei, Shandong, Jiangsu and other places, making numerous military contributions during his years of service. In the initial period of the Battle of Jingnan, Zhu Di was in severe danger, being far outnumbered by the Jianwen emperor's forces, which numbered hundreds of thousands. In a battle that took place at Zhengcunba, near Beiping (a former name of Beijing), Ma He offered to lead a cavalry unit to launch a surprise attack on the enemy's command camp. Attacked by these valiant generals and warriors, the Jianwen emperor's troop commander, Li Jinglong, did not know the size of the attacking force, so, in confusion, he commanded his troops to retreat. Zhu Di took the opportunity to attack, crushing the enemy. The Zhengcunba Battle relieved Beiping from the siege of the Jianwen emperor's troops, marking the turning point at which the Jingnan troops turned from a passive position to an active one, thanks in large part to the military contributions of Ma He. According to Zhu Guozhen in *Major Decisions of the Ming Emperors*, 'In the initial period of the Jingnan Battle, there were numerous famous generals and brave, wise imperial officials. Zheng He, also named Sanbao, was an official who had made wondrous military contributions in repeated battles ever since the Jingnan rebellion of the Prince of Yan.'[5]

In 1403 Zhu Di proclaimed himself emperor in Nanjing, changing the title of the reign to Yongle, known in history as Ming Chengzu, or Emperor Zhu Di of the Ming Dynasty. On 1 January of the following year, Zhu Di rewarded the heroes of the Jingnan Battle, praising them as 'bear-like veteran generals and strategic masterminds'. Ma He was promoted to the post of imperial eunuch and the emperor bestowed on him the surname Zheng. He was known as Zheng He from then on. As is recorded in *The History of Ming*, 'Zheng He, of Yunnan origin, known as Sanbao Eunuch, who served the Prince of Yan at Fandi and made military contributions in an uprising, was promoted to be an imperial eunuch.'[6]

Why did the emperor bestow a new surname on Ma He? A proverb in Zheng He's home town says, 'A horse (*ma*) is out of place in an imperial court, so Ma He was given the surname Zheng.' An imperial official was an intimate servant of the emperor, but a horse, pronounced *ma* in Chinese, was an inelegant companion, so he was renamed.

Another Yunnan legend says, 'The emperor wrote the character 郑 (*zheng*) for him, as large as a bucket, to replace the surname Ma.' Why Zheng instead of another surname? It seems no one has researched this. As I understand it, when Zhu Di took the throne, he was filled with mixed feelings when he rewarded his meritorious ministers. The rewarding ceremony reminded him of the Zhengcunba skirmish during the Jingnan Battle, the turning point in the war, in which Ma He had fought so bravely. It was his close involvement in the battle of Zhengcunba that made 'Zheng' a natural choice for his new surname.

Because Zheng He's residence was in an alleyway beside North Avenue at an intersection in the Xicheng District of Beijing, it became known as Father Sanbao Alley and, later, Old Sanbao Alley. Over time, by the end of the Qing Dynasty, the pronunciation was corrupted from 'Sanbaolao' to 'Sanbulao'. Since the founding of the new China, this is what the alley has been called.

According to the historical records, there was an alley called the Flying Dragon Bridge Alley in Nanchizi, Beijing, where a white marble arch, the Flying Rainbow

Bridge, spans the alley. The bridge was in part constructed of stones Zheng He had brought back from his voyages across the ocean. There were engraved with patterns of fish, dragons, lions, shrimps and other animals. The architectural style was greatly influenced by Western architecture, as reflected in the Ming Dynasty poem by Tao Chongzheng, which reads: 'The Imperial Eunuch Sanbao sailed the Western Seas and brought back the white jade beam of this fairy bridge. The armoured wings fly with the wind, and the eyes are dazzled by its brilliance.'[7] The word *hong* (rainbow) was corrupted to *long* (dragon), which is why we have the Flying Dragon Bridge Alley there today.

Regardless of the fact that it is derived from a mispronounced word, the current Flying Dragon Bridge Alley and Sanbulao Alley are connected with Zheng He. These sites are constant reminders of Zheng He, the Sanbao eunuch.

MISFORTUNE BEFALLS THE JINGHAI TEMPLE

After taking the throne, Zhu Di adopted a good-neighbour policy to promote 'domestic peace, friendly relations with neighbours, and equal and peaceful relations with all countries'. After bestowing the new surname on Zheng He, the emperor ordered him to make preparations for his voyage on the Western Ocean. Why did the emperor choose Zheng He for this task? According to historical records, the main reason was his appearance: 'Sanbao is unmatched in good looks and wisdom among my chamberlains. Judging from his rosy complexion, he is truly trustworthy.'

Jiangsu was where Zheng He's ocean expeditions were planned and launched. From 4 to 6 July 2005, Jiangsu Province held the International Academic Forum, marking the 600th anniversary of Zheng He's navigations. I attended the forum.

Following arrangements, participants visited the Tian Fei Palace and the Jinghai Mosque in Nanjing, attended the opening ceremony for the Longjiang Treasure Shipyard Relics Park, paid respects at Zheng He's tomb, went to Taicang to visit the Zheng He Museum and the port where Zheng He's voyages began, and attended the opening ceremony of the Third China Festival of Zheng He's Ocean Voyages, held in Taicang.

Zhu Di had great respect for the goddess Tian Fei. To mark the triumphant return of Zheng He from his first voyage, the Yongle emperor, in the fifth year of his reign (1407) 'constructed a new Longjiang Tian Fei Temple' at Dasheng Pass, outside Andemen, by the city walls of Nanjing. In the seventh year of his reign (1409), 'Tian Fei was bestowed the title "Great Benevolent (Hongren) Deity Goddess Blessing the Nation and the People," and a board was inscribed with the words "Hongren's Blessing Palace."' In the spring of the 14th year of Yongle (1416), another resplendent Tian Fei Palace was constructed at the foot of Shizi Shan ('Lion Mountain') outside Yifengmen in Nanjing (modern-day Xing Zhong men). The emperor himself made the inscription for this palace, which read, 'Imperial Monument to the Blessed Hongren Goddess Tian Fei'. This inscription marked the safe return of the officers and men who made the voyage on the Western Ocean. In the 17th year of the Yongle reign (1419), the emperor again ordered the 'rebuilding of the Tian Fei Temple outside Yifengmen in Nanjing'.[8]

In 1925 the Tian Fei Palace was destroyed. Its only surviving monument was later moved to the Jinghai Temple. The Tian Fei Palace we see today is a reconstruction, as is the Tian Fei Palace Monument in the Monument Pavilion.

The Jinghai Temple, adjacent to the Tian Fei Palace at the south-western foot of Shizi Shan, outside Nanjing's Yifengmen, was named after Jinghai, a title bestowed by the emperor. It was a Buddhist temple built in the early period of the Ming Dynasty to mark the success of Zheng He's voyage. The temple housed treasures he brought back from his journeys, including the *malus micromalus Makino* (midget crabapple tree), as recorded in the *Encyclopaedia of Works Past and Present*, which states: 'The Jinghai Temple houses water and land Arhat figures drawn in Western countries, brought to China by Imperial Eunuch Zheng He and his men. When they were displayed in summer, many people vied to see them.'[9] *Guest gossip*, by Gu Qiyuan of the Ming Dynasty, records: 'The Jinghai crabapple, brought back during the Yongle reign by the imperial eunuch Zheng He from areas in the Western Ocean, is newly planted in this newly built temple.'[10] The *Local Annals of Shangyuan – Jiangning* describes the crabapple in the Jinghai Temple in these words: 'When in blossom, the Malus crabapple, shading acres of land, is as beautiful as brocade.'[11]

The Jinghai Temple has twice undergone major repairs, once during the Zhengde reign of the Ming Dynasty and once during the Qianlong reign of the Qing Dynasty. Unfortunately, during the Xianfeng reign of the Qing Dynasty and during the Japanese occupation of Nanjing in 1937, its main buildings were burnt down in the fighting. The incomplete stone stelae in the temple that bore records of Zheng He's voyages and sea travel of the Ming Dynasty were all destroyed. The Jinghai Temple stone stelae were the most important evidence of Zheng He's voyages. Their loss during the War of Resistance Against Japanese Agression was a crime committed against the Chinese people by the Japanese.

The Jinghai Temple that is there today was rebuilt at the end of the 20th century, with the new addition called the Nanjing Treaty Historical Documents Exhibition Hall. The Treaty of Nanjing between China and Britain, the first of what the Chinese refer to as the 'unequal treaties' in China's modern history after the Opium Wars, was drawn up in the Jinghai Temple, adding weight to its already considerable historical significance.

On the 600th anniversary of Zheng He's navigation on the Western Ocean, the Longjiang Treasure Shipyard Relics Park was opened to the public. I attended the opening ceremony and visited the relic site. The Nanjing Treasure Shipyard of the Ming Dynasty was an important shipyard in ancient China, where a large number of ships for Zheng He's fleet were built. With the centuries that have passed since the Ming Dynasty, this shipyard was gradually abandoned and most of the area became farmland or was under water. Standing by the huge docks, one can visualise the great shipyard and the vessels of Zheng He's fleet. After the founding of the new China, shipbuilding materials and ship components and tools have been discovered in the docks, which are called shipyards by the local people. Of the various objects discovered, a huge rudder is the most notable.

The rudder, 11.07 m in length, was unearthed from the sixth shipyard site in May 1957. The upper part is nearly rectangular in shape, the middle section cylindrical, and the lower 6-m-long section flat. The rudder's upper section has two oblong holes to house the rudder tooth used to operate the rudder. The flat section was slotted for fitting the rudder blade. The entire rudder stock was made of ironwood, hard in texture with lines of bagasse. I saw the rudder when I visited the 600th Anniversary Commemorative Exhibition of Zheng He's Navigations on the Western Ocean.

While I was visiting the relic site, two more exhibits caught my interest. One was a replica of a treasure boat from Zheng He's fleet, with some smaller boats inside it. This corroborated the story I had heard on Pate Island about the shipwreck, when the sailors had let down lifeboats to escape from the sinking vessel.

The other item was a rare stone, which had been labelled 'Zheng He on his Western Voyage'. It was a large Yangtze Three Gorges pebble, weighing in at 1 kg. Formed from hundreds of millions of years of erosion by river water, the patterns and lines on the pebble bore a vivid resemblance to the grand scene of Zheng He's voyage, with numerous boats sailing in single file along a large river toward the vast ocean. This piece, formed naturally into a perfect, fascinating pattern, was labelled the 'most valuable treasure in the museum'.

I went to Zheng He's tomb and attended the tomb-sweeping ceremony. The tomb was situated at the beautiful Niushoushan ('Ox Head Hill') in the Qinhuai Scenic Tourist Area, surrounded by a beautiful landscape of undulating hills. Zheng He's tomb, originally made of earth, was rebuilt in 1985 according to Islamic funeral rites and customs, preserving the Islamic features. To mark the 600th anniversary of the voyages of the world's first ocean navigator, the Central Committee of the Communist Party of China and the government of the Nanjing Jiangning District rebuilt and enlarged the original structure of Zheng He's tomb, and built a 4-km road and a new square at the tomb's entrance.

The tomb that day was covered in fresh flowers and fronted by wreaths laid by people from all walks of life. An 'Elegiac Address on Zheng He' at the tomb reads:

On 4 July 2005, with great sincerity, we worship the spirit of Zheng He, the outstanding Ming Dynasty navigator and diplomat of our nation. Zheng He, of noble Islamic birth, born in Yunnan, performed meritorious deeds in Shi Cheng. On seven ocean voyages, he defied death and danger. He visited thirty countries and proved a worthy imperial envoy. He spread the Chinese spirit and world peace, explored marine routes, made friends with neighbouring nations, benefitted generations, and won worldwide prestige. Our national envoy sacrificed his life on an alien land. His soul has returned and is now resting in Jinling. The majestic Niushoushan takes care of our national essence. A handful of yellow earth links China and the world. Zheng He's ocean voyage of 600 years ago is a cause that lasts forever. When our nation aims far and high, our ancestral saint is as bright as the sun and moon.

What is in the tomb of Zheng He under Niushoushan in Nanjing? Is it his clothing? His remains? This question is widely debated in academic circles, one that is provoked by conflicting accounts in two different county annals. According to the Jiangning County annal in the Kangxi reign of the Qing Dynasty,

> the tomb of Eunuch Sanbao is at the western foot of Niushoushan. Sanbao was ordered to sail the Western Ocean. In the early period of the Xuande reign, he was again ordered to sail the Western Ocean. He died in Calicut State, where his caps and clothes were buried, according to imperial order.[12]

However, the annals of Shangyuan County and Jiangning County, compiled in the Tongzhi reign, record that 'Zheng He was ordered to sail the Western Ocean during the Yongle reign and reported his completion of the voyage in the early period of the Xuande reign. He died in Calicut State and was buried at the foot of Niushoushan, as the emperor ordered.'[13] The answer to this much debated question still awaits convincing evidence, which might be obtained through further excavation.

A sudden, light rain coincided with my arrival at Liujiagang, a port on the southern bank of the Yangtze Estuary south-west of Taicang City. Standing in the River-Viewing Pavilion, built in commemoration of Zheng He's voyages on the Western Ocean, looking out at the horizon where water meets sky and imagining the grand occasion of Zheng He setting sail, one could not help but marvel at the dramatic historical changes. As early as the Yuan Dynasty, Liujiagang had been known as the 'eastern metropolis' and the 'first harbour under heaven'. Zheng He's oceangoing fleet started its navigations from the Longjiang Pass in Nanjing, headed toward the sea after Liujiagang, and then anchored at Changle in Fujian to wait for the navigation monsoon.

'CHINESE STUDENT' HAPPY AT HOME

Recognising me at first sight, she smiled, nodded shyly and asked how I was – a phrase she had just learnt in Chinese. As I raised my camera to take her photo, she looked excited and a little tearful. She was thinner than she had been two years earlier, and even prettier than before. Her name was Mwamaka Sharif, the Kenyan Chinese student, a descendant of Zheng He's crew.

When I visited Pate Island in Kenya in March 2002, I had learnt that this Chinese student, Mwamaka Sharif, was at school in Lamu Island. In May the following year, I visited Lamu Girls' Secondary School, where she was studying, and interviewed her. She was studying at the time to prepare for her college entrance exam. Because I wanted to encourage her and help reduce her financial burden, I gave her 10 000 Kenyan shillings (about RMB 1 000, or $120) to pay her tuition fees. I was not sure why, but she had gone back home rather than going to college. Perhaps my donation had made her feel warmer towards her 'motherland' and inspired her to study in China. She plucked up the courage and wrote a letter saying she wished to study in China, as she was descended from a Chinese person. Guo Chongli, the Chinese ambassador to Kenya, informed the relevant Chinese departments of her wish. The Ministry of Education in China gave Mwamaka a special place at a Chinese school, paid for by financial assistance from China.

In March 2005, a reporter from Phoenix Television and officials from Taicang City in Jiangsu Province were informed by Ambassador Guo of Mwamaka's wish. The Taicang officials offered financial aid for this 'Chinese student' to study in China. It was at their invitation that Mwamaka and Alfred Muramba, the mayor of Malindi, were present at the Third Chinese Taicang Zheng He Navigation Festival.

Being 'home' a great joy

Mwamaka said that, from the moment she got off the plane and set foot in China, she felt as if she were at home. 'China is larger and better than I had imagined. I am very happy to be at home,' she said.

Most of the Chinese people who saw her said that Mwamaka looked every inch a Chinese person herself. On 3 July, she was invited to attend the launch ceremony for the eight-part television series *Zheng He's Navigations on the Western Ocean*, produced by the Nanjing Television Station. When she went up to the rostrum, a Zheng He expert, who was at the International Academic Forum for the 600th Anniversary of Zheng's Navigation on the Western Ocean, said enthusiastically, 'She is our child.' It was true. A descendant of a member of Zheng He's crew, she had set foot 600 years later on her homeland to identify with her roots. Everyone there was excited. In Nanjing, Mwamaka praised the beauty of the city she was in. 'I love China,' she said in Chinese, a phrase she had only recently learnt.

While visiting the newly opened park at the Zheng He treasure-boat relic site and feeling curious about everything exhibited there, Mwamaka asked numerous questions. When she saw the 11-m-tall mast of Zheng He's treasure boat, she sighed in admiration. Most of the fishing boats she saw on Pate Island had much shorter masts. Mwamaka was stunned by the rare stone with the beautiful image of a hundred boats struggling on the open sea. To satisfy her curiosity, a museum administrator allowed her to touch the stone.

Now that she had come from Kenya to China, Mwamaka had become a star. Taicang City put up slogans to welcome her home. She was invited to the home of Xue Wei, a third-year student at a local high school. Chatting with a girl her own age, Mwamaka said cheerily, 'I feel like I've come home. It's good to be home.'

She also told Xue Wei that she had learnt about her Chinese origin from her maternal grandmother. As they chatted, they sang songs for each other. Excited, Mwamaka asked Xue Wei to teach her to write Chinese characters with a brush. She learnt to write the characters 我回家了, meaning 'I've come home'. The strokes were heavy, revealing her inner self.

Maintaining Chinese origins
Whatever the reason Zheng He's fleet sailed to Pate Island – whether it went there for trade or to exchange gifts for giraffes to bring back to the imperial court – the crew ended up at Shanga Village, which was closest to the site of the wreck, settled there, married local women and were gradually integrated into local society.

When I had visited Mwamaka's home during my quest for information about Zheng He's voyage to Africa, her mother told me that, to maintain the purity of Chinese blood, they had an unwritten rule among them that, when they married black women, their children should marry another person of Chinese descent to pass on the Chinese line. Later, when most of those of Chinese descent had gradually left Pate Island for foreign shores, the scarcity of Chinese people on the island was a constraint on the marriage options for the younger generation, leaving them with no choice but to marry local people.

Mwamaka's father made his living from fishing. Living in such a poor family, Mwamaka's mother placed all her hope on her youngest daughter, then in her last year at high school. 'I am done in this life. My hope is that my daughter will be a success,' she had told me when we met.

International sisters
The 39-year-old guide from the Taicang Zheng He Museum, Zhou Mianyu, was a descendant of Zhou Wen, who accompanied Zheng He on six of his voyages. Zhou Mianyu said that Zhou Wen had been to East Africa on several voyages, and had always stayed for some time. The younger Zhou had a special place for

Africa in her heart. Learning that the 19-year-old Mwamaka had come to China, Zhou Mianyu was very excited and wished to 'adopt' Mwamaka as a sort of sister. She said, 'We are both descendants of Zheng He's sailors. We started sharing a fate 600 years ago. I will tell her stories of Zhou Wen, prepare her delicious home cooking, and buy her beautiful clothes.' Very pleased with this news, Mwamaka looked forward to meeting Zhou Mianyu.

Zhou Wen's tomb was in Taicang Park. According to the Taicang County annals, Zhou Wen was a lower level official in charge of one thousand households. The title of his epitaph reads: 'Epitaph of Zhou Wen the Military Strategy General and Taicang Official, Shanghou Shengyuan'. The tomb inscription reads: 'Alas Western nations are thousands of *li* from China, over dark, remote, desolate waves, in dangerous uninhabited places. Few returned alive, and those who did were bestowed wealth and position.' This tomb reflects the hardships Zheng He's fleet experienced in its voyages on the Western Ocean.

Everything that Mwamaka saw and heard in China filled her with excitement. She had not imagined that her motherland was so beautiful and its people so warm.

It was during the time that she was seeking her roots in China that Taicang and Malindi, Kenya, became sister cities. During Zheng He's travels, the king of Malindi presented a giraffe to the Chinese emperor, a tale that is often retold. This time, a student seeking her roots in China became a new tie of friendship between China and Africa. This sisterly affection marked a continuation of the old tale of Zheng He's voyages west, starting a new chapter of friendly ties between China and Africa.

FASCINATED BY TRADITIONAL CHINESE MEDICINE

We were in Nanjing in November 2009. It seemed we were destined to encounter similar circumstances, whether in Kenya or China.

On 1 November, a Sunday during the period I was attending the First Forum of Science and Civilisation in China, I paid a special visit to Mwamaka at the Nanjing University of Chinese Medicine, accompanied by Han Xikun, a postgraduate student at Nanjing Agriculture University. Unlike my previous visit as a reporter, this time I came as a friend. 'Mr Li, you are the one who changed the path of her life. You are her saviour, and the only family she has in China,' Han said to me. There was some truth to this, but I was still surprised Mwamaka called me *shu shu*, Chinese for 'uncle', when we met.

The temperature had suddenly dropped below zero when a cold front made landfall in Nanjing that day. The driver stopped at Nanjing Medical University and we hurried into the medical school campus to avoid the cold. As it was the weekend, we had some difficulty locating the international students' dormitory. We pressed on towards the Nanjing University of Chinese Medicine, determined to find Mwamaka one way or another. Two years earlier, I had been put in touch with Mwamaka through Yang Huanhuan so I could give her a book, but I had been unable to contact her by phone this time.

I did not expect that room 510 of the on-campus Jinxing Hotel would be closed to us. I confirmed that this was her room, then left her a message in English, thinking, as I had four years earlier, that I had to find her. We are friends – even family!

In the evening we went back to her room. As the door opened, she smiled. Compared with how she looked in the past, she was slimmer, more spirited and more mature. She was dressed like a typical Chinese student and spoke fluent Chinese, making it difficult to connect her with that girl we had known from the small Kenyan island.

In September 2005, the Chinese government had helped Mwamaka come to China as an international student at the Nanjing University of Chinese Medicine. Now, having grown accustomed to university life, she was sitting on her bed, saying jocularly that she felt she was living in a dream and that she was very fortunate to have the opportunity to study in China and to have received the aid to make it possible. She spoke these words with gratitude. The great changes I saw between her present and past lives seemed even more fantastical than her dreams.

When I asked about her studies, she said she had spent two years learning Chinese, followed by studying specialised courses, including acupuncture, Chinese internal medicine, Western diagnostics and a physical-education course in shadow boxing. 'I am a quick learner of shadow boxing,' she said. 'I'm more nimble and box at a higher standard than the other international students.'

'Don't forget, you're a Chinese student,' I replied. She smiled sweetly in response.

Mwamaka told me frankly that she was under a lot of pressure with her studies, losing weight during each exam period. I looked at her class schedule: Theory of Yin-Yang and the five elements, twelve meridians and collaterals. These were all difficult subjects. She added that other challenging subjects included treatise on fevers, the Inner Classical Canon of Huangdi, and classical Chinese language. Classical Chinese is overwhelming even to Chinese-speakers. I told her she should study hard and pay attention to exercise and nutrition too. I reminded her that an orderly lifestyle and sound health were the guarantees for good performance in her studies. She nodded earnestly.

She told me she had adjusted to campus life and that the university treated her well. Because her homeland was hot year round, she was accustomed to summer in Nanjing. Though her dorm room was equipped with an air conditioner and telephone, she did not use them. She had heating to keep her warm when needed and an en suite bathroom. She had bought some cooking utensils to allow her to cook during holidays as a form of relaxation.

During her five years of studying in China, she had been back to her homeland only in 2007, taking some Chinese specialities for her family. 'I was very excited to go home after such a long time away,' she said. 'My family all missed me very much, especially my mother. When the people in my village saw I had come back from university, they all said, "I want to go to China. I'm a descendant of Zheng He too."' Saying that, she burst into laughter, bringing warmth to the chilly room.

'What are you going to do after you graduate?' I asked. 'Are you going to be a doctor, as you originally dreamed?'

'Yes,' she replied. 'I've kept all the textbooks I've used. I will teach others when I'm back home. Doctors are badly needed there.'

The first time we met, she had expressed her wish to study at medical school, to master the skills of medicine and cure people of diseases. With her situation now very different from before, I believed she would have a great future with her persistent pursuit of professional skills. After she graduated, I believed the flowers of China–Africa friendship would be more vibrant and colourful than ever.

THE FALLACY OF THE CHINA THREAT

Some 600 years after Zheng He's travels, some ill-intentioned Westerners were stirring up a clamour about a 'China threat'. This fragile theory was not only unworthy of attention from the Chinese people, but was also a ridiculous fallacy in the eyes of more broad-minded people in Western countries. Anyone with even a sketchy understanding of Chinese history knows that the world after the 15th century would have been very different from the present white-dominated world if it had been ruled by the Chinese instead. Judging by Zheng He's unprecedented grand deeds in his seven voyages, this conclusion must surely be correct. A comparison of the purpose of Zheng He's travels with those of later Western navigators makes this fact even more evident.

What motivated Zheng He to travel? The views held by Chinese and other experts in Zheng He studies include several theories: the trade theory, the imperial-tribute theory, the diplomacy theory, the Jianwen emperor theory, the giraffe theory and the luxury theory.

The trade theory suggests that the initial period of the Ming Dynasty was a continuation of the tradition from the Yuan Dynasty of attaching importance to foreign trade. The Ming Dynasty established foreign-trade offices in Taicang, Quanzhou, Guangzhou and other cities to manage foreign trade. After ascending the throne, Ming Dynasty Emperor Zhu Di took measures to encourage the development of foreign trade. He ordered Zheng He's fleet to sail across the Western Ocean to expand and maximise foreign markets.

If one adheres to the imperial-tribute theory, then, befitting the fame of their sovereignty, the Ming emperors ordered Zheng He to lead a fleet to show off their 'military strength and material wealth'[14] to other countries to gain tribute from foreign countries as a way of gathering rarities and treasures from all over the world.

The diplomacy theory holds that, around the time of Zheng He's travels, areas in South East Asia were unstable and there was rampant opposition to the Ming Empire. The dispatch of envoys was a means of control through conciliation intended to create a close connection with foreign governments and of civilising subordinate nations for the purpose of stabilising domestic territories and those in the areas immediately surrounding China's borders. This strategy aimed to enhance the Yongle emperor's prestige by 'giving more and taking less'.

The Jianwen emperor theory posits that, after taking the throne through armed revolt, the Yongle emperor feared that the deposed Jianwen Emperor and his queen had not been killed in a fire, but had fled overseas. Fearing they might stage a return from a foreign stronghold, he dispatched Zheng He to search out the whereabouts of the Jianwen emperor.[15]

The giraffe theory advocates the notion that Zheng He's expedition to Africa was made in search of giraffes. When people saw giraffes in Bangladesh, they mistook the creatures for the mythical kylin, a precious, auspicious animal and a symbol of royal grace. Later, when people found out that Kenya had giraffe populations, they set off on an expedition in search of the animal.

The luxury theory says that all the overseas trade carried out by Zheng He's fleet was meant to collect luxury items from all over the world, such as precious stones, sandalwood, scented wood, agilawood, spices and other rarities for the imperial eunuchs, nobles, concubines and officials. According to Dai Wenda:

> As an imperial eunuch in earlier years, Zheng He was ordered to make these tours to purchase luxuries for the imperial court. If I am correct in saying so, then it was for the sake of purchasing luxury products for the imperial concubines of the Ming Dynasty that these voyages were made.[16]

Clearly, each of these theories follows its own train of thought and, like the proverbial blind man with the elephant, takes a part for the whole. In fact, Zheng He's travels were both motivated and achieved by many factors, an overlap of economics, politics, culture and other factors. Complicated as the motivations behind Zheng He's travels were, one indisputable fact is that they were not made for the purpose of plundering other people's property or wealth, nor for occupation of their territory, but for 'moralising and caring for distant peoples'[17] through peaceful, civilised, friendly deeds – not by fighting, and not by aggression, as thieves do. Facts have proven that Zheng He's travels promoted friendly communication between China and the countries he visited, especially trade relations between China and Africa, realising material exchanges between them. The Chinese people, in their exchanges with others, proceeded on the principle of 'not bullying the minority or the weak'.[18] This way, they became informed about the locations of other nations, learnt their social customs, and accumulated valuable, abundant first-hand information that contributed to the world's knowledge of navigation. Zheng He's nautical chart is a treasured geographical map left for the generations that came after him.

Foreign sinologists believe that Zheng He led his fleet on a voyage across the Western Ocean 50 years before the end of the 15th century, launching the Age of Discovery. His fleet was broad in scale, its power vast and mighty, its organisation tight and its shipbuilding technology superb, especially considering the lack of a rudder and the gunwales. The fleet led the world in its time, and it was not until World War I, 500 years later, that the West built a fleet that compared with Zheng He's. The comprehensive national strength and navigational technology in China made the establishment of a world hegemony a real possibility for the Middle Kingdom, but, despite its ability to wield this power, China did not choose to do so.

Sinologists have also pointed out that there were many factors behind the fact that China missed the opportunity for international development. Of the many possible reasons for this, the idea of 'two and a half' factors is most significant. The basis for the first factor is that China lacked greed. Being dominated by Confucian scholars, the old China was not geared for expedition. Confucian teaching held that 'while the parents are alive, the children should not travel far'.[19] Throughout history, the Han ethnic group did not launch any large-scale expeditions. Chinese agricultural civilisation centred on spring sowing and autumn harvesting, and self-reliance and self-sufficiency, not on plundering from others for development. For this reason, it lacked the urge to occupy the territories of other people. The great Tang Dynasty poet Du Fu admonishes that 'a state that limits killing will naturally have its own borders',[20] a perfect testimony to the view of Confucian culture. With their emphasis on agriculture, Confucian societies restrained commerce and valued justice over material gain. The Zheng He fleet gave boatfuls of treasures to foreign leaders as gifts, not for profit. This is in sharp contrast to the insatiable greed of some European colonial empires. The second factor was blind greed. According to Nicholas Kristof,

> Chinese elites regarded their country as the 'Middle Kingdom' and believed they had nothing to learn from barbarians abroad ... The Chinese could easily have continued around the Cape of Good Hope and established direct trade with Europe. But as they saw it, Europe was a backward region, and China had little interest in the wool, beads and wine Europe had to trade.[21]

In other words, arrogance, conceit, self-satisfaction, self-admiration, conservativeness, the worship of authority, resistance to new ideas, and the view of themselves as 'number one' made the Chinese short-sighted and ignorant.

The 'half factor' was the feudal ethics of the old China. China was a centralised feudal state. Once conservative forces dominated the imperial court, its ban on maritime travel and other erroneous policies were disastrous to the whole nation. To keep its maritime ban intact, they made every effort to destroy the records of Zheng He's fleet, downplayed his merits and achievements, and dismissed this unparalleled maritime force in support of the new emperor.

Unlike the causes behind the abrupt cessation of Zheng He's expeditions, the 'two and a half factors' that spurred the continuous overseas expansion and occupation by European colonists were extreme greed and the endless drive for overseas expansion.

Firstly, in the 15th century, the Portuguese opened a new sea route for acquisition of an important commodity – spices. Motivated by profits, Portuguese fleets sailed south to the West African coast, round the Cape of Good Hope, and finally to Asia. This sea route was highly profitable. Magellan's fleet once made a profit of 10 000 times the cost price for 26 tonnes of cloves. Since the Portuguese lived by the sea and made their living by fishing, they had to find a way to conquer the seas of the East to obtain wealth when Spain and other countries blocked Mediterranean Sea trade. By the 16th century, many European countries adopted policies that were as good as economic suicide, leading Portugal to adopt conservative policies, savagely killing Jews, burning heretics and expelling scientists. At this historical juncture, Holland and Britain took the opportunity to step into the role of European aggressors. They not only filled the vacancy in maritime expeditions, but exceeded their forerunners in both momentum and method.

It may be concluded that the conservative, conceited and narrow-minded Confucian culture was the root cause of the abrupt end to Zheng He's voyages. In such a society, China's lack of greed and lack of the urge to conquer other peoples would clearly not constitute a threat. Historical facts prove that the well-equipped, invincible fleet of Zheng He never plundered other people's property or occupied their territory. His travels bring to mind the Great Wall of China, 10 000 *li*[22] in length, first constructed in the Qin Dynasty and later lengthened and reinforced by subsequent dynasties, whose sole purpose was to defend against invaders. The Great Wall is convincing evidence that China is more a defensive than an expansive nation, unlike Western countries, which created military capacity to attack others. Kristof writes:

> If ancient China had been greedier and more outward-looking, if other traders had followed in Zheng He's wake and then continued on, Asia might well have

dominated Africa and even Europe. Chinese might have settled in not only Malaysia and Singapore, but also in East Africa, the Pacific Islands, even in America. Perhaps the Famao show us what the *mestizos* of such a world might have looked liked, the children of a hybrid culture that was never born. What I'd glimpsed in Pate was the high-water mark of an Asian push that simply stopped – not for want of ships or know-how, but strictly for want of national will. All this might seem fanciful, and yet in Zheng He's time the prospect of a New World settled by the Spanish or English would have seemed infinitely more remote than a New World made by the Chinese. How different would history have been had Zheng He continued on to America? The mind rebels; the ramifications are almost too overwhelming to contemplate. So consider just one: this magazine would have been published in Chinese.[23]

This being the fact, can we help but ask what is meant by the 'China threat' fallacy? Does it mean a threat from China or a threat to China, the ill intent of those advocating this fallacy?

THE GLORIOUS ZHENG HE EPIC

Six hundred years ago, the great navigator and diplomatist Zheng He began his seven ocean voyages, 'navigations for peace', opening up an important 'Maritime Silk-Porcelain Road' and recording a beautiful epic. Over hundreds of years, Zheng He, the ambassador of peace, has been loved and revered by people of the countries he visited and he has become a symbol of peaceful diplomacy and friendly ties.

Peace was the main theme of the grand epic of Zheng He's voyages. In the early period of the Ming Dynasty, pirates appeared now and then in the South China Sea area, endangering marine safety and trade. The mission of Zheng He's navigations was to ensure marine safety, to maintain stability in South East and South Asia, and to keep sea routes running safely for the purpose of equal trade with countries to the west. It was for peace and justice that he made his voyages. In the 28 years of his travels, he fought only three defensive battles, and that was because he had no alternative. Wherever they went, he and his men treated people with courtesy, respected local customs and carried out transactions on equal terms without taking advantage of the weak. They disseminated civilisation and brought home advanced culture, science and technology, providing diplomatic success through 'rule by virtue', gaining trust and respect from local people.

This 'peace mission' was a reflection of the broad-mindedness and great tolerance of the Chinese nation, and was a conversation between different civilisations. Zheng He's fleet, 'with sky-high sails, navigated day and night under blazing sun or starry skies, riding the turbulent tides as if on a grand road'.[24] This great momentum was sufficient to 'manifest military power over aliens', but Zheng He's fleet did not resort to such actions in dealing with any country it visited, even a small, weak African city state, nor did it occupy an inch of another country's land or other people's property. They did not trade a single African slave either. In these peaceful ocean voyages and cultural exchanges, China 'did not conquer and plunder, but not because it was unable to do so'.[25] This peaceful navigation and exchange gave full expression to the traditional virtue of the polite, peace-loving Chinese people, as some scholars abroad have emphasised. For example, in Gavin Menzies's words, 'What was most remarkable about Zheng He was that he represented the best of the human soul, the spirit of equality for all people, rich or poor, old or young, noble or humble. China has every reason to feel proud of his achievements.'[26]

These 'navigations of peace' won trust and friends for China, and respect and love for Zheng He from the nations and regions he visited. Some South East Asian countries revere Zheng He as a kind of god of peace, and have built temples and shrines to him. The names Zheng He and Sanbao are seen in cities, streets, harbours, water wells and stelae everywhere. According to the figures, there are 17 Zheng He temples in South East Asia. The road of peace opened up by the great mariner gave birth to prosperity, with Asian and African envoys coming and going for visits.

In the equal, friendly, mutual relations with Africa, Zheng He's fleet, though magnificent in size, was never arrogant in its dealings with African countries. After Zheng He had come and gone, some European fleets treated the African people as if they were not even human, insulting and humiliating them as they pleased. They even went so far as to strike up a noisy debate over whether African people were humans or animals, in an attempt to degrade the colonised people and justify their own colonialist crimes. By contrast, it was only natural that Zheng He, the 'ambassador of peace', was revered. President Thabo Mbeki once said: 'Why did the king of Malindi present the Chinese emperor with a giraffe instead of an elephant, lion, or leopard? This was because he respected the Chinese king's far-sightedness and broad-mindedness in dispatching an oceangoing fleet to visit Africa for courteous, reciprocal dealings with African nations.' Mbeki said at the forum marking the 10th anniversary of the founding of the democratic South Africa and the establishment of the China–Africa partnership:

> History tells us that hundreds of years ago, no Africans or Asians saw one another as barbarians. Seas and oceans apart, Africans and Asians saw that their own happiness depended on the happiness of the other. The basic idea reflected in these goodwill relations is the brilliance of human nature. It was based on goodwill that the 15th-century Chinese fleet arrived in African

seaports, ushering in cooperation and mutual benefit, not the destruction and despair brought about by the slave trade and colonialism when the Arabians and Europeans arrived later.[27]

This peaceful navigation, such a contrast from the early voyages of Western countries, has provided a mirror for people to understand history and to perceive the world. As Engels once said:

> What the Portuguese were after in coastal Africa, India, and the Far East was gold. The word 'gold' was an incantation that drove the Spanish across the Atlantic Ocean to America. Gold was the first thing sought after by white peoples as soon as they set foot on any newly discovered coast.[28]

After Zheng He's expeditions, sailors from Portugal, Spain and other countries appeared one after another, vying for rule of the seas by use of sword and fire all over the globe, pursuing cold-blooded colonialist plunder and cruel exploitation. Those vicious deeds and Zheng He's peaceful navigation can hardly be mentioned in the same breath. They are as different as day and night, as starkly contrasted as black and white.

The epic navigational exploits of Zheng He's fleet have become a symbol of peaceful mutual exchange, a symbol of equality and mutual benefit, and a symbol of friendly, neighbourly relations. It is a manifestation of the concept and practice of China's traditional peaceful diplomacy. This navigational wonder is a demonstration to the world that China, once the powerful ruler of the sea, never threatened or intimidated other countries, nor did it occupy their territory or plunder their property. On the contrary, the powerful Chinese nation helped spread human civilisation, gave impetus to the development of humanity's productive forces, and benefited all countries of the world through win-win development in mutual benefit and shared peace. It is based on this historical fact that African countries are sincerely looking forward to the advent of a second Zheng He era.

Zheng He belongs to China, and to the whole world. The ideals and practices of Zheng He's fleet are a precious historical experience to which we can refer when contemplating peaceful world development, harmonious human coexistence and friendly relations between nations. The unprecedented Zheng He epic is a clear demonstration to the world that in human history, the law of the jungle, conquest, plunder, destruction and occupation, as embraced by Western social Darwinism, is not the only way for humankind. Rather, mutual benefit, peaceful development and harmonious coexistence, as embraced in an Eastern development mode, has more to recommend itself and is more widely appreciated.

Celebrating the 600th anniversary of Zheng He's voyages on the Western Ocean was done to revitalise China and inspire it to stick to the path of peaceful development so as to benefit China, the world and the future development of humankind.

16

A historical record of China–Africa relations

FROM LEGEND TO NEW FINDINGS THROUGH EXCAVATION

The earliest known interactions between China and Africa occurred between the 10th and 2nd centuries BC, through indirect contact that was recorded in mythology and through the silk trade. For example, according to the *Biography of King Mu*, in the 17th year of his reign (10th century BC), King Mu of Zhou rode eight steeds west to meet the Western Mother Goddess and 'the King offered the Mother Goddess wine by the Jade Pool'.[1]

The *Bamboo Annals*, discovered in a tomb from the Wei Kingdom dating from the Warring States period, also say that, 17 years after he ascended the throne, King Mu of Zhou met the Western Mother Goddess on Mount Kunlun during his expedition.[2] The scholar Alfred Forke believes that the Western Mother Goddess refers to the Queen of Sheba, who lived during Solomon's reign and who, during her prime, visited King Mu. Renowned Dutch sinologist Jan Julius Lodewijk Duyvendak, on the other hand, holds that this conjecture is nothing more than 'a fine matter to amuse scholars'.[3]

Scientific research must rest on evidence, not mythology or legend. Silk fabrics discovered in an ancient Egyptian tomb throw light on the meeting of King Mu of Zhou and the Western Mother Goddess, hinting at the possible existence of a land route from China to Egypt via central and western Asia as early as the reign of Mu. In 1993 a team of Austrian scientists discovered some foreign matter in the hair of a specimen when they were researching the remains of a female Egyptian mummy dating from Egypt's 21st Dynasty (1070–945 BC). Electron microscope analysis revealed that the foreign matter was cocoon fibres, suggesting that silk fabrics were used by the Egyptians at a time when China was the only silk-producing country in the world.[4]

The discovery of silk in Egypt suggests that at least indirect contact between China and Egypt had begun by the 10th century BC, though it is not yet clear how the silk was transported to Egypt. Before the discovery of the silk, a stone relief dating from the Han Dynasty had been discovered in Jiawang, Xuzhou Province, in 1979, depicting figures of the kylin resembling African giraffes.[5]

Xuzhou, the home of Liu Bang, founding emperor of the Han Dynasty, had always been a water and land transportation hub in China, and an important place for the Western and Eastern Han dynasties, inhabited by imperial relatives, eastern aristocrats, scholars, Taoists, architects, sculptors and artists. The Han Dynasty stone reliefs originated, developed and thrived in a social milieu based on feudal nobles' worship of gods and spirits, elaborate funeral rites and great materialism. The stone reliefs depict many themes reflecting aspects of society at that time. Thematically, they can be classified into imagery that reflects social strata, production, literature, art, mythology, legend, superstition, and so forth, and include items such as the kylin, the vermilion bird, the tortoise, the azure dragon and the white tiger engraved onto tomb gates, tomb pillars or coffins to ward off evil spirits and ghosts. The unearthing of the Han Dynasty stone reliefs provides evidence of China's partial knowledge of African animals.

The earliest record of the lion in historical works from the Han Dynasty

It is common knowledge that the lion is not native to China, but to Africa. Nevertheless, the Chinese people have known about the lion for a long time, loving it as king of the beasts hailing from an alien land. The lion has long been important to China's cultural life.[6]

Lion imagery is familiar to every Chinese home, where one finds them crouching at sides of a mansion's door, dancing on jubilant occasions or being drawn to suit children's tastes. There are Chinese records of lions dating back to the Warring States period. The unearthed Western Jin Dynasty *Biography of King Mu* narrates the Zhou king's travels in the western region, and mentions a tiger-like animal called the lion.[7]

According to scholarly studies, this animal's name is a foreign word transliterated from a western regional dialect.[8] The 1989 edition of *Cihai* defines the word *suanni* thus: 'Suanni means lion. In the *Biography of King Mu*, Volume 1, "Suanni covers 500 *li* a day, like a wild horse."'[9] Guo Pu notes: 'Suanni is another name for lion. *Erya: Interpretation of Animals* says, "Suanni: a tiger-eating leopard."'[10] *Erya* is the oldest Chinese dictionary, edited in the period between the Warring States and the Western Han Dynasty, which includes the term *suanni*, a word similar to the name of a short-haired tiger.[11] The appearance of the word 'lion' in *Erya*, the earliest record of ancient Chinese writing, is evidence that the Chinese people had seen lions and knew of them as early as the Warring States period, or at least the time between the Warring States and the early Western Han Dynasty. Because there were no lions native to China, the date of their arrival can be inferred from *Erya*.

The 2002 edition of *Ciyuan* gives almost the same definition for *suanni* as that found in *Cihai*, emphasising that it is an 'animal name'. *Erya* adds a note to its definition, reading, 'Was the lion produced in the Western Region? During the reign of Han Dynasty Emperor Shundi, the king of Shule presented buffaloes and lions to the Chinese emperor.' According to the *Dongguan record of the Han Dynasty*, 'In the second year of the Yangjia reign, the king of Shule dispatched an envoy, Wen Shiyique, to pay respects to the Chinese emperor and to present buffaloes and tiger-like yellow lions with big whiskers and bushy tail ends.'[12]

The definition for *suanni* given in *Ciyuan* provides us with new information that suggests the lion was introduced to the central part of China as a gift from the Western Region during the reign of the Han Dynasty Emperor Shundi. This information involves definitions of the two geographical concepts of the 'Western Region' and 'Shule', as well as insight into the etymology of the Chinese character 出 (*chu*, '[to go] out').

The book *Western Region Place Names* suggests that the Western Region 'includes China's Xinjiang and the vast areas of Central Asia and the Mediterranean to the west and the Indian Ocean to the south'.[13] Because the term 'Western Region' is a general reference to China's Xinjiang and the vast western areas beyond, the Western Region's place names in this authoritative reference include those in parts of East and North Africa. 'The research scope of this book is this area in the broad sense: from Yumen in the east to Europe and Africa in the west, except the South China Sea and the Vietnam Peninsula.'[14] In other words, the term 'Western Region' is defined in two senses, a narrow sense that refers to Xinjiang, and a broader sense that includes Africa and Europe.[15]

The term 'Shule' is much more complicated than 'Western Region'. In the Complete Map of the Western Han Dynasty Period and in the Complete Map of the Eastern Han Dynasty, 'Shule'[16] is in the territory of China, under the administration of the 'Western Region Protectorate' in the Western Han Dynasty period, and later under the administration of the 'Western Region Governor' in the Eastern Han Dynasty period. However one looks at it, the situation in the Western Region was complicated throughout the entire Han Dynasty, especially the middle years of the Eastern Han Dynasty, with constant changes in administrative subordinations.

> For instance, in the middle of the Eastern Han Dynasty, 'in the 3rd year of the Yongyuan reign of Emperor Zhihe (AD 91), Ban Chao conquered the Western Region and was appointed protector over 50 states within the territory of China. Sixteen years later, at the beginning of Emperor An's reign (AD 107), all the states staged rebellions and the protector was dismissed. After another

16 years, in the 2nd year of Emperor Yanguang's reign (AD 123), Ban Yong was appointed governor of the Western Region and established a military station in Liuzhong (today's Lukqun in Turpan, Xinjiang). Ban Yong conquered 17 states, including Qiuci, Shule, Yutian and Shache, which submitted as vassals. The area west of Usun and Congling remained disconnected. The 70 or 80 years after Emperor Huan marked a period of great changes in territorial and administrative division.'[17] Such writing demonstrates that the reign of Han Dynasty Emperor Shun (AD 126–144) coincided with the period between the reign of the Yanguang emperor and that of Emperor Huan (AD 147–167), while Shule was a subordinate of the Central Empire, under the administration of the Western Region governor in China's territory. Because the king of Shule was a local official subject of the emperor, the gift he presented to the emperor was not a 'tribute from a foreign country'.

In the Chinese language, the term *chu* (出) in *chu xi yu* (出西域) has two meanings. The first is 'to produce' (for example, 'produced in the Western Region') and the other is 'to originate' (as in 'originated in the Western Region' or, simply, 'from the Western Region'). In the context of the current discussion, this term could indicate either that lions were produced in the Western Region or that they were introduced from the Western Region. As no records have ever been found in Chinese history of lions 'produced' in Xinjiang, the Shule lions must have come to China from an alien land. The king of Shule expressed his friendliness to the emperor by offering not a local speciality, but an exotic gift.

So where did Shule's lions come from? Following the 'unprecedented travel' of Zhang Qian[18] in the Western Han Dynasty, which opened up the Silk Road, Western produce and culture constantly entered China. As a critical section of the Silk Road, Shule was the only access point through which lions could have been introduced. These lions must have come from a foreign land, possibly as a tribute paid to Shule. In AD 123, when Shule 'subordinated' itself to the Central Empire, the king of Shule, fearing attack from the powerful Han Empire, presented lions to the emperor during the reign of Emperor Shun.

But, even before Emperor Shun, there were records of the Western Region presenting lions as a tribute as in the first year of Emperor Zhang He's reign in the Eastern Han Dynasty (AD 89), recorded in *The Book of the Later Han: Western Region Records*, suggesting that it was more logical for the king of Shule to retain tributes.[19] Historically, retaining tributes was not uncommon, including repeated instances of retaining special tributes, such as lions. As recorded in Yang Xuanzhi's *Records of Temples and Monasteries in Luoyang* in the Northern Wei Dynasty,

> at a bridge south of the Eastern Road, there are two lanes, the White Elephant Lane and the Lion Lane. The lion was tribute presented to the Chinese emperor

by the king of Persia. The lion was retained by Mo-ch'i Ch'ou-nu and kept by the bandits. At the end of Yong'an, Ch'ou-nu was defeated and the lion sent to the capital.[20]

There are dozens of records addressing the question of where the lions came from in the *Twenty-four books of history*. The six most representative are:
- Ban Gu's *Book of Han*, which records:

    Alexandria Prophthasia is 12 200 *li* from Chang'an, and not under the administration of the governor. It is a state with a large population. Situated a 60 days' walk north-east of the governor's office, west of Kawmira, south of Badakshan, east of Alexandria, and west of Antiochia. It takes more than 100 days to travel from there to Antiochia. This state is adjacent to the West Sea, with a humid climate and rice fields. Alexandria Prophthasia is sultry, vast and flat. Its plants, livestock, fruit, vegetables, grains, cuisine, palace chamber, markets, currency, arms, gold and jewels are the same as those of Kawmira, in addition to the lion and rhinoceros. Being so far away, Han envoys seldom travelled there. Starting from Yumen and Yangguan and proceeding southward to Pigan, Alexandria Prophthasia can be reached at the southern terminus. Parthia can be reached by travelling north and east. Parthia, under King Hecatompylos, 1 600 *li* from Chang'an, is not under the administration of the governor. It is south of Qangly, west of Alexandria Prophthasia, and east of Antiochia.[21]

- The *Book of Wei*, by Wei Shou in the Northern Qi Dynasty, records: 'The State of Persia, with Susa as capital, is in Niumixi, the ancient Antiochia, home to steeds, donkeys, and camels, as well as white elephants, lions, and large bird eggs.'[22]
- Xu Ke edited the *Qing Bai Lei Chao*, which describes the lion as 'a ferocious animal produced in Africa and Brazil, in South America'.[23]
- In the Ming Dynasty *Luodong Liujiagang Goddess Tian Fei overseas communication records monument*, we read: 'In the 15th year of the Yongle reign (1417), a fleet was sent to the Western Region, where it introduced lions, leopards and western horses from Hurmuz, along with giraffes and lions from Mogadishu.'[24]
- In *Wonders overseas*, Ma Huan writes:

    In the 19th year of the Yongle reign (1421), the emperor dispatched the Imperial Eunuch Li [Feng Chengjun notes: probably Li Xing] and other officials to grant clothing and caps to tribal chiefs. In Sumatra, a branch of the fleet was led by Imperial Official Zhou [missing character in text] to the destination [Feng Chengjun notes: three treasure boats in Wu edition], where the tribal head gathered his officials at the seaside to accept the grant. The king told his people that they were permitted to sell and exchange their treasures. A large piece of cat's-eye jade weighing up to 6 grams, various precious jade pieces, large pearls, and several coral trees up to 2 feet tall, 5 boxes of coral branches, gold foil, rose distillate, kylin, lions, spotty cat deer, leopards, and white cuckoos were purchased and brought back.[25]

- The Ming Dynasty's Tian Yiheng writes in the *Young diary excerpts*:

The *Book of Han* records that Alexandria Prophthasia produces lions. Meng Kang says, 'Lions are like tigers, but pure yellow with whiskers and large bushy tail ends.' The *Erya* writes, 'Suanni is like a light-coloured tiger, eating tigers and leopards, and walking 500 *li* a day.' This is a common animal, not a strange one. In the Wushu year of the Chenghua Emperor's reign (14th year of the Chenghua Emperor, 1478), Western States presented lions to the Chinese emperor as tribute, and a senior official from the capital saw the animals. In the 42nd year of the Jiajing Emperor's reign (1563), lions were presented again, and the emperor's half-brother, Zhang Ziwen, Governor of Shanxi, saw them with his own eyes, saying it was yellow, like a golden dog, with a long, powerful tail. The tribal people fastened the animals with two iron chains and kept them in an iron cage. When ordered to release the animals, the people sank a 2-metre iron pile into the ground, then let it go round fastened to the stake. They were kept from dogs and horses, for fear they might grow furious. The elderly people of Shanxi say there had been two similar lions presented as tribute 50 years earlier. These proved to be lions presented at Jiayu Pass in the Wushu year of the Chenghua reign (1478). The Western Region also produces black lions and performance lions, whose droppings [contained] storax and whose tendons could be made into strings. Their hides were made into drums, which were louder than all stringed instruments, and whose tails were made into fly swatters to keep mosquitoes and gnats away.[26]

These six records all have several features in common. Firstly, they are historical books written across a great time span (from the Han to the Ming Dynasty). Secondly, the first three indicate 'producing' sites – Alexandria, Persia and Brazil – places where in ancient times lions and other large cats were once found. The third to the fifth point tell of means by which the lions came to China and, finally, the last record describes both 'producing' sites and means of arrival, as well as giving descriptions of the animal's colours.

Of the four 'lion-producing' sites, the first three names (Persia, Africa and Brazil) are clear geographical indicators. The fourth, Alexandria, remains unclear in terms of its precise geographical location, and is therefore worthy of further scrutiny. As recorded in the *Book of Han: History of the Western Region*, the

Chinese people had come to know Alexandria as a place where there were lions, and they knew the place was adjacent to 'Liqian in the West'. According to sinologist Paul Pelliot and other scholars, Liqian, also known as 'Alassanda' in Chinese and 'Alikasundra' in the Pali language, referred to the Egyptian Alexandria. In other words, Liqian was Alexandria in translation.[27] Upon further consideration, even if Alexandria state was not Alexandria city, but 'situated to the west of Liqian', it still places Liqian adjacent to Alexandria city, i.e., in present-day Egypt. In addition, the famed Sphinx was adjacent to the Egyptian pyramids, demonstrating the great significance of lions in ancient Egypt.

The record in *Young Diary Excerpts* indicates that 'Western States presented lions ... as tribute'. The *Excerpts* also indicate that the *Book of Han* recorded that Alexandria was a place that 'produced' lions. This suggests that Alexandria was one of the places described as 'present[ing] lions as tribute'. Lions were apparently bred in Alexandria, in ancient Egypt. *A brief history of Wei: Western Rong history* says:

> The Daqin Empire's Liqian is in Parthia, west of Antiochia and the Western Sea. The west part of the sea is directly accessible by water from Angu City at the Parthian border, with two months of favourable winds each year in which the wind is mild, and two months every three years if windless. The country west of the sea is known as Haixi. A river flows out from the country, and a large sea lies west of the country. Heading straight north from Chisancheng, Haixi, to Wudan City, there is a river to the southeast. It takes a whole day to cross the river by boat. There are three large cities in all. A northward land trip from Angu City to the north of the sea, followed by a direct westward trip to the west of the sea and a direct southward trip will lead to the city of Wu Chisancheng.[28]

Yu Taishan said that, in the text above, 'the city Chisancheng' situated in 'Haixi' should in fact read, 'The Chisan County is situated in Haixi', saying that 'chisan' and the following 'Wudan' and 'Wuchidan' are misspellings of Wudanchisan. The phrase, 'a direct southward trip will lead to the city of Wu Chisancheng' was changed to '... the city Wuchisandan' by Yuan Haojing in his notes in the *Book of Han sequel*, Volume 80, saying that the four characters were linked into an integral word involving Wudancheng, so 'chisancheng' should thus be corrected. 'Wuchisandan' is the complete translation of Alexandria 'proceeding directly northward from the country to Wu[chisan]dancheng', and hence indicates a northward trip from the southern end of the Great Qin Empire to Alexandria, Egypt.[29] Yu Taishan's note indicates that 'Wuchisandan' in the *Brief history of Wei* should denote Alexandria, the complete translation of the name for Egyptian Alexandria.

This definition conforms to the description of 'Wuchisandan' in the *Brief history of Wei*. In short, Alexandria is the Egyptian city of Alexandria.

Western Region Place Names gives almost the same interpretation as that found in *Collected Interpretations of Place Names on the Ancient South China Sea*, taking it for a transliteration of Alexandria. For a clear interpretation of the issue, the full text of Feng Chenjun's discussion of the issue is quoted here:

> Alexandria is a city name in *Records of Ancient Greek Place Names*, similar to many other names, of which two are found in Chinese history books. One is the country Alexandria in the *Book of Early Han* and the country Wuyi in *Brief History of Wei*, or modern-day Herat in Afghanistan. The other is Liqian in the *Book of Early Han* and in the *Brief History of Wei*, Liqian in the *Book of Later Han* and the *Book of Jin*, and Lijian in the *Historical Records*, the *Brief History of Wei*, and the *History of the Northern Dynasties*. This place name might be a general reference to Greek or Roman colonies, in the same way Yavana refers to Greeks in Sanskrit or Alasandra in Pali, a transliteration of present-day Alexandria City.[30]

The two authoritative dictionaries of place names, *Western Region Place Names* and *Collected Interpretations of Ancient Place Names on the South China Sea*, have given identical interpretations for 'Alexandria'. In other words, the name refers to modern-day Herat in Afghanistan or to the Egyptian Alexandria. Other possibilities have not yet been identified.

At this point, what is certain is that four areas of the ancient world where lions or other large cats were indigenous – Alexandria, Persia, Africa and Brazil – can be named, as Alexandria was in Africa.

In the *Book of Han*, Ban Gu also says that Parthia could be reached by 'travelling north and east' from Alexandria state, making it impossible for the term to be a reference to Herat, Afghanistan. If Alexandria was the Afghan Herat, then its position does not agree with the text, since the place reached by 'travelling north and east' from there is China.

Some people have expressed doubts about Parthia having lions, based on the description that 'Parthia can be reached by travelling north and east', suggesting that the lions presented to the Chinese emperor by Parthia probably came from Africa. Following that line of reasoning, all lions found along the Silk Road originated from Africa. Since Persia and Parthia were in the reaches of the Tigris and Euphrates, in present-day Iraq, and Herat is in Afghanistan, all three were on the Silk Road. Was it possible that all the lions there were tributes retained from Africa? That lions were indigenous to Africa we know, but whether they were found in Asia is questionable. However, the following points may affirm the presence of lions in Asia in ancient times:

- Though the Sphinx is a time-honoured relic, lions are also seen in ancient Persian culture, as evidenced by several facts, primarily the appearance of lions in the imagery of ancient Iranian carpets and in literary works. Scenes of Persian kings are found in stone works in Persepolis (the ancient palace of the Persian Empire), and before the Iranian Islamic Revolution, lion patterns appeared in the national flags, royal crowns and kings' costumes in the region. Lion culture was passed down through generations in Iran, as evidenced by lion patterns observed in coins of the Pahlavi period.
- Iranian lions, also called Asian lions, are remarkably different from African lions. They are smaller, have shorter hair and are yellow. The male lion's mane is short and dark yellow, and does not cover the ears, and there is a cluster of long black hair at the end of a long tail. African lions' ears are covered with a long mane. An Iranian lion's belly skin is longitudinally wrinkled, whereas an African lion's is not.[31] Asian lions and African lions are of a different breed.

These two points seem to offer sufficient proof that lions were also found in Asia. The difference between the two breeds seems to result from different food chains and different climates. African lions vary in species and tastes, taking a wide range of prey, which enables them to grow large without wrinkles along the belly. In Africa's tropical grassland, regions that experience great variance in temperature, African lions need longer hair to adapt to these temperature swings.

If, then, Asia, along with Africa and Latin America, is a region where lions were found, China's lions must have come from either Asia or Africa (as Latin America is the region furthest from China).

Since their introduction to China, lions have become a symbol of Chinese culture and a favourite creature of the Chinese people for several reasons. Firstly, lions originally came to China as tributes, and so were treated as a national treasure. They were fed in palatial gardens and became royal pets beyond the reach of ordinary people, kept only by those in higher social positions, giving them a mystical, imperial feel.

Furthermore, lions were renowned for their great might, instead of being merely 'notorious', like tigers. The people wanted a beautiful animal that could conquer the tiger, and lions filled this aesthetic vacancy, catering to popular taste. They were strong, awe-inspiring, and upright figures, holy and auspicious, just as the people had hoped to find. In addition, the Han and Tang dynasties were China's golden age, known for the people's reverence for the vigour and power of heroes. The brave, invincible lion became an ideal animal for guarding mansions and warding off evil spirits.

The introduction of Buddhism into China and the positive image of the lion gave impetus to the worship of vigour. The image of the lion became very popular

– familiar to every household – during this period. Finally, anything rare is treasured. The lion, as an exotic speciality, became a popular favourite, and its inaccessibility left space for the imagination.

The artistic beautification that followed made the lion seem a little naive and very vigorous, as seen in the traditional lion dance fashionable all over China. The popularity of the lion dance rests on its dual function, catering to the people's psychological need to overcome the strong, while also serving as a form of recreation. Though lions are not native to China, lion dances have been popular for a long time over vast parts of the country. The 1989 edition of *Cihai* defines the lion dance, in its various manners and styles, as a 'folk dance of the Han ethnic group since the Han Dynasty'.[32]

Furthermore, as a welcome folk recreation, the lion dance was probably also associated with Africa. As recorded in historical books, most of the lion dancers were black people. *The Book of Han: Records of Rites and Music* reads: 'Elephant men, like those playing shrimp, fish, and lions.'[33] However, out of a fear of lions, the Chinese did not immediately start performing lion dances in the early period. Instead, lion dances were often performed by black people, the *kunlun*, who were from the same land as the lions.[34]

Up until the Tang Dynasty, the costumes of the lion dancers were those of the *kunlun*. *The Book of* kunlun: *Music 2* points out that

> the *Melody of Peace* is also known as the five-direction lion dance. The lion, a ferocious animal, is produced in the southeastern foreign country India Sinhala and other foreign countries. Covered with artificial fur, people move this way and that. With rope and whisk, two people play tricks in their own manner. One hundred and forty people sang *Melody of Peace*, assisted by dancing feet and the rope holders in kunlun costume.[35]

In the great Tang Dynasty poet Bai Juyi's (AD 772–846) poem 'New Yuefu', there is a description of the dance: 'Xiliang dancers acted as masked foreigners and masked lions. With carved wood for heads and silk for tails, with gilded eyes and silver teeth, dancers quickly shook their fur and ears, like sand flowing from afar.'[36]

Bai says that the lions came 'from afar' and that the lion dancers acted as 'masked foreigners'. The word 'foreigners' in Bai's poem is a reference to black-skinned foreigners. The poem tells of the fact that, until the Tang Dynasty, lion dancers were still acting as black people, indicating that the lion dance custom was introduced to China from foreign countries, a 'foreign pastime' introduced together with the lions.

This description shows that lions were not from China, but an animal brought from Africa, that African lions came to China a very long time ago, and that their introduction held great significance for the Chinese people. The lions described in the Han Dynasty were 'pure yellow' and lion dancers acted as '*kunlun*'. Up until today, the lion costumes that the Chinese use in dances are yellow from head to tail. There are very few that are black. Lions are vivid examples of the long communication between China and Africa.

Earliest records of African animals in history books from the Tang Dynasty

The earliest records of African animals seen by Chinese people are found in Tang Dynasty historical records. Two historical writings from that era mention animals in their descriptions of African customs or produce, Du Huan's *Record of travels* and Duan Chengshi's *Miscellaneous morsels from Youyang*.

Du Huan says that the state of Molin (modern-day Morocco) was inhabited by Muslims and Christians who 'do not eat the meat of pigs, donkeys, or horses'.[37] In the fourth volume of *Miscellaneous Morsels from Youyang*, Duan Chengshi writes:

> [In] the state of Berbera, situated in the Southeastern Sea, [they eat] no grains, only meat, often drawing blood from cattle, mixing it with milk, and drinking it raw. They are naked, only covered around the waist with sheepskins. The females, who are spotlessly white and pretty, are often captured by their own people and sold to foreigners at exorbitant prices. The land only yields ivory and anbar ivory; wild ox horns are used to make weapons of war, including long spears, armour, arrows, and bows. It has an army of 200,000 foot soldiers, and is often attacked by Dashi.[38]

Berbera is in present-day Somalia. Five animals are mentioned in this passage: ox, sheep, elephant, whale and buffalo. 'Anbar' refers to ambergris, thus named because of its resemblance to amber, a waxy, flammable substance produced in the digestive tract of the sperm whale. Noted for its sweet, earthy fragrance, similar to isopropanol, ambergris was long used as a fixative in perfume products, though it has now been replaced by synthetic chemicals.

Ambergris was discovered in China as early as the Han Dynasty. Fishermen would scoop up this substance where they found it drifting in the sea, usually weighing several kilograms. It had a fishy smell that turned into a lingering fragrance when dried and burned, an aroma stronger than musk. Local officials presented it to the emperor as a treasure. It was transformed into imperial perfumes and medicines, and was highly valued. The imperial chemists and alchemists claimed that it was the solidified saliva of a sleeping 'sea dragon'.

Song Dynasty writer Zhou Qufei points out in the seventh volume of *Answers from outside the ridge* that

> Dashi's Western Seas team with dragons, which rest their heads on rocks, letting their saliva float in the water to accumulate into a hard solid. Divers probe for

this most valuable of treasures. White when it is new, it turns purple after a while, and eventually grows dark. I had seen it in Panyu, neither fragrant nor stinking, and light as pumice. People say it has an exotic fragrance, or that it is fishy or gives out different odours. These sayings are all untrue. Dragon saliva does not add or reduce fragrance, but does gather smoke. Green smoke lingers in the air when a bit of dragon saliva incense mixture is burned, so thick it can be cut through with scissors, just like buildings in a mirage.[39]

Scientific and technological progress has since revealed many mysteries of nature. Because the notion that ambergris was dragon saliva was not believed, numerous fantasies emerged to explain it. Some said it was a deep-sea concretionary wave; some that it was weathered bird droppings from islands. It was also believed to be marine sediment or a sea fungus, like mushrooms or truffles growing on tree roots. Marine biologists affirmed through research that it was an intestinal secretion of a huge marine animal – but which animal long remained a mystery. This being the case, some people tried a different route, asserting that it was the excrement or sperm of a whale. In *Views from a starry mast*, Fei Xin gave his account of the explanations of ambergris:

> Dragon Saliva Island stands in the South Sea, beautiful amidst the waves. In spring, dragons gather there, playing and spitting their saliva. Barbarians land on the island in canoes to gather the saliva before returning home. If there is a storm, they all jump into the water, one hand holding the side of the canoe and the other paddling to shore. Such saliva, a dark yellow fishy jelly when fresh, gradually turns muddy. As it is obtained from the body of a huge fish, it is a huge ball, smelling fishy when fresh, but pleasantly fragrant when burned. Its market price in Sumatra is high, one ounce being worth 12 bullion of the state, and 1 jin worth 192 bullion, or about 49 000 Chinese copper coins.[40]

It was the fishermen of Socotra Island in the Arabian Sea who uncovered the mystery of ambergris. These fishermen make their living catching sperm whales. Once, an elderly fisherman discovered a lump of ambergris in the intestinal tract of a whale when he was carving up his catch. This drew the attention of marine biologists, who, through in-depth research, solved the mystery. The horny jaws and hyoid teeth of giant squid and octopus are indigestible. This undigested material remains in the intestines and stomach of the whale. When the intestine gets irritated, it secrets a special waxy substance that coats the residue and, over time, turns it to ambergris. Scientists point out that some sperm whales vomit out a coagulated substance, while others secrete it from their body. In only a few instances does it remain inside their bodies.

The sperm whale (systematic name *Odontoceti*) is known as the pilot whale for its huge head. Ambergris, tasting sweet, sour and fishy, is used in China as a condiment and as medicine to promote qi (or chi), activate blood, remove stasis, relieve pain, alleviate water retention, and treat stranguria, coughing, shortness of breath, and heart or stomach pain. It is for this reason that it has always been highly valued.

Earliest record of giraffes in Northern Song Dynasty writings

The earliest record of the giraffe in ancient Chinese writing comes from the Northern Song Dynasty. In his *Natural history sequel* (Volume 10), Li Shi records: 'In the state of Barbera, there are strange animals called camel cattle, with skin similar to that of a leopard, hoofs similar to that of cattle, and without humps. They are 9 *chi* from head to tail, and over 10 *chi* in height.'[41]

The state of Barbera was in present-day Somalia, and the strange animal described here, the camel cattle, was the giraffe.

After Li Shi, Southern Song Dynasty writer Zhao Rugua, in his diary of his travels abroad, *Records of Foreign Peoples*, often mentions African animals, including the giraffe. In the first volume, 'Barbera', he writes:

> This land produces camels and sheep. Camel meat, milk and grilled cakes are people's everyday food. This land is also noted for ambergris, elephant tusks and rhinoceros horns. The tusks weigh 100 *jin*, and the horns over 10 *jin* ... This land also produces the camel crane, with head and neck up to 2 metres. It is winged, but does not fly high. Another animal is called the zula. It is the size of a camel and the shape of cattle. Yellow in colour, its forelegs are as tall as 5 *chi*, its hind legs 3 *chi*. Its head is held high, and its skin is an inch thick. There are also mules, with alternating stripes or lines of red, white and black. These are all wild beasts, most probably a variation of the camel.[42]

The last three animals described above, the camel crane, zula and mule, are the ostrich, giraffe and zebra.

Barbera, or 'Barbara' in Arabic, a derivation of the Latin 'Barbari', is a reference to indigenous people among Latin urban dwellers. Refusing to accept the Latin language, they were called 'Barbarians', or 'savages'.

All scholars agree Barbera is in Somalia. Some say it is the Somali region of Berbera; some say Zaila, Seylac or Zaylac; and others say Mogadishu or its southern neighbour, Brava. Since all three of these areas are in Somalia, Barbera is in some part of present-day Somalia. Scholars all agree that the 'zula' is the giraffe, which was called *zurapa* in the Persian language, *zarafa* in Arabic and *giri* in the Somali language. 'Zula' can be called a transliteration of the Persian word *zurapa*. In the section titled 'Aden' in *Wonders Overseas*, the giraffe, called 'kylin', is undoubtedly another transliteration, from the Somali *giri*, while 'zulava' in *Views from a starry mast* is a transliteration of *zula*.

As for the zebra, in *Views from a Starry Mast*, Fei Xin writes: 'The state Brava produces the animal maha, looking like a musk deer, and coloured like a deer. It is like a coloured donkey.'[43] Brava is a transliteration of maha; the 'maha' is the big antelope; and the coloured deer is the zebra. In Somali, the zebra is called faro, which is transliterated into *fulu* in Chinese. The Ming Dynasty book *Illustrated Record of Strange Animals* provides pictures of this animal. According to the records in the Loudong Liujiagang Stone Inscription Monument to the Goddess Palace Foreign Affairs, built by Zheng He's crew, 'in the 15th year of the Yongle reign (1417), Mogadiscio presented a coloured deer and a lion to the emperor as tribute. Brava presented a thousand-*li* camel and a camel chicken to the emperor.'[44] The 'camel chicken' is the ostrich. The story of the giraffe given as a tribute by the king of Malindi to the Chinese emperor in 1415 is of even greater interest.

These various records of African animals in ancient Chinese texts added to the Chinese people's knowledge of African animals, increased their understanding of African animals, and promoted friendship between China and Africa. At the same time, they serve as evidence of the long-standing relations, exchange and friendship between the two.

OFFICIAL AND NON-OFFICIAL COMMUNICATIONS

The second stage of China–Africa relations (from the 2nd century BC to the 15th century AD) was a period of direct communication between governments and people, both by land and by sea. This long historical period can be divided into two phases: a phase of land-based communication lasting from the 2nd century BC to the 6th century AD, and a phase of land and sea communication from the 7th to the 15th century AD.

Land communication, 2nd century BC to 6th century AD

Before the period of indirect communication between China and Egypt, there were ancient states around the Nile in Africa and around the Yellow River in China, the civilisation centres of their respective continents. In the 6th to 4th centuries BC, the Persian Empire rose in the Middle East, situated between the world's two centres of civilisation. In 529 BC, the Persian Empire occupied Bactria (northern Afghanistan) and, after that, captured Egypt. In 332 BC, the Greek Macedonian King Alexander defeated the Persian army, occupied Egypt, and marched his invincible troops all the way to western and central Asia, founding the Alexandrian Empire and building a land bridge between the two centres of civilisation.

When Alexander died in 323 BC, his empire was divided into three parts. The Ptolemaic Dynasty, which remained in Egypt, had its capital at Alexandria. In ancient Chinese texts, Alexandria is expressed in two ways: Liqian in *Historical Records*, *Book of Wei*, and *History of the Northern Dynasties*; and Lijian in the *Book of the Later Han* and the *Book of Jin*.[45]

In 139 BC, the Han Emperor Wudi dispatched Zhang Qian to lands in the west to form an alliance with Da Yuezhi to fight the Huns, their common enemy. Thirteen years later, Zhang Qian returned home after a tortuous journey and reported to the emperor that he had visited Dayuan (the region of the present-day central Asian Fergana Basin), Da Yuezhi (in present-day Amu Darya River), Bactria (a Greek name), Qangly (an area between present-day Lake Balkhash and the Aral Sea), Uisin, Alanian, Parthia (Persia), Antiochia, Liqian and Sindhu.[46] Attaching great importance to Zhang Qian's report, Emperor Wudi 'established the Jiuquan Prefecture to facilitate communication with western and northern countries, and dispatched officials to visit Parthia, Alanian and Liqian'.[47] Most scholars in the history of China–Africa relations are of the opinion that Liqian, referred to by Sima Qian and Ban Gu, is Alexandria City.

Very possibly, the Han Dynasty diplomatic envoy Zhang Qian may not have reached Egypt, as there is no historical record of it in ancient Chinese texts. Nevertheless, his journey marks the beginning of official China–Africa diplomacy. During the same period, an Egyptian magician was sent to Xi'an by the Parthian king after Zhang Qian's second mission to visit western lands. In 115 BC, during his travels, Zhang Qian sent an assistant to Parthia: 'The Han envoy returned with a Parthian envoy following him. Seeing that Han was such a large country, the egg of a large bird and the magician were given to the Han emperor as tribute.'[48] This account is the earliest record of a visit to China by an African, through a rather circuitous route. Besides Egypt, China had indirect contact with Kush, in the upper reaches of the Nile, and the kingdom Aksum, in modern-day Ethiopia.

Zhang Qian's journeys to the west opened up the earliest Silk Road, which started from Chang'an, ended up at Alexandria and was later extended to Europe, by way of the Yumen Pass, central and western Asia, Damascus, Gaza and the Sinai Peninsula. Unfortunately, this passage was soon blocked by wars. In 64 BC, Rome occupied Syria and, in 30 BC, went on to conquer Egypt. Roman troops marched east in 53 BC, when the triumphant Marcus Licinius Crassus marched his seven Roman legions to Parthia across the Euphrates. However, the Romans were met with strong resistance from Parthian troops.

The next year, there was a fierce battle near Carrhae between the two armies. The Roman legions faced disastrous defeat, with over 20 000 of Crassus's soldiers killed and 10 000 captured. Crassus's oldest son made a successful escape with about 6 000 soldiers following him, fleeing to Qangly in central Asia, where they sought refuge with Zhizhi Chanyu[49] and the Huns. Among the deserters were many soldiers recruited from Egypt by the Roman legions.

The fate of Crassus's son was no better than that of his father. In 36 BC, 20 years after he had fled to Zhizhi Chanyu's region, the Han Western Region administrator was ordered to dispatch an army of 40 000 soldiers to suppress Zhizhi Chanyu, and the two armies engaged in a deadly battle close to Zhizhi's city (Zhambyl, in modern-day Kazakhstan). The Han army won the battle, 'capturing 145 soldiers and accepting over 1,000 soldiers who surrendered'.[50] In this battle, the Han soldiers found that the enemy used a round-shield battle formation that was like fish scales, forming a double fence around the city wall. This mode of military operation, unique to the Roman legions, suggests that there were Romans in Zhizhi Chanyu's troops, most likely deserters from the army of Crassus.

The Han Dynasty established Liqian County (present-day Yongchang County) in Zhangye, in north-west China, for the settlement of Roman captives, including Egyptians. Over the past 2 000 years, these prisoners of war married local women in those settlements, merging into local society and greatly changing their own appearance and customs. But careful observation reveals their physical characteristics and their customs, such as the high, rosy cheeks of the people in the hills of Yongchang, and their Roman noses, deep-set eyes, curly hair, strong build and golden-yellow hair, all of which are rare in China. It is said that Zhelaizhai Village,[51] close to Lixuan, is home to the greatest concentration of people of Roman descent, about 300 residents in all. Most have a markedly European appearance. Some children of Asian parents in the area have blue eyes.

Their daily habits are also different from those of the people in neighbouring villages. For example, at funerals the dead are buried with the head facing north in surrounding villages, but here they face west. The local people revere cattle and have a special liking for bullfighting. During the Spring Festival, for sacrifices, the villagers make buns in the shape of bulls' heads, which they call 'cattle noses'. When they graze their cattle, herdsmen take delight in bringing bulls together and provoking fights between them, as did the ancient Romans.[52]

Land–sea communications, 7th century to 15th century

Most scholars researching the history of China–Africa relations believe that Zhang Qian's travels to western countries marked the beginning of China–Africa relations, despite the much earlier indirect, non-official contact between the Chinese and Egyptian people. As Ai Zhouchang and Mu Tao put it, 'Only since then did the Chinese come to know of the Egyptian Alexandrian Lixuan and begin to dispatch envoys to Lixuan.'[53]

The time around the 7th century was an eventful period for China and Africa. After a long-term separation between the two Jin dynasties and the Northern and Southern dynasties in the Three Kingdoms period, China started to move towards unification. As a feudal empire, China grew much stronger in the Song,

Yuan and Ming dynasties, experiencing unprecedented economic development and political stability.

In Africa, after the end of the Roman Empire, the Arab Empire grew in strength. North Africa became Arabic, and the western and eastern coastal areas were dominated by Islamic city states. A number of commercial city states were founded north and south along the east coast of Africa. At the same time, China experienced rapid growth in shipbuilding and navigational know-how. This historical setting prepared China and Africa for commercial and communication contact, spurring upsurges of development in China–Africa relations that would last 900 eventful years.

The Tang Dynasty writer Du Huan's *Record of Travels*, the first scholastic work on west Asia and Africa written by a Chinese person, gives an account of the state Molin (Morocco today). This is the earliest description of Africa in Chinese historical records, the first travel record of west Asia and Africa, and the earliest record of Islam in the Chinese language. In the 10th year of the Tianbao reign (AD 751) of the Tang Dynasty Emperor Xuanzong, the Zhenxi military commissioner Gao Xianzhi made an expedition to western countries and was engaged in armed conflict with the state of Chach (present-day Uzbekistan). Defeated, Chach begged the Arabian state of Dashi for military assistance, and Gao Xianzhi marched his troops into the state, reaching Taraz (present-day Taras), where 'he encountered Dashi troops, persisted for five days, and was attacked on two sides by the Karluk rebels and Dashi troops. Gao Xianzhi was utterly defeated, and all but a few thousand of his soldiers were killed.'[54]

Du Huan was 'captured by Dashi in this battle and sent to Xihai in the same year. In the early Baoying years (AD 762), he returned to China on a commercial vessel by way of Guangzhou and wrote *Record of Travels*.'[55] Du Huan was one of the 20 000 soldiers captured at the Battle of Taraz during the defeat of the Gao Xianzhi troops, among whom were widely talented individuals, including silk spinners, gold- and silversmiths, and artists, as described in *Record of Travels*. Some of China's great inventions, particularly paper making, were introduced to the West via the Battle of Taraz. Joseph Needham says: 'Chinese inventions paved the way for the European Renaissance.' He was referring to the introduction of paper making to the West.[56]

The *Record of Travels* was followed by Duan Chengshi's *Miscellaneous Morsels from Youyang*. Born in Zouping, Linzi District, Shandong Province, Duan Chengshi was the son of Duan Wenchang, who served as prime minister in the last years of the Yanhe reign. Duan Chengshi, being a man of extensive learning with a good memory and diligent in his research, became an imperial librarian and governor of Jiangzhou. He collected anecdotes and folk tales and, between AD 850 and 860, wrote *Miscellaneous Morsels from Youyang*. Consisting of 10 volumes and 10 sequels, this profound, comprehensive book was warmly received by readers and has been quoted by scholars over the past thousand years. Volume 4 of the book is a detailed account of the state of Berbera, including information on its produce and customs. The place described in the book is modern-day Berbera, Somalia.[57]

Black Africans first came to China during the Tang Dynasty. There are records of Arabs selling black African people to China in the *Book of Tang* and the *New Book of Tang*, appearing as 'kunlun slaves' in these books. In 1954 pottery figurines of black Africans were unearthed in the tomb of a young female member of the Tang Dynasty Pei family in the southern suburbs of Xi'an and in a Tang Dynasty tomb in Dazhao Township, Chang'an District, Xi'an, in 1986. The former is in the collection of the Xi'an City Museum, the latter in the Shaanxi Provincial Museum's collection. In addition, black African images have also been found in mural paintings of the Dunhuang Mogao Grotto. At the same time, Chinese Tang Dynasty porcelain ware has been unearthed in East Africa.

By the period of the Song Dynasty, marine trade between China and Africa became more active, with increasing numbers of visitors from both sides and an ever greater depth of communication. In the Song Dynasty, two books appeared that recount China–Africa communication: *Answers from Outside the Ridges*, completed in 1178 by Zhou Qufei, and *Records of Foreign Peoples*, completed in 1225 by Zhao Rugua. In these two books, the authors give accounts of the locations, social customs, products and climates of some African countries.

By the Yuan Dynasty, another book, *Records of Exotic Lands*, by Zhou Zhizhong, appeared, providing more detailed information on African countries. This book features records unprecedented at the time, all born of the author's personal observations and from lost books. What merits attention is the fact that, by the Yuan Dynasty, there were three marine routes between China and Africa: the China–North Africa route through China, India, Aden and Egypt; the China–East Africa route through China, the Maldives and East Africa; and the China–Madagascar Route, which was subdivided into two routes, one through China, Socotra Island and Madagascar, and the other through China, the Malabar Coast and Madagascar.[58]

The opening up of new navigation routes during the Song and Yuan dynasties activated official and grass-roots-level communications, initiating a positive trend in bilateral relations. In great part the result of the attention given to overseas trade by the Chinese emperors of two dynasties, this development was also a reflection of world history, and an especially important stage in China–Africa relations. There were envoys, more frequent official communications, direct non-governmental contact and mutual understanding between China and Africa.

Entirely unlike the Song Dynasty writers Zhou Qufei and Zhao Rugua, who based their work on what they had heard and learnt, the Yuan Dynasty writer Wang Dayuan made two voyages to Africa himself, once from 1330 to 1334, and then again from 1337 to 1339. His *Brief on Exotic Islands*, completed in 1349, a record of his personal experiences and observations, provides us with rare information. Wang Dayuan was the first Chinese traveller to 'tour' Africa.

During the same period, the Moroccan Muhammad Ibn Battuta, a great African traveller and contemporary of Wang Dayuan, visited China in 1346, touring Quanzhou, Guangzhou, Beijing and other cities. Ibn Battuta's *Travel Notes* (originally, *Survey of Exotic Wonders*) is a collection of travel notes published according to Ibn Battuta's oral accounts, recording what he saw and heard in China. Wang set out in 1330, when he was 19 years old, and Ibn Battuta in 1325, at the age of 21. To an extent, this coincidence is evidence of a strong wish for mutual understanding and observation. Official envoys first started going between the two lands about this same time. According to Marco Polo's record, the Yuan Dynasty Kubla Khan dispatched envoys to Madagascar.

The effect of this communication was that by the time of the Yuan Dynasty, China was more informed about Africa than was any other country in the world. This finds convincing expression in the fact that three Chinese artists had drawn up the most accurate maps of Africa at that time. These included the world map drawn by renowned painter Zhu Siben; the *Large-Coverage Revelation Map*, drawn by Zhu's contemporary the geographer Li Zemin; and the anonymous Complete map of the Ming. The latter is the earliest world map that accurately depicts the shape and profile of the African continent.

In the early years of the Ming Dynasty, founded by Zhu Yuanzhang, a great number of envoys were sent overseas, travelling by both sea and land, to show neighbourliness and develop trade. Later, to avoid possible collaboration between outlaws going to sea and Japanese pirates, strict orders were issued to prohibit oceanic voyages.

After Emperor Yongle ascended the throne, Zheng He's hugely influential voyages across the Western Ocean began, and, thereby, China–Africa relations were brought to a new historic level. The geographical features of the countries visited by Zheng He are described in three important works written by attendant translators: *Views from the Starry Mast* by Fei Xin, *Wonders Overseas* by Ma Huan and *Records of Foreign Countries* by Gong Zheng. Fei Xin's text records the local conditions and customs of three African regions – Djibouti, Mogadiscio and Brava, which were all in modern-day Somalia.

UNUSUAL COMMUNICATIONS UNDER THE CONTROL OF WORLD POWERS

The period of abnormal relations under Western powers lasted from the 16th century to 1949, when the new China was founded. This period is divided into two stages, the first from the 16th century to 1911, demarcated by the 1911 Revolution, spanning the late years of the Ming Dynasty and the entire Qing Dynasty.

This period was characterised by the suspension of official communication and control, and suppression of limited non-governmental communication. The second period, from 1911 to 1949, the republican period, was characterised by control and obstruction of China–Africa relations by colonisers, and by solidarity and mutual support between the people of China and Africa in their struggle against imperialism and colonialism.

Late Ming and Qing dynasties, 16th century to 1911

In 1433, Zheng He's grand voyages came to an abrupt end. In 1441 (the sixth year of the Ming Dynasty Zhengtong reign), the Egyptian Mamluk Sultanate dispatched envoys to 'pay tribute, presenting mules, horses and local specialities' to the Chinese emperor, but the envoys 'never came again'.[59] Very little official communication between China and Africa was recorded in the annals of history, and official communications were discontinued at this time. Nevertheless, the maritime-trade ban in the late Ming and Qing dynasties did not completely curtail non-governmental communications between China and Africa.

Apart from internal causes for the disruption of official communications between China and Africa, the cessation was mainly a result of an external factor: the obstruction of sea and land transportation. Zhang Qian's unprecedented travels opened up the Silk Road, which served as a land bridge, as it were, between Europe and Asia, and played an immeasurable historical role in promoting the progress of humankind and the development of that era. Despite several booms during this period, the Silk Road experienced a decline in importance after the Song Dynasty. Following the collapse of the Yuan Dynasty in 1368, the Silk Road's 'intestinal obstruction' became more prominent. In 1453, 20 years after the end of Zheng He's voyages, the Ottoman Empire captured Constantinople and conquered large areas of Asia and Africa, including the reaches of the Tigris and Euphrates, Syria, Pakistan, Egypt and Algeria, putting the Silk Road – and consequently all trade between east and west – under the control of the Ottoman Empire.

To the south, the Maritime Silk Road and the Porcelain Route underwent a historic change. After Zheng He's voyages, the feudal rulers practised isolationist policies, and Chinese fleets were no longer seen on the seas. The Indian Ocean, once thriving with thousands of boats, became deserted and empty. This void in China–Africa maritime communications provided an opportunity for rampant colonialism on the Indian Ocean. In February 1488, Portuguese navigator Bartolomeu Dias sailed around the Cape of Good Hope. In November 1497 another Portuguese navigator, Vasco da Gama, again rounded the Cape, headed east, and reached Calicut, India, before returning to Portugal on the eve of 1500.

Soon after that, Portuguese colonialists occupied the East African coastal cities of Zanzibar, Kilwa and Mombasa, the Indian coastal cities of Goa, Diu, Daman and Bombay, and other areas. In 1509, the Portuguese defeated the allied Egyptian-Indian fleet and gained control of the Indian Ocean side of the east–west maritime route. In 1511 the Portuguese colonialists seized Malacca (in modern-day Malaysia), looting passing ships and making it dangerous for merchants and commercial vessels, with few commercial boats sailing there. The sea route was almost cut off, and the Pacific side of the east–west route fell into the hands of the Portuguese colonialists. After that, European colonialists initiated a new sea lane to the east, seized command of navigations on the Indian Ocean, and manipulated the shipment of Chinese commodities to Egypt and East Africa and their transfer to Europe by way of East Africa. The traditional sea lanes linking the Arab, Persian and Chinese peoples were sabotaged, blocked and replaced by colonialist-controlled sea lanes. In this world ruled by Western powers, China–Africa relations continued progressing in an indirect way against an abnormal diplomatic backdrop.

Having gained control of the Indian Ocean, the Western colonialists transported Chinese people to Africa and African people to China, to serve their own wishes. The Chinese people transported to Africa in the early years, whether freely or as labourers, were brought in colonial ships. In the same way, Africans who went to China were in one of two categories. The smaller number were those who came for their own ends or out of religious fervour. The others, a fairly large group, were sold as slaves. In 1517, soon after the Portuguese occupation of Macau, China, African slaves and soldiers were transported there. The chapter titled 'Situation' in Yin Guangren and Zhang Rulin's *A Brief History of Macau* (Volume 2) gives the following description: 'Westerners in Macau came in the 30th year of the Jiajing reign (1551), both masters and black slaves.'[60] The book goes on to point out that the rapidly increasing numbers of black people in Macau included not only men, but also women. Black soldiers were so numerous that they made up the bulk of the Portuguese forces. Saishang-a, vice-minister of the Qing, presented the following account of the situation in Macau: 'There are over 300 foreign guards here [all black people], training year-round, whether hot or cold.' According to historical records, the population of Macau reached 7 000 in 1635, of whom 5 100 were black African slaves. *Macau in the Recovery Period* records: 'In 1635, there were 850 Portuguese with their *casados* [families] in Macau, each having six armed slaves, of whom the largest and most outstanding families were *cafre*.[61] There were also people of other races.'[62]

In 1624 Dutch colonialists occupied Taiwan, China. In 1661, when recovering Taiwan, Zheng Chenggong reorganised the captured Africans into a troop of black soldiers and sent them to fight the Dutch, armed with weapons seized from the Dutch forces.

The African soldiers impressed the Chinese with their combativeness, loyalty, bravery and fighting skills. Even so, the black soldiers were not rewarded with corresponding political, economic or social status. Dissatisfied, many of them fled to pursue new opportunities with the Ming border generals. According to statistics, 'over 200 *pretos* [black people] fled to Anhai from Macau' in 1647.[63]

Quite a few fled to the Southern Ming-controlled areas and became loyal soldiers of the Southern Ming emperor. The Southern Ming Emperor Longwu took the throne in Fuzhou, relying on an officer, Zheng Zhilong, Zheng Chenggong's father, who was the most influential leader of the armed merchants in the south-eastern coastal areas. He had a troop of 300 black soldiers under his command, loyal, reliable Christians from southern Africa. This troop was trusted and appreciated by both the elder and the younger Zheng. During an all-night Christmas celebration, the soldiers once sounded bugles and fired guns, startling Zheng Zhilong, who took it for a surprise enemy attack. After learning what was happening, Zheng did not punish them, but instead 'ordered that the soldiers be treated to drinks and cakes, and favoured them with silver so they could continue the celebration the following day, while warning them not to fire their guns, so as not to disturb the local residents'.[64] The officers and men were deeply moved by the gesture.

There were both white European and Japanese soldiers in Zheng Zhilong's troops, but the black officers and men 'obtained by Zheng Zhilong from Macau and other places' were not only 'fiercer than the white devils', but also good at foundry work and the use of firearms, providing Zheng's army with arms and support. The Franciscan priest Buenaventura Ibáñez recorded: 'In Anhai, the officer has a company of black soldiers, recruited from Macau and other places. They are Christians, and have wives and children. They have come to visit us. Their company commander is Luis de Matos, a clever, intelligent black man.'[65] Also, 'there are some black men from Macau there [Anhai], Christians, soldiers under that officer [Zheng Zhilong]'.[66] He added: 'The abovementioned officer has a large number of brown[67] Christians to serve him. He has great trust in them, and uses them as bodyguards and soldiers. When we landed, some of them came to welcome us. We had come to know some of them in Macau.'[68]

After Zheng Zhilong surrendered to the Qing, the black officers and men remained loyal to Zheng Chenggong, serving as a foreign mercenary bodyguard troop. When Zheng Chenggong attacked Nanjing, elite all-black squads fought the Qing army at the city wall and on the banks of the Yangtze River. In Zheng Chenggong's operation to recover Taiwan, the black troops fought dauntlessly against the stubborn enemy entrenched on the island and succeeded in persuading some Dutch officers and men to surrender. According to *Forgotten and Harmed Taiwan*, 'Two black troops in Zheng Chenggong's forces attacked Dutch fortresses. Some were former slaves of the Dutch, and were trained to use flintlocks.'[69]

In the third lunar month of 1661, Zheng Chenggong led his army of 25 000 soldiers and hundreds of warships to recover Taiwan. The unstoppable army swept the Penghu Islands, landed at Heliao Port in southern Taiwan (which was neglected by the Dutch), wiped out the Dutch troops and took the port. Growing bolder, the spirited soldiers of Zheng not only destroyed Dutch reinforcements, but also besieged the Dutch strongholds of Chikan City and Taiwan City. While besieging the cities, Zheng Chenggong enforced strict discipline, ensuring peace for the residents and promising swift retribution for any violations. He issued orders to reclaim the wastelands for military supply purposes and visited the Gaoshan ethnic tribe in their residential areas. With hearty support from the local people, Zheng's army absorbed Taiwanese fighters who armed themselves and helped drive out the colonialists.

Zheng Chenggong also adopted psychological tactics to weaken enemy forces. Based on a strong military threat, Zheng Chenggong shook the morale of the besieged or defeated enemy forces by sending them battlefield information, messages, statements, urging them to surrender. With skilful use of such tactics, Zheng Chenggong arranged for his black soldiers to secretly communicate with their counterparts in the Dutch army, inciting the black troops under Dutch command to surrender. These soldiers of slave origin in the Dutch army, daily oppressed by the colonialists, welcomed this instigation to rebel, spurring the surrender of black soldiers in the Dutch army. At the same time, the disadvantaged, unsupported Dutch troops in Taiwan City, unwilling to surrender, attempted a desperate battle, hoping that reinforcements would come to their aid. It was at this decisive moment that Zheng Chenggong ordered his troops to launch a general attack, during which they took an important fortress outside Taiwan City, Utrecht. Seeing the hopeless situation, the more than 600 defending soldiers in Taiwan City readily surrendered. On 1 February 1662, the head of the Dutch colonial forces, Frederick Coyett, signed the surrender treaty.

The recovery of Taiwan by Zheng Chenggong was a double gain. On the one hand, after 38 years of Dutch occupation, Taiwan was returned to China; on the other, the black slave soldiers in the Dutch army were liberated. These clever soldiers had contributed to both the recovery of Taiwan and their own liberation. Even more significantly, during the rule of Zheng Jing, Zheng Chenggong's son, in Taiwan, another black army offered its loyal service as palace guard. The soldiers from this force were buried in this exotic land where they had spilt their blood.

During the period in which large numbers of Chinese labourers were transported to Africa, another notable phenomenon occurred: Chinese merchants and scholars began travelling in Africa, leaving behind writings about the continent and insightfully introducing Africa to the Chinese people. Examples of the former include Fan Shouyi's *Records of a European Tour*; Chen Lunjiong's *Experiences*

Overseas; Xie Qinggao's *Records of the Seas*; and Wang Dahai's *Anecdotes on Sea Islands*. Later examples include Yung Wing's *My Life in China and America*; Zhang Deyi's *Navigation Wonders*; and Ding Lian's *Notes on Travels in Three Continents*. These were followed by Lin Zexu's *Cyclopedia of Geography*; Wei Yuan's *Records and Maps of the Oceanic Nations*; and Xu Jishe's *A Brief Record of the World*.

Compared to the works on other continents, these works on Africa seem sketchy and less informative. For instance, *Records of the Seas*, dictated by Xie Qinggao and recorded by Yang Bingnan, consists of three volumes, the first describing the Chinese mainland, the second describing the coastal lands around the Chinese mainland and the countries in the South China Sea, and the third describing three continents: Europe, America and Africa.

The section on Africa is brief, typified by descriptions such as the following: 'Africa, just to the west of Mauritius, can be reached within a month. Its boundary is unknown. It is home to over 100 nations.' The African people are described as being 'as black as liquor, with curly hair'. The situation in Africa is described as 'seized by Western powers, with some Africans capturing their own compatriots and selling them to foreign countries as slaves'. Further descriptions include: 'Its soil yields grain, ivory, rhinoceros horns, seahorse teeth, oranges, and watermelons.' The author, citing a description of Africa from *Experiences Overseas*, adds: 'The record in this section is not as detailed as that in *Experiences Overseas*.'[70] In discussing the authorship and content of the book, it records, 'Qinggao, a merchant and supposedly illiterate, is mostly reliable in his diction and broad observation, but not entirely so, despite the fact that he had been travelling for 14 years.' The book also notes: 'The names of nations, approximately pronounced in a Western accent, not in written form, might have been far-fetched and not quite authentic.'[71]

The republican period, 1911–1949

Just over a century ago, the 1911 Revolution did not bring about radical change to the fate of China or to the general framework of relations between China and Africa. These changes came only with the founding of the new China. Nevertheless, China–Africa relations in the republican period were marked by new conditions, problems and issues.

Primarily, so-called official relations between China and Africa, to a certain extent, developed in scope, in the number of nations involved, and in terms of the geopolitical situation. A minister-counsellor level of diplomatic relations was established between China and Egypt. Both nations with ancient civilisations, these two countries were quite similar, with each also having experienced a ground-shaking revolution in the early 20th century. The 1911 Revolution in China overthrew the Qing Dynasty and turned a new page in history, while the dynamic national independence movement forced the UK to give up its protectorate in 1922, paving the way for national independence for Egypt. As an independent state, the stage was set for Egypt to reinstitute its traditional diplomatic relations with China.

The two countries began negotiations to establish diplomatic relations in 1928, reaching an agreement to institute minister-counsellor-level diplomatic relations. In June 1935, the Nanjing government appointed Qiu Zhuming as Chinese consul to Cairo and, in May 1942, appointed Lin Haidong as Chinese minister counsellor to Egypt, with Qiu Zhuming reassigned as second legation secretary in charge of Cairo's consular affairs. In 1945 the Alexandrian consulate was established with Chen Kaimao formally appointed as consul. In 1944 the Egyptian legation was established in China and the first consul dispatched to China.[72] The re-establishment of China–Egypt diplomatic relations provided an opportunity for economic, cultural and personnel exchanges for the continuation and development of friendly relations between the two countries. For instance, China dispatched students to Egypt, with an exchange of teachers. The Egyptian government sent two doctors to China during a disastrous flood that occurred along the Yangtze River in 1931. They were warmly welcomed and praised by the Chinese people.

When the revolution took place in 1911, Liu Yi, the Qing imperial court consul general to South Africa, returned to China for leave. After the revolution, due to the upheaval caused by fighting among the warlords and unrest among the people, the Republic of China failed to dispatch consuls to South Africa in a timely manner, until the reappointment of Liu in 1920. Liu was so hard up financially that he depended on donations from Overseas Chinese for a living. During my own research into South Africa in August 2011, I had a conversation with Ye Huifen (Melanie Yap), author of *Colour, Confusion and Concessions: The History of the Chinese in South Africa*. I browsed through a good deal of original information she had collected, including letters of thanks to the local Chinese residents, written with an ink brush by Liu Yi. In his letters, Liu called the local Overseas Chinese donors his brothers and expressed his heartfelt thanks for their generous donations. On the one hand, this demonstrates the patriotism of the Chinese community in South Africa. On the other, it demonstrates the truth that a poor country is nothing in diplomatic relations.

Besides dispatching a consul general to South Africa, China also established consular relations with Algeria, Mauritius and Madagascar.

A characteristic of this stage in the history of China–Africa relations was a fluctuation in the limited level of trade, caused by external factors. During the republican period, China's trade with Africa focused on South Africa, Mauritius, Egypt and other North African countries. Limited as it was, trade was affected by the world recession of the 1930s and by the War of Resistance Against Japanese Aggression. According to statistics from a Mauritian Blue Paper, in the period between 1911 and 1920, Mauritian imports from China were valued at

4 379 947 Mauritian rupees; from 1921 to 1930 the figure was 10 369 778 rupees; and between 1931 and 1938, 4 099 544 rupees. The marked discrepancy is an indication of the close connection between Mauritian imports and the Chinese political landscape. After the death of the Empress Dowager Cixi in 1907, China experienced dramatic political changes, and Mauritius experienced a corresponding dramatic decline in its imports. After the founding of the Republic of China, Mauritian imports from China rose, then declined again when Sun Yat-sen handed over the presidency to Yuan Shikai. When Sun came back into power, imports from China into Mauritius started climbing again. In 1931, when the Japanese invaded three north-eastern provinces in China, Chiang Kai-shek adopted a policy of 'stabilising the domestic situation to resist foreign invasion', opposing the nationalist sentiment of the Overseas Chinese community, as they saw the communists as their brothers and the alien Japanese as foreign aggressors, of a kind with Western colonisers who bullied and oppressed China. From this time, Mauritius decreased its imports from China, a possible indication that it was not in favour of Chiang's policy.[73]

Another factor to consider is that the Chinese and African nations, sharing a similar destiny, supported each other in their struggle against imperialism on one hand and colonialism on the other. Being Third World countries, enslaved and oppressed, and closely united in a common destiny, China and Africa have been encouraging and supporting each other in their struggle against colonialism and imperialism: it's as if they composed their revolutionary songs of triumph together as they struggled heroically side by side.

On 5 December 1934, the Italian Fascists abruptly crossed the Somalia–Ethiopia border, killed over 100 Ethiopian soldiers and wounded dozens more. The Fascists even demand apologies and compensation from Ethiopia. Flatly refusing these unreasonable demands from Italy, Ethiopia prepared for an armed counterattack to defend its territory. The records state:

> Their action and spirit is enough to turn our faces red from ear to ear, and to make us sweat with shame. The Italo-Abyssinia[74] War and China-Japan conflict are parallel in line and action. The present situation in Abyssinia reflects our past which, though not making us 'sweat with shame', only makes us 'ashamed for our lack of heat'.[75]

The Ethiopian people's resolute actions and spirit in resisting foreign invasion was a great encouragement to the Communist Party of China and to the Chinese people, who were saving China by resisting Japanese invasion. In a declaration, the Communist Party of China said:

> Dear compatriots, China is our motherland! The Chinese nation is a compatriot to us all! Can we sit by watching the extermination of our nation and family? No! Absolutely not! Abyssinia, with its eight million people, is able to wage a heroic struggle against the Italian imperialists' aggression, defending their territory and people. Can China, a great nation of 400 million people, sit helpless, waiting for death?[76]

The righteousness and heroic spirit of the Ethiopian people frightened the Italian aggressors and kept Italian troops beyond the border, not having the nerve to invade, for half a year. Then, on 3 October 1935, Italy started a war of aggression against Ethiopia, attacking from three sides. Ethiopia mobilised the whole country to offer stiff resistance to the aggressors. The Chinese Workers' and Peasants' Red Army, approaching its successful completion of the Ten Thousand *Li* Long March, published an open letter to the Ethiopian people, expressing support for the war they had just waged to resist Italian aggression, praising the Ethiopian people for their staunch national spirit, and pointing out that imperialism was the common enemy of the Chinese and Ethiopian peoples. On 1 December 1935, the Chinese government joined in the international stand against Italy, announcing economic sanctions.

China–Africa relations in this period were controlled, obstructed and suppressed by the colonialists, with official bilateral exchanges and non-governmental contracts all restricted by the colonial powers. In this respect, there are three points to be noted. Firstly, because of the control over the traditional China–Africa navigational routes by the colonialists, China–Africa personnel exchanges and trade were realised only with permission from the colonisers.

Secondly, despite nominal diplomatic relations established between China and some African countries, these relations were in fact channels serving the colonial rulers, as clearly evidenced by the China-Congo Special Chapter, signed by China and Belgium, and the Labour Protection Regulations, signed by China and Britain.

Finally, African countries were represented by colonialists, and the Qing Empire was at their mercy, as demonstrated by so-called diplomatic rights. The Labour Protection Regulations was signed in London and the China-Congo treaty drafted in Brussels and represented by the Belgians in negotiations and signing. What was even more absurd was that the Chinese consul to Mozambique was a German nominated by Portugal. In short, in the 500-year history of China–Africa communications, the two subjects of communication – China and Africa – were not initiators or decision-makers, but their relations were controlled and manipulated by Western powers. Facts have demonstrated that communication, cooperation and diplomatic affairs were impossible between the weak semi-colonial China and the African countries under colonial rule. Nevertheless, their shared historical experience, common goal, interlinked national sentiment, and their friendship in the joint struggle brought them together and prepared the ground for the establishment of equitable, mutually beneficial, sincere diplomatic relations.

INDEPENDENT, LOYAL, FRIENDLY PARTNERS: 1949 TO PRESENT

The period from 1949 to the present was one of development from independent, strategic partnership to direct diplomacy. The founding of the new China opened up a new chapter in China–Africa relations. From its founding, the new China's relationship with Africa entered its greatest period of development, with direct official and non-official communication by air and sea with stable, healthy, well-rounded development and greater scale, speed and frequency of communications.

This period can be divided into three stages. In the first, from 1949 to 1978, the foundation was laid for normal development. The second stage, from 1978 to 2000, saw several adjustments and more rapid development. The final stage, from 2000 to the present, witnessed systemisation and all-round development.

The first stage of development occurred in two steps. The first, laying of the foundation, lasted from October 1949, when the People's Republic of China was founded, until 1959, when China established diplomatic relations with Guinea. The People's Republic of China was greatly concerned with the various national liberation movements and actively supported them. The Asian-African Conference, held in April 1955, provided a good opportunity for China to establish direct diplomatic contact with Africa. The following year, Egypt became the first African country to establish diplomatic relations with China, opening up modern diplomatic relations between the two regions. Three years later, in 1959, China-Africa relations crossed the Sahara Desert, with Guinea becoming the first African country south of the Sahara to establish diplomatic relations with China, launching a phase of more comprehensive development in the relations between China and the African continent, and laying a solid foundation for more diplomatic initiatives.

Over the next 20 years development prevailed, with China–Africa relations growing at a steady, rapid pace. By 1979 China had established diplomatic relations with 44 African countries. During this period, China gave active support to the national independence and national liberation movements taking place across Africa, and offered newly independent African countries enthusiastic assistance for the development of their national economic agendas. At the end of 1978, China started its own great historical programme of Reform and Opening Up, a dramatic historical shift of national focus from class struggle to economic construction. Its international focus during this period moved away from revolution and war to peace and development.

Against this historical backdrop, China–Africa relations entered a second phase, in which adjustments and rapid development took centre stage. Politically, China gradually de-emphasised the ideological aspects of China–Africa relations.

Economically, financial assistance gradually shifted towards mutually beneficial economic trade and cooperation. At the same time, China carried out activities in the fields of culture, medicine, and science and technology, promoting exchange and cooperation. As a result, bilateral relations saw rapid development in this stage, and China–Africa trade increased each year, with a large number of Chinese enterprises entering Africa. By 1999, over 800 Chinese companies were operating in 40 African countries, Chinese investment in Africa had reached $466 million and, conversely, African investment in China $520 million, with 662 projects operating in China.[77]

The establishment of the Forum on China–Africa Cooperation (FOCAC) in 2000 marked the beginning of a new era, in which China–Africa relations set off on a path towards all-round systematic development, with greater depth, scope and vigour at higher levels, in a broader field, and through more channels, creating a multidimensional, multilayered, wide-ranging development trend. On 19 July 2012 Thomas Boni Yayi, president of Benin and then acting chairman of the African Union, said in his speech at the opening ceremony of the 5th Ministerial Conference of FOCAC, speaking on behalf of all African countries, that FOCAC had become an important platform for collective dialogue and a practical, effective mechanism for cooperation. In the three-year period before that speech, the joint efforts of Africa and China had lent great impetus to the achievements of the 4th Ministerial Conference of FOCAC, particularly in the execution on both sides of the eight cooperation policies. Boni Yayi said, 'The cooperation between Africa and China is expressed in many plans, projects, and their follow-up implementation and achievement. For this, we should extend our great respect to the Chinese people and their leaders.'[78]

South African President Jacob Zuma, co-chairman at the following session of the forum, expressed his great appreciation for the selfless long-term assistance China had given to Africa. He stated that China's devotion to Africa had found expression in many achievements and in great cooperation between the two, especially in terms of human-resource development, debt reduction and investment: 'The efforts made by China to assist the development of Africa have been affirmed by many African countries, and the mechanism of FOCAC has made it possible for Africa and China to cooperate even more closely as strategic partners for the benefit of the African and Chinese peoples.'[79]

At the 4th Ministerial Conference of FOCAC in 2009, held in Sharm el-Sheikh, Egypt, the Chinese premier, Wen Jiabao, said:

> Since its establishment nine years ago, FOCAC has played an important role in leading and promoting the development of China–Africa relations, bridging the deepening friendship between China and Africa, and serving as a platform

for strengthened cooperation. Especially since the Beijing Summit held three years ago, both China and Africa are committed to the establishment of a new strategic partnership based on political equality and mutual trust, and on win-win economic cooperation. This has opened up new prospects for China–Africa cooperation.[80]

Premier Wen provided evidence of the growing relationship between China and Africa by citing specific examples and figures in terms of growing mutual trust in the political arena, deepening cooperation in trade and economics, and greater cultural exchange and mutual learning. He referred to the substantial results of Chinese aid to Africa, and the vigorous development of cultural and educational exchanges. He listed numerous examples of China–Africa relations and trade, which served to illustrate the strengthening of China–Africa relations.

For instance, during the period 2001 to 2010, China–Africa economic and trade relations experienced all-round rapid development, with bilateral trade values increasing by 28 per cent as China became Africa's largest trade partner. China has continually supported and assisted Africa's independent development through investment and aid, on the basis of equality, mutual benefit and joint development. At the same time, a pattern of cooperation that is multilayered, broad-ranging and comprehensive has been forged by the two. This plays a significant role in promoting the economic development and social progress of both sides.[81]

Over the previous decade or more, economic and trade relations between China and Africa experienced rapid development with a pattern of cooperation featuring comprehensive coverage beginning to emerge. This pattern played an irreplaceable role in the economic and social development of both sides. The Chinese Ministry of Commerce has identified five characteristics inherent in China–Africa relations:

- Rapid development of bilateral trade, which increased by 28 per cent from 2001 to 2010 to ultimately hit $126.9 billion and saw China become Africa's largest trade partner.
- A substantial increase in China's direct investment in Africa. By the end of 2010, China's direct investment in Africa had reached $13 billion, with over 2 000 Chinese enterprises investing in Africa. In the first three quarters of 2011, China's direct non-financial investment amounted to $1.08 billion, registering an 87 per cent year-on-year increase and establishing a momentum of significant growth.
- Stable development of cooperation in infrastructure construction. Chinese companies completed $132.5 billion worth in contracted projects by the end of 2010. This accounts for 30 per cent of China's overseas project turnover, which was expanded in the first three quarters of 2011 with the signing of

- contracts worth a further $25.2 billion and the completion of another $23.7 billion worth of contracts.
- Gradual expansion in the scope of cooperation, with a sound development trend emerging in finance, telecommunications, tourism and shipping. There are many Chinese financial institutions operating in Africa and many Chinese and African airlines operating direct flights between the two.
- The perfecting of a guarantee system, with FOCAC serving as an important mechanism for the promotion of the development of bilateral economic and trade relations. The economic and trade measures put forward by China in the framework of the forum have become important systems that give impetus to greater economic and trade cooperation. China has established joint economic and trade committees with most African countries, and has signed agreements for trade and investment protection.[82]

When speaking of the latest developments in China–Africa relations at the 5th Ministerial Conference of FOCAC, Chairman Hu Jintao cited several statistics. He pointed out that China–Africa trade values reached $166.3 billion in 2011, twice the figure seen in 2006. By 2012, China's total direct investment in Africa had reached over $15 billion, with projects in 50 African countries, and the China-aided African Union Conference Centre, in Addis Ababa, was completed in 2012.

Through steady growth of aid to Africa, China has built over 100 schools, 30 hospitals, 30 anti-malaria centres and 20 agricultural technology demonstration centres. China has fulfilled its promise to provide Africa with $15 billion in preferential loans. It has also trained 40 000 African personnel in various fields and provided over 20 000 government scholarships.

Through joint efforts, China and Africa have established 29 Confucius Institutes or Confucius Classrooms in 22 African countries. Twenty well-known institutions of higher education in Africa and China are involved the China–Africa College 20 + 20 Cooperation Program. Chairman Hu emphasised that

> facts have proven that the new China–Africa strategic cooperation is a continuation of the traditional friendship between China and Africa, is to the most basic benefit of both China and Africa, and conforms to the trend of the times, a trend toward peace, development, and cooperation. The establishment of this China–Africa relationship has opened up a new historical period for the development of a new relationship between China and Africa, and has lent vigour and vitality to this bilateral cooperation.[83]

FIVE FEATURES OF CHINA–AFRICA RELATIONS

In conclusion, there are several striking features of China–Africa relations. The first is that the relationship has a long history over several centuries. The entire process of China–Africa communication can be roughly divided into four periods, alternating between indirect and direct communications. There were five peaks of communications during these periods, in the Han Dynasty, the Tang Dynasty, the Song-Yuan Dynasty, the early Ming Dynasty and the period after the founding of the new China.[84] In this long historical process, Zheng He's visits to Africa marked a high point in ancient China–Africa relations, a trend that is echoed in the rapidly developing relations between the two regions since the founding of the new China.

This gradual development of China–Africa relations over the ages has been full of twists and turns, influenced by many factors, both internal and external, and by changes both in the domestic situations in China and Africa and in the international situation. The general trend and orientation of the development of the relationship has been markedly slow. In terms of communication channels, non-official communications were followed by official pairings. In terms of communication routes, land communication was followed by sea communication. In terms of geography, North Africa preceded East Africa. In terms of scope, simple personnel and trade exchanges preceded rapid development. This trend in the development of China–Africa relations is evident. It was also characterised by a series of rises and falls, and by alternating active and passive factors. For instance, the control of the exchange of personnel and goods by Western colonialists after the Portuguese gained control of the sea trade routes led to Western manipulation of China–Africa relations, with neither side being free to take initiative in their dealings. The founding of the new China marked a new round of rapid, all-round development of China–Africa relations.

The mutual understanding and shared characteristics between China and Africa serve as an emotional basis for mutual respect and equitable treatment that are distinctly reflected in the five peaks of communication between the two regions. In the period of the divided Han Dynasty, Zhang Qian returned to China after suffering great hardships in western countries. Being warmly received by the Han Emperor Wudi for his report, he was sent on another diplomatic mission to the west. Upon arriving in Wusun, Zhang Qian ordered his assistant Gan Ying to continue his westward travel in an effort to contact countries in western Asia and North Africa. Years later, when the Han envoy started its return journey, the Parthian king ordered an envoy to accompany him. This envoy 'presented large bird eggs and Liqian magicians to the Han emperor'.[85]

In the Tang Dynasty, Du Huan was sent accidentally to Africa, and left behind the earliest Chinese record of personal experience in Africa. During the same period, black Africans travelled to Chang'an, as evidenced by clay figurines unearthed from two Tang Dynasty tombs in Xi'an. By the Yuan Dynasty, the great Chinese traveller Wang Dayuan travelled through more than 10 African countries, writing his *Brief on Exotic Islands*. A few years later, the great African traveller Ibn Battuta went to China and produced *Travels of Ibn Battuta*. The Ming Dynasty eunuch Zheng He made four visits to Africa during his travels on the Western Ocean, and African countries sent envoys to pay return visits to China, travelling aboard Zheng He's ships. The king of Malindi respectfully presented giraffes to the Chinese emperor in this way.

In modern times, the Chinese and African nations have, through shared joy, sorrow and adversity, assisted and supported each other in their long, bitter struggles against imperialism and colonialism. Such reciprocal exchanges, interactions and mutual support, happening almost simultaneously, are convincing evidence that China and Africa – even as far apart as they are – are of one mind and spirit, enjoying mutual understanding, shared aspirations, great potential and enthusiasm for communication, and common prospects. Given time, such mutual understanding and opportunities will translate into both internal and external motivations for the rapid development of China–Africa relations.

The founding of the new China marked a new era of development in China–Africa relations, realising the hopes of the peoples of China and Africa. Their similar pasts, their close mutual affection, and the shared task of development that lay before them bound them closely on the basis of political equality, mutual trust, mutually beneficial economic cooperation, cultural exchange and mutual learning. Now, people in China are increasingly talking about Africa, more Chinese companies are investing in Africa and more Chinese tourists are visiting Africa. The African people are likewise appreciative of China for its brilliant economic achievements, with the 'China mode' and the 'China path' being hot topics of conversation in Africa. The African continent is 'looking eastward'.

One simple fact that verifies the mutual understanding and emotional connection between the people of China and Africa is that every Chinese person who has worked in or visited Africa, whether sent by the government or at his or her own expense, has become a great enthusiast of the African continent and its people, maintaining a special affection for Africa that only intensifies over time. This deeply ingrained affection for the continent keeps the Chinese people eager to do their part for the African people. This is as true of those who have been away from Africa for a long time, as it is of those who just left. This special affection is often called the 'African complex'. The Chinese government's special representative for African issues, Liu Guijin, once said, 'In the past 26 years, I never left Africa or African affairs.' Liu often says, 'I deeply love Africa, this lovely land under my feet, and have great affection for it.'[86]

Many African people who visit China are likewise warmly received by the local people. In June 2011 the West Asia and Africa Institute of the Chinese Academy of Social Sciences received a delegation of African scholars, making arrangements for them to participate in discussions at various central and local institutions. In the opening speeches, leaders from these institutions unanimously extended their warm welcome to the African scholars, calling them friends in an expression of the long-standing affection the Chinese people have had for the people of Africa. This sincerity and warmth deeply moved the African scholars, closing the emotional distance between the Chinese and African nations.[87]

Throughout the history of development in China–Africa relations, the two have treated each other with sincerity, equality and wholehearted assistance, as friends, partners, and important members of the international community. Taking the African continent as an integrated whole, China gives equal treatment to all African nations, large or small, powerful or weak. In terms of economic cooperation, China emphasises mutual benefit and win-win cooperation, wholeheartedly assisting African countries in enhancing their capabilities for independent development and improving the livelihood of their people. China emphasises mutual learning, each taking from the other's strong points to make up for its own weaknesses for the sake of joint development. In international affairs, China has always attached importance to the benefit of African countries and supported their concerns.

The normal development of China–Africa relations was, and still is, to some extent, disrupted and influenced by external factors. This finds expression in three main areas. Firstly, the important contributions China–Africa communications have made to the world are, unfortunately, being concealed, neglected or even forgotten. For instance, of the four great medieval travellers acknowledged by the West, three are Italians, and one is the African Ibn Battuta, while Du Huan and Wang Dayuan, both from China, are ignored by some. Another instance is the east–west navigational route, supposedly discovered by Vasco da Gama, at least half of which was opened up by Zheng He.

A second area was the intrusion of Western colonialists into the Indian Ocean, causing communications between China and Africa to decline into a recession that lasted five centuries. The effects of this situation have lasted through to the present day, with China and Africa still striving to build mutual understanding and trust. The third area is the continued pressure exerted by the West on contemporary China–Africa relations, with the ongoing development of those relations constantly subjected to a clamour of voices from the West.

The history of China–Africa relations is a reflection of the evolution of human history and the world's development path. Du Huan and his comrades introduced great Chinese inventions to Europe by way of Africa, promoting human progress. Zheng He opened up the oceangoing navigation era of humankind, marking the advent of a new era with his four visits to Africa. The independence and liberation of China and Africa marked the end of Western colonialism. The economic development of China and African countries suggests that we are witnessing the advent of a brand-new world economic order today.

17

The Chinese in Africa

DISTRIBUTION OF THE OVERSEAS CHINESE

The history of the world is characterised by continuous migration for the sake of survival and development. For early immigrants, the primitive instinct to adapt to nature and to seek arable lands gradually developed into conscious behaviours aiming at achieving new benefits and pursuing new lifestyles. It is this primal impulse that dominates and determines people's mobility, a drive towards greater heights.

Immigration trends and behaviours drove the Chinese to the Western Pass or places east of Shanhaiguan[1] or to coastal areas of China, and encouraged them to venture to the Southern Ocean, or the Americas as humankind entered an era of international migration.

According to the UN Immigration Database, the number of transnational migrants increased from 155 518 065 in 1990 to 178 498 563 in 2000. In 2010 it had grown to 213 943 812 – an increase of over 58 million in 20 years. In the same period, while the world population continued to grow, the global migrant population increased from 2.9 per cent to 3.1 per cent of the population.[2]

In this global era of migration, no country can avoid the migration phenomenon. Overseas Chinese[3] form a large proportion of the world's migrant population, while Chinese people in Africa constitute a small part of the total Chinese emigrant community.

By the middle of the 20th century, the geographical distribution of the Chinese diaspora was uneven, with great concentration in some places and sparser dispersion in others. Two facts demonstrate this. Firstly, about 90 per cent of the Chinese emigrant population was concentrated in South East Asia, especially Indonesia, Thailand, Malaysia and Singapore, each of which was home to about 5 million Overseas Chinese (about 75 per cent of Singapore's population were ethnic Chinese). And, secondly, about half of the remaining 10 per cent reside in North America, with the other half scattered across north-east Asia, Latin America and

Oceania.[4] The ethnic Chinese in Africa make up a small portion of the total Overseas Chinese population.

For a long time, the actual number of Overseas Chinese was not known. In the early years of the new China, the government's estimates suggested that there were 13 to 15 million, of whom over 85 per cent lived in South East Asia. In 1984, several years after the launch of Reform and Opening Up, General Secretary of the Chinese Communist Party Hu Yaobang and Executive Secretary Xi Zhongxun cited figures of 30 million Overseas Chinese. Since then, Chinese leaders have been using the imprecise term 'tens of millions' when speaking of the overseas population.

Table 17.1 *Total population of Overseas Chinese, 1950–2008*

	Early 1950s	1980	1999/2000	2008
Population (millions)	12.09	21	39.75	48

Sources: *Overseas Chinese population reference material*. Beijing: Research Society on Overseas Chinese, 1956; State Council's Overseas Chinese Affairs Cadre School of the Overseas Chinese Affairs Office, *Summary of Overseas Chinese* (2005), 'Global Overseas Chinese population data at the end of the 20th and beginning of the 21st centuries'.
Note: The newest data, from 2008, is estimated from comparisons and summaries prepared by the Global Chinese Entrepreneurs Development Report Group of the China News Agency.

Table 17.2 *Distribution of Chinese diaspora, 1950–2000*

Area	Early 1950s		1999/2000	
	Chinese population (millions)	%	Chinese population (millions)	%
Asia	11.667	96.45	32.94	82.85
Americas	0.256	2.12	4.33	10.90
Europe	0.037	0.31	1.45	3.66
Oceania	0.098	0.81	0.78	1.98
Africa	0.037	0.31	0.24	0.61
Total	12.097	100.00	39.75	100.00

Sources: *Overseas Chinese population reference material*. Beijing: Research Society on Overseas Chinese, 1956; State Council's Overseas Chinese Affairs Cadre School of the Overseas Chinese Affairs Office, 2005, *Summary of Overseas Chinese*, 'Global Overseas Chinese population data at the end of the 20th and beginning of the 21st centuries'.

The estimates of the number of Overseas Chinese made by domestic authorities and academics are widely different, varying from 30 million to 87 million.[5] The following data, based on the 2008 *Global Overseas Chinese development report*, issued at the beginning of 2009 by a research group from the China News Service, shows the variations in the reported numbers of Overseas Chinese in various periods of the new China.[6]

The China News Service report suggests that in 2008, the Overseas Chinese population was about 6 million.[7] This estimate indicates several points. Firstly, the figures from the various authorities have not been reconciled. Due to the regional mobility of Overseas Chinese people, marriage between different ethnic groups, and various limitations, research institutions and government bodies are not able to carry out comprehensive, detailed demographic censuses among the Overseas Chinese scattered throughout the world. Of the censuses provided, some were carried out by the relevant national authorities, while most were carried out by Chinese embassies, consulates, Overseas Chinese Affairs offices, and Overseas Chinese associations, often resulting in disparities in terms of the time the censuses were conducted and the population size reported.

Secondly, the Overseas Chinese Affairs Office estimates that the Overseas Chinese population totalled 39.76 million at the turn of the new century, 2 million of whom were a new generation of migrants who had left mainland China in recent decades, since 1978. Another estimate of the total Overseas Chinese population is taken from an annual statistics report produced in 2007 by the Taiwanese Overseas Chinese Committee, stating that the Overseas Chinese population totalled 38.794 million.

Thirdly, in estimating the total number of Chinese living in 2008, this research group adopted data from the 2005 edition of *Summary of Overseas Chinese*, published by the State Council's Overseas Chinese Affairs Cadre, School. The total population reported in 2000 was 40 million, a fairly reliable figure, since it came from respected statistical research carried out by the editorial group in various countries.

Finally, calculated in light of the world population growth rate of 1.2 per cent between 2000 and 2005, the number of Overseas Chinese should have grown from 40 million in 2000 to 44 million in 2008, an increase of 4.17 million in a nine-year period. By 2008 the total number of Overseas Chinese should be estimated at 48 million.[8]

The *Annual Report on Overseas Chinese Study* (2011)[9] states that, in the 30 years since Reform and Opening Up, about 4.5 million people have emigrated from China, with about 2.5 to 3 million of them emigrating to developed countries. The report puts the total worldwide Overseas Chinese population at 45.43 million, with 33.48 million living in South East Asia, making up 6 per cent of the population in that region and 73.3 per cent of the global Overseas Chinese population. These figures are the result of elaborate estimations made of the worldwide Overseas Chinese population by the research group under the leadership of Professor Zhuang Guotu of the Nanyang Institute, Xiamen University, a task entrusted to the group by the State Council's Overseas Chinese Affairs Office. This research group arrived at its results systematically, according to historical statistical data and taking into account the natural population growth rate, mechanical growth rate and other factors, with consideration given to the impact of new migrants since Reform and Opening Up. After the announcement of these research results, the Overseas Chinese Affairs Office of the State Council of the People's Republic of China formally announced in June 2010 that the Overseas Chinese population was 45 million, the largest migrant population in the world.[10]

I have come to the following conclusions, based on my analysis of the data cited above:
- Despite variations in the sources of these figures and in research methods, the total number of Overseas Chinese people is between 45 and 48 million, with the official estimate of 45 million in this range seeming to be the more objective conclusion.
- In the roughly 30 years since Reform and Opening Up, great changes have taken place in China, and the geographical distribution of Overseas Chinese has changed as a result. The proportion of ethnic Chinese living in South East Asia has fallen from 90 per cent of the total Overseas Chinese population to 73 per cent – a decrease that can be explained by the fact that new emigrants have opted to depart for developed countries.
- For a combination of reasons, the precise figure for the number of Overseas Chinese people living in Africa is not available.

THE OVERSEAS CHINESE POPULATION IN AFRICA

Because the Chinese mainland's academic circles are so little involved in studying the Overseas Chinese community in Africa, especially compared with studies of the Chinese population in South East Asia, Europe and the Americas, Professor Li Anshan's treatise, the *History of the Overseas Chinese in Africa*, published in 2000, can be regarded as the most authoritative work on the subject. In 1996 Li estimated that the total population of Overseas Chinese in Africa was 136 000.[11]

The figure given for the population of Chinese in Africa at the turn of the century, according to the 2008 Global Chinese Entrepreneurs Development Report, is 240 000. The Overseas Chinese Blue Paper (2011) cites Zhu Huiling's figures as 250 000, and Wang Wangbo and Zhuang Guotu's figures for 2006/07 as 500 000, but this does not include those migrating from Taiwan, Hong Kong and Macau. The total Overseas Chinese population in Africa, including those from Taiwan, Hong Kong and Macau, is 550 000.[12] This report puts the total number of Overseas Chinese worldwide at 45.43 million.[13] The official figure announced by the Chinese authorities is the result of this research.

Table 17.3 *Overseas Chinese population and distribution by continent, 2006–2007*

Continent	Number (10 000)	Percentage of global Overseas Chinese population (%)	Continent	Number (10 000)	Percentage of global Overseas Chinese population (%)
Asia	3 548	78.10	Oceania	95	2.09
America	630	13.87	Africa	55	1.21
Europe	215	4.73	World	4 543	100.00

Source: Wang Wangbo and Zhuang Guotu (eds), *2008 Description of the Overseas Chinese*. World Knowledge Press, 2010, p. 7.

Table 17.4 *New Overseas Chinese population and distribution by continent, 2006–2007*

Continent	Number (10 000)	Percentage of global Overseas Chinese population (%)	Continent	Number (10 000)	Percentage of global Overseas Chinese population (%)
Asia	400	11.27	Oceania	60	63.16
America	350	55.56	Africa	50	90.91
Europe	170	79.07	Total	1 030	22.67*

Source: Wang Wangbo and Zhuang Guotu (eds), *2008 Description of the Overseas Chinese*. World Knowledge Press, 2010, p. 7.
* The figures in this table indicate the proportion of new Overseas Chinese against the total Overseas Chinese population. The percentage by continent indicates the proportion of that continent's Overseas Chinese population in relation to the worldwide Overseas Chinese population.

Scholars often cite the Overseas Chinese in their studies about China, and often report on the size of that population group. It is unanimously agreed that it is impossible to work out an exact number of the Overseas Chinese population, and that estimates must suffice. It is generally accepted that the Overseas Chinese population in Africa was between 0.4 and 0.6 million at the end of the last century.[14] Since this figure is somewhat elastic, the Western media usually rely on an average of 0.5 million living in Africa.

So, how many Overseas Chinese are actually living in Africa? To address that question, it is important to categorise the Overseas Chinese population there and analyse why it is so difficult to work out a precise figure. From there, it is possible to make an estimation according to the categories and, on that basis, to estimate the population of Overseas Chinese in Africa and examine the trends.

Categorising the Overseas Chinese population in Africa

The term 'Overseas Chinese in Africa' can mean various things, with broad and narrow definitions, including earlier and more recent migrants, those from mainland China as well as those from Hong Kong, Taiwan and Macau. In its broadest sense, the term refers to all ethnic Chinese who are born, living or working in Africa, whether government-sponsored or self-supported, from the mainland, Taiwan, Hong Kong or Macau, regardless of occupation, personal identity, residency or citizenship, as long as they have Chinese blood.

In the narrowest sense, it refers to people from the Chinese mainland who emigrated to Africa since the beginning of Reform and Opening Up in 1978 for business, employment or education. This category is often called the 'new Overseas Chinese'. It does not include government-funded personnel, those from Hong Kong, Macau or Taiwan, or those who arrived earlier. This latter group forms the largest number of Chinese people in Africa, having come for business, employment or to study, with very few of them becoming citizens in their countries of residence.

The Overseas Chinese in Africa can be divided into the following three categories: government-sponsored personnel, self-supporting personnel and contract workers. They can also be further divided into categories such as early migrants, mixed race and new migrants.

Among the Overseas Chinese in Africa, there are public-sector employees sent there by Chinese government departments, enterprises and other institutions, including embassy workers, employees of Chinese businesses, experts, doctors, journalists, students, volunteers, Confucius Institute teachers, peacekeeping troops and other personnel. Motivated by various factors, the self-supporting category of personnel in Africa work in a range of occupations, with many running hotels, stores, factories, construction companies, international trade companies, travel agencies, newspapers and clinics. Most of this group are employees or small-business owners. Very few have succeeded as major entrepreneurs. The past several years have seen an increase in contract workers employed in infrastructure, building roads, houses and dams, for example, encouraged by the growth in Chinese investment and assistance in Africa.

The earlier Overseas Chinese comprise those who came to Africa to make their living shortly before or after the founding of the new China, as well as their descendants. The mixed-race groups are the descendants of Chinese-African couples, the descendants of earlier Overseas Chinese-African couples, the descendants of new Overseas Chinese-African couples, and their children. All Chinese people of mixed race in Africa, albeit a small number, fall into this category. Those who have gained citizenship in their African countries of residence also form a very small group. Of these, the earlier Overseas Chinese form the majority, with an overwhelming proportion of them living in South Africa, Mauritius, Madagascar and Réunion (an overseas *département* of France).

Africa's Chinese population can therefore be roughly divided into two categories: new Overseas Chinese and earlier Overseas Chinese. Most new Overseas Chinese are residents, but not citizens, in their countries of residence, whereas the earlier Overseas Chinese are now citizens and part of the larger African family, having been there for generations.

Difficulties in sourcing accurate data

As a special community growing in number and influence, the Overseas Chinese presence in Africa is increasingly attracting attention with the rapid pace of development of China–Africa relations. There is therefore great interest in gaining accurate data on the Overseas Chinese population in Africa. This interest has been expressed by the Chinese government, African governments, international media, researchers and the African Overseas Chinese community itself. Each of these groups wants an exact figure for its own motives and objectives but, in practice, putting a precise figure on the size of this group is difficult – a problem that will not be solved in the short term.

Obstacles to acquiring an exact figure for the Overseas Chinese population in Africa include the difficulty in agreeing on a definition, difficulties in obtaining quantitative statistics, and the difficulty of organising and managing the data – a triumvirate often referred to in Chinese as the 'three difficulties'.

The first, the challenge of agreeing on definitions of terms, relates to identifying personal status in the broader or narrower sense. This concerns residential status, with duration of stay distinguishing the individual as either a short-term visitor or resident. Some suggest that one year should serve as a demarcation line, but this is arbitrary, and is particularly hard to pin down, as so many of the Overseas Chinese travel back and forth between African countries or between the African and Asian continents. Another difficulty arises from the issue of self-identification, particularly in instances such as children born out of wedlock who, for whatever reason, may not identify as Chinese. Other issues, such as switching from government-funded to self-supporting status, can lead to confusion in one's identity as well. The major difficulty in defining an identity lies in assertion, categorisation and affirmation, which are often called the 'three suppositions' in Chinese.

The major challenge to quantifying the numbers is rooted in the mobility, dispersion and diversity of the Chinese population in Africa. Whether for business development or simply for making a living, some Overseas Chinese continually move from one African country to another, between Africa and China, or between Africa and other parts of the world, varying the length of time and location of their stays, some maintaining residential status, or perhaps holding different passports.

This great degree of mobility, typical of the Overseas Chinese people in Africa, is often seen among contract workers, presenting another challenge to the gathering of statistics. Alongside this mobility, the dispersion of the Overseas Chinese is seen in the scattered locations of their settlements. For instance, in South Africa, there is a concentration of Chinese people who live not only in the major urban areas, like Johannesburg, Durban, Pretoria, Cape Town, Port Elizabeth and Bloemfontein, but also in several other towns and in more remote and isolated areas. Many contact the consulates in Johannesburg, Cape Town and Durban only if they experience trouble. Compounding the situation, there is a great diversity in the occupations among the Overseas Chinese people in Africa, who perform any occupation one can imagine – and many one cannot.

But the real challenge of gathering statistics on the Overseas Chinese population in Africa does not lie primarily in their mobility, dispersion or diversity, but in the lack of organisation and management. This difficulty is seen in the poor management of their countries of residence, which leads to a great deal of illegal immigration and the vague definition of the rights, responsibilities and obligations of Overseas Chinese organisations and the related Chinese authorities. In other words, any description of the difficulty of management and organisation does not indicate a shift of responsibilities and performance on the part of the concerned authorities. Rather, the difficulties are a result of the characteristics of Overseas Chinese communities, due to the limited functions of their organisations, the limited diplomatic powers of their missions, the limited domestic channels, and a lack of distinct definition of management roles in the countries in which the Overseas Chinese live.

The Overseas Chinese have established and developed associations, societies and communities in their adopted countries of residence based on where they live, affiliations and professional relationships. Over time, with the growing numbers of Overseas Chinese and their social progress, Overseas Chinese organisations have adapted to keep up with the times, establishing an increasing number of technological and political societies in the process. Active as they are in organising and managing the Overseas Chinese population, these organisations have a relatively loose structure, lacking a binding force. They are too malleable for exact membership to be kept, despite the basic stability of their leadership.

China has established embassies in all the African nations with which it has diplomatic relations[15] and has consulates with offices or personnel appointed to deal with Overseas Chinese affairs in several African countries. However, the exact size of the Overseas Chinese population is of little concern to embassies and consulates, as an approximate figure suffices for their needs. The five central committees of the Overseas Chinese Affairs Office are greatly concerned about Overseas Chinese affairs, but their communication with the Overseas Chinese communities is limited and their work for the Overseas Chinese people is mainly carried out through the embassies and consulates.

In managing the Chinese communities, their countries of residence are also confronted with many practical challenges. Given the low percentage of Chinese people in their overall population, most of these countries do not have special items in their population censuses to account for ethnic Chinese people, and some categorise Chinese in the broader group of Asians. Furthermore, the global problem of illegal immigration is a huge issue for most countries, creating difficulties in locating data and exact figures for official population statistics.

In short, in the current environment, it is virtually impossible to gain an exact figure of the number of Overseas Chinese people living in Africa.

Statistics related to Africa's Overseas Chinese population

As mentioned, the Chinese community in Africa in the period 2006 to 2007 is given as 550 000, with the earlier Overseas Chinese population segment making up about 50 000 of that number. I am of the opinion that this number is on the low side.

The primary reason I have reached this conclusion is that the figure underestimates the new Overseas Chinese population in Africa, the segment that forms the overwhelming majority within the Chinese community in Africa, with clusters of Chinese present in almost every African country, many of whom are new migrants.

In interviews that I conducted among the Overseas Chinese community in South Africa, it was estimated that there were 250 000 Chinese people living in the country from 2006 to 2007, with new Overseas Chinese forming a huge majority, at about 210 000. Therefore, the continental figure of 550 000 is clearly an underestimate, if one bears in mind that South Africa's Chinese community has long made up about a third of the Chinese population of the whole continent. Taking this into account, I attempted to calculate the figures based on the fact that there were then 53 African countries whose Chinese population varied in size from several hundred to hundreds of thousands, but this calculation method is too simple and too general to yield any meaningful results, leaving great disparities in the total number of Chinese people living in Africa.

A second factor in my thinking is that the official number of earlier Overseas Chinese is likewise an underestimation. The approximate number of 50 000 overseas people from Hong Kong, Macau and Taiwan, out of Africa's total of 550 000, is also a low figure. The number of this group during this period is closer to 90 000. In South Africa alone, home to the largest Overseas Chinese population on the continent, the number of earlier Overseas Chinese and the new Overseas Chinese from Taiwan each approached 20 000 in 2006 to 2007, not including those from Hong Kong and Macau, which formed, at any rate, a smaller number.[16] The countries that were home to the largest population of earlier Overseas Chinese were Mauritius,

Madagascar and Réunion. In fact, the total number of Overseas Chinese in these three countries alone, combined, exceeded 50 000 at the time of China's Reform and Opening Up, when there were 12 000 living in Madagascar in 1977, 31 000 in Mauritius in 1978, and 13 500 in Réunion in 1979[17] – a total of 56 500.

Overseas Chinese population in Africa, 2012

In more recent years, with the strengthening of China–Africa trade and increasing personnel exchanges, the number of Overseas Chinese in Africa has been growing at a rapid rate, with a noticeable rise in the number of new Overseas Chinese, particularly short-term Chinese labourers in Africa. To meet the demands of this growing trend, China Southern Airlines introduced a Beijing–Dubai–Lagos route in December 2006, and a direct flight from Guangzhou to Luanda, Angola, in 2007. In 2009, Hainan Airlines introduced direct flights to Johannesburg from Beijing and Shanghai.

Having analysed data from various sources, I am of the opinion that the total Overseas Chinese population in Africa was a little over 1 million by the end of 2012. The sources for this data include information obtained during my visits to 30 African countries, my estimates and those of my Chinese associates in light of my experience with the Chinese communities in several African countries, information from African embassies to China, and data from news media. On the basis of this information, I divide Africa's Overseas Chinese population into four categories, given the uneven distribution and great disparity in population among the communities.

The first category includes three countries with a Chinese population of over 100 000: South Africa, Angola and Nigeria. South Africa, which is arguably the largest African economy and serves as the gateway to the continent, hosts the largest concentration of Overseas Chinese, officially numbered at 250 000 in 2006 to 2007, and approaching 300 000 in recent years. Angola has seen the most rapid increase in its Overseas Chinese community, rising from just tens of thousands to numbers closer to those seen in South Africa. According to a report, 'the Angolan Ministry of Internal Affairs shows that the Chinese in Angola, close to 260 000 in number, are playing an important role in the Angolan economy'.[18] Nigeria is the most populous African country, with over 100 million people, over 200 000 of whom are Overseas Chinese. In an interview in August 2012, an official from the Nigerian Embassy jokingly asked if I was interested in official or actual numbers. The former was given as 180 000; the latter, which included illegal immigrants, was about 220 000. Our discussion brought us to the conclusion that the real number of Overseas Chinese in Nigeria in 2012 was 200 000.

These three countries are home to the largest, most concentrated Overseas Chinese communities in Africa. The total combined Chinese population of these three countries was about 760 000, accounting for 75 per cent of the total number of Overseas Chinese living on the African continent.

The second category includes countries with a Chinese population of 30 000 to 50 000, including Mauritius, Madagascar, the Democratic Republic of the Congo (DRC), Ghana, Tanzania and Réunion. These countries, having a long history of Chinese people living within their borders, see an overwhelming number of earlier Overseas Chinese in their numbers, particularly in Mauritius, Madagascar and Réunion.

According to a 2010 Xinhua News Agency report, 'over 400 Chinese companies are registered in Ghana, and the total Overseas Chinese population there is 30 000'.[19] Among the Overseas Chinese residents in the DRC and Tanzania in 2012, some permanent residents and businesspeople who had been living and working there for many years told me that the Chinese population in each country was about 30 000. The report cited above puts the Chinese population of Mauritius at about 40 000, or 3 per cent of the population, as of June 2006.[20] The total Overseas Chinese population in Madagascar is 40 000, with about 10 000 (including 100 holding Taiwanese passports) in Tamatave Province, 10 000 in Antananarivo Province and 5 000 in Toliara Province.[21] These figures are based on a June 2006 report. A 2004 report in the *People's Daily* overseas edition states that 'Réunion, situated in the southwestern part of the Indian Ocean and 2 500 square kilometres in area, is home to 30 000 Overseas Chinese people'.[22]

The period in which the above figures were reported ranges from 2004 to 2012. Strictly, statistical calculations put the number of Chinese in these six countries at 200 000. Dynamically calculated based on an average of 40 000 in each country, the total actually comes to 240 000.

The third category is countries with a Chinese population ranging from 1 000 to 10 000, such as Egypt, Algeria, Sudan, Ethiopia, Kenya, Uganda, the Republic of Congo, Mali, Zambia, Zimbabwe, Namibia, Mozambique, Lesotho and Seychelles. There are about 20 African countries with Chinese populations that fall within this range. Due to the great disparity of the Chinese population in these countries, estimations are difficult. A sketchy estimate puts the total number of Chinese living in countries grouped in this category at somewhere between 50 000 and 100 000.

Three countries serve as examples of the challenge of estimating these figures. One 2010 report states that the 'current total number of Overseas Chinese in Egypt is about 5 000, small in scope and number'.[23] In 2008 the Chinese ambassador to Kenya, Zhang Ming, said that there were over 5 000 Chinese in Kenya, most of them in the major cities.[24]

In the Republic of Congo, according to incomplete statistics, 'the total number of Chinese people working or operating businesses in Brazzaville totals 4 000'.[25]

The fourth category comprises over 20 countries with a Chinese population up to several hundreds, mostly in West Africa, though some are in other parts, such as Tunisia, Morocco, Central African Republic, Somalia, Rwanda, Burundi, Malawi, Swaziland and Comoros. The size of the Chinese population in such countries is, as a rule, below 1 000, and in a few cases, even below 100. The total estimate for the Overseas Chinese population in these countries is 15 000.

There is therefore clearly an unequal distribution of Chinese across Africa, ranging from over 100 000 in some countries to below 1 000 in others. With the total for the continent being an estimate, those with a Chinese population below 1 000 are negligible for calculation purposes. In the third category of countries, the total population is estimated at between 50 000 and 100 000, a very elastic number that has a limited impact on the total. Clearly, the decisive factors determining the number of Overseas Chinese people living in Africa are the countries in the first two categories, which come to a total of 1 million.

This is, of course, an approximate number. When the countries in the third and fourth categories are also included, Africa's total Overseas Chinese population easily tops 1 million, and is probably about 1.1 million.

Africa's Overseas Chinese population: Changing trends

Within this graduated, uneven distribution of Overseas Chinese throughout Africa, the overwhelming majority – about 90 per cent – are new Overseas Chinese. Of this group, about a quarter are short-term workers. Here follows an analysis of the tendency for potential changes in the major Overseas Chinese communities in Africa, serving to predict the future direction of this group of people.

Firstly, the earlier Overseas Chinese and government-sponsored personnel will see a slow increase in number. Government-sponsored personnel work within specific terms of service, usually on a three- or five-year rotation basis. As a rule, the total number of this group is stable, but with the increased pace of economic development and cultural exchange, government-sponsored personnel will see a long, slow rise in numbers, less than the natural population growth rate.

Secondly, self-supporting personnel, especially businesspeople, will see a rise in number. As Africa's economic growth continues to stimulate the local consumer market, African demand for Chinese commodities attracts more Chinese businesspeople to the continent, bringing about the establishment and development of small and medium-sized businesses. Institutions of higher learning in South Africa, Sudan and Egypt are attracting increasing numbers of Chinese students, and self-funded students have become a notable source of enrolment. With Africa's deepening understanding of China, Chinese culture is growing in popularity, and many Chinese doctors, martial-arts teachers and language teachers will seize the opportunity to enter the African market and disseminate Chinese culture, enhancing bilateral exchange. In the near future, an increasing number of private businesses and personnel will undoubtedly increase their presence in Africa at a slow, steady pace, rather than in an abrupt spike.

Thirdly, a decrease in the number of short-term workers will lead to a decrease in the total number of Chinese. The rising numbers of Overseas Chinese over the past few years was largely due to the sharp increase in the number of contract labourers. In 2011 China withdrew 35 860 Chinese nationals from Libya, most of whom were workers. In Rwanda, there were about 900 Chinese residents in 2012, two-thirds of whom were employees of Chinese companies engaged in contract or foreign aid projects; the remaining third were individual Chinese traders and their family members. The Chinese enterprises included those under China's central government, local enterprises, foreign aid enterprises, and enterprises focused on contract projects. Despite the fluctuation in the number of the employees of these enterprises, recent years saw a general increase in their overall number. This was true in other African countries as well. Even so, the situation in 2012 might suggest that a revision is soon to come, for the following reasons:

- With economic development and market changes, Chinese enterprises were no longer able to recruit cheap labour at home, creating numerous problems connected to employee benefits and management.
- African countries complained about the large proportion of Chinese workers employed by Chinese businesses, putting a strain on those nations' relationships with China, though the Chinese government has taken measures to address the imbalance.
- With the improved livelihood of the Chinese people at home, many have simply lost the desire to venture abroad for work. This being the case, there will be a marked decline in the number of Chinese workers in Africa, which will have a significant impact on the total number of Chinese people living on the continent.

Lastly, aside from factors such as natural population growth rates and mechanical growth rates, several points should be taken into consideration. Firstly, most businesspeople within Africa's Overseas Chinese community are single men, some of whom do not stay for long. It is a Chinese tradition for men to be more adventurous in their careers, most of them young or middle-aged. Of the latter group, a man is only able to live abroad with his wife and children if he already enjoys some level of success. Once abroad, the average Chinese man often finds it different from what he had imagined, and often curtails his time overseas. Younger men and women, lacking experience in life, often feel frustrated or discouraged when confronted with difficulties associated with living in a foreign land. This is common among the new Overseas Chinese in Africa.

Secondly, in recent years, many of the new Overseas Chinese who went to Africa in the 1990s have subsequently returned to China. Then, after some career success, they may travel back and forth to Africa for business. They cannot therefore be considered in the category of new Overseas Chinese in the truest sense. This Chinese tradition of 'going back to one's roots' is often closely associated with the domestic conditions in African countries. For instance, many of the Overseas Chinese living in South Africa left because of concerns over their security.

Thirdly, some Overseas Chinese have emigrated to North America or Oceania, driven by considerations for their children's education or by unsatisfactory conditions in Africa, such as economic recession or crime. And, finally, with the growing number of new Overseas Chinese, some African countries, such as South Africa, Angola and Nigeria, in the process of cracking down on illegal immigrants and regulating immigration from neighbouring countries, have also tightened their visa requirements for Chinese guests and residents.

Based on this analysis, I predict that, in the near future, the Chinese population in Africa will not only experience a slower rate of increase, but will show a mild decrease. Whether this number will eventually rise again depends on developments and changes in the economic situations in China and Africa.

HISTORY OF THE OVERSEAS CHINESE IN AFRICA

The history of the Overseas Chinese in Africa is closely related to that of the Overseas Chinese worldwide, especially in South East Asia, as the earliest Overseas Chinese in Africa were transported there from South East Asia by Western colonialists. The earliest Overseas Chinese residents in Africa can be categorised as free immigrants and contract labourers.

According to Beijing University's Dr Li Anshan, the free immigrants among Africa's Chinese population came from three points of origin:

- Some came to Africa by boat from South East Asia or China, including helpless farmers, and exiled patriotic Chinese unhappy with the Qing Dynasty rule.
- Some were former prisoners released from Batavia (modern-day Jakarta) to Cape Town. Some of these were unable to return home for fear their imprisonment would be prolonged; some were willing to stay as residents; some were unable to leave without permission; and some missed their homebound ships for various reasons.
- The final group included those who chose to stay when their contracts were completed, feeling that their prospects abroad were better than at home.

During the slave-trade period, the Chinese, like the Africans, were major targets for slavery. After intruding on China's territorial waters, the Portuguese sold Chinese nationals as slaves, as recorded in the *Memoir of Emperor Wuzong of the Ming*

Dynasty (Volume 149), which claims the colonialists were 'seducing and recruiting desperate refugees and purchasing people's children'. After usurping Macau, they redoubled their crimes, 'kidnapping and plundering men and women from the cities, selling them to foreigners for money, and earning enormous incomes every year' – as recorded by Guo Shangbin in his *Imperial Censor Guo's memoir* (Volume 1).

In 1604 and 1607, the Dutch twice forced Guangzhou to open trade, but were 'obstructed by the Portuguese in Macau'. In 1622 the Dutch navy general Kornelis Rayerszoon attacked Macau with 15 warships and 2 000 soldiers, retreating after a defeat and occupying the Penghu Islands to the east. In 1624 they occupied Taiwan and built Fort Zeelandia in Anping Port. In 1662 they were expelled by Zheng Chenggong, an unprecedented event that saw eastern forces defeating Europeans who had invaded.[26]

The Dutch and the Portuguese were two of a kind. During their invasion and occupation of the Penghu Islands and Taiwan, neither stopped harassing the coastal areas of Fujian and Zhejiang, seizing cheap, able-bodied labourers – even women and children served as victims to be held for ransom money.

According to Dutch historical records, when Dutch colonialists set foot on Java, the Chinese people living on the island had already formed a vigorous community centred on the pepper market, rice cultivation, and the production of cane sugar, and had become quite wealthy. Hoping to gain some inroads with the Chinese, the Dutch East India Company's governor general, Jan Pieterszoon Coen, named a Chinese resident, Su Mingguang, one of his officials in 1620.[27] But Coen was up to no good. Seeing that Chinese labourers were diligent and made good progress, he spared no effort in capturing Chinese slaves to develop his lands. In 1623, Coen wrote to his successor Pieter de Carpentier:

> Batavia, Moluccas, Ambon, and Vanlan are very much in need of labour and money to generate rich profits to return home. The Chinese are unmatched for our purpose. Trade is no place for friendship; it is high time we dispatch battleships to the coast of China to capture Chinese men, women, and children and bring them to the Netherlands. In case of war with China, it is even more necessary to capture the Chinese, especially women and children. They should be transferred to Batavia, Moluccas, Ambon, Vanlan, and other places. As the ransom for each Chinese is as much as 80 ryals, it is absolutely necessary to keep them within the company administration, and to keep the Chinese women from going home. Instead, they are to be transferred to the above-mentioned places.[28]

This accords with Li Changfu's assertion, in his *Chinese colonial history*, that the Portuguese and Dutch regarded the Chinese in the same way they did the Africans.

He writes: 'It is only natural that the later Europeans came to China to vend the Chinese as they do the piglets.'[29]

The earliest Chinese immigrants to Africa were therefore likely to have been prisoners transported by the Dutch colonial authorities from South East Asia. In 1593 the Portuguese brought Chinese people to South Africa. In May 1638, the first Dutch governor of Mauritius transported some Chinese people to Mauritius from Indonesia, and in 1654, another three Chinese people were transported to Mauritius by the Dutch. These are early recorded incidents of Chinese immigrants to Africa.

It was the diligence and obedience of the Chinese labourers that incited Dutch Cape colony pioneer Jan van Riebeeck to repeatedly ask the Batavian authorities to send Chinese labourers, though these requests were not granted. For the same reason, his successor Zacharias Wagenaer was also eager for Chinese labourers. On 6 June 1662, in a letter to the authorities in Batavia, he proposed that 25 or 30 poverty-stricken Chinese people be dispatched to Africa, provided they were skilled farmers. He estimated that one Chinese farmer could replace 50 disobedient, lazy farmers in the Cape. Two years later, he made the same request. When Chinese labourers were finally sent to Cape Town by the Dutch East India Company, however, they were not the skilled farmers the governor had hoped to attain, but prisoners or political exiles.

According to reports, 'in the early 17th century, only one or two persons were expelled every year, but beginning in the 1680s, the number increased. It seems the first expelled Chinese was named Ytcho Wancho. He was transported to the Cape of Good Hope in 1660 aboard the ship *Arnhem*.'[30]

Ytcho Wancho was the first recorded Chinese settler in Africa. He was later sent to prison on Robben Island after attacking a female slave with a knife. There, he was punished by whipping and attempted to hang himself.

In the early 18th century, free Chinese immigrants appeared in Africa, marked in the history books with the 1702 christening of a Chinese man named Tuko de Chinees, and later renamed Abraham de Vyf when he became a Protestant.[31]

This so-called contract Chinese labour was in fact a cover under which the colonialists 'recruited' 'willing' Chinese labourers and sent them to African colonies for hard labour. After the abolition of slavery, this was just a variation of slavery, and it was legal. This was particularly true in France and Portugal. At the time, China was weak and under corrupt rule, so it was easily reduced to an ideal source of labour for the colonialists. As a rule, a contract labourer could be freed only after he had done 14 years of hard labour.

Mauritius was the first destination for Chinese contract labourers. In 1760 the French transported Chinese people to work on the plantations there. During the Anglo-French war, the first batch of 300 Chinese were captured and taken to

Mauritius from South East Asia as hostages by the French navy officer Charles Hector, comte d'Estaing. The Frenchman intended to have these Chinese people do hard labour on the sugar plantations, but the Chinese refused, on the pretext that they were businessmen and so not skilled in farming. The hapless Frenchman repatriated the Chinese the following year, though it seems some were left behind on the island. In 1762 Hector 'recruited' the next batch of labourers directly from China, a watershed event that opened the way for an influx of Chinese labourers to Mauritius, Réunion, Saint Helena, Madagascar, South Africa, Tanganyika and other parts of Africa.

In China a labourer (coolie) was called a 'piglet',[32] and the corresponding coolie trade was called the piglet trade. Like slaves, the coolies were a ragtag assortment of suppressed, exploited people. A coolie's terms of indentured labour could vary from three to eight years. Because of this arrangement, Engels called them 'hidden coolie slaves'. As the Qing Dynasty continued the Ming Dynasty's ban on maritime trade, the Portuguese colony Macau became the base for the coolie trade. The colonialists recruited Chinese coolies from inland China, sent them to Macau, then transported them by boat to Africa and South America. According to the *1634–1834 East India Company* chronicle of trade with China, edited by Hosea Ballou Morse, before 1811, a batch of Cantonese stonemasons and carpenters were transported to Saint Helena by way of Macau. After that, more Chinese labourers were sent to southern Africa.

After the Opium War, China's overall national strength was further weakened and Western forces ran rampant, doing as they pleased. They began trafficking Chinese labourers directly from the interior of China to Africa. In 1845 and 1846, two batches of Chinese labourers were transported from Xiamen to the French Réunion. Foreigners described the misery of the Chinese labourers, calling their boats a 'floating hell'. Major Sir Maurice Cameron describes the misery of the Chinese labourers in the south seas:

> The death of the Chinese labourers was a loss to the boat owners, but not capital. The more labourers a boat carried, the more profitable the journey. A boat with a capacity of 300 was loaded with 600 coolies. Even if 250 died on the way, it was still more profitable than transporting 300 without any deaths. While the marketable number was 350, the rated number was 300.[33]

Sun Yat-sen hit the nail on the head when he said:

> Foreign capitalists recruited Chinese labourers for their diligence and low cost. With the ban on maritime trade still in effect, the Chinese government prohibited labourers from going abroad. That being the case, the Westerners had to hire labourers from Macau, which saw hundreds of thousands of

labourers go abroad every year. Such labourers were swindled from China's interior, lured by honeyed words, desirable gains, and imagined wealth. Once the labourers were cheated into the 'piglet sty', they were confined there until they were sold at high prices to foreigners by the 'head piglet' (piglet vendor), transported abroad, and made to do hard labour. Such labourers did hard manual work all their lives, suffering pains, whippings, and humiliations as a way of life, like suckling pigs subjected to killing and butchering. In the fullest sense, they were sold as 'piglets'.[34]

In 1886, gold ore was discovered in the Rand. This was followed by a gold rush all over the world, with many Chinese people joining in the fray through various access points. Most arrived at the mines under the Labour Protection Regulations signed in 1904 between the British government and the Qing imperial court. The period from 1904 to 1910 saw an upsurge of contracted Chinese labourers being introduced to Africa. According to statistics, by 1910, the total number of contract labourers had reached 142 000, increasing 'the immigration of Chinese labourers to South Africa, begun in 1904 with a total of 55 000 recruited by Britain for gold ore mining'.[35]

In reality, the actual number of Chinese labourers in South Africa far exceeded this figure. For instance, statistics from the Gold City Museum indicate that, in the period from 1904 to 1906, there were about 63 000 Chinese labourers in the country.[36] I made several visits to Gold City, South Africa, and the images of the hard life of labour that those miners endured were unpleasant. It called to mind the descriptions: 'Cheeks smoked dusty, hair grey, and fingers black';[37] 'ploughing one thousand *mu* of land and harvesting one thousand chests of grain, I am exhausted, but who will pity me?'[38]

The contribution to gold mining made by those vast hordes of Chinese labourers is evident, inestimable and indelible. But they led miserable lives, experiencing great hardship, living like dogs.

Li Anshan divides the history of the Overseas Chinese in Africa into four stages:
- 1800–1910, when contract labourers outnumbered free immigrants.
- 1930–1940, when Japan invaded China and many from the coastal regions were forced to flee abroad to avoid being enslaved.
- The early years of the new China, when the emigration policy was relaxed and the earlier Overseas Chinese had gained enough of a foothold to invite relatives and friends to come from China to make a living.
- The 1980s, when China joined the global immigration surge to Africa, keeping pace with Reform and Opening Up.[39]

The Overseas Chinese make up a large portion of the global migrant population. The present situation suggests that there are Chinese residents in almost every African country, with the bulk residing in those countries that have historically hosted great numbers of Overseas Chinese, including South Africa, Mauritius and Madagascar. In light of this information, I have drawn the following conclusions:

- Mauritius was most likely to have been the first African destination for Chinese migrants, possibly because of its location and historical background, and the fact that the first Chinese labourers here were brought by colonialists for the development of the sugar industry.
- The earliest free Chinese immigrants were likely to have been prisoners who had completed their sentences.
- The earliest record of Chinese immigrants to Africa was in 1654, and the earliest Chinese settler in Africa arrived in 1660.
- Chinese immigrants came to Africa in number and scale from 1762, the first batch being contract labourers who were transported there.
- Dutch and French colonialists initiated the trafficking of labourers from China to Africa.

THE EARLIEST CHINESE VISITORS TO AFRICA

The earliest Chinese visitors to Africa were a distinctly different group from Chinese immigrants. The first recorded Chinese visitor to Africa was the Tang Dynasty traveller Du Huan in AD 751–762, whereas the first Chinese immigrations to Africa, moving from individuals to large-scale immigration, took place during the Qing Dynasty, from 1654 to 1762, a period spanning 108 years.

We are not interested here in the pull or push factors often discussed in the theoretical study of the history of global migration, or in the connections and contrasts between contract labourers and free migrants. Nor is this present study concerned with the internal and external causes of immigration to Africa. Chinese migrants' arrival in Africa spanned four dynasties, the Tang, Song, Yuan and Qing, and they were motivated by various reasons, encompassing those of individual travellers to those of settlers. This is the basis for the view commonly shared among scholars of China–Africa relations that 'the first Chinese immigration to Africa took place in the Qing Dynasty'.[40]

Zheng He's shipwreck

No written records or material evidence has yet been discovered to prove that the Chinese sailors in the East Africa shipwreck (mentioned in earlier chapters) were the officers and men of Zheng He's fleet. However, despite differing opinions, scholars generally believe that the 'Chinese' on Pate Island must be the descendants of Zheng He's crew – a view that has been supported in the present book. I believe it can be inferred from known historical facts that the shipwreck near Pate Island took place during the time of Zheng He's voyages across the Western Ocean. There are several reasons for this theory.

Firstly, had the shipwreck happened before Zheng He's journeys, the survivors would not have heard about the giraffes from the outside world, given the challenges to transportation and communication on the remote island where they stayed.

Secondly, had the shipwreck pre-dated Zheng He's travels, the survivors would have tried everything they could do to connect with the huge fleet when they learnt of it passing near the East African coast. In that case, Zheng He's ships would have taken these Chinese people home, a reasonable response out of patriotic sentiment, and not unfeasible as a practical operation.

Next, before Zheng He's travels on the Western Ocean, it was less probable that a direct visit could have been made from China to Africa by ship, since maritime communication between China and Africa was generally managed by Arabian merchant ships at that time. This fact is reflected in several works on China–Africa relations, including *Answers from Outside the Ridges* and *Records of Foreign Countries*.

Furthermore, had the shipwreck happened after Zheng He's travels, the survivors could not have settled at Shanga Village, because it was destroyed sometime in 1440, shortly after Zheng He's final journey, as evidenced by excavations by Mark Houton, a British archaeologist and professor at Cambridge University.[41]

Finally, after Zheng He's voyages, the imperial family's ban on maritime trade made it impossible for large ships to cover the distance between China and Africa. What was worse, after Zheng He's journeys, Western colonialists controlled the Indian Ocean, making it impossible for Chinese ships to reach Africa unimpeded.

Despite the lack of unequivocal evidence, such as written records, renowned Zheng He studies expert Zheng Yijun, after studying reports and information, believes that the descendants of Chinese people now living on Pate Island are undoubtedly descended from members of Zheng He's crew. He believes that the waters off Pate Island were the only passage by which Zheng He could have reached Malindi. It must have been during the time of Zheng He, and not at any other time, that these sailors reached this place, and they arrived as part of Zheng He's fleet. After Zheng He's travels on the Western Ocean, China's self-seclusion policy, the ban on maritime trade, the repression policy adopted by the Ming and Qing dynasties, and especially Western colonialist countries' expansion of control over the Indian Ocean and the concomitant threat of gunboats, when added together, reduced the Ming Dynasty's former vassal states to colonies of Western powers, constituting a threat to China's oceangoing operations and forever disabling China's development on the Indian Ocean.

This fact is evident in records of China's maritime activities, such as *Records of the East and West Oceans*, by Ming Dynasty writer Zhang Xie, which describes areas east of Sumatra, *Records of Overseas Nations*, by Qing Dynasty writer Chen Lunjiong, and *Records of the Sea*, by Xie Qinggao, all of which convey the fact that Chinese ships were no longer seen heading west through the Strait of Malacca.

Maritime activities in the Eastern Ocean left room for development, and sea routes to the Philippines and Japan were developed in the middle and later period of the Ming Dynasty. Zheng Yijun indicates that, before Zheng He's voyages west, maritime communication between China and Africa was sparse and detailed written records were never made. It is likely that travel in sections of western Asia and along the East African coast were controlled by Arab ships, meaning that very few Chinese people would have been able to travel to Africa for hundreds of years while the maritime ban was in effect, curtailing China–Africa communications.

This being the case, the Chinese sailors who settled down to live in Shanga Village in ancient times were undoubtedly crew members from Zheng He's fleet.

The shipwrecked sailors: Earliest Overseas Chinese in Africa

A current popular belief among scholars of the history of China–Africa relations is that the earliest Chinese immigration to Africa took place in the Qing Dynasty, when the first Chinese contract labourers were sent to Africa in 1760. As mentioned, Charles Hector, comte d'Estaing, plundered more than 300 Chinese hostages from South East Asia and took them to plantations in Mauritius, where he tried to force them to do hard manual labour. The plundered Chinese people refused to do his farm work, claiming that they were businesspeople unskilled in farming. Most were repatriated home. In 1762, another batch of Chinese labourers were transported directly from China to Africa by the French. Before that, there had been migrations from China to Africa, but they were scattered and small in number. The Chinese labourers in Mauritius, a fairly sizeable population, are recognised as the earliest Overseas Chinese settlers in Africa.[42]

We know that the fourth of Zheng He's seven voyages on the Western Ocean, in which he aimed to reach Africa, began in the 11th year of the Yongle reign (1413), and the seventh ended in the sixth year of the Xuande reign (1433). Therefore, the shipwreck near Kenya's Pate Island must have occurred between 1414 and 1433. Even if it happened during Zheng He's seventh voyage (1430 to 1433), the fleet's sailors would have been the first Chinese settlers in Africa by 330 years, and would have arrived 200 years before individual free immigrants.

Shipwrecks are inevitable in global navigation, and Zheng He's seven voyages were no exception. His fleet's usual routes along the African coast were in an area where shipwrecks were common. For fleets sailing along the unknown African coast, it would have been likely – even inevitable – that one or two ships would have struck a reef. One ship from Zheng He's fleet was wrecked on the reef near Kenya's Pate Island, and hundreds of Chinese sailors escaped to the island, settled down, married local women and had children, living a friendly, harmonious, multi-racial life as an integral part of the community.

These Chinese sailors, though sturdy and in possession of treasures, were not as arrogant or prejudiced as the Chinese Empire, but were modest, gentle people who saw the locals as their equals.[43] The local island residents likewise did not refuse or reject these alien visitors, but warmly accepted them, with generosity and tolerance. The Chinese sailors exchanged their belongings, including silk, tea, porcelain and other treasures, for basic produce and daily necessities from the local residents, gaining a foothold and ensuring their survival. In that special historical setting, this attitude and practice of equality were truly praiseworthy.[44]

In their new country, the Chinese sailors began to serve the local community with their special skills, which helped them overcome the language and cultural barriers, winning them understanding, trust and tolerance from the public before they could be fully integrated into local society. The medical officials and doctors among them began to collect and prepare traditional Chinese herbs to cure the local people of diseases, heal the wounded and rescue the dying. At the same time, they passed their medical skills on to the local people. Even now, the Chinese doctors on Pate Island are still curing the sick. The craftsmen among them, including blacksmiths and carpenters, used local materials and made tools and utensils with their own hands, as is still evident in the work of the blacksmiths on Pate Island today. The architects among them joined in the local construction industry, building houses for themselves and others. The houses belonging to the Chinese families on Pate Island today are of a different layout from the others. They are in a style typical of Chinese architecture, with a yard. Archaeologists believe that quite a few structures, especially the walls and decor of the Grand Mosque, are distinctively Chinese.

These sailors, bringing the excellent traditional Chinese culture and virtues of the Chinese nation with them, won the trust of the locals and were praised for China and its people. Such traditional culture and merits are expressed in words such as 'harmony', 'diligence' and 'helpfulness'. As a friendly, harmonious part of local society, they created a better life with wisdom and diligence, becoming a great help to those around them. Hundreds of years have passed, but their descendants, now part of the larger African family, still have traditional Chinese culture, remembering their Chinese blood. TCM physicians still serve the people with their customary medical skills, often without charging a cent. Though small in number, these people have made a lasting impact in the places where they reside, representing a positive image of Chinese people and winning the respect of the African public.

THE CHINESE ARE NOT COLONISTS

The members of the Zheng He fleet who settled in Africa and the Chinese migrants who came much later, though both hailing from China and sharing many common characteristics and features, obviously had different reasons and motives in terms of their migration to Africa, as well as different outcomes. Even more so, Overseas Chinese who travelled to Africa for various reasons are so different from Western colonialists that the two groups can hardly be mentioned in the same breath.

Settlers from Zheng He's fleet and early Overseas Chinese

The unfortunate shipwreck victims from Zheng He's mission became settlers in Africa by accident. They are both different from and similar to the early Overseas Chinese in Africa. All of them arrived on the continent by chance through what must have seemed an inevitable journey. However, they differ in several ways.

For a start, they had different motivations. The shipwreck victims travelled to Africa under order from the imperial court hoping to accomplish the greatest sea voyages in human history, whereas the early immigrants travelled to Africa either to escape hardship or because they were forced into going to Africa and were never allowed to return.

Their methods were also different. The sailors travelled to Africa directly from China, on a mission that was organised by the Chinese imperial court, whereas the later group travelled to Africa indirectly, mostly transported there by Western colonialists.

There were differences in their routes. The shipwreck victims went directly from China to Africa, whereas the later Overseas Chinese generally went by way of a third country.

Finally, there were differences in results. Those from Zheng He's fleet generally married local black people and became part of the local community, though they never forgot their Chinese background and remained deeply rooted in traditional Chinese culture. Over the centuries, they were ultimately integrated into African society; they became typical Africans. The later Overseas Chinese, however, lived as in an alien land, even if they were there for a very long time. They remained in Chinese communities, finding it difficult to change their traditional Chinese lifestyle and customs. They hardly ever married local residents, suffering a bitter, circuitous path before merging into local society.

In short, Zheng He's fleet was travelling on a journey of great initiative, even though some crew members were forced to land and stay on an island as shipwreck victims. The later Overseas Chinese, on the other hand, were passive and poverty-stricken, tricked or cheated by Western colonialists. Even so, despite these obvious differences between the two groups, they are all Chinese people who were profoundly nurtured by traditional Chinese culture. Bestowed with fine Chinese national qualities, they won a good reputation for the Chinese people among Africans by their diligence and hard work.

Differences between Overseas Chinese and European colonialists

As the earliest Overseas Chinese in Africa, the crew from Zheng He's fleet gained a good reputation for the Chinese people by their actions. This is in sharp contrast to the European colonialists who later came to Africa. As African residents living together with the local people, the Chinese people were different from the European colonisers and white immigrants in several ways:

- In relation to the local African residents: equality vs oppression
- In relation to Africa's natural resources: sharing vs plundering
- In emotional connection with the local people: intimate vs remote; centripetal vs. centrifugal
- In relation to traditional African culture: integration vs rejection
- In compact with the African historical process: weak vs strong
- In purpose of visit and settlement in Africa: friendship vs aggression; trade vs occupation; accidental vs inevitable

The stark difference between Africa's Overseas Chinese population and its European colonists and white immigrants, which grew out of the respective Eastern and Western cultural traditions, has had a direct impact on their respective relations with and policies towards Africa. Mutual respect and equitable treatment have always been the foundation for the development of China–Africa relations, which was beyond the ken of the colonial mindset.

The former colonisers regarded themselves as the top authority on earth, and they observed African affairs and addressed the African people from a commanding position, that of a suzerain. Until today, some Europeans remain stuck in their colonialist mindsets, regarding Africa as their 'backyard', while always pointing at others in reproach regarding African affairs. The newest member of the BRICS grouping, South Africa has been deeply impressed by this throughout its own experience. President Jacob Zuma said, 'We have a place among the BRICS countries, feeling that Africa is courteously accepted, our points of view are treated equally, and the African continent is by no means neglected.'[45]

Some European countries poke their noses into African affairs, and point a finger at other nations' relations with African countries. In addressing economic and cultural cooperation between China and African countries, the former colonisers have made some unreasonable and irresponsible remarks on the one hand, and, on the other, indicate that they intend to learn from China. However, these politicians, who have succeeded in their old colonialist ideas, are not willing to let go of their lofty airs, and so find it difficult to treat Africa with sincerity and equality and to observe China–Africa relations with a peaceful, open mind.

It is fortunate that some visionary Europeans are undergoing a change in their traditional values, and are learning to view China–Africa relations from a more practical perspective. For instance, a news report in the *People's Daily* in April 2012, covering Chinese products in the African market, reported that the benefit to the African consumer has been great after the influx of inexpensive Chinese commodities into the African market about a decade ago. Today, with Chinese enterprises moving to the higher streams of the value chain, high-end Chinese commodities, like cellphones and farm threshers, are likewise winning favour from African consumers.[46]

The article goes on to cite a March 2012 report from Standard Bank stating that, since 2002, Chinese commodities have more than tripled in the African market and that, in 2011, Chinese imports accounted for 16.8 per cent of the total value of imported commodities in Africa. Over the previous four years, Chinese enterprises profited most through the sale of machinery, motor vehicles and electronics. At the same time, the value of commodities imported from Italy, Spain, Germany, UK and Japan dropped below 2008 figures. China–Africa relations expert Anna Katrina Stahl, of the Brussels Institute of Contemporary China Studies, believes that the steady growth of Chinese commodities imported into Africa means greater competition for the European Union (EU), that China–Africa relations are an undisputed success, and that the mutual, win-win cooperation between the two is a revelation to the EU, urging its Africa policy towards reason and good practice.[47]

The West ignores China and its rise

During the period when the colonialists' racist regimes were rampant in Africa, the Overseas Chinese were oppressed and exploited, just like the local African people, since racist regimes categorised all non-white races as the same, partly due to China's weakened international position at the time.

Like Africa, China had been reduced to a colony or semi-colony of the West, under imperialist oppression and colonialist exploitation. Over the past two centuries, the domination by the West, first by Europe, then by the US, planted in Westerners a sense of superiority and a habitual way of thinking that is Western-centred. This view presumes that the West is the source and origin of human wisdom, and that Westerners are born superior to people of any other place. The belief is that the Western mode is the only applicable access to any success for any people, that Westernisation is the sole effective mode of access to modernisation, and that China will be an inevitable failure, its success unsustainable. Professor Martin Jacques of the London School of Economics and author of *When China*

Rules the World: The Rise of China and the Fall of the Western World, in an article published on 25 March 2012 in the *Observer*, put it clearly when he said:

> We think of ourselves as open-minded but our sense of superiority has closed our minds. We never entertained the idea that China could surpass the US. Backward, lacking democracy, bereft of Enlightenment principles, the product of a very different history, it was not western. So how could it? We were the universal model that everyone else had to embrace to succeed. The only form of modernisation that worked was westernisation. China would inevitably fail: the project was unsustainable. By insisting on seeing China through a western prism, we refused to understand China in its own terms. Our arrogance bred ignorance: we were not even curious.[48]

In 'Why do we continue to ignore China's rise? Arrogance', another of Jacques's articles, he cites examples of two groups – Westerners learning Chinese and British trade partners – to show that the Western attitude towards China is one of arrogance, negligence and near-sightedness. He points out that Westerners keep saying that teaching Chinese should be made more available in schools, though very few actually offer it as an option. And, he says, the British economy 'exhibits the same morbid symptoms', with Britain exporting more to Ireland than it does to China, India, Russia and Brazil combined.

Jacques emphasises that, unless solutions are found to these problems, the West will be sidelined. As the world's economic centre is shifting from the developed world to the developing world, with China playing a leading role, the end result will be a rapid decline in the developed world, which will require a restructuring of global organisations, particularly the International Monetary Fund and the World Bank.

In these articles, Jacques points out that in 1978, China's economy was one-twentieth the size of that of the US. But after two decades of double-digit growth, its global influence has outstripped competitors. This story is now not only China's story, because its rise has begun to change the whole world. Only in 2008, when the global financial crisis began, did the Western world become somewhat aware of the influence of China's rise. When Western economies were mired in depression and stagnation, China was extraordinarily optimistic. Goldman Sachs predicted in 2009 that China's economy will exceed that of the US by 2027. In March 2012, the British *Economic Weekly* predicted that it would happen by 2018.

18

Significance of China's long history in Africa

DEBUNKING THE FALLACY THAT EUROPEANS DISCOVERED AFRICA

The discovery of when Chinese immigration to Africa first started shows it is a fallacy that Europeans discovered Africa. The visit of Zheng He's majestic fleet to the African coast is a resplendent chapter in world history, yet Westerners either evade or dilute this historical fact, arguing that it was Bartolomeu Dias who sailed around the Cape of Good Hope in 1486 and Vasco da Gama who discovered the new sea route to the East in 1498. They promote this popular misunderstanding with their stories, trying to erase the fact that the Chinese were the earliest in Africa, and trying to erase time-honoured African history, imagining that 'Africa had no history' or that African history began with the continent's first contact with Europe.

Ghana's first post-independence president, Kwame Nkrumah, aptly noted in his speech on 12 December 1962 at the first African Studies Scholar Conference:

> Such earlier European works are motivated by the economy, not science. They are related to the unbalanced ivory and gold trades, and to the lawless human trafficking which they have to justify. I would like to point out here that at that time, most of the European and American works on Africa were defensive in nature, written in an attempt to justify their slavery system and their continuous plunder of African labour and natural resources. That prepares a justification for their economic and political enslavement of Africa. That deprives Africa of its future, and of its history. Such words imagine that the history of Africa was born as a result of the contact between Africa and Europe and, in a logical sequence, the history of Africa is but an extension or an expansion of European history, to the extent that even the awesome reputation of Hegel[1] has been exploited to support their fiction that Africa has no history. Defenders of imperialism and colonialism cannot wait to add Hegel to the development of their fiction.[2]

After drawing attention to the long history and profound culture of Africa, Nkrumah went on to say:

> The Chinese published their earliest significant records of Africa in their Tang Dynasty period (AD 618–907). There were academic communications between China and Egypt as early as the 18th century. And Chinese knowledge about Africa is not limited to their knowledge of Egypt. They also possessed detailed knowledge about Somalia, Madagascar, and Zanzibar, having traversed vast areas in Africa.[3]

Chinese explorations over large parts of Africa included Zheng He's four large expeditions to the continent. The fleet's visits and the fact that some of his crew members settled on African islands is convincing evidence of the fact that the Chinese were not only the first 'discoverers' of Africa, but also the first foreign settlers there. This is clearly a decisive blow to the notion of a European discovery of Africa.

Scholars and other far-sighted people who have become aware of this respect these historical facts. Many African scholars and political figures are making efforts to safeguard these facts, but informing and changing minds that have become preconditioned is a long process, requiring continuous effort. As a rule, people find it difficult to change established habits of thought, preferring to be carried along by a sort of intellectual inertia. For instance, the so-called Arabic numerals are in fact Indian numerals, since they were first used in India. But because these numerals were introduced to Europe by way of the Arab world, Europeans mistook them as an Arab invention, and this misinformation was passed down through the generations.[4] It is difficult to estimate how many people in the world have been misinformed, but I am sure it is a common misconception even among Chinese people today.

SUPPORTING AFRICA'S EASTWARD ORIENTATION

Historical evidence surrounding the start of Chinese emigration to Africa provides a historical basis and theoretical support for the development of China–Africa trade relations, and what one might call the 'eastward orientation' of Africa.

The voyages Zheng He's fleet made to Africa were for the purpose of friendship, trade and to nurture exchanges. It follows that direct trade between China and Africa began during the period of Zheng He's travels, against the political and economic backdrop of the early Ming Dynasty, and was closely associated with the Chinese tradition of encouraging agriculture and restricting trade. During the Tang Dynasty, the peak of Chinese feudal society, though the imperial court welcomed foreign merchants to their business operations and provided them with a variety of preferential policies, domestic trade and commerce were still restricted. For instance, the Great Tang Western Market in the Tang Dynasty capital Chang'an was a well-known prosperous international market, bustling with shops, commodities and merchants. Even so, Chang'an's residents and other Chinese nationals were somewhat restricted from entering this international market. Most of them went to the Eastern Market, a domestic market, for their needs. Hundreds of years later, the Great Ming Empire followed the conventions of the Tang Dynasty, emphasising openness to the outside world and restricting domestic commerce. At the same time, Zhu Yuanzhang, the first emperor of the Ming Dynasty, made innovative reforms of the tribute system, integrated the tribute and commercial systems, and stipulated a new integrated tribute-commerce system. The new system thoroughly replaced foreign trade with tribute trade, prohibited the Chinese people from taking part in international commercial and trade activities, and brought foreign trade under the full control and operation of government authorities.

The so-called tribute trade was divided into domestic and overseas trade. The former referred to foreign trade when foreign countries' diplomatic corps travelled to China to pay tribute to the Chinese emperor; the latter was the converse – foreign trade where Chinese diplomatic corps visited foreign countries. Tribute trade was official trade. More specifically, China's foreign trade was controlled by the imperial court, conducted at a certain time and place when foreign envoys paid tribute to the Chinese emperor under the supervision of the imperial court's Ministry of Rites or the foreign shipping department of a port, in an open and fair process known as 'bilateral equal trade'. Overseas trade was conducted in host countries during the Chinese imperial court's diplomatic visits to foreign lands. Foreign trade, domestic and overseas, restricted in terms of time, location, commodity type and quality of goods, was conducted on a commercial basis on the principle of bilateral equal trade.

Tribute trade was a special form of foreign trade under the maritime ban policy. Because China's coastal areas were often invaded by Japanese pirates and harassed by other seafaring outlaws, Zhu Yuanzhang closed all foreign-trade ports in the early years of the Ming Dynasty, issuing a strict 'maritime ban' to prevent ships and Chinese citizens from taking to the sea, even for fishing. He also banned all foreign ships, except those of diplomatic corps, from visiting China, prohibiting foreign ships from approaching China's coast. Under this strict maritime ban, the only channel for foreign trade was official trade. In this context, the trade conducted by Zheng He's fleet during its voyages on the Western Ocean has attracted more attention.

There are various theories about the motives for Zheng He's travels – whether they were political, economic or cultural. In economic terms, the motives included the purchase of foreign goods to enrich the domestic market, solidify the imperial court's position in tribute trade, and maintain the domestic price system that had been formed by tribute trade. It might have been to trade Chinese treasures for overseas items, including rarities and valuables favoured by the Chinese emperor, and for the enjoyment of the members of the imperial family; and trading Chinese specialities, such as silk, porcelain and tea for gold and silver to replenish the state treasury and increase China's strength.[5]

Despite the various possible motives and bartering modes of trade, complementary 'equal trade' was always a basic principle of Zheng He's dealings. With this sort of fair and equal trade, Africa's local specialities were naturally favoured by the fleet in its trade along the East African coast. This corroborates the fact that fair and complementary direct trade between China and Africa had begun before European colonialists arrived in Africa, that Africa's 'eastward orientation' and China's entry into Africa began 600 years ago, and that trade and cooperation between China and Africa today are an extension, continuation and development of a 600-year-old relationship.

From July 2010 to October 2014, China and Kenya conducted a joint archaeological research study in an effort to locate the shipwreck. This joint study has attracted a great deal of attention from the media. In a report titled 'Could a rusty coin rewrite Chinese-Africa history?', the BBC said that findings from this archaeological research might not only change people's understanding of East Africa, but could also trigger a re-evaluation among East African countries about the role of contemporary China. On this subject, Dr Herman Kiriama, from the National Museums of Kenya, said:

> We find that the Chinese are very different from the Europeans in their attitudes toward East Africa. They dispatch envoys with gifts. This indicates that they treat us as equals, and that Kenya, as an active sea power, had close connection with the outside world long before the arrival of the Portuguese. That will have a far-reaching impact on Kenyan thinking about our current relationship with the East. China began its trade connection with East Africa much earlier than the Europeans. The current development of China's trade in Africa is but a continuation of this long tradition. For a long time, the East African coast was open to the East, not the West. These findings will provide solid ground for statesmen to stick to their 'Eastward Orientation', as we have always done.[6]

SETTING AN EXAMPLE FOR THE OVERSEAS CHINESE COMMUNITY IN AFRICA

That crew members from Zheng He's fleet settled in Africa sets a positive example for Overseas Chinese people in Africa, demonstrating a spirit of putting down roots and integrating themselves into African society.

The Chinese 'entry into Africa', in its fullest sense, began in the contemporary era when the European colonialists exited Africa. From the time when Chinese medical teams were dispatched to Africa to the time when the TAZARA Railway was constructed with Chinese assistance, and from the time when Chinese construction companies entered Africa to the time when Chinese private enterprises were registered in Africa, an increasing number of Chinese have headed to the distant shores of Africa. Today, Chinese people are seen in almost every African country. But with issues such as language, social custom, dietary habits and other constraints, Chinese integration into local society has been a slow, difficult process. Of course, this is true not only of Chinese people living in Africa, but is a common occurrence among Chinese people in other countries as well. Even those who have lived overseas for many years still speak Chinese, eat Chinese food, and play mahjong with other Chinese people, finding it difficult to enter local society, especially mainstream society.

Zheng He's four visits to Africa were the greatest oceangoing navigational achievements known to humankind, and still serve as a historical emblem for the Chinese people emigrating to Africa today. As I see it, there are three points deserving special attention: language, similar customs and equality in social position.

According to the Zheng family genealogy: (First preface), Zheng He's remote ancestor was King Su fei-erh, of the Kingdom of Bukhara,[7] in what was known then as the Western Region. The king submitted to the Song Dynasty imperial court in the third year of the Xining reign of the Song Dynasty Emperor Shenzong (AD 1070). He was appointed department manager and conferred the titles of Marquis Ningyi, Duke Qing and King of Chaofeng at the time of his death. His eldest son, Saifuddien, was appointed Prince Zhaoqing, and his second son, Sayan, inherited the title Marquis Ningyi and was promoted to Duke Ju. Titles were passed on to Sayan's son, Suzusha; his son, Shams al-Dīn 'Umar al-Bukhārī; and Shams al-Dīn 'Umar al-Bukhārī's son Kamal al-Din. After the collapse of the Song Dynasty, Kamal al-Din's son, Sayyid Ajjal Shams al-Din Omar, was ordered to station at Xianyang as Imperial Grand Expedition Marshal, General Left Premier and Manager of Government Affairs. Between 1274 and 1279, he served as Yunnan Provincial Manager of Government Affairs and at his death was granted the title Prince Xianyang, for his meritorious administration. His eldest son, Nasr al-Din, was ordered to station in South Yunnan. Nasr al-Din's son Bayan was granted the title Prince Huai'an, and his son, Charameddin, was given the title Marquis Danyang. Charameddin's son, Mir Tekin, was father of Ma Sanbao, also called Zheng He. Zheng He made his elder brother, Ma Wenming's son, his heir, naming him Zheng Ci, with the title Enlai.[8] Some of the Zheng family's descendants after Zheng Ci lived in Kunyang, Yunnan, for a time, then moved to Dongying, in Yuxi City. Some moved to Chiang Mai, Thailand, and a smaller number moved to Nanjing, Beijing, Shanghai, Suzhou and other places. Zheng He's descendants now live in Yuxi, Nanjing, and Thailand, in three main branches of the family.

Some of the details of Zheng He's life, such as the relationship of his clan with Islam and the time and place of his birth in Yunnan, remained a mystery for hundreds of years, as the *History of Ming: Biography of Zheng He* contained only the five characters 郑和, 云南人 (Zheng He, from Yunnan). It was not until 1912 that renowned scholar Yuan Jiagu learnt from his friend Su Xiaoguan that there was a 'Hajji Ma Tomb' in Kunyang, the tomb of Zheng He's father. Yuan went to Yueshan in Kunyang County for a survey, verified the existence of the 'Hajji Ma Tomb' and the epitaph of Mr Ma, inscribed a postscript for the epitaph and printed it in his *Snow bedroom anthology* and *Yunnan inference*. During his research, Yuan learnt that Zheng He was from the Ma clan and a descendant of the Hui ethnic group, and that his grandfather and father had made pilgrimages to Mecca, thus earning the term of respect *Hajji*.[9] It was his strong faith that prompted Zheng He's grandfather to make the long, arduous pilgrimage to Mecca. This is evidence that the Ma clan had been of the Islamic faith at least from the time of Zheng He's grandfather.[10]

In the 11th year of the Yongle reign (1413), on the eve of his fourth voyage, on imperial orders, Zheng He was sent on a diplomatic mission to the 'Arabian countries in the Western Region [...] by way of Shaanxi'. He went in search of translators who would be a part of his mission to Arab countries. Through a careful selection process, he chose the imam of the Qingjing Mosque, Hassan, as his attendant on his expeditions on the Western Ocean. At the Zheng He Monument in Xi'an's Daxuexi Alley, the Inscription for the Reconstruction of the Qingjing Mosque records:

> By April of China's 11th year of the Yongle reign (1413), the eunuch Zheng He was sent under imperial orders to Arabian countries in the Western Region. He went to Xi'an in search of translators of the Arabian language and found Imam Hassan of this mosque. Zheng presented this information to the imperial court, and the imam became his attendant.[11]

The fact that the Ming Dynasty Emperor Yongle entrusted Zheng He with an important diplomatic mission, naming him an envoy because of his Islamic heritage, demonstrates his recognition of the importance of a common language and customs shared between Zheng He and the lands he was to visit. Before his fourth voyage to Arab countries, Zheng He paid a special visit to Xi'an in search of Arabic-language translators to serve as his attendants. This indicates that a linguistic connection was vital to the success of the mission. At the time the sailors of Zheng He's fleet became stranded on the remote island, they were able to integrate themselves into the local society, indicating their awareness of the need to treat these foreign people with courtesy and equality. Common customs, language and social status ensured that Zheng He and his attendants could integrate themselves into African society. This experience is a pioneering example for contemporary

Chinese people who go to Africa, providing a model by which they can look to integrate themselves into local societies and become more globalised.

The way Zheng He's officers and men managed to successfully integrate into African society is testimony to China–Africa friendship. When seen from Kenya's perspective, China–Africa friendship has been expressed in a flesh-and-blood relationship. A Kenyan citizen once said in his communications with the Chinese Embassy in Kenya, 'We were friends before; now we are brothers.'[12]

REFUTING CHARGES OF NEW COLONIALISM

The verification that there was a Chinese presence in Africa even earlier than previously known provides a hearty refutation to the notion of a 'China threat' and so-called new colonialism. Zheng He's fleet arrived in Africa much earlier than the European colonial fleets, and members of his crew settled down in Africa long before the colonisers. These two facts offer further refutation of notions of a China threat and new colonialism.

Zheng He's journeys were made during a prime period in China's history, a time when China owned one-third of the world's wealth. In his National Construction Strategy, Sun Yat-sen vividly depicted China's comprehensive national strength, saying, 'That is why China was able to build 64 huge ships in 14 months, with a capacity of 28 000 sailors to demonstrate its national strength to foreign countries. This was a great deed, and has never been surpassed in China's history.'[13]

Chinese history provides clear evidence that the powerful, prosperous Great Ming Empire did not resort to military power, nor did it show off its power to subdue other countries. Developing China is also convincing evidence that a powerful China is not arrogant, nor is it a military threat to others. Why, then, are so many people today talking of a China threat and new colonialism? Perhaps here a definition of colonialism is needed and the difference between the present situation and the colonial past can be examined.

The definition of 'colonialism' in the *Concise Encyclopaedia Britannica* reads:

> Colonialism: Modern colonialism began around the year 1500. By the end of the 15th century, the Europeans discovered the sea routes to the Indian Ocean and to the Americas. Since then, the commercial and trade centre gradually shifted from the Mediterranean Sea to the Atlantic Ocean, and there rose such colonialist countries as Portugal, Spain, Netherlands, France and Britain. Their colonies and expansion covered the world and, at the same time, disseminated the European system and culture.[14]

The *Encyclopaedia of China* (2nd edition) interprets colonialism and new colonialism as follows:

The aggressive polices and deeds adopted by capitalist countries were to invade, enslave, and exploit weaker or smaller countries, nations, and backward areas in order to turn them into colonies or semi-colonies by military, political, or economic means ... In different periods of capitalism, colonialism finds expression in different forms. In the period of primitive accumulation of capital, undisguised violence was generally adopted. In the non-monopoly capitalist period, 'free trade' was the major form to turn developing countries, nations, and regions into their commodity markets, raw material production bases, investment outlets, and sources of cheap labour and mercenary soldiers. In the imperialist period, alongside the above-mentioned means, capital export became the major means of exploiting developing countries, nations, and regions. By the end of the 19th century and beginning of the 20th, the countries and areas that had been reduced to colonies and semi-colonies were under the imperial colonialist system. After the Second World War, national independence movements surged to a peak in colonies and semi-colonies, and a large number of Asian and African countries won national independence, collapsing the imperialist colonial system. The countries still pursuing their colonialist policies turned to indirect, covert, and more deceptive means to maintain and achieve new colonialist benefits. Politically, while permitting and acknowledging the independence of colonies and semi-colonies, they attempted to realise control by training and fostering their agents. Economically, they tried every conceivable means to control key sectors of the economy and plunder those countries through 'aid' attached to harsh conditions, unequal trade, and multinational corporations. Militarily, they tried to realise military occupation by providing military 'aid', establishing military bases, stationing troops, dispatching military advisors, and training soldiers. To achieve their strategy, they even incited *coups d'états*, stirred up evil wars, and fostered puppet regimes. Taken as a whole, these strategies are known as 'new colonialism'.[15]

These definitions shed light on the fact that the main features of colonialism are military conquest by naked violence and armed occupation of other countries and regions; political control and enslavement of other peoples by imposing colonialist ideology and superstructure; economic plundering of other countries' natural resources by destructive exploitation and development; and cultural destruction by forced dissemination of (Western) languages, transplantation of (Western) values, reckless destruction of indigenous cultures and distorting the history of other countries.

New colonialism, or neocolonialism, is a development and evolution of colonialism in new situations and conditions, a disguised form or variation of colonialism in a new historical period. The term 'neocolonialism' first appeared at the 20th Congress of the Communist Party of the Soviet Union, held in 1956, and was also mentioned in the 1957 Moscow Declaration. In March 1959 the editorial board of the Soviet Union journal *International Life* and the editorial board of the Chinese journal *World Knowledge* held a joint seminar on the theme 'The collapse of the imperialist colonial system after the Second World War'.

In China, the Communist Party's Central Committee's academic journal, *Red Flag*, published the article 'US imperialist foreign aid' by Gu Yiji, on 1 July 1959. This article points out that US imperialist international 'aid' after World War II was an important weapon for US expansion and 'a new American way to carry out colonialism'. The July 1961 article by Bei Pyrrha in the 7th issue of *African Communist* argues:

> The adoption of the new colonialist policy does not mean a change of mind or a decision to discard their sinister past, but a disguised mode of exploitation they have to take under the conditions of rapid development of the world's socialist system and the surging national independence movement. Today, the wheel of history is driven by the strength of socialism and national independence movements, not by imperialist powers as before.[16]

Japanese scholar Okakura Koshiro says:

> Neocolonialism is a unique presentation of imperialist colonial policy in the third phase of [the] capitalist crisis. As is widely known, in the third phase of the overall crisis, i.e., the period after 1957, the world socialist system was seeing rapid growth in strength and international influence, while the colonialist system was obviously heading towards collapse due to the attack from the national liberation movements; the total collapse of the colonialist system was inevitable. It is a natural occurrence that appears on the eve of the collapse of colonialism, imperialism's death kick as it tries to maintain the dying colonialist system.[17]

Soviet scholar Y. Bochkarov aptly notes:

> The nature of neocolonialism may be presented as follows: giving minimum political freedom to colonies in return for maximum opportunity for economic benefit through exploitation on the part of the colonisers. Neocolonialists do not give anything to the people, but only spend large sums of money bribing the privileged stratum which occupies governmental posts, hoping to turn that stratum into the pillar of their 'mute' rule of the areas that are no longer under their direct control. They even go so far as to instigate rulers of the former colonies to remove political dissidents under various pretexts so as to strengthen the position of the privileged stratum.[18]

Since the 1960s the African people have seen through neocolonialism. At an early date, far-sighted Africans had become aware of Western cultural assimilation, spiritual enslavement, political division, economic dissimilation and military softening tricks used against Africa. For example, in March 1961 the All-African Peoples' Conference, held in Cairo, carefully studied the African situation at that time and passed certain resolutions on neocolonialism. These stated that

> neocolonialism is a revitalisation of the colonialist system that reduces newly independent countries to victims of the indirect, tricky political, economic, social, military, and technological control. The Conference is aware that neocolonialism finds expression in colonialist economic and political interference, in threatening and blackmailing, and in preventing African countries from adopting political, social, and economic policies to develop their own natural resources and to benefit their people.

The conference's resolutions claimed that the US, the German Federal Republic, Israel, Britain, Belgium, the Netherlands and France were the major countries relying on neocolonialism. The resolutions listed and condemned the following eight manifestations of neocolonialism in Africa:
- The establishment of puppet governments in African nations
- Trying to associate African countries, before or after independence, with imperialist power
- Balkanising some African countries
- Economic infringements on African countries before independence and fostering economic dependence of African countries after independence
- Merging African countries into colonialist economic groups
- Foreign economic infiltration after independence
- Direct economic dependence
- Establishing military bases

The conference unmasked six active agents of neocolonialism:
- Colonialist embassies and delegations
- So-called foreign or UN technical aid planners and executors
- Military personnel and advisors serving in military and police forces
- Agents of imperialist and colonialist countries working under the guise of religion, charity organisations, or cultural, trade-union or youth organisations
- Vicious propaganda in news media under imperialist or colonialist control
- Puppet governments used by imperialists for execution of neocolonialist agendas

The resolutions put forward methods for opposing neocolonialism, including mobilising the African people, seeing through the nature of neocolonialism and uprooting imperialism. For this purpose, the conference condemned 'Balkanising countries before or after independence, with Balkanising defined as maintaining colonialism in Africa', and condemned 'all conditional aid'. It urged 'all independent African countries with foreign military or semi-military bases in their territory to remove such bases'. In addition, the conference demanded immediate establishment of the 'All-African Trade Union Confederation as an effective means of counter attack against neocolonialism'.[19]

With the progress seen over the passage of time, neocolonialism has adopted various modes, patterns and statuses as it has adjusted and adapted to new situations. But for all its changes, it remains the same in nature, adhering to the original political system and economic benefits of the colonisers, not giving a single thought to the will of the African countries or peoples.

France, for example, has always attached great importance to Africa. Georges Pompidou established the Franco-African Summit Conference; François Mitterand proposed the establishment of the Summit Conference of French-Speaking Countries; Jacques Chirac vigorously promoted the establishment of a Europe-Africa Summit Conference; and Nicolas Sarkozy put forward the Union for the Mediterranean. All these French initiatives were made in an attempt to establish a dialogue mechanism that would maintain a French presence in Africa, with Franco–African relations as a focus of French diplomacy. All the importance France has attached to Africa and all the efforts it has made to position Africa have been done to change its own disadvantageous situation and keep it from falling further from power. Since the beginning of the 21st century, Africa's vitality, potential, and influence are attracting great attention; France's own advantageous position in Africa has seen a decline, shaking its foundation as a major power. Such being the case, France is unwilling to stand idly by, even though it is unable to increase its investments and is unwilling to lose its existing economic benefit. In 2010, France decided to turn the Franco-African Summit Conference into an 'Innovation Summit Conference', aiming to put forward new measures by discussing a new theme, hoping to strengthen the traditional France–Africa relationship. The African people paid no heed to French efforts to 'improve' the African image.

Senegalese economist Sanou Mbaye says that, in former French colonies, 'people are still under the influence of the disastrous political and economic policies. They have a long way to go to free themselves from the spiritual fetters before their psychological wounds are healed.'[20]

Colonialism and neocolonialism have resulted in unprecedented disasters and terrible wounds for the African people. This is a historical fact that is acknowledged even by former colonial states. With the healthy, rapid development of relations between China and Africa, some Westerners attempt to stir up ill-intentioned confusion in the relationship between Africa and China by associating China with new colonialism.

Has China constituted a threat to Africa? Is China's engagement with Africa an instance of new colonialism? Is it true that China is pursuing relations with African countries in a move to gain access to oil and other resources?

In addressing these questions at a press conference in Egypt during his 2006 visit to seven African countries, Premier Wen Jiabao made clear that

> 'new colonialism' is an absolutely wrong label for China's activity. From the time of the Opium War in 1840, China suffered under colonial aggression for 110 years. The Chinese nation experienced the pain brought to it by colonialism and knows well the need to fight against colonialism. That is the primary reason we have always supported the national independence and revitalisation of African countries. It is widely known that China is an oil trade partner to several African countries, but our trade relations are cooperative, open, transparent, regular, and beneficial to all partners. Last year, the oil China imported from Africa was not even one-third of that imported by some large nations.[21]

It is important to listen to the voice of Africa. In recent years, China–Africa relations have become a topic discussed by African people in all walks of life, including African scholars. At the 13th conference of the Council for the Development of Social Science Research in Africa (in 2011), China–Africa relations became a hot topic and was the theme of two group meetings. In their speeches and reviews, conference participants unanimously made positive comments on relations between China and Africa. Cameroonian scholar Herman Touo said in his speech ('Does the African economy fear China?'):

> In recent years, more and more Chinese have been coming to our country, Cameroon, for various business operations. They have brought great convenience to our daily lives and have sped up the construction of our infrastructure. Does the African economy fear China? Do Africans fear Chinese? Our answer is a clear 'no'. We welcome the Chinese! Africa welcomes Chinese investments.

His speech received loud applause. As host of the group meeting, Senegalese scholar Mamadou Diouf said: 'China–Africa cooperation is a win-win, mutually beneficial cooperation. Africa and China should continue with their cooperation and should make daring advances, letting others say what they please.'[22]

The voices of African leaders have also been heard on the subject. For example, in September 2011, Alpha Condé, then newly elected president of Guinea, at the Summer Davos Forum held during his first visit to China, granted an interview to Lifen Zhang, chief editor of the *Financial Times* Chinese website. Addressing attacks on China's African policies made by some Western countries, Condé stated that China is not engaged in 'new colonialism'. He said that Guinea was the first sub-Saharan African country to acknowledge China and that it had always supported China in the UN. In 1996, when Guinea was constructing a large dam, China was a cooperation partner. According to Condé, relations between Guinea and China have been a win-win cooperation, not a relation of exchange but of long-term vigorous cooperation between partners. He said:

> We must discard such outdated clichés. We Guineans do not believe that China is a new colonialist or hegemonic power. China is not colonising any foreign country nor plundering foreign natural resources. In fact, we welcome the presence and participation of China. I have said that China is a country that respects the sovereignty of other nations, and it also treasures its own independence. China is earnestly practising what it advocates as a great respecter of other nations. It is a great pleasure for us to communicate with China. The Guinean people do not fear China. They know what China can do for them. For this, we are grateful. Africans are not in any way hostile to Chinese investment in Africa, and this is especially true in Guinea. I am curious about the motives behind the fear of Chinese presence in Africa and in Guinea. History tells us that certain countries had been colonialists in Africa before. Are they worried China will someday replace them? As Guineans, we are not worried. [...] I would like to repeat my view that China provides an opportunity for Africa, and Africa provides an opportunity for China too. I do feel that China has provided present-day Africa with new prospects. Many African countries have not gained their due development because some former Western colonialist countries do not wish to see their development. Now that China is in sight, we have the possibility of a counterbalancing weight to keep these existing powers in balance.

Condé believes that his view is shared by many African leaders: 'For instance, my friends the Angolan President José Eduardo dos Santos, South African President Jacob Zuma, and Malian President Amadou Toumani Touré all share my view. We are considering signing a number of multilateral agreements with China. This is the general trend.'[23]

Many African people are of the opinion that China–Africa relations are a win-win partnership. A member of staff at the Kenyan Investment Authority, Emanuel Ollie Neuilly, said:

> The Chinese have come as investors. In the world today, all investments are good news for us. China will become a very important country in a few years. They are not only takers. They are building our infrastructure and have been doing so ever since they came. They are our friends and good investors.[24]

Many African people, leaders, officials and scholars agree that China is not a threat to Africa or to the world, and that what China is doing in Africa is not a form of neocolonialism. Why are there people who maintain this is the case, using terms like the 'China threat' and 'new colonialism'? Are they blind to what China is doing in Africa and other parts of the world? Are they deaf to the voices of justice from China and Africa? Perhaps we need to rehash here the history of colonialism.

Throughout history, European colonial expansion was divided into two phases. The period from 1450 through 1763 was the first phase of European colonial expansion. After Zheng He's oceangoing navigations, China utterly secluded itself from the outside world, while for Western Europe, the introduction of the compass, the development of the shipbuilding industry, and the advancement of geographical knowledge made oceangoing voyages possible. This was a strong stimulation to the Europeans, who were eager to search for wealth from the East.

After the middle of the 15th century, Portugal colonised Madeira and the autonomous region of the Azores. With the discovery of the sea route to the East, Portugal occupied Goa in India in 1510 and extended its colonies further afield in Asia and America, and in 1553 it occupied Macau. After 1492, when Spain began its rampant expansion to America, there was a conflict between the two colonisers. In 1494, under arbitration by the pope, the two colonial powers signed the Treaty of Tordesillas,[25] defining their respective scopes of power and carving the world between them. After that, in order to establish an enormous colonialist empire, Spain ruthlessly butchered the indigenous people in South America, reducing their population from 50 million when the Spanish arrived to 4 million by the 17th century. In the mid and late 16th century, the rising colonial powers – the Netherlands, Britain and France – started to vie with Spain and Portugal for control of the world. The Netherlands occupied China's Taiwan Province in 1624, ruling the island for 38 years, and continued with its expansion to North America, establishing the Dutch West India Company. France began its colonisation in the 16th century and, in 1603, established its colony in North America. In 1533, Britain established its Muscovy Company and, in 1600, established the East India Company for further expansion on the Indian subcontinent. To satisfy the needs for expanding colonisation, the colonial countries revived the slave system that had been active in the Mediterranean area in the Middle Ages. In 1442 the Berbers were reduced to slavery by the Portuguese. In 1502, the Spanish began trafficking black Africans to America to make up for the labour shortage after the massacres there. In 1562 Britain began its slave trade, and the Netherlands followed suit in 1619. By the middle of the 18th century, the slave trade had reached its peak. In 1763 alone, Britain traded about 40 000 black slaves from Africa, transporting them in 150 ships.

The period after 1763 marks the second phase of European colonial expansion. In the first phase, trade in the colonies supplied Europe with coffee, chocolate, tea, tobacco, spices and potatoes, changing the eating habits of Europeans. But with the start of the Industrial Revolution, trade in the colonies took a back seat, despite the fat profits the colonialists had gained from it. The colonisers attempted to turn their colonies into production bases for their raw materials and grains, as well as markets for their industrial products. For that reason, they moved large numbers of their nationals to the colonies and massacred or drove indigenous people from the colonies to make room for the development of agriculture and industry, subduing or transforming the indigenous people to fit the demands of colonial expansion.

It has been estimated that as many as 50 million Europeans emigrated in the 100 years after 1820. Their advanced science, technology, and railway-led traffic and communications system, while serving the colonial agenda, wounded the souls of the colonised peoples by impressing on them that the colonisers were advanced and superior while the colonised were backward and inferior. In the century between 1763 and 1875, Britain was at the forefront of colonial expansion, and by the 19th century, its monopoly trade developed into free trade. In the period between 1875 and World War I, the competition among colonial powers intensified, not only among the old established powers, but also among new players, such as Germany, the US and Japan. As many as 15 Western powers participated in the notorious Berlin Conference (1884–1885) to carve up Africa. After the conference, in just 20 years, almost the whole African continent had fallen victim to Western powers.[26]

Labels such as the 'China threat' and 'new colonialism' are nothing more than a product of the colonialist mode of thought. First of all, the former colonisers take for granted that when China enters Africa, it is stepping into their shoes, and therefore practising neocolonialism. Secondly, the former colonisers are accustomed to regarding Africa as their 'backyard' or 'hunting reserve', their own sphere of influence, one that is forbidden to others. Thirdly, the healthy and rapid development of China–Africa relations has turned some envious Westerners into troublemakers. It is evident that China–Africa relations have progressed greatly in the 21st century, moving from the field of politics, as was the norm when the Chinese mainland had to win over diplomatic partners from Taiwan, to the field of economics. The figures show this: bilateral trade value has increased nine times, reaching $107 billion in 2008, an annual increase of 45 per cent. China–Africa trade value surpassed that of Africa–US trade for the first time. China's direct investment in Africa increased from $490 million in 2003 to $7.8 billion in 2008.[27]

Reference to history brings wisdom. From 5 to 8 July 2010, the First International Academic Conference on Zheng He was held in Malacca, Malaysia, with the theme 'Zheng He and the Afro-Asia world'. Tun Datuk Seri Utama Mohd Khalil bin Yaakob, head of Malacca State and a self-proclaimed 'super-fan of Zheng He', said at the opening ceremony that during its voyages on the Western Ocean, 'Zheng He's fleet was able to conquer everyone, but did not conquer anyone, bringing peace wherever it went. In the eyes of the world, Zheng He was a messenger of peace, revered and admired for his style as a general and for his superior strength.'[28]

Professor Liao Jianyu, director of the Singapore Chinese Heritage Centre and International Society for the Study of the Chinese Overseas, said in his keynote speech at the conference, 'Zheng He of the World and Zheng He of Asia and Africa', that the economic development and continuing rise of China over the past 30 years have aroused the concern of the Western world. The West's concern about Zheng He is in fact a concern about China, a fear that its strength will present a threat to world peace. He said: 'Though predicting the future by the past is not very precise, the uniqueness of Chinese culture and history, and the notion of peace and harmony Zheng He brought to the world are of great significance and influence, and are indispensable in a regional context.'[29]

Professor Liao went on to say that, viewed from the perspective of religion, Zheng He was exemplary in his interactions with other religions. At the time, Islam was spreading peacefully across South East Asia, existing discreetly alongside other religions. This history of peaceful coexistence between religions is very evident in Malacca. But in the Portuguese period in Malacca (1511–1641), when it was under a religious government, Catholicism spread, while other religious activities were suppressed. The Dutch period brought in new rule by Protestants, and British rule brought in Anglican authorities. While the British were generally more accommodating rulers than the Portuguese, when it came to religion, they could not compare to Zheng He. These two examples cited in the speech are sufficiently strong evidence to refute any notion of a China threat or new colonialism.

It is very important to make a clear distinction between fallacies such as the China threat and new colonialism, and China's activity in maintaining its own interests and its active participation in international affairs and the promotion of world peace. With the rise of globalisation and China's increasing exposure to the world, China is gaining depth, wisdom, and vitality in its integration into the world and its communication with the international community. It is apparent that, with the number of Overseas Chinese on the rise in various countries, the protection of Overseas Chinese people is becoming an increasingly important issue. For instance, in March 2011, 35 000 Chinese citizens had to be withdrawn from Libya. At the same time, with the expansion of its commercial activities, China needs to protect its own overseas interests. In December 2008, the Chinese navy started to escort Chinese merchant ships, in an effort to ensure their safety.

Peace, development and cooperation are the call of our times and are in the common interest of all the world's countries. China's participation in international affairs and its motivation to maintain its own interests are different from the so-called China threat and new colonialism. Equating the two is to view China through a distorted lens. Or perhaps there is an ill-intentioned confusion in some people's minds; perhaps some people harbour the preconceived notion that anything China does is somehow suspect, and that its achievements are a violation of the rules. This could arguably be more accurately termed a threat to China than a China threat, and one that is meant to keep China in a predefined box. It is perhaps more reasonable to define this so-called new colonialism as a restriction placed on China in an attempt to hold it back. It is apparent that these guises and fallacies, like all other attempts to hold China down, have been fabricated in vain and will be exposed for what they are.

Zheng He's fleet was the earliest to visit Africa and its crew members were the earliest foreign settlers on the continent. The experience of the first group of Chinese immigrants in Africa shows the world that China has never intended to be colonialists. Had China wanted to colonise Africa at that time, it would have merited the label of the oldest colonising country in the world. In that case, the Europeans, who came later, would have been the new colonialists. In fact, it is the Western countries that practised colonial oppression and exploitation, plundering Africa and enslaving the African people. They are at once the authentic old colonisers and the neocolonialists too.

Six hundred years ago, Zheng He's fleet sailed to Africa all the way from China. An unexpected shipwreck left some of its crew there, and the limited options for transportation and communication meant they remained there forever, never to return to China. They became integrated into their society, put down roots in African soil, and spread Chinese culture as the earliest Chinese residents in Africa. The peaceful diplomatic policies of the Ming Dynasty's imperial court, which Zheng He observed, were a diplomatic practice that reflected the traditional philosophy of the Chinese nation and an expression of its love of peace, admiration for harmony, practice of kindness and pursuit of beauty. The peaceful diplomatic policies followed by the new China are a continuation of this Chinese culture, and an integral part of the core values of the Chinese people, a brilliant crystallisation of the civilisation and wisdom of humankind.

Postscript: Final reflections

EARLY WINTER 2012, BEIJING

Winter arrived early this year. The world was moving forward at such a rapid pace that even the Siberian cold snap lost patience and refused to wait for its appointed time. As the old poem says, 'A strange wind bursts urgently upon us, lighting the lawn with moonlight. The art of nature and humans makes of the waters carved flowers afloat on the breeze.'[1] The north wind was cold, and snowflakes filled the sky. The pure blanket of silvery white over the earth created a beautiful scene in northern China.

At that same moment, the world looked very different thousands of miles away on the Kenyan coast. There, a scorching sun floated over blue seas, and lush vegetation encroached on the sandy beaches. Following China's land archaeological excavation team was a second wave of underwater researchers from China, rushing to conduct their archaeological explorations.

The China–Kenya joint research programme was conducted according to agreements signed by the two nations. An introduction to the background of this project is called for here. In 2005, on the 600th anniversary of Zheng He's voyages on the Western Ocean, China held a series of commemorative activities with the theme 'Love for the motherland, good neighbourliness, and scientific navigation'. The local and overseas editions of the *People's Daily* issued a series of reports titled *The Search for Zheng He's Footprints in* Africa, which garnered great attention from other media organisations and the public. Prompted by public enthusiasm for the project, State Councillor Chen Zhili instructed Minister of Culture Sun Jiazheng and head of the National Relics Bureau Shan Jixiang to invite experts and scholars to participate in relevant research projects.

At the same time, the Kenyan National Museum's Department of Archaeology expressed its hopes for joint archaeological excavation projects. The China National Relics Bureau sent experts to study in Kenya. The two countries signed a cooperation agreement for the archaeological study, as reported by Xinhua News Agency's Lin Zhishen. Lin's article follows:

> China and Kenya signed a cooperation agreement to conduct archaeological research of the Kenyan coast near the city of Mombasa, with plans to search the

coastal area for a 'Zheng He Monument' and uncover the mystery surrounding East African residents of Chinese descent. This is the first reported agreement of cooperation for archaeological research signed between China and an African country.

The Chinese delegation included the head of the National Relics Bureau, Shan Jixiang, who visited Kenyan Minister for National Heritage, Suleiman Shakombo, to sign the agreement on behalf of their governments. The agreement, which binds the two nations to a joint exploration of the Kenyan coast and the Lamu Archipelago from 2006 through 2009, includes provisions for underwater excavations, searches for the tomb of the legendary Chinese crew, and other archaeological research.

At the conclusion of the signing ceremony, Shakombo said that there is a long, rich history of cultural exchange between China and Kenya, with the historical fact of Zheng He's voyages on the Western Ocean and the legendary tales of his crew members being shipwrecked in the Lamu Archipelago being key features. The China-Kenya joint archaeological research project will decode ancient mysteries and will further strengthen cultural exchange between the two nations, promoting China-Kenya friendship for generations to come. The cooperation agreement is a matter of extraordinary significance.

At the signing ceremony, Shan Jixiang said, 'Though situated tens of thousands of miles apart, the two nations have close connection in politics, economics, culture, and other fields. This joint archaeological research project is for the purpose of promoting cooperation in cultural heritage protection in China and Kenya, and for broadening the scope of China-Kenya cultural communication through archaeological excavation and research. Though this archaeological research programme is challenging, we believe that our joint efforts will be rewarded with fruitful scientific findings and will contribute a new chapter to the history of friendly communication between the Chinese and Kenyan peoples.'

Chinese Ambassador to Kenya Guo Congli and Director of the Underwater Archaeological Research Centre of the National Museum Dr Zhang Wei attended the signing ceremony, alongside their counterparts from the Kenyan National Heritage Ministry and the Kenyan National Museum, officials from the Lamu region, and about one hundred representatives from Kenyan coastal provinces.

It was reported that three conclusions have been reached by Chinese and Kenyan archaeologists after several years of preliminary investigation in the Lamu Archipelago. First, there are still people of Chinese descent living on Lamu Island, descended from Zheng He's crewmen. Second, the Lamu area is a virtual storehouse of ancient Chinese porcelain ware, and is one of the most important of the 40 known relic sites where Chinese porcelain is found. Finally, there might be sunken Chinese vessels near Pate Island in the Lamu Archipelago. Experts have pointed out that this China-Kenya joint archaeological research project might shed some light on historical mysteries.[2]

Five years into the China–Kenya joint archaeological research agreement, after a period of investigation and verification, Chinese archaeologists travelled to Africa for simultaneous land excavation and underwater archaeological research. The following report by Zhang Ran appeared in the *Beijing Times* on 24 February 2010:

> Yesterday morning, the China National Museum, the Archaeology Department of Beijing University, and the Kenyan National Museum held an agreement signing ceremony. Through investigation and excavation of cultural relics, relic sites, and underground and underwater remains in the Kenyan Lamu Archipelago, experts from the two countries will provide access to the historical mysteries of the cultural exchange and economic and trade communications between ancient China and Kenya. Chinese experts will also search for sunken ships from Zheng He's legendary fleet. Zhao Hui, President of the Archaeology Department of Beijing University, says that this project is being launched after five years of investigation, verification, and preparation. This research project includes archaeological investigation, exploration, and excavation of cultural relics in the Kenyan Lamu Archipelago and its immediate waters, archaeological excavation of ancient relic land sites in Kenya's Malindi City and its surrounding area, and investigation of Chinese cultural relics unearthed in the Kenyan coastal area.
>
> The joint archaeological research project will reportedly last for three years, and the Ministry of Commerce will donate 20 million yuan in international aid. The Chinese side will dispatch experts and personnel to Kenya to work for two to three months each year. The local climate permits excavation only during its two dry seasons, in June through September and December through February. The curator of the Kenyan National Museum, Dr Idle Omar Farah, announced that an advance Chinese team will arrive in Kenya for preparation before the main group arrives.
>
> According to Zhao Jiabin, Director of the China National Museum Underwater Archaeological Research Centre, in the process of archaeological excavation and investigation in the five Kenyan coastal areas, including Malindi, some fragments of sunken ships and a great deal of ancient Chinese porcelain ware have been unearthed, including pieces from as early as the Yuan Dynasty through the Qing Dynasty.

'It is not yet known whether these porcelain pieces were brought in by Chinese or Arabian ships,' says Dr Farah, adding that most of the ancient Chinese porcelain ware is currently in the Kenyan National Museum. All the relics unearthed in archaeological projects may be borrowed by China for research and exhibition purposes, upon signing further agreements in accord with international conventions.[3]

The Kenyan land excavation started in July 2010, focusing on archaeological excavation of ancient relic sites in the vicinity of Malindi, Kenya. This excavation project was executed by a joint archaeological team consisting of nine Chinese experts from the Archaeology Department of Beijing University, and eight Kenyan experts and workers from the Kenyan National Museum's Coastal Archaeology Department, the strongest working team to tackle Kenyan archaeological research history. Lasting two months, the field excavation was the largest archaeological activity in Malindi's coastal area. An abundance of ancient relics have already been discovered, displaying great variety and providing new materials for study by historians of the Malindi Kingdom. Two years later, the Chinese research team continued with large-scale excavations in the Malindi area from 11 July through 21 September 2012, conducting archaeological investigations of ancient Chinese porcelain.

The achievements of the joint China–Kenya archaeological research group have been extensive. The team's excavation work, the first activity Chinese archaeologists have conducted abroad, has gained the attention of both local and Western media outlets, particularly the BBC, whose report 'Coin that could re-write Chinese-African history found' and the accompanying video recordings have been most influential and extensive. The report states: 'A tiny copper coin has subverted our knowledge about the early history of East Africa, and should challenge us to rethink contemporary China's role in East Africa.'[4]

From an academic perspective, the major contributions of the land excavations and the investigation of the Chinese porcelain are:
- The Yongle copper coin, the Ming Dynasty official kiln porcelain and the Longquan porcelain, all discovered and unearthed in the Mambrui archaeological stratum, have provided convincing evidence of the arrival of Zheng He's mission at the north-eastern Kenyan port, an academic question long awaiting an answer.
- The capital of the ancient kingdom of Malindi has been confirmed. It is most likely that the ancient seat of government in Malindi was Malin or Malindi, as recorded in the Chinese Yuan and Ming Dynasty documents, a significant place for Zheng He's fleet to visit on the African continent. This discovery puts an end to the centuries-long dispute over the precise location of the ancient capital of Malindi.

- The discovery of slag, crucibles, blast pipes and other iron-making relics has provided evidence of frequent iron-making activities over a long period of time. This matches both oral and written records indicating that Malindi was a major centre of ironware exports, providing convincing evidence of the development of the iron-making skills seen in Kenya.
- The discovery of large amounts of Chinese porcelain along the Kenyan coast provides evidence that the Lamu Archipelago was the earliest site for maritime trade, providing a scientific basis for more in-depth research into trade on the Indian Ocean in ancient times, including China–Africa trade in the period during which Zheng He journeyed on the Western Ocean. In conclusion, these land excavations have provided material evidence for records found in Chinese and foreign literature.

Before the joint archaeological research project began, I had not met Professor Qin Dashu of Beijing University, but we have become friends through this project. My most recent meeting with him took place when he had just returned from Kenya. We spoke about the great achievements made by the China–Kenya joint research project. He grew excited as we spoke, saying, 'This clearly shows that such international archaeological research activities, once earnestly executed, will prove to be an advantage to Chinese scholars in understanding and researching our culture, history, and cultural relics, and will prove to foreign scholars our superiority in gaining knowledge and making achievements.'

To throw more light on this issue, Professor Qin quoted what the Kenyan National Museum experts had said to him: 'Just as the excavation of the Shanga relic site by the Englishman Mark Horton[5] refreshed our understanding of the history of the Lamu Archipelago, your discovery has renewed our understanding of the history of the Malindi area.'

The archaeological research project was carried out on land and under water simultaneously. According to the research agreement, a Kenyan underwater archaeological team was formed, consisting of 12 underwater archaeological researchers from Beijing, Shanghai, Zhejiang, Fujian and Jiangxi, dispatched by the China National Museum, and two professionals from the Kenyan National Museum. From 26 November 2010 to 23 January 2011, the research team conducted underwater archaeological investigations and excavations in coastal areas of Kenya, focusing on the waters off Lamu and Malindi. The second phase of underwater research was carried out from 2 December 2012 to 13 January 2013. As required by the terms of the project, the 2012 Kenyan archaeological research team comprised 18 top researchers from the China National Museum and two professionals from the Kenyan National Museum.

Zhao Jiabin, director of the China National Museum Underwater Archaeological Research Centre, said that work in 2012 focused mainly on large-scale investigations of waters in the Lamu Archipelago region, and included systematic underwater archaeological excavations at the Shela underwater relic site, discovered in 2010. The investigative excavations were carried out in strict accordance with archaeological fieldwork regulations, with detailed written, graphic and video records, and completing the collation of previously collected data and cultural relics.

According to the preliminary research, the pottery refloated from this relic site includes pieces with Arab and Swahili features, some with traces of repair and use. Most of the refloated fragments were blue and black porcelain, similar to the Chinese porcelain discovered at places such as Pate Island in the Lamu Archipelago, their surfaces showing evidence of use. These are most likely to be products from kilns in southern Fujian, dating from the middle and late Qing Dynasty. Zhao says that various advanced instruments were employed to scan and measure items recovered from the Shela relic site, so as to obtain accurate information about the geographic and geomorphic conditions there. In addition, at the time of writing, the archaeological team intended to conduct underwater investigations and mapping of the Ngomeni sunken-ship relic sites, located in the waters off Malindi. Because boards from ships, glazed pottery, pottery fragments and much coagulum have been found there, it is suspected that this is a shipwreck site.

The joint research team is to be commended for its great achievements. A large quantity of Chinese porcelain fragments were discovered during the excavations of the Lamu Archipelago's waters. These serve as precious material evidence of ancient China–Africa commerce and trade. In September 2013, I made my fifth visit to Lamu, arriving at Manda Kiwanda Island and visiting the archaeological site there. As an old Chinese poem says, 'An auspicious snow tells of a bumper harvest.'[6] As the China–Kenya joint underwater research project entered its second year, snow fell in Beijing, telling of exciting discoveries to come. My own enthusiasm has prompted me to compose a poem:

> Fifteen years in Africa
> Bound to the sunken Sanbao craft
> Searching on land and on sea
> Longing to set its wonders afloat

On 14 March 2013, more good news came from Kenya. On Manda Island, scientists discovered a 600-year-old copper coin, a new piece of evidence supporting Zheng He's visits to East African that rewrites the history of international trade.

The UK's *Daily Mail* reported that the working team of Chapurrukha Kusimba, from the Field Museum in the US, and Sloan Williams, from the University of

Illinois, discovered the 600-year-old Chinese copper coin. The piece is a Yongle copper coin, issued during the Yongle reign (1403–1424). This important discovery will have a great impact on our understanding of history. The coin, a small disc of copper and silver with a square hole in the centre, so it could be worn on a belt, proves that there were commercial communications between China and East Africa decades before the arrival of European explorers in Africa. Kusimba says:

> Zheng He was, in many ways, the Christopher Columbus of China. It's wonderful to have a coin that may ultimately prove he came to Kenya. We know that Africa has long been connected to other parts of the world, but this copper coin has raised the question of the relationship between China and the coastal lands on the Indian Ocean.[7]

The report also points out that Zheng He's great fleet reached other areas of the Indian Ocean. Soon after the death of the Yongle emperor, China secluded itself and broke off its connections with all these areas, giving European explorers an opportunity to lead the era of great geographical discovery and expand their territories. Before this Chinese copper coin was discovered, it was believed the earliest European to reach the area of present-day Kenya was the Portuguese navigator Vasco da Gama, who arrived in Mombasa in 1498. It was believed da Gama went northwards from Mombasa to Malindi, but no evidence of this northward journey to the Lamu Archipelago has been found.

Manda Island and Pate Island are both part of the Lamu Archipelago. From 200 to 1430, Manda Island was prominent in the area, with trade playing an important part in its development. The discovery of this Yongle copper coin is further evidence of the importance of trade. After 1430, Manda Island was deserted, remaining uninhabited. This deserted island has recently become a tourist attraction, with a small airport to facilitate visitors to the Lamu Archipelago.

In addition, from July to September 2010, a Peking University archaeological team found a 'Yongle Tongbao' in the Malindi archaeological excavations, along with some Jingdezhen blue-and-white tiles. That December, the finds were confirmed by experts as Jingdezhen official kiln products from the Ming Dynasty Yongle period. In addition, in July to September 2012, the Peking University archaeological team found a piece of celadon at the same site, and an inspection in 2013 confirmed that the tiles were Longquan celadon products from the Ming Dynasty Yongle period. During the Ming Dynasty, the 'official kiln' referred to all the government kilns. Management of these kilns was very strict, and the products produced were for exclusive use by the emperor or the queen. It was so tightly controlled that even defective products would be broken and buried, and were not allowed into circulation. As a result, such tiles were likely to be found exclusively in diplomatic porcelain. Since Zheng He's was the only large-scale diplomatic mission in the Yongle period, the discovery of these tiles can be seen as evidence that Zheng He's fleet had been here. Archaeologists at Peking University also found other porcelain kilns near Malindi.[8]

These discoveries are no ordinary finding. They prove several historical facts. Firstly, it is now evident Zheng He's fleet arrived in the East African coastal areas in the period between 1405 and 1433, decades earlier than Da Gama. The myth that Europeans discovered Africa, once believed so firmly, has been exposed as sheer nonsense. Secondly, we can now see that commercial communications between China and Africa began at least 600 years ago, and China–Africa trade is a continuation and development of this historical commerce. Furthermore, the relationship between China and the countries in the immediate vicinity of the Indian Ocean has a long history worthy of further research. Finally, it is evident that the African continent, particularly the East African coastal area, will provide us with new evidence of the arrival of Zheng He's fleet, and that the story of Zheng He and Africa will always live, frequently recorded in our words over time.

Notes

Prologue

1. (Tang) Liu Yuxi, 'A poem in praise of autumn'.

Chapter 1

1. First printed in 1931, this was the earliest Chinese newspaper in Africa, with an inscription on the masthead by Chiang Kai-shek. It ceased publication for unknown reasons in March 2004.
2. It is said in note 1 on page 11 of *A Tentative Analysis of Sino-Africa Transportation History* (published by SDX Joint Publishing Company, September 1973) that 'one of my friends in Kenya told me that he had heard of Chinese people reaching Lamu and Mombasa (Manbasa on Zheng He's navigational chart) about 500 years earlier. There are similar legends throughout Kenya, telling the story of Chinese people arriving there for trade in the 15th century.
3. Nicholas D Kristof, 1492: Prequel, the *New York Times Magazine*, 6 June 1999. Kristof was a reporter for the *New York Times Magazine* and a specialist in Chinese studies. He took the Chinese name Ji Sidao. Around the beginning of the millennium, he became interested in Zheng He's voyages on the Western Ocean. While he was serving as the chief of bureau for the Tokyo branch of the *New York Times Magazine*, he visited Kenya's Pate Island to investigate the situation there.
4. Louise Levathes, *When China ruled the seas*. New York: Oxford University Press, 1994. Levathes, who took the Chinese name Li Luhua, was a long-time staff writer for *National Geographic* in the US. In 1988 she interviewed leading British sinologist Joseph Needham, author of *Science and civilisation in China*.
5. Joseph Needham, *Science and civilisation in China*. Cambridge: Cambridge University Press, 1988.
6. Louise Levathes, *When China ruled the seas*. New York: Oxford University Press, 1994, p. 21.
7. Tu Peilin, a journalist with the *People's Daily*, wrote in 'Friendship between the Chinese and Somalian people' (*People's Daily*, 17 October 1962) that there is a populous village in Brava, Somalia, that is often called the 'China village'.

8 Wang Dayuan was born in 1311 (the fourth year of Zhida in the Yuan Emperor Wuzong's reign) in Nanchang, Jiangxi Province. At the age of 20, he began travels that led him to sail the Eastern and Western oceans, spending eight years on his journeys. In 1349 (the ninth year of Zhizheng in the Yuan Emperor Shundi's reign), he wrote *A Brief Record of the Islands*, which lists 220 place names, including some East African cities.
9 Mombasa is labelled 'Manbasa' on Zheng He's nautical charts.
10 See Carolina Sassoon's *Chinese porcelain in Fort Jesus*, published in Mombasa by the National Museum of Kenya in 1975.
11 For further information about the connection between Gedi and China, see James Kirkman's *Gedi* (8th ed.), published in Mombasa, 1975.
12 (Qing) Zheng Yingyu (ed.) et al., *The history of Ming*. Zhonghua Book Company, 2003, pp. 8451–8452.
13 See Edmond Bradley Martin, *The history of Malindi: A geographical analysis of the East African coastal town from the Portuguese period to the present*. Nairobi: East African Literature Bureau, 1973, pp. 12–13.
14 For further details, see He Tingwu and Xia Daizhong (eds), *The Zheng He epic*. Yunnan People's Press, Yunnan Fine Arts Press and Aurora Press, 2005, p. 354.

Chapter 2

1 J de V Allen, Siyu in the 18th and 19th centuries, *Transafrican Journal of History (1979)*, 8(1): 11–35.
2 Ibid.
3 Ibid.
4 See Mark Herton, Helen W Brown and Nina Mudida, *Shanga: The archaeology of a Muslim trading community on the coast of East Africa*. British Institute in East Africa, 1996, p. 22.
5 Ibid. p. 16.
6 (Qing) Ji Yun, 'The excellent landscape from Fuchun to Yanling'.

Chapter 3

1 Richard Seymour Hall, *Empires of the monsoon: A history of the Indian Ocean and its invaders*. Harper Collins, 1996.
2 'Shangaa' describes astonishment; the second 'a' serves to emphasise the high level of astonishment.
3 Translator's note: The Cultural Revolution began in 1966 and lasted until 1976.
4 Project Hope is a Chinese welfare charity that aims to financially support the children of the poor in basic education.
5 (Song) Ye Yin, 'Lament of the female machine worker'.

NOTES

Chapter 4
1. (Ming) Wang Shizhen, 'Late autumn village scenes'. In *300 Ming poems with detailed annotations*, edited by Zhu Anqun and annotated by Ma Xuesong et al. Baihuazhou Literature and Art Publishing House, 1997, p. 338.
2. In 1974 a farmer in Lintong, in China's Shaanxi Province, came across a 'human head' while digging a well in his home. The whole family agreed that it was something sinister, so they buried it again, refilled the unfinished well, and kept it a strict secret. The head was that of a terracotta figurine. It was not until the Terracotta Warriors were discovered to be of great historical significance that the family shared their secret. Had they shared their findings when they initially discovered it, the Terracotta Warriors would have been discovered earlier.

Chapter 5
1. Fatma Shapi and Katie Halford, *A Lamu cookbook*. The Lamu Society, 1981.
2. *Journey to the west* is a Chinese novel, published in the 16th century. It is attributed to the Ming dynasty writer Wu Cheng'en. The novel is one of the four great classical novels of Chinese literature. See Wu Cheng'en, *Journey to the west*, 3 volumes. Beijing: People's Literature Press, 1991.

Chapter 6
1. 'Tukul' is the term used in the local language for the type of dwelling called 'gojo' in Amharic. A tukul or gojo is a hut made of branches, with a conical roof covered in dried grass. The scarcity of rain in the region makes dried grass an effective cover for houses.
2. From a billboard of the UN High Commissioner for Refugees representative office in Ethiopia, December 2000.

Chapter 7
1. This hotel was attacked by al-Shabaab militia in 2015.
2. It is often suggested by various people in China that absolute freedom is a good thing. My experience of such freedom in Somalia, however, suggested that it would bring about more chaos than convenience.
3. The Chinese-African medical teams provided free aid to Africa, sent by the Chinese government, and supported by the province, cities and municipalities as counterpart aid. There are Chinese medical teams stationed in 47 African countries. The medical team in Somalia was supported by Jilin Province, which withdrew when civil war broke out in Somalia. It has not returned since.
4. Computerised tomography, a scanning technology.

5   *Marvellous views from a starry mast.* Beijing: Zhonghua Book Company, 1954, pp. 69–70.
6   Xu Dongda (ed.), *A complete collection of ancient poetry for children.* Aurora Press, 2001, p. 205.

Chapter 8
1   Hu Yanwu and Xia Daizhong (eds), *The Zheng He epic.* Yunnan People's Press, Yunnan Fine Arts Press and Aurora Press, 2006, p. 128.
2   Ibid.

Chapter 9
1   Tanzania–Zambia Railway Authority.
2   Zoe Marsh and GW Kingsnorth, *An introduction to the history of East Africa.* Shanghai: Shanghai People's Publishing House, 1974, p. 9
3   B Davidson, *The lost cities of Africa.* New York: Back Bay Books, 1959, p. 146, quoted in Dr Xia Nai, Porcelain: Evidence of communication and relation between China and Africa, *Cultural Relic* 1, 1963, p. 19.
4   The Zanzibar Islands lie 25 to 50 km from the mainland. The two largest islands – Unguja, commonly referred to as Zanzibar Island, and Pemba – have an area of 1 651 km² and 980 km², respectively. Zanzibar/Unguja is the main island.
5   'The East is red' is a patriotic Chinese anthem from the time of Chairman Mao's Cultural Revolution.
6   The author was a member of the delegation. This quotation is taken from his notes.
7   Chen Dunde, *Mao Zedong – Nixon in 1972.* Liberation Army Art Press, 2002, p. 307.
8   *The history of Ming,* Volume 304: *The biography of the eunuch Zheng He.* Zheng Hesheng and Zheng Yijun, *Zheng He's western navigation document collection* (addendum), Volume 2. Maritime Press, 2005, p. 1132.
9   *The history of Ming* Volume 326: *History of Maldives,* p. 934.
10 Feilang (ed.), *Arabic, Persian, and Turkic oriental document annotation,* Volume 2. Geng Sheng and Mu Zhanglai, trans. Zhonghua Book Company, 2001, p. 681.
11 TA Chumovsky, *Três roteiros desconhecidos de Ahmad Ibn-Madjid o piloto árabe de Vasco da Gama* (Three rutters [sailing manuals] of Ibn Majid, the Arab pilot of Vasco da Gama). Lisbon: Comissão Executiva das Comemorações do V Centenário da Morte do Infante D. Henrique, 1960, p. 40. In Wu Zhiliang and Jin Guoping, The ultimate destination of Zheng He's voyage: An investigation on Bila and Sunla, *Zheng He Studies* 1, 2004, 55–62.

12 Maura Quatorze and Machado Da Graça, Sunken treasure brings a tidal wave of trouble, *The Sunday Independent*, 13 June 2004.

Chapter 10

1   A Guandi Temple is dedicated to Guan Yu, a general in the late Eastern Han Dynasty. As one of the best-known Chinese historical figures throughout East Asia and in Chinese communities around the world, Guan Yu has been deified and referred to as a mighty warrior with wisdom, courage, and the precious qualities of loyalty and dedication. It is a Chinese belief that he can bring courage, wealth and success to people. Guandi Temples, meaning literally 'Emperor Guan Temples', and shrines to him are found around the world wherever Chinese people live.
2   Tamatave is the former name of Toamasina. Overseas Chinese tend to use the former name.
3   This estimated data was given by the local organisation of Overseas Chinese in Tamatave.
4   In the Chinese community, 'Old Overseas Chinese' is used to designate Chinese Africans born in Africa. They are the second, third or later generations of Chinese immigrants, and some of them can no longer speak Chinese. 'New Overseas Chinese', by contrast, is the term used to refer to the first generation of Chinese immigrants in Africa.
5   (Ming) Zhou Hui, *Jinling trivia*, Volume 3: *Grain tree*.
6   (Qing) Chen Wenshu, Preface to the *Grain tree poems*, *Moling collection*, Volume 6.
7   (Qing) Chen Wenshu, *Grain tree poems*, *Moling collection*, Volume 6.
8   Gavin Menzies, *1421: The year China discovered the world*. Shi Yanqun, trans. Jinghua Press, 2005.
9   (Ming) Anonymous, *Fair winds for escort*, in *Two classics on navigation by compass*, collated and annotated by Xiang Da. Beijing: Zhonghua Bookstore 1960, p. 25.
10 (Song) Zhu Yu, *Pingzhou talks*.
11 (Ming) Gong Zheng, *Records of Western Ocean countries*, author's Preface.
12 Joseph Needham, *Civilisation in China* (Chinese edition), Volume 5, Fascicle 1. Science Press, 1971, p. 169.
13 Gavin Menzies, *1421: The year China discovered the world*. Shi Yanqun, trans. Jinghua Press, 2005, pp. 307–309.

Chapter 11

1   Joseph Needham, *Science and civilisation in China*. Cambridge: Cambridge University Press, 1954.

2   Li Anshan, *History of the Overseas Chinese in Africa*. Beijing: Chinese Overseas Publishing House, 2000, p. 127.
3   Melanie Yap and Dianne Leong Man, *Color confusion, and concessions: The history of the Chinese in South Africa*. Hong Kong: Hong Kong University Press, 1996, p. 10.
4   Ibid., p. 14.
5   Ibid., p. 37.
6   Cultural ties since 220 AD, *The Star*, 1 October 2003.
7   Malcolm Turner, *Shipwrecks and salvage in South Africa: 1505 to present*. Cape Town: Struik, 1988, pp. 11, 29.
8   Ibid., p. 29.
9   (Ming) Gong Zhen. *Records of Western Ocean countries*, author's Preface.
10 *The history of Ming*, Volume 304: *The biography of the eunuch Zheng He*.
11 *Zheng He: Record of the divine goddess*. Zheng Hesheng and Zheng Junyi, *Document collection of the Zheng He Western Ocean Voyage* (updated), Volume 1. Maritime Press, 2005, p. 18.
12 Gavin Menzies, *1421: The year China discovered the world*. Shi Yanqun, trans. Jinghua Press, 2005.
13 Gavin Menzies, *1421: The year China discovered the world*. New York: Bantam, 2003, pp. 115–118.
14 Ibid., p. 138.
15 Ibid., pp. 212, 248.
16 The four great technological inventions from ancient China are widely celebrated in Chinese culture: the compass, gunpowder, paper making and printing.

Chapter 12

1   Douglas L Wheeler and René Pélissier, *Angola*. Shi Lingshan, trans. Commercial Press, 1973.
2   Karl Marx, *Das Kapital*, Volume 1, in *Collected works of Marx and Engels*, Chinese version. Beijing: People's Publishing House, 2009, pp. 860–861.
3   Mao Zedong, A declaration of support to the American black people in their struggle against racial discrimination, in *Mao Zedong's collected diplomatic works*, compiled by the Ministry of Foreign Affairs of the People's Republic of China, Communist Party of China, Central Committee Literature Research Office, Central Committee Literature Press, 1994, p. 496.
4   Patrice Lumumba, *Congo, my country*. Praeger, 1962.
5   Quoted in Tang Pingshan, National hero, Lumumba of Zaire, in Chen Gongyuan, Tang Dadun and Yuan Mu (eds), *African celebrities*. World Knowledge Press, 1989, pp. 293–306.

6 Ibid.
7 After Mobutu took office, he changed the name of Stanleyville to Kisangani; the capital, Léopoldville, to Kinshasa; Elizabethville to Lubumbashi; and Congo, the name of the state, to Zaire.
8 Patrice Lumumba: Soldiers fighting for freedom in Africa. Moscow Advance Press, pp. 155–157, in Chen Gongyuan, Tang Dadun and Yuan Mu (eds), *African celebrities*. World Knowledge Press, 1989, pp. 300–301.
9 Communist Party of China, Central Committee Literature Research Office, *Collected poems of Chen Yi*, Volumes 1 and 2, Central Committee Literature Press, 2011, p. 512.
10 Published in *People's Daily*, 16 February 1961.
11 Gavin Menzies, *1421: The year China discovered the world*. New York: Bantam, 2003.
12 Gavin Menzies, *1421: The year China discovered the world*. New York: Bantam, 2003, pp. 134–136.
13 Gavin Menzies, *1421: The year China discovered the world*. Shi Yanquan, trans. Jinghua Press, 2005, p. 62.
14 See Tariq Hasan, *Colonialism and the call to Jihad in British India*. New Delhi: Sage Publications India, 2015; Thomas FX Noble et al., *Western civilization: Beyond boundaries*, Volume 2: *Since the 1950s*, 7th edition. Boston: Cengage Learning, pp. 688–689; Arnold Wright (ed.), *Southern India: Its history, people, commerce, and industrial resources*. New Delhi and Chennai: Asian Educational Services, 2004 (reprint of 1914–1915 edition). London: The Foreign and Colonial Compiling and Publishing Co.
15 See The State of Cochin, in Arnold Wright (ed.), *Southern India: Its history, people, commerce, and industrial resources*. New Delhi and Chennai: Asian Educational Services, 2004 (reprint of 1914–1915 edition). London: The Foreign and Colonial Compiling and Publishing Co., p. 366.
16 Ibid., p. 260.

Chapter 13

1 A *mu* is a Chinese unit of measurement; 1 *mu* = 0.067 hectares.
2 (Song) Ouyang Xiu, An oration in memory of Cai Duanming. In *Collected works of Ouyang Xiu*, Volume 50. Shanghai: Shanghai Bookstore 1989, n.p.
3 See Preben Kaarsholm, The past as a battlefield in Rhodesia and Zimbabwe: The struggle of competing nationalisms over history from colonization to independence, *Collected Seminar Papers. Institute of Commonwealth Studies* 42(1992), 156–170.
4 Li Zhaoxing et al. (eds), *World affairs almanac 2004/2005*. Beijing: World Knowledge Press, 2005, p. 316.

Chapter 14

1. Revisiting Kaunda, *People's Daily*, 14 September 2001.
2. Zhou Boping, *My career as a diplomat in harsh times (1964.9–1982.1)*. Beijing: World Knowledge Publishing House, 2004, p. 132.
3. Translator's note: This date is right at the beginning of the Cultural Revolution (1967–1977). Much writing in the West suggests that China was completely closed off to the outside world during the decade of the Cultural Revolution, and that there is complete silence during that era in the subsequent records. The dates of many African dignitaries' visits to China and Chinese dignitaries' visits to African nations, as well as the records of those events, demonstrate that this claim is false.
4. In May 2003, as a journalist, the author conducted this interview in Dar es Salaam. This quote was from a person on site during the interview. See Li Xinfeng, Journalist investigated the TAZARA railway three times in Tanzania and Zambia: How is it now?, *Global Times*, 17 March 2004.
5. Du Fu, 'Lament at river head'.
6. The exchange rate between RMB and US dollars fluctuated greatly during this period, so it is hard to calculate an exact amount. The US dollar–RMB exchange rate was about 1:1.88 in 1976, and about 1:8.28 in 2004.
7. The Tanzanian people call it the Uhuru Railway, from the Swahili *uhuru*, a word meaning 'freedom' and 'national liberation'.

Chapter 15

1. (Ming) Yuan Zhongche, *Insights of ancient and modern times*, Volume 8. In Zheng Hesheng and Zheng Yijun (eds), *Collected documents on Zheng He's navigations of the Western Ocean*, addendum, Volume 1. Ocean Press, 2005, p. 21.
2. (Tang) Li Bai, 'Difficult road', in *Selected poems by Li Bai*, selected and annotated by Yu Yanyin. Shanghai: Minzhi Bookstore, 1934, p. 28.
3. Preparatory Committee for the Celebration of the 580th Anniversary of the Great Navigator Zheng He's Navigation of the Western Ocean and China Maritime History Research Society, *Zheng He family genealogy documents*. China: Communications Press, 1985. p. 3.
4. Liu Xu was a successful candidate in the highest imperial examinations. When composing the inscription, he was a candidate for an official position in Zhejiang Province. Liu Ruqi was a young scholar. Yan Zhenqing (AD 709–784) was an official and famous calligrapher in the Tang Dynasty. He created what has been later referred to as 'the style of Yan Zhenqing', which has often been imitated.
5. (Ming) *Major decisions of the Ming emperors*, Volume 7.

6   *The history of Ming*, Volume 304: *Biography of the eunuch Zheng He*, Volume 7.
7   Zheng Hesheng and Zheng Yijun (eds), *Document collection of Zheng He's voyages on the Western Ocean*, addendum, Volume 2. Maritime Press, 2005, p. 1021.
8   Hu Tingguang and Xia Daizhong (eds), *The Zheng He epic*. Kunming: Yunnan People's Press, Yunnan Fine Arts Press and Aurora Publishing House, 2005, p. 108.
9   Zheng Hesheng and Zheng Yijun (eds), *Document collection of Zheng He's voyages on the Western Ocean*, addendum, Volume 2. Maritime Press, 2005, p. 1019.
10 Ibid., p. 1021.
11 Ibid., p. 1022.
12 Hu Yanwu and Xia Daizhong (eds), *Zheng He epic*. Yunnan People's Press, Yunnan Fine Arts and Aurora Press, 2005, p. 111.
13 (Qing), Mo Xiangzhi and Wang Shiduo, *Annals of Shangyuan County and Jiangning County, compiled during the reign of Emperor Tongzhi*, Volume 3: *Mountains*, in Zheng Hesheng and Zheng Yijun (eds), *Document collection of Zheng He's voyages on the Western Ocean*, addendum, Volume 2. Maritime Press, 2005, p. 1030.
14 *The history of Ming*, Volume 304: *Biography of the eunuch Zheng He*.
15 Ibid.
16 Dai Wenda, *African discoveries made by Chinese people*. Commercial Press, 1983, pp. 28–29.
17 (Ming) Zheng He: Record of the goddess Tianfei, in Zheng Hesheng and Zheng Yijun (eds), *Collection of documents on Zheng He's navigations on the Western Ocean* (updated), Volume 1. Maritime Press, 2005, p. 535.
18 (Ming) Zhu Di: Imperial decree for overseas seigniors and leaders, in Zheng Hesheng and Zheng Yijun (eds), *Collection of documents on Zheng He's navigations on the Western Ocean* (updated), Volume 1. Maritime Press, 2005, p. 531.
19 Analects of Confucius, Benevolence. See *The Analects,* http://classics.mit.edu/Confucius/analects.1.1.html. For the whole book, see http://classics.mit.edu/Confucius/analects.html.
20 (Tang) Du Fu, 'On the frontier'.
21 Nicholas D Kristof, 1492: Prequel, *The New York Times Magazine*, 6 June 1999.
22 *Li* is a Chinese unit of length. One *li* is approximately 500 m. The Great Wall is often referred to as 'the 10 000 *li* Great Wall' in Chinese, while the total length of great walls built in the history of China was 21 196 km, according to

a report by the State Administration of Cultural Heritage of China. See Zhang Hang, The total length of the Great Wall is 21 196.18 km, *Beijing Evening News*, 5 June 2012.
23　Ibid.
24　(Ming) Zheng He: Record of the goddess Tianfei, in Zheng Hesheng and Zheng Yijun (eds), *Collection of documents on Zheng He's navigations on the Western Ocean* (updated), Volume 1. Maritime Press, 2005, p. 18.
25　Liang Huiwang. *Mencius*. Volume 1.
26　Gavin Menzies, *1421: The year China discovered the world*. Jinghua Press, 2005, Preface.
27　Thabo Mbeki, Speech at the 10th Anniversary in Commemoration of Democratic South Africa and China–Africa Partnership Forum. Special issue jointly published by *People's Daily* and the South African Embassy in China, 30 April 2004.
28　Frederick Engels, *On the collapse of feudalism and the origin of nations*, in Volume 4 of *Collected works of Marx and Engels*, complied by the Communist Party of China Central Committee's Compiling Bureau of Marx, Engels, Lenin and Stalin's Works. People's Press, 2009, p. 217.

Chapter 16

1　Zhang Yun (ed.), *Mountain and sea classics: Biography of King Mu*. Yue Lu Publishing House, 2007, p. 220.
2　See Ai Zhouchang and Mu Tao, *History of China–Africa relations*. East China Normal University Press, 1996, p. 1.
3　JJL Duyvendak, *The discovery of Africa by the Chinese*. Commercial Press, 1983, p. 3.
4　Ai Zhouchang and Mu Tao, *History of China–Africa relations*, pp. 2–3.
5　Xuzhou Museum, On Xuzhou Han Dynasty reliefs, *Cultural Relics* 2, 1980, p. 55.
6　See this description in Su Shi's poem: 'At the roaring of a lion on the eastern bank of the river, I am at a loss, nearly dropping my walking stick.' Later, a 'roaring lion on the eastern bank of the river' came to refer to a jealous, unreasonably angry wife.
7　According to the *Modern Chinese dictionary*, the term is pronounced *suanni*, referring to a 'legendary ferocious animal'. *Modern Chinese dictionary*. Beijing: Commercial Press, 2002, p. 1206.
8　In the Persian language the word for 'lion' was pronounced *sheer*. 狮 (*shi*) in Chinese evolved from *sheer*. One opinion is that the word comes via the Sogdian language, since there was no modern Persian language at that time, and Sogdian is a branch of the eastern Persian language. The word 'lion' in the

ancient Western Region's Sogdian and Khotan Saka languages is pronounced *skrukh* or *shrkhu*, respectively, both coming from the same Persian language source. This means that the word *sheer* in Persian is not a foreign import. Persian documents show that there were many lions in the southern and south-western areas of Iran. In 1983 groups of two to five lions were seen in the bush south of the Iranian Persian Shush area.

9   *Biography of King Mu*, annotated by (Jin) Guo Pu, Volume 1. Shanghai: Shanghai Ancient Books Publishing House, 1990.
10 *Erya: Explaining beasts*, annotated by (Jin) Guo Pu. Beijing: Zhonghua Book Company, 1985.
11 *Erya* is a comprehensive dictionary edited according to meaning, completed in the time between the Warring States period and the early Western Han Dynasty.
12 (Eastern Han) Liu Zheng (ed.) and Wu Shuping, *Annotation of the Dongguan record of the Han Dynasty*. Zhonghua Book Company, 2008, p. 112.
13 Feng Chongjun (ed.) and Lu Junling, Preface, *Western Region place names* (updated). Zhonghua Book Company, 1982.
14 Ibid.
15 The Western Region is a geographical concept in Chinese historical writings. As the Western Region varies in scope in different books, people today have different understandings of this term. Aside from the usual definitions, some take it to refer to ancient central Asia in the broad sense, and Xinjiang in the narrow sense. Others say that it refers to the vast areas west of the Yumen and Yangguan passes, including central Asia, with which China's Xinjiang region is contiguous.
16 Shule was one of the 36 states in the Western Region in the early period of the Han Dynasty, located in today's Kashgar, Xinjiang. The Shule city seat was a communication hub and the juncture of the southern and northern Silk roads, a meeting point of Eastern and Western culture, where Persian, Indian and central Chinese culture intersected. Shule was also the first station of Buddhism's introduction into China from India.
17 Tan Qixiang (ed.), *A Concise atlas of Chinese history*. Chinese Atlas Press, 1996, p. 23.
18 Zhang Qian (d. 113 BC) was a Chinese official and diplomat. He travelled to central Asia and brought the Chinese emperor information about the region, which had been unknown to the Chinese. His travels helped open the way for China's interaction with central Asia.
19 (Southern Song Dynasty) Fan Ye, *The book of the Later Han: History of the Western Region*.

20 (Northern Wei) Yang Xuanzhi, *Records of Buddhist temples in Luoyang*, Volume 3. South City.
21 (Han) Ban Gu, *Book of Han: History of the Western Region*, Volume 66, Part 1.
22 (Northern Qi) Wei Shou, *Book of Wei: Collected biographies*, Volume 90: *History of the Western Region: History of Persia*.
23 Xu Ke (Ed.), *Qing Bai Lei Chao*, Volume 12: Zhonghua Book Company, 2000, p. 5506.
24 Zheng Hesheng and Zheng Yijun (eds), *Collected documents on Zheng He's navigations of the Western Ocean* (updated), Volume 1. Ocean Press, 2005, p. 18.
25 (Ming) Ma Huan, *Wonders overseas*, (updated), in Zheng Hesheng and Zheng Yijun (eds), *Collected documents on Zheng He's navigations of the Western Ocean* (updated), Volume 1. Ocean Press, 2005, p. 592.
26 (Ming) Tian Yiheng, *Young diary excerpts*, Volume 3: *Lion*, in Zheng Hesheng and Zhang Yijun (eds), *Collected documents on Zheng He's navigations of the Western Ocean* (updated), Volume 1. Ocean Press, 2005, p. 752.
27 See Chen Jiarong, Xie Fang and Lu Junling, *Collected interpretations of place names on the ancient South China Sea*. Zhonghua Book Company, 1986, p. 898. This book states that 'Alexandria was a city named in the *Record of ancient Greek place names*. Many ancient cities are so named. This is one of the two cities in Chinese historical books. One is Alexandria in the *Book of former Han*, and the other is Alexandria in the *Brief history of Wei*, present-day Herat in Afghanistan. The other is Liqian in both of these volumes.' This interpretation of the place name says that Pelliot verified that 'Liqian' is 'the Pali language Alassanda, or Alasandra in Chinese, referring to the Egyptian Alexandria. Liqian is a translation, just as Yavana refers to the Greeks in Sanskrit, and is used as a general reference to Greek or Roman colonies.'
28 (Wei) Yu Huan, *Wei Lüe, Xirong commentaries*, in Zhang Xinglang, *Collected materials on the history of East–West transportation*. Beijing: Zhonghua Bookstore, 1977, p. 38.
29 See Yu Taishan, Book of Wei, Xirong commentaries, *China's Borderland History and Geography Studies* 16(2), June 2006.
30 Feng Chongjun (ed.) and Lu Junling, *Western Region place names* (updated). Zhonghua Book Company, 1982, p. 3.
31 See http//www. irandeserts.com/cms/searchResult. aspx? query = % D8% B4% DB% 8C% D8% B1% 20% D8% A7% DB% 8C% D8% B1% D8% A7% D9% 86% DB% 8C.
32 *Cihai*. Shanghai: Shanghai Dictionary Press, 1990, p. 925.
33 See the *Book of Han: Records of rites and music*, Meng Kang notes.

34 For interpretations of the word *kunlun*, see Zhang Xinglang, Kunlun and kunlun slaves research, in *Collected historical materials about the transport between China and Africa*, edited and annotated by Zhang Xinglang, collated by Zhu Jieqin. Beijing: Zhonghua Book Company, 2003, pp. 574–582; Ge Chengyong, The origin of black people in Chang'an in the Tang Dynasty, *Studies on Chinese Literature and History*, 2001 (65), pp. 1–27; and Sun Ji, Kunlun and Zengzhi figures of the Tang Dynasty, in Sun Ji, *Sacred Chinese fire: Several questions on Chinese ancient cultural heritage and the cultural interaction between East and West*. Shenyang: Liaoning Education Press, 1996, pp. 251–260.

35 *Book of Kunlun Music 2*.

36 Huo Songlin, *Translation and analysis of Bai Juyi's poems*. Heilongjiang People's Publishing House, 1981, p. 182.

37 (Tang) Du Huan, edited by Zhang Yichun, *Record of travels*. Zhonghua Book Company, 2006, p. 23.

38 (Tang) Duan Chengshi, Fang Nansheng (ed.), *Miscellaneous morsels from Youyang*. Zhonghua Book Company, 1981, p. 46.

39 (Song) Zhou Qufei, edited by Yang Wuquan, *Collection of answers from outside the ridge*. Zhonghua Book Company, 2006, p. 266.

40 (Ming) Fei Xin, edited by Feng Chengjun, *View from a starry mast*, collation. Zhonghua Book Company, 1954, pp. 26–27.

41 (Song) Li Shi, edited by Li Zhiliang, *Natural history sequel*. Bashu Publishing House, 1991, p. 144.

42 (Song) Zhao Rugua, edited by Yang Bowen, *Foreign county records, collation and interpretation*. Zhonghua Book Company, 2008, p. 102.

43 (Ming) Fei Xin, edited by Fang Chengjun, *View from a starry mast*, collation, Zhonghua Book Company, 1954, p. 25.

44 (Ming) Qian Gu, *Wu capital essay collection sequel*, Volume 28: *Taoist temples*, in Zheng Hesheng and Zheng Yijun, *Collected documents from Zheng He's navigations on the Western Ocean* (updated). Maritime Press, 2005, p. 18.

45 See Xu Yongzhang, *Research on relations between China and Asian-African countries*. Hong Kong Social Sciences Press, 2004, pp. 40–42.

46 (Western Han) Shima Qian, *Historical records: History of Dawan*. Beijing: Zhonghua Book Company, 1959, pp. 3157–3181.

47 (Eastern Han) Ban Gu, *Book of Han: Biography of Zhang Qian*. Beijing: Zhonghua Book Company, 1964, pp. 2687–2707.

48 (Eastern Han) Ban Gu, *Book of Han: History of the Western Region*. Beijing: Zhonghua Book Company, 1964, pp. 3871–3932.

49 Zhizhi Chanyu (d 36 BC) was a Chanyu (chief) of the Xiongnu (Huns). At his time, the Xiongnu was separated into two parts, Southern Xiongnu and Northern Xiongnu. Zhizhi Chanyu held the northern part.
50 (Eastern Han) Ban Gu, *Book of Han: Biography of Chen Tang*. Beijing: Zhonghua Book Company, 1964, pp. 3001–3035.
51 The word is a cross between 'Liqian' and 'Lixuan', probably due to accent or pronunciation.
52 See *Roman village in the Chinese interior*, 30 March 2009; also Du Chen, Suspected Ancient Roman descendants discovered in eastern Gansu, *Morning News*, 24 June 2005.
53 Ai Zhouchang and Mu Tao, *History of China–Africa relations*. East China Normal University Press, 1996, p. 1.
54 Du You, *General laws*, Volume 216: *10th year of the Tianbao reign*, in Du Huan and Zhang Yicun (eds), *Record of travels*, collation. Zhonghua Book Company, 2006, p. 1.
55 Zhang Xinlang and Zhu Jieqin (eds), *Collected documents on China–West communications*, Volume 2. Zhonghua Book Company, 2003, p. 566.
56 See Du You, *General laws*, Volume 216: *10th year of the Tianbao reign*, in Du Huan and Zhang Yichun (eds), *Record of Travel*, collation. Zhonghua Book Company, 2006, p. 2.
57 Zhao Rugua and Feng Chenjun (eds), *Foreign county records*, collation. Zhonghua Book Company, 1977, p. 55.
58 Ai Zhouchang and Mu Tao, *History of China–Africa relations*, East China University Press, 1996, pp. 53–54.
59 *The history of Ming*, Volume 332: *History of the Western Regions*.
60 Quoted in Huang Chen, Dianne, 'Zheng Chenggong's black foreign gun squad's great service in recovering Taiwan', http:www.stnn.cc/culture/reveal/t20060323_172387.html.
61 *Cafre, caffre* or 'kaffir' in English means: 1) Bantus; 2) a racist term for a black person in South Africa; 3) a general Muslim term for non-Islamic people.
62 *Macau in the recovery period*, p. 28, in Jin Guopin and Wu Zhiling, *On the history of Macau in the early period*. Guangdong People's Publishing House, 2007, p. 378.
63 Roman Jesus Society Archives, Japan-China file 122, p. 264, in Jin Guopin and Wu Zhiling, *On the history of Macau in the early period*, p. 379.
64 *South China Jesus Society annals 1644*. See *China annals*, p. 251.
65 *Records of the Franciscans in China*, Volume 7, p. 32, in Jin Guopin and Wu Zhiling, *On the history of Macau in the early period*, p. 377.
66 *Records of the Franciscans in China*, Volume 2, pp. 362–363, in Jin Guopin and Wu Zhiling, *On the history of Macau in the early period*, p. 377.

67 'Brown' is the term used as a euphemism for black people. The outdated European term for black people, 'negro', is similar to 黑鬼 (black devil) in Chinese.
68 *Records of the Franciscans in China*, Volume 2, p. 367, in Jin Guopin and Wu Zhiling, *On the history of Macau in the early period*, p. 377.
69 See Cao Yonghe and Leonard Blusse, The disappearance of aborigines on Lamay Island: The beginning of a lost page in Taiwan's history, in *Collected Pingwu Research Essays*. Rice Fragrance Press, 2004, pp. 413–444.
70 Xie Qinggao and Yang Bingnan, Feng Changjun (ed.), *Sea Record Collection*. Zhonghua Book Company, 1955, p. 77–78.
71 Ibid, Preface.
72 See Ai Zhouchang, *China–Africa relations in the republican period (1911–1949)*. Beijing University Historiography, Beijing University Press, 1993, pp. 96–97.
73 Fang Jigen, *Collected documents on the history of the Chinese in Africa*. Xinhua Publishing House, 1986, pp. 110–111, 114.
74 The Chinese name for Ethiopia at the time.
75 Mu Yujun, A Perspective of the Italy-Abyssinia War, *Diplomacy Monthly* 7(5), 1 November 1935, p. 66.
76 A letter to all compatriots for national salvation from Japanese aggression, 1 August 1935.
77 See Ji Peidong (ed.), *Fifty years of China–Africa friendly cooperation*. Beijing: World Knowledge Publishing House, 2000, p. 99.
78 Thomas Boni Yayi, Speech at the opening ceremony of the 5th Ministerial Conference of FOCAC, Beijing, 19 July 2012.
79 Jacob Zuma, Speech at the opening ceremony of the 5th Ministerial Conference of FOCAC, Beijing, 19 July 2012.
80 Wen Jiabao, Promoting a new style of all-round China–Africa strategic partnership, speech at the opening ceremony of the 5th Ministerial Conference of FOCAC, *People's Daily*, 9 November 2009.
81 See Cui Peng, China has become the largest trade partner for Africa, *People's Daily*, 17 November 2011.
82 See Guo Caiping, Ministry of Commerce: China–Africa trade values reach a new high this year, *China Economy Network*, 16 November 2011, http//intl.ce.cn/specials/xxxx 201111/16/+20111116_22842858.shtml.
83 Hu Jin Tao, Opening a new type of strategic partnership between China and Africa: A speech at the opening ceremony of the 5th Ministerial Conference of the China–Africa Cooperation Forum, *People's Daily*, 20 July 2012.
84 See Zhang Xiang, Four upsurges in ancient China–Africa communications, *Nankai University Historiography*, 2nd Issue, 1987, pp. 118–131.
85 *Historical record*, Volume 113: *Historical Record of Dawan*.

86 Special Representative Liu Guijin on Africa and Darfur, *World Knowledge*, 26 November 2007.
87 The author of this book participated in the delegation's reception and all discussions.

Chapter 17

1 'Western Pass' refers to the western end of the Great Wall, where access to Mongolia was available for the Chinese people who lived on the Central Plain. From the 16th century to the early 20th century, a large population emigrated from the Shanxi, Shaanxi, and Hebei to Mongolia. Shanhaiguan (or the Shanhai Pass) is one of the major passes in the Great Wall. The Shanhaiguan was the entrance to north-eastern China, commonly known as Manchuria. In the 19th to the early 20th century, many people emigrated to the north-east from the Central Plain, especially Shandong.
2 UN Immigration Database, www.http://esa.un.org/migration/index.asp?panel=1.
3 Under the People's Republic of China's Returned Overseas Chinese Protection Law, the term 'Overseas Chinese' refers to Chinese citizens residing abroad who retain their Chinese nationality, Chinese people who have settled abroad and taken up a new nationality, ethnic Chinese descendants born abroad, and returned Overseas Chinese. The term 'Overseas Chinese' was first seen in the 1883 Northern Commerce Minister Fu Li-Jardine, Merchants and Swire Contract memorial book, penned by Xiangshan, Guangdong natives Zheng Guanying and Li Honngzhang: 'Most Overseas Chinese in Southeast Asia outside the port cities gradually arranged to send ships to deal with outsiders to create greater competitiveness.' In the late 19th and early 20th centuries, the term was used widely by Sun Yat-sen and other Alliance members, leading to its spread.
4 See Li Minghuan, International migration trends and changes of the Overseas Chinese, in Zai Qiujin (ed.), *Overseas Chinese research report*. Social Sciences Literature Press, 2011, p. 12.
5 See Li Minghuan, General trends in international migrations and new changes in the Overseas Chinese situation, in Zai Qiujin (ed.), *Overseas Chinese and ethnic Chinese Blue Paper* (2011). Social Sciences Literature Press, 2011, p. 29.
6 China News Agency, Global Chinese Entrepreneurs Development Report Group, *2008 Global Chinese entrepreneurs development report*, http://www.chinaqw.com/news/200902/02/144817.shtml, tables 1 and 2.
7 The new Overseas Chinese includes those migrants who went abroad after the establishment of the New China up until the era of Reform and Opening Up. Because of the historical background, only a few Chinese people were allowed to settle abroad during this period. Data shows that between 1949 and 1978,

the Chinese government approved only 21 million. The number of settlers who went to Hong Kong, Macau and Taiwan was also small. According to the author's experience working in Africa, the 'new Overseas Chinese' and 'Chinese immigrants' were together termed 'new Overseas Chinese', and the earlier immigrants called 'earlier Overseas Chinese'. The terms are precise, so the author has opted to use them here.

8   China News Agency, Global Chinese Entrepreneurs Development Report Group, *2008 Global Chinese entrepreneurs development report*, http://www.chinaqw.com/news/200902/02/144817.shtml.

9   *Annual report on Overseas Chinese study*. Beijing: Social Sciences Academic Press, 2011.

10 Li Minghuan, General trends in international migrations and new changes in the Overseas Chinese situation, p. 30.

11 Li Anshan, *History of the Overseas Chinese in Africa*. Chinese Overseas Publishing House, 2000, p. 569.

12 Publisher's note: There are divergent views on the status of Taiwan's and Macau's sovereignty. Many countries regard Taiwan and Macau as sovereign states and do not align with the views of the author expressed here.

13 Li Minghuan, General trends in international migrations and new changes in the Overseas Chinese situation, p. 24; Gui Shixun, Overseas Chinese and their contributions to the motherland, *Overseas Chinese Blue Paper* (2011), pp. 55, 62.

14 See Martin Jacques, *When China rules the world*, Li Longsheng (ed.), Zhang Yi'an (trans). Lianjing Publishing Industry Co., 2010, pp. 504–505.

15 There are currently 54 countries in Africa, 49 of which have diplomatic relations with China. Those that have not established diplomatic ties are Burkina Faso, Gambia, Swaziland, São Tomé and Príncipe, and Chad.

16 In recent years, a large portion of earlier Overseas Chinese, including those from Taiwan, have emigrated to North America and Australia, mostly because of the social order, economic conditions or employment pressures in South Africa, or out of consideration for their children's education. The number of early Overseas Chinese in South Africa has decreased rapidly. By the end of 2012, the total number was around 250 000. This is the number I estimated during my visit to South Africa in February 2012, after much consideration.

17 Li Anshan, *History of the Overseas Chinese in Africa*. Chinese Overseas Publishing House, 2000, pp. 563–567.

18 A Chinese businessman in the shadow of a Chinese gang in Angola, *Culture and Arts Newspaper*, 13th edition, 14 September 2012.

19 Bai Jingshan, Ghana's Overseas Chinese celebrate the Lantern Festival, 28 February 2010, http://news.xinhuanet.com/world/2010-02/28/content_13070448.htm.

20 Overview of the Overseas Chinese in Mauritius, 30 June 2006, http://www.chinaqw.com/news/2006/0630/68/34596.shtml.
21 Overview of the Overseas Chinese in Madagascar, 30 June 2006, http://www.chinaqw.com/news/2006/0630/68/34599.shtml.
22 Wang Zhihao, Islanders are not old timers – Remembering the Chinese General Chamber of Commerce reunion, *People's Daily* overseas edition, 21 July 2004.
23 Egypt's Overseas Chinese development status outlook, 12 May 2010, http://www.jsqw.com/html/dv_453153152.aspx.
24 Kenya riots not seedlings of Overseas Chinese, *Beijing Morning Post*, 4 January 2008.
25 Han Bing, Congo (Brazzaville) welcomes Overseas Chinese for the 'Double Festival', 13 September 2010, http://news.xinhua-net.com/world/2010-09/13/c_13492745.htm.
26 Li Changfu, *Chinese colonial history*. Shanghai Bookstore, 1984, p. 161.
27 The year 1602 cited in *Chinese colonial history* is understood to be a printing error, with '1620' being the correct version.
28 Li Changfu, *A history of Overseas Chinese in Southeast Asia*, in *Series of publications of the Republican Period*, Volume 3. Shanghai: Shanghai Bookstore, 1991, pp. 33–34.
29 Li Changfu, *Chinese colonial history*. Shanghai Bookstore, 1984, p. 161.
30 Fang Jigen. *History of Africa's Overseas Chinese*. Xinhua Publishing House, 1986, pp. 29–31.
31 See Melanie Yap and Dianne Leong Man, *Colour, confusion and concessions: The history of Chinese in South Africa*. Hong Kong University Press, 1996, pp. 6–7.
32 The English word 'coolie' comes from Tamil, referring to a manual labourer. In Chinese, the meaning and pronunciation are the same, so it is translated into 苦力 (*kuli*). Nevertheless, the term 'coolie' in English refers to Chinese people who were sold to Europe and America to work as slaves. Foreign language books and files all refer to Chinese workers as 'coolies', but in Chinese they are called 'piglets' (猪仔). Existing research shows that the term 'piglet' first appeared in the 1820s. See Zhang Xintai's *Minor records of Guangdong*, compiled in 1827: 'In Guangdong, ignorant people are seduced and sold as piglets.' On 24 July 1839, in his memorial speech to the Ministry of Foreign Affairs, Lin Zexu said, 'Over ten years ago (1820), there were successive years of famine, and thousands of people went abroad. When they were onboard ship, they were called to eat with a loud cry that resembled the call for pigs used in the inland areas, leading to these boats being called pig-vending boats.'
33 Major Sir Maurice Cameron: Malaya, in Chen Lite (ed.), *History of the Chinese diaspora*. Zhonghua Book Company, 1946, p. 80.

34 Sun Yat-sen. Reporter book (Asahi Shimbun). Shanghai: *China Daily*, 2nd edition, 24 June 1919, http://zhan.renren.com/guanzhuzhexieshier?gid=3602888498031345875&from=post&checked=true.
35 Chen Lite, *History of Overseas Chinese migrations*. Zhonghua Book Company, 1946, p. 34.
36 This data was obtained from the exhibits at the Gold City Museum in South Africa.
37 (Tang) Bai Juyi, The old charcoal seller, in *A complete collection of Tang poetry and Song Ci*, annotated by Zhang Zhiying. Beijing: China Textile Press, 2015, p. 127.
38 (Song) Li Gang, Ill cattle, in Miao Yue (ed.), *Dictionary of Song Ci appreciation*, Shanghai: Shanghai Dictionary Publishing House, 2015, p. 841.
39 Li Anshan, *History of the Overseas Chinese in Africa*, pp. 36, 83–89, 124, 127–128.
40 See Chen Gongyuan, *Friendly communication between ancient Africa and China*. Beijing: Commercial Press, 1985, p. 49; Li Anshan, *History of the Overseas Chinese in Africa*. Chinese Overseas Publishing House, 2000, pp. 89, 626; Zhang Xiang, New relations from the long history of relations between China and Africa, *West Asia and Africa* 6 (2006), p. 54.
41 See Nicholas D Kristof, 1492: Prequel, *The New York Times Magazine*, 6 June 1999.
42 See Chen Gongyuan, *Friendly communication between ancient Africa and China*. Beijing: Commercial Press, 1985, p. 49; Li Anshan, *History of the Overseas Chinese in Africa*. Chinese Overseas Publishing House, 2000, pp. 89, 626; Zhang Xiang, New relations from the long history of relations between China and Africa, *West Asia and Africa* 6 (2006), p. 54.
43 This information was acquired from Ghazzal H Swaleh, assistant director of the Malindi Museum. In May 2003, the author and Swaleh went to Pate Island together, and this information was collected from the conversation between them.
44 Ibid.
45 See *Reference News*, 12th edition, 4 April 2012.
46 Ibid.
47 Sun Tianren, Adjustments in the European attitude toward Chinese investment in Africa, *People's Daily*, 3rd edition, 7 April 2012.
48 Martin Jacques, Why do we continue to ignore China's rise? Arrogance, 26 March 2012, http://world.people.com.cn/GB/157278/17483643.html.

Chapter 18

1. Hegel, in his book *The philosophy of history*, arbitrarily states that since the dawn of history, Africa was closed to the outside world, and that black people always remained in a primitive human state, veiled in dark night until his time, void of the light of history, and that their performance proves that they are barbarous, untamed, natural people – inhuman. See Hegel, *The philosophy of history*, Wang Zaoshi, trans. Beijing Sanlian Press, 1956, pp. 136–139.
2. Ghanaian Kwame Nkrumah's speech at the First African Studies Scholars Conference, Le Shan, trans. *Collected Translations on Asia and Africa* 3 (1963), pp. 2–3.
3. Ibid., p. 1.
4. In AD 825, renowned Persian mathematician, astronomer and geographer Muhammad ibn Musa al-Khwarizmi wrote *On calculation with Hindu numerals* in Arabic, which was later translated into Latin and introduced to Europe, bringing the current use of numerals into the European body of knowledge. The Europeans mistook these as Arabic numerals, not knowing who had actually created them.
5. See Wang Yuxian, *600 years of Chinese commercial groups*. China CITIC Press, 2011, p. 42; Dai Wenda, *Chinese discoveries about Africa*. Commercial Press, 1983, pp. 36–40.
6. Qin Dashu, Beijing University–Kenya archaeological study and its achievements, Culture and Health Department of the Civic and Municipal Affairs Bureau, Macau Special Administrative Region. Model lectures: 2010–2011 lectures delivered by renowned archaeologists on the Heming Haujiang Excavation, *Macau Xingyuan selected works*, December 2011, pp. 84–95.
7. The state of Bukhara in the ancient Western Region is translated into Chinese as *Buhuo* or *Buhu* in *The book of Tang*, into *Buha'er* or *Puhua* in the *History of the Yuan Dynasty*, and into *Buhala* in the *History of Ming Dynasty*. Its location was near Xinjiang in present-day Uzbekistan.
8. *Zheng He's genealogy* reports: 'By the 6th Year of the Xuande reign (1431), Zheng He was granted the title Sanbao Eunuch. Zheng made his elder brother Zheng Wenming's son his heir, naming him Ci.'
9. In Islamic custom, *Hajji* is a respectful title for a male pilgrim who has visited the Islamic holy city of Mecca. The Chinese term for *Hajji* is a translation from the Arabic term meaning 'visitor to the sacred land', or pilgrim. Zheng He's grandfather and father both earned this title. As Zheng had been taken away when he was a child, his father's name may have faded in his memory; he called his father 'Hajji Ma', according to Islamic custom. Because Zheng He was about 10 when his father died, his father's funeral was conducted by Zheng's elder brother, Ma Wenming. In the third year of the Yongle reign, Zheng He

was promoted to Grand Imperial Eunuch. He invited Li Zhigang, grand secretary and minister of rites, to write an epitaph for his father's tomb. Because it was the eve of his first voyage to the Western Ocean, he posted the epitaph to Kunyang in Yunnan and erected the inscribed tombstone at his father's tomb. In the later period of the Qing Dynasty, Zheng He's descendants in Kunyang joined in the Hui uprising and, after failing to meet their goals, escaped to Shi Gou Tou Village in Yuxi County. Fearing that the epitaph of Mr Ma would be damaged, they buried the tombstone in front of Hajji Ma's tomb. In the last year of the Qing Dynasty, the Hui people discovered the tombstone in a deserted location when they were building tombs on the western slope of Yueshan. The tombstone was restored to its original location, where it stayed until it came to the attention of the public after Yuan Jiagu's verification in 1912.

10 See He Yanwu and Xia Daizhong (eds), *The epic of Zheng He*. Yunnan People's Press, Yunnan Fine Arts Press and Aurora Press, 2005, pp. 31–41.
11 See *Record of the reconstruction of the Qingjing Mosque*. Located in the Mosque in Daxuexi Alley, Xi'an. The local Hui people call the tombstone the Zheng He Monument.
12 Di Lihui, Searching for Zheng He's wrecked ship in East Africa, *Science News* 6 (2010), p. 46.
13 Sun Yat-sen, National Construction Strategy, in Hu Yanwu and Xia Daizhong (eds), *The epic of Zheng He*. Yunnan People's Press, Yunnan Fine Arts Press and Aurora Press, 2005, p. 14.
14 *Concise Encyclopaedia Britannica,* Volume 9. Encyclopaedia of China Press, 1995, p. 441.
15 *Encyclopaedia of China* (2nd edition), Volume 28. Encyclopaedia of China Press, 2009, p. 397.
16 See Sugiyama Ichitaira, The deepening and development of the concept of neocolonialism, *African Studies Monthly*, September 1961, in *Asia-Africa Renditions* 3 (1963), pp. 38–39.
17 Okakura Koshiro, On colonialism, *Asia and Africa Studies Monthly*, September 1961, in *Asia and Africa Translation Collection* 3 (1963), pp. 37–38.
18 Y Bochkarov, The practice of French neocolonialism in Africa, *New Times* 14(15) 1964 (English edition), in *Asia and Africa Translation Collection* 7 (1964), pp. 23–24.
19 See Resolutions on neocolonialism, in *Collection of Third All-African Peoples' Conference documents*, World Knowledge Press, 1962, pp. 310–313.
20 Gu Yuqing and Pei Guangjiang, France–Africa 'Innovation Summit' strengthens economic relations, *People's Daily*, 1 June 2010.
21 Wen Jiabao holds press conference in Egypt, *People's Daily*, 19 June 2011.

22 On 5–9 December 2011, the 13th conference of the Council for the Development of Social Science Research in Africa was held in Rabat, Morocco, with 'Africa and the 21st-century challenge' as the conference theme. It was attended by 400 African-affairs experts and scholars from Africa and other parts of the world. I attended the conference by invitation and, at a group meeting, made a speech titled 'China–Africa relations in the 21st century'.
23 See Guinean president, after first visit to China, indicates China is not 'new colonialist', *Reference News*, 14th edition, 23 September 2011.
24 Rapid development of China–African relations a source of envy for the West, *Reference News*, 1st edition, 9 November 2009.
25 The Treaty of Tordesillas was an agreement signed between Spain and Portugal in the Spanish town Tordesillas in Castilla. The agreement aimed to carve up the New World. It stipulated that the two countries would jointly monopolise the world outside of Europe and that the north–south meridian 300 leagues (approximately 1 770 km or 1 100 miles) west of the Cape Verde Islands and 46°37' west longitude would be the demarcation line of power between the two countries. The area west of the demarcation line belonged to Spain, and east of the line to Portugal. This is why Spain was more influential in the western hemisphere, and Portugal more influential in Brazil, Africa and the Far East. Spain approved the treaty on 2 July, and Portugal on 5 September, 1494. When Magellan circumnavigated the globe, these two countries signed another treaty, the Treaty of Saragossa, to define demarcation in the Pacific Ocean.
26 See *Concise Encyclopaedia Britannica*, Volume 9. Encyclopaedia of China Publishing House, 1995, p. 441.
27 Rapid development of China–Africa relations a source of envy for the West, *Reference News*, 1st edition, 9 November 2009.
28 Mohd Khalil Yaakob, Speech at the opening ceremony of the First International Academic Conference on Zheng He, 5 July 2010, Malacca, Malaysia.
29 Liao Jianyu, Keynote speech at the First International Academic Conference on Zheng He, Zheng He of the world and Zheng He of Asia and Africa, 5 July 2010, Malacca, Malaysia.

Postscript

1 Lu Chang's Tang Dynasty poem 'A surprising snow'.
2 China signs first archaeological agreement with African nation, 24 December 2005, http://news.xinhuanet.com/world/2005-12/24/content_3963619.htm.
3 Under China-Kenya joint archaeological research agreement, Chinese experts to search for Zheng He's sunken ships in Africa, Beijing Times, 24 February 2010.

4   Coin that could re-write Chinese-African history found, *BBC News Africa*, 18 October 2010, http://www.bbc.co.uk/news/world-africa/11562927.
5   See Mark Horton, *Shanga: The archaeology of a Muslim trading community on the coast of East Africa*. London and Nairobi: British Institute of East African Studies, 1996. While studying for a doctoral degree at Oxford University, Mark Horton carried out six large-scale archaeological excavations in Shanga from 1980 to 1988, excavating important mosques, markets, residences of nobles, and all major functional areas at the relic sites, except for the vast areas of cemeteries.
6   (Tang Dynasty) Luo Yin, 'Snow'.
7   The 600-year-old coin that proves China was trading with East Africa before Europeans arrived, Daily Mail, 14 March 2013, http://www.dailymail.co.uk/sciencetech/article-2293189/600-year-old-coin-proves-China-trading-East-Africa-BEFORE-Europeans-arrived.html/#ixzz2Qs7Zjtwl.
8   Ding Yu, Zheng's fleet to East Africa? *Surging News*, 13 September 2016, http://www.thepaper.cn/newsDetail_forward_1511142.

Bibliography

CHINESE LANGUAGE PUBLICATIONS

Ai Zhouchang (ed.). *Selected essays on China–Africa relations.* East China Normal University, 1989.

Ai Zhouchang & Mu Tao. *History of China–Africa relations.* East China Normal University Press, 1996.

Chang Feng. The friendship between peoples of Asia and Africa, seen from a museum – Notes on Quanzhou City Overseas Communication History Museum. *Traveler* 2, 1960.

Chen Cenren. Researches in Zheng He's seven West Ocean navigations (10) – Zheng He stayed twice in North Africa. *Great Achievements* 59, October 1978.

Chen Dunde. *Mao Zedong – Nixon in 1972.* Liberation Army Art Press, 2002.

Chen Gongyuan. Zheng He's Western Ocean navigation and China–Africa friendship. *Maritime History Studies* 3, 1981.

———. *Ancient friendly communications between Africa and China.* Commercial Press, 1985.

Chen Gongyuan, Tang Dadun & Yuan Mu (eds.). *African celebrities.* World Knowledge Press, 1989.

Chen Hansheng. 'Piglets' going abroad – How 7 million Chinese labourers were cheated to foreign countries. *Encyclopedic Knowledge* 5, 1979.

———. (ed.). *Collected historical materials on Chinese laborers abroad* (Volume 4): *A comprehensive book in Chinese and foreign languages on Chinese labourers working abroad.* Zhonghua Book Company, 1981.

———. (ed.). *Collected historical materials on Chinese laborers abroad* (Volume 9): *A comprehensive book in Chinese and foreign languages on Chinese labourers working abroad, Chinese labourers in Africa.* Zhonghua Book Company, 1981.

Fan Shuzhi. Zheng He travelled to Somalia. *Xinming Evening News*, 26 December 1960.

———. Zheng He and 'Somalia'. *Action Weekly* 80, January 1961.

Feng Zuozhe. An unforgettable page in the history of friendship between China and Somalia – Records of Zheng He's visits to Somalia in historical books. *Guangming Daily*, 20 April 1978.

Fujian Province Government Information Office. *Zheng He's West Ocean navigations*. China Intercontinental Press, 2005.

Guang Wen. Historical friendship between peoples of China and Africa. *History Teaching* 3, 1966.

Guang Yao. Historical connections between China and Somalia. *People's Daily*, 18 July 1962.

Hou Renzhi. Marine communications between China and East Africa before the so-called discovery of the new navigation route. *Chinese Science Bulletin* 11, 1964.

Hu Yanwu & Xia Daizhong (eds). *Epics of Zheng He*. Yunnan People's Publishing House, Yunnan Art Press and Aurora Press, 2005.

Jin Guoping et al. Textual research in Bila and Suna – The endpoint of Zheng He's navigation. In Wang Tianyou and Wan Ming (eds) *Selected essays in Zheng He studies in the past 100 years*. Beijing University Press, 2004.

Li Anshan. *History of the Overseas Chinese in Africa*. Chinese Overseas Publishing House, 2000.

Li Defu. Geographical basis of Zheng He's oceangoing navigation to Africa. *Collected essays on Zheng He's West Ocean navigation* (2nd collection). Compiled by the Preparatory Committee for the 580th Anniversary of the Great Navigator Zheng He's West Ocean Navigation and by the Chinese Navigation History Studies Society. China Communications Press, 1985.

Li Jie (ed.). *A dictionary of Mao Zedong's works*. Zhejiang Publication United Group and Zhejiang People's Press, 2011.

Li Shihou et al. (eds). *Genealogical materials about Zheng He*. China Communications Press, 1985.

Liao Jianyu et al. (eds). *Zheng He and the Asia–Africa world*. Jointly published by Malacca Press and the International Zheng He Society, 2012.

Lu Tingen. *Collected essays on African issues*. World Knowledge Press, 2005.

Lu Tingen & Ai Zhouchang (eds). *General history of Africa*. East China Normal University, 1995.

Ma Wenkuan et al. *Discovery of ancient Chinese porcelain in Africa*. Forbidden City Press, 1987.

Mu Yujun. A perspective of the Italy-Arab War. *Diplomacy Monthly*, November 1935.

Qiu Jin (ed.). *Reports on the Overseas Chinese (2011)*. Social Sciences Literature Press, 2011.

Shandong University History Department, China–West Communication Research Center. *Zheng He's West Ocean navigations*. China Communications Press, 1985.

Shen Fuwei. Zheng He's treasure fleet navigation to East Africa. In *Collected essays on Zheng He's West Ocean navigation* (1st collection). Compiled by the Preparatory Committee for the 580th Anniversary of the Great Navigator

Zheng He's West Ocean Navigation and by the Chinese Navigation History Studies Society. China Communications Press, 1985.

———. *China and Africa, 2000 Years of China–Africa relations*. Zhonghua Book Company, 1991.

———. *Records of cultural exchanges between China, West Asia, and Africa*. Shanghai People's Press, 1998.

Shen Guangyao. History of communications between ancient China and East Africa. *World Knowledge* 1, 1963.

Shu Shizheng. *Record of Zheng He's southern expedition*. Shengli Publishing House, 1941.

Song Zhuping. Quanzhou – An ancient city recording historical friendship between Asia and Africa. *Fujian Daily*, 20 August 1961.

Sun Guangqi. *Navigation history of ancient China*. Ocean Press, 2005.

Sun Yuanzhi & Zheng Yijun. *On Zheng He after investigations in Southeast Asia*. Beijing University Press, 2008.

Wang Tianyou & Wan Ming (eds). *Selected essays in Zheng He studies in the past 100 years*. Beijing University Press, 2004.

Wang Zhaomo. The Italy-Arab problem in the past half year. *Diplomacy Monthly*, November 1935.

Xia Nai. Long-standing friendship between China and Africa. *People's Daily*, 19 September 1962.

———. Porcelain as evidence of relations between ancient China and Africa. *Cultural Relics* 1, 1963.

Xiang Da (ed.). *Zheng He's nautical chart*. Zhongha Book Company, 1961.

Xu Yuhu. Studies in navigation charts of Africa in the early years of the Ming Dynasty. *African Studies* 2, 1973.

Zhang Junyan. *Ancient maritime communications between China and West Asia and Africa*. Ocean Press, 1986.

Zhang Tieshan (ed.). *Preliminary studies in China–Africa communication history*. Sanlian Bookstore, 1965.

———. *A road of friendship – Records of Chinese aid to the construction of the Tanzania–Zambia Railway*. China Foreign Economic and Trade Press, 1999.

Zhang Tiesheng. A probe into the historical relations of communication between China and Africa. *New Construction* 1, 1963.

Zhang Xinglang & Zhu Jieqin (eds). *Collected documents on China–West communications*. Zhonghua Book Company, 1978.

Zhang Xun & Zheng Yijun (eds). *History of Chinese navigation science and technology*. Ocean Press, 1991.

Zheng Hesheng. Verification of the years of Zheng He's West Ocean navigation based on new historical evidence. *Ta Kung Pao History and Geography Weekly* 57, 25 October 1935.

———. Notes on visiting Changle Blessing Goddess Tianfei Tombstone. *Ta Kung Pao History and Geography Weekly* 110, November 1936.

———. Treasure ships of the Zheng He mission. *Oriental Magazine* 40(23), 1944.

———. *Zheng He*. Shengli Publishing House, 1945.

———. *Collected anecdotes of Zheng He*. Zhonghua Book Company, 1946.

———. Postscript for Guan Jinchen's essay: Ships of Zheng He's West Ocean navigation fleet. *Oriental Magazine* 43(1), 1947.

———. Friendly relations between China, Asian and African countries in the early years of the 15th century. *Literature, History and Philosophy* 1, 1957.

———. Political, economic and cultural relations between China, Asian and African countries in the early years of the 15th century. *Journal of Shandong University (Philosophy and Social Sciences)* 1, 1957.

Zheng Hesheng & Zheng Yijun. *Collected documents on Zheng He's West Ocean navigations* (Volume 1). Qilu Publishing House, 1980.

———. A brief comment on Zheng He's West Ocean navigation. *Journal of Jilin University (Philosophy and Social Sciences)* 1, 1983.

———. *Collected documents on Zheng He's West Ocean navigations* (Volume 1). Qilu Publishing House, 1983.

———. *Collected documents on Zheng He's West Ocean navigations* (Volume 2). Qilu Publishing House, 1983.

———. *Collected documents on Zheng He's West Ocean navigations* (Volume 3). Qilu Publishing House, 1989.

———. On Zheng He's West Ocean navigation. *Maritime Communication Studies* 5, 1983.

———. A brief review of Zheng He's West Ocean navigation fleet ships. In *Collected essays on Zheng He's West Ocean navigation* (1st collection). Compiled by the Preparatory Committee for the 580th Anniversary of the Great Navigator Zheng He's West Ocean Navigation and by the Chinese Navigation History Studies Society. China Communications Press, 1985.

———. New historical evidences of Zheng He's West Ocean navigation. *Journal of Chinese Literature and History* (3rd collection), 1985.

———. *Collected materials on Zheng He's West Ocean navigation* (updated edition), Volume 2 of 3. Ocean Press, 2005: 1148–1149.

Zheng Shiqu & Chen Wutong (eds). *A general history of Chinese culture* (Ming Dynasty volume). Beijing University Press, 2009.

Zheng Yijun. Contributions to China's marine sciences made by Zheng He's West Ocean navigation. *Marine Science* 2, 1977.

——. Zheng He died in the year 1433. *Guangming Daily*, Historiography supplement, 16 March 1983.
——. *On Zheng He's West Ocean navigations*. Ocean Press, 1985.
——. *Zheng He*. China Youth Press, 1991.
——. Zheng He's Western Ocean navigation and the development of marine economy in the early years of the Ming Dynasty. *Kunming Social Sciences* 6, 1992.
——. Zheng He's Western Ocean navigation and marine development in the early years of the Ming Dynasty. In *Collected essays in Zheng He studies* (Volume 1). Dalian Maritime Transportation College Press, 1993.
——. Contributions made by Zheng He's West Ocean navigation to China's oceanic geography. *Traditional Culture and Modernization* 1, 1994.
——. *Studies in group structure in Zheng He's West Ocean navigation – Also on the sayings about Zheng He's ten West Ocean navigations*. Sea Tide Press, April 1996.
——. Contributions to Maritime Silk Road made by dissemination of Islamic culture in the period of Zheng He's West Ocean navigation. In *Maritime Silk Road Studies 1: Maritime Silk Road and Islamic Culture*. Fujian Education Press, 1997.
——. 'Group structure' in Zheng He's West Ocean navigation and its modern significance. *Journal of Qingdao Ocean University (Philosophy and Social Sciences)* 2, 1998.
——. A brief comment on the characteristics of marine development strategy in Zheng He's West Ocean navigation. In *Zheng He and the sea*. China Agriculture Press, 1999.
——. *A long history of marine civilization*. Yellow River Press, 2000.
——. Zheng He: A great navigator earlier than Columbus and Magellan. *China Ocean News*, 12 March 2002.
——. Historical position and contribution of Taichang in the period of Zheng He's West Ocean navigation. *Zheng He Studies* 2, 2003.
——. Zheng He's Western Ocean navigation and China–Africa friendship. In Fan Jinming et al. (eds) *Zheng He: An ambassador of good neighbors*. Sea Tide Press, 2003.
——. *History of Chinese oceanography*. Shangdong Education Press, 2004.
——. On Wang Jinghong's historical contributions. In *Zheng He's West Ocean and collected essays in Fujian*. Fujian People's Publishing House, 2004.
——. *A complete biography of Zheng He*. China Youth Press, 2005.
——. Contributions of Zheng He's Western Ocean navigation to the development of world civilization in the early period of the 15th century. In *Collected*

essays of the International Academic Seminar on World Civilization and Zheng He's Expedition. Beijing University Press, 2005.

———. *The great navigator and diplomat Zheng He.* Aurora Press and Yunnan Art Press, 2005.

———. Great practice of peace in the transition period of human history. In *Collected essays of the Nanjing International Academic Conference.* Social Sciences Press, 2005.

———. *On Zheng He's West Ocean navigations* (updated edition). Ocean Press, 2005.

———. Zheng He's Western Ocean navigation and the development of the Maritime Silk Road. *Quanzhou Port Studies* 3, 2005.

———. A brief comment on Zheng He's sea power theory. *Collected essays from the 2006 Founding Conference of Shanghai Zheng He Studies Center.*

———. Development of China's marine industry in the period of Zheng He's West Ocean navigation and my pondering on it. In *My pondering on Zheng He's West Ocean navigation.* Science Press, 2006.

———. Zheng He's oceangoing expedition and the formation of the peaceful development pattern of an oceanic Asia. In Liu Hong (ed.) *The interaction between an oceanic Asia and the Overseas Chinese world.* Singaporean Chinese Descendants Center, 2007.

Zheng Yijun & Fan Jingxi. A brilliant chapter in diplomatic relations. In *Zheng He: History and reality.* Yunnan People's Press, 1995.

Zhou Yusen. *Textual researches in Zheng He's navigation routes.* Taibei Ocean Shipping Press, 1959.

Zhu Xie. *Zheng He.* Sanlian Bookstore, 1956.

———. Zheng He's navigation which discovered equatorial Africa. *Wenhui Daily,* 30 March 1957.

OTHER LANGUAGES

Chang Kuei-Sheng. A re-examination of the earliest Chinese map of Africa. *Papers of the Michigan Academy of Science, Arts and Letters* 42, 1956.

Davidson B. *Discovery of the ancient Africa* (Chinese edition, trans. Ge Ji and Tu Erkang). Sanlian Bookstore, 1985.

Debre F. *Overseas Chinese* (Chinese edition, trans. Zhao Xipeng). Xinhua Publishing House, 1982.

Duyvendak JJL. *Ma Huan re-examined.* Amsterdam, 1933.

——— *Voyages de Tcheng Houo (Cheng Ho) à la côte orientale 1416–1433.* In Yusuf Kamal *Monumenta Camal Monumenta Cartographia Africae et Aegipti* 4, 1939.

——— *Chinese discovery of Africa.* Commercial Press, 1983.

Fripp CE. Chinese medieval trade with Africa. *Native Affairs Department Annual* 18, 1941.

Gamarra Z. *Vie et prodiges du grand amiral Zheng He*. Paris: Mazarine, 2000.

Goodrich LC. A note on Prof. Duyvendak's lectures on China's discovery of Africa. *Bulletin of the London School of Oriental and African Studies* 1(2), 1952.

Ibn Battuta (dictated), Abdul Hardy Tuch (ed.) & Li Guangbin (trans.). *Wonders on an alien land – Ibn Battata's Travel Notes* (full translation). Ocean Press, 2008.

Lelievre D. *Le dragon de lumière: Les grandes expéditions des Ming au début du XVème siècle*. Paris: Empire, 1996.

Levathes L. *When China ruled the seas: The treasure fleet of the dragon throne, 1405–1433* (Chinese edition, trans. Qiu Zhonglin, 2000). Oxford University Press, 1994.

Marsh Z & Kingsnorth GW. *A concise history of East Africa* (Chinese edition, trans. Wu Tongzhi). Shanghai People's Publishing House, 1974.

Mayer MF. Chinese explorations of the Indian Ocean during the 15th century (partly a translation of His –Yang Chao Kung Tien Lu of Huang Sheng–Tseng, 1520). *China Review* 3 (1874): 219, 321; (1875): 61, 173.

Menzies G. *1421: The year China discovered the world* (Chinese edition, trans. Bao Jiaqing, 2003). Bantan Books, 2002.

———— *1434: The year a magnificent Chinese fleet sailed to Italy and ignited the Renaissance*. (Chinese editions, trans. Yang Lixin, 2012). Harper Collins, 2008.

Mikami T. *A road of pottery and porcelain* (Chinese edition, trans. Li Xijing & Gao Ximei). Cultural Relics Publishing House, 1984.

Mills JV. Note on early Chinese voyages. *Journal of the Royal Asiatic Society* 3, 1951.

Pelliot P. *The great Chinese oceangoing navigation in the early years of the 15th century. Les grands voyages maritimes Chinois au début du 15ème siècle.* T'oung Pao, 1933.

Porter J & Anzovin S. *The steps of civilization – Explorers who influence the world*. Zhonghua Book Company, 2007.

Schwarz EHL. Chinese connection with Africa. *Journal of (Royal) Asiatic Society of Bengal* 4, 1938: 175.

Sivin N. Eighty years before Columbus a Chinese armada with 27 000 men reached Africa. *Scientific American*, January 1972.

UNESCO. *A general history of Africa* (Volumes 1 and 2). China Translation and Publication Corporation, 2003.

Willets W. The maritime adventure of General Eunuch Cheng Ho. *Journal of Southeast Asia History* 2.

Yamamoto T. A textual research in Zheng He's West Ocean expedition (Chinese edition, trans. Wang Gulu). *Wuhan University Literature and Philosophy Quarterly* 2 and 4(4), May and June, 1935.

Index

A
Acupuncture, ix
Africa
  see under names of African countries; Overseas Chinese; Sino–African relations; China, Emigration and immigration; Colonialism; *Zheng He*; Refugees; Slave trade
African National Congress, v
Ambergris, 245–247
ANC *see African National Congress*
Angola, 169–173, 195, 279
Animals, 245–248
  Giraffes, 7–12, 39, 84, 247–248
  Lions, 191, 236–245
Arabic language and culture, 71, 112, 135, 301
Arabs, 17, 28, 51, 53, 134–135, 251–252 *see also Islam; Sino–African relations*
Archaeology, 299, 313–320
Architecture, 17, 46, 76

B
Bangladesh, 7–10
Belgium, 174–178, 189
Buganda *see Uganda*
Burundi, 185–187

C
Cape Colony *see Cape of Good Hope*
Cape of Good Hope, 141, 148, 161, 163–166, 229, 285, 296
Chairman Mao *see Mao, Zedong*
China
  Emigration and Immigration (*see Overseas Chinese*)
  Han and Eastern *Han* Dynasty, 72, 236–238, 244–245, 249–250, 266
  History (*see China, history of; Sino–African relations*)
  Ming and *Qing* dynasties, 25, 41, 152, 213, 227, 254, 298
  Relations with Africa (*see Sino–African relations*)
  Shule region, 237–238
  Song Dynasty, 214, 252–254, 300
  Tang dynasty, 252, 266–267, 297–298
  Western Region, 236–242, 300–301
  Yuan dynasty, 252–254, 266–267
China, history of, 235–268 *see also China*
  1911–1949 era, 258–262
  1949 to present, 262–265
  Historical record of, 235–268
  Land communications era (*see 2nd century BC to 6th century AD*)
  Land–sea communications era (*see 7th century AD to 15th century AD*)
  2nd century BC to 6th century AD, 248–250
  7th century AD to 15th century AD, 250–253
  16th century to 1911, 254–258
China Village *see Shanga Village*
China–Kenya joint archaeological research agreement, viii
Chinatown, Mauritius, 142–143
Chinese–African relations *see Sino–African relations*
Chinese emigration and immigration *see Overseas Chinese*
Chinese language, 41–42, 54–55
Chinese medicine *see Traditional Chinese medicine*
Chinese Titanic *see Shipwreck near Pate Island*
Chinese Village
  See Shanga Village
Colonialism, 170–175, 189, 254–257, 260–261, 283–286, 293–294, 302–312 *see also Explorers and navigators, European*
  Neocolonialism, 303–312
  New colonialism (*see Neocolonialism*)
Comoro Islands, 144–145
Comoros *see Comoro Islands*
Congo *see Democratic Republic of Congo*

D
Da Gama, Vasco, 3–4, 64
Democratic Republic of the Congo, v, 170, 174–180, 261, 280–281
Diaspora, Chinese *see Overseas Chinese*
Donkeys, 73–77
Dragon jars *see under Porcelain ware*
DRC *see Democratic Republic of the Congo*
Dynasties *see under China*

E

Education *see Schools and education*
Emigration and immigration *see Overseas Chinese*
EU *see European Union*
European explorers and navigators *see Explorers and navigators, European*
Executive management committee, v
Expatriate Chinese *see Overseas Chinese*
Expeditions and fleets *see under Zheng He*
Explorers and navigators, European, 25, 65, 152–153, 163–166, 230, 254–255, 320 *see also Colonialism*

F

Famau *see Wafamau*
Faza village and district, 52–55, 76
 Relic sites (*see under Relic sites*)
Fleets *see under Zheng He*
FOCAC *see Forum on China–Africa Cooperation*
Following Zheng He's Footprints Through Africa, viii, 68
Forum on China–Africa Cooperation (Focac), 263–265

G

Games, 122–126
Gedi, 5, 63–65
 Relic site (*see under Relic sites*)
Ginwala, Frene, 153–156
Giraffes *see under Animals*
Great Zimbabwe *see Zimbabwe*
Guandi temple, Madagascar, 137–141

H

Han and Eastern Han Dynasties *see under China*
Hospitals *see Medicine and medical treatment; Traditional Chinese medicine*
Somali (*see under Somalia and Somali people*)

I

Indian Ocean, xi *see also Western Ocean*
International development of, 229
Islam, 51, 74–75, 118, 215–216, 221–222, 251, 300–301 *see also Arabs; Mosques; Sino-African relations*

J

Jinghai Temple, 219–220

K

Kaunda, Kenneth, 130–132, 195–198
Kenya
 Attacks on, 35
 Relic sites (*see under relic sites*)
Kismayo, 78–80, 84, 88–89, 113–114, 116–122
Kylin *see Giraffes under Animals*

L

Lamu archipelago, 13, 33, 52
Lamu Girls' Secondary School, x, 44, 74, 223
Lamu Island, x, 3, 13–14, 33, 71–78
Lamu Museum *see under Museums*
Lamu Old Town, 35–36, 73–77
Lions *see under Animals*
Longjiang Treasure Shipyard Relics Park *see under Relic sites*
Lumumba, Patrice, 174–179

M

Madagascar, 137–141
Mah- jong *see Games*
Malindi, 5–12, 25
 Malindi Museum (*see under Museums*)
Mandela, Nelson, 133, 187
Mao, Zedong, 112, 131–134, 196–197
Maps, 152–156, 165–166, 253
Mauritius, 141–144, 260, 279–280, 286–288, 290
Medicine and medical treatment, 31, 62, 90–91, 108–109, 147, 226–227, 291 *See also Traditional Chinese medicine*
Ming Dynasty *see under China*
Mmaka, Fakii, viii, 47, 59–63
Mogadishu *see Somalia and Somali people*
Mombasa, 3
Mosques, 5, 54, 215–216, 291, 301 *see also Islam*
Mozambique, 131–132, 135–136
Museums
 Gedi, 5, 64–66
 Lamu, 8, 71, 77, 126–127
 Malindi, 8, 25
 National Museum of Tanzania, 129–130
 Rwanda, 188–189
 Slavery, 130, 172–173
 Zanzibar, 130–131
Muslims *see Islam*
Mwamaka *see Sharif, Lali Mwamaka*

N

Namibia, 167–168
Nanjing University of Traditional Chinese Medicine, viii, x
Neocolonialism; New colonialism *see under Colonialism*
NGO *see non-governmental organisation*
Non-governmental organisation, v, 91
Nyerere, Julius, 130, 196–198

O

Overseas Chinese, 137–143, 146, 161–163, 259–260, 270–288, 311
 Difference to colonialists, 293–295
 Differences to shipwreck survivors, 291–292
 Difficulties in assessing numbers, 276–278

Distribution and population tables, 271, 274
Earliest, 290–292
Employment of, 282–288
New Overseas Chinese, 162–163, 274, 275–276, 278–279, 281–283
South Africa, 278–279

P
Pate Island, vii, x, xi, 1–2, 25, 30, 34
  Relic sites (*see under* Relic sites)
  Shipwreck on (*see* Shipwreck near Pate Island)
Plants, medicinal *see* Medicine and medical treatment
Porcelain ware, 65, 129–131, 135–136, 182–183, 315–320
  Dragon jars, 36–38, 56–57, 126–128
  Kenya, 4–5, 9, 71–72
  Portugal, 4, 25, 165–166

R
Refugee camps, 82, 85–94 *see also* Refugees; UN Refugee Affairs
Refugees, 85–94, 188, 190 *see also* Refugee camps; *see under* United Nations
  Education of, 86–87
Relic sites
  Fawa village relic site, 53
  Gedi relic site, 63–65
  Kenya, 39
  Longjiang Treasure Shipyards, 219–220
  Pate relic site, 17
  Shanga relic site, 27–29, 39
  Siyu relic site, 20, 22, 26, 43
  South–east Asia, 83
Rwanda, 188–190

S
Schools and Education, x–xi, 44–45, 60–61, 86–89, 107–108, 225–226
Seychelles, 144–146
Shanga Rocks, 29, 39, 68, 70–71
Shanga Village, viii, x, 14–22, 24–29, 31–33, 38–54
  Relic sites (*see under* Relic sites)
Sharif, Lali Mwamaka, vii, x, 44 223–226
Ships and sailing *see under* Zheng He
Shipwreck near Pate Island, 17–18, 28–29, 39, 68–71, 79–80, 288–293
Shule region *see under* China
Silk, 3, 47–48, 235–236 *See also* Weaving
Silk Road, 72, 238, 249, 254
Sino–African relations, 71–72, 113–116, 137–144, 185–187, 213, 223–227, 297–299
  1911–1949 era, 258–262
  1949 to present, 262–265
  Difference to European–African relations, 296–297

Historical record of, 235–268
Kenya, 7–8, 28, 31–32, 47–48
Land communications era (*see* 2nd century BC to 6th century AD)
Land–sea communications era (*see* 7th century AD to 15th century AD)
Ming and Qing Dynasties era (*see* 16th century to 1911)
2nd century BC to 6th century AD, 248–250
Religious aspects of, 39, 43, 51, 74–75, 251, 301, 311
Republican era (*see 1911–1949 era*)
Tanzania and Zambia, 130–134, 196–201, 205–211, 262–269
7th century AD to 15th century AD, 250–253
16th century to 1911, 254–258
Siyu Village, 15–18, 20–22, 24–29
  Population, 25
  Relic sites (*see under* Relic sites)
Slave trade and slavery, 76, 130–132, 170–174, 255–257, 283–287, 309
Slavery Museums *see under* Museums
Somalia and Somali people, 2, 78–82, 86–88, 93, 95–123 *see also* Refugee camps
  Chinese embassy in, 100–103
  Hospitals, 105–107
South Africa, 152–169, 195–196, 259, 277–281, 283, 285–288
Suanni *See* Lions (*under* Animals)

T
Tang dynasty *see under* China
Tanzania, 129–131
  National Museum of Tanzania (*see under* Museums)
Tanzania Zambia Railway, v, 129–132, 195–211
Tanzania Zambia Railway Authority *see* Tanzania Zambia Railway
TAZARA railway *see* Tanzania Zambia Railway
TCM *see* traditional Chinese medicine
Tourists and tourism, 17, 35, 74–77, 267
Trade and trading, 83, 227–231, 252–254, 259–265, 295–299, 310, 317–320
  Slave trade (*see* Slave trade and slavery)
Traditional Chinese medicine, v–x, 23–24, 29–32, 61–63, 147, 225, 291 *see also* Medicine and medical treatment

U
Uganda, 190–192
UN *see* United Nations
UNESCO *see under* United Nations
United Nations, v, 82, 84
  UN Educational, Scientific, and Cultural Organization (UNESCO), v, 73–74
  UN Refugee Affairs, 82, 85–87, 89–93

W
Wachina *see Wafamau*
Wafamau, 18, 26–27, 46–47, 49–52, 65–67
Weaving, 45, 47–48, 72, 186–187 *see also Silk*
Western Ocean, xi *see also Indian Ocean*
Western region *See under China*

X
Xia, Ruidu *see Sharif, Lali Mwamaka*
Xiao, Xia *see Sharif, Lali Mwamaka*

Y
Yuan dynasty *see under China*

Z
Zanzibar, 130–131, 255
  Museums (*see under Museums*)
Zheng, He, vii, xi, 7, 11, 23, 83, 212–222
  Fleets and trade expeditions, vii, xi, 83–84, 165–166, 227–234, 297–302, 319–320
  Monument in *Xi'an*, 215
  Ships and sailing, 1–2, 64, 83, 149–151, 164–165, 220–221, 302
  Shipwreck of *Zheng He* ship (*see Shipwreck near Pate Island*)
  Zheng He Monument, Malindi, 4–6
  Zheng He Villages, 2, 78, 80, 116
    South Africa, 161–163
Zimbabwe and Great Zimbabwe, 182–185
Zulu people, 157–160
  King of (*see Zwelithini, King Goodwill*)
Zwelithini, King Goodwill, 158–161